On the Success of Failure

A Reassessment of the Effects of Retention in the Primary Grades, Second Edition

This book is about the practice of grade retention in elementary school, a particularly vexing problem in urban school systems, where upward of half the students may repeat a grade. *On the Success of Failure* addresses whether repeating a grade is helpful or harmful when children are not keeping up. It describes the school context of retention and evaluates its consequences by tracking the experiences of a large, representative sample of Baltimore schoolchildren from first grade through high school. In addition to evaluating the consequences of retention, the book describes the cohort's dispersion along many different educational pathways from first grade through middle school, the articulation of retention with other forms of educational tracking (like reading group placements in the early primary grades and course-level assignments in middle school), and repeaters' academic and school adjustment problems before they were held back.

Karl L. Alexander is John Dewey Professor of Sociology at Johns Hopkins University.

Doris R. Entwisle is Professor Emerita in the Department of Sociology at Johns Hopkins University.

Susan L. Dauber is Senior Program Officer at The Spencer Foundation in Chicago, Illinois.

On the Success of Failure

A Reassessment of the Effects of Retention in the Primary Grades

Second Edition

KARL L. ALEXANDER
Johns Hopkins University

DORIS R. ENTWISLE
Johns Hopkins University

SUSAN L. DAUBER
The Spencer Foundation

CAMBRIDGE
UNIVERSITY PRESS

PUBLISHED BY THE PRESS SYNDICATE OF THE UNIVERSITY OF CAMBRIDGE
The Pitt Building, Trumpington Street, Cambridge, United Kingdom

CAMBRIDGE UNIVERSITY PRESS
The Edinburgh Building, Cambridge CB2 2RU, UK
40 West 20th Street, New York, NY 10011-4211, USA
477 Williamstown Road, Port Melbourne, VIC 3207, Australia
Ruiz de Alarcón 13, 28014 Madrid, Spain
Dock House, The Waterfront, Cape Town 8001, South Africa

http://www.cambridge.org

First published 2003

Printed in the United Kingdom at the University Press, Cambridge

Typeface Palatino 10/13 pt.   *System* LATEX 2_ε [TB]

A catalog record for this book is available from the British Library.

Library of Congress Cataloging in Publication Data

Alexander, Karl L.
   On the success of failure : a reassessment of the effects of retention in the primary
      grades/ Karl L. Alexander, Doris R. Entwisle, Susan L. Dauber – 2nd ed.
   p. cm.
   Includes bibliographical references and index.
   ISBN 0-521-79064-6 – ISBN 0-521-79397-1 (pbk.)
   1. Grade repetition – United States.   2. Education, Primary – United States.
      I. Entwisle, Doris R.   II. Dauber, Susan L.   III. Title.
   LB3063 .A54 2003
   371.2′8–dc21   2002020180

ISBN 0 521 79064 6 hardback
ISBN 0 521 79397 1 paperback

Contents

Preface to the Second Edition

On The Success of Failure, published in 1994, evaluated academic and socioemotional sequelae of early grade retention from the vantage point of our long-term research project, the Beginning School Study (BSS). Baltimore-based and still ongoing, the BSS in fall 1982 began monitoring the educational progress of a panel of city schoolchildren just as they were starting first grade. The study group was mainly low-income (two-thirds) and just over half African-American (55% – all but a few of the rest were White). Over the elementary years many were held back – 40% through fifth grade. *Success* sought to determine how the decision to have these children repeat a grade affected them. Was it helpful, as intended, or harmful, as critics of the practice contend? The question has great practical import, especially for children like the BSS participants – disadvantaged, minority youth who often struggle at school.

Success covered the first 8 years of the group's schooling. It reviewed not just grade retention but also the ways other forms of educational tracking (e.g., special education and ability grouping) shape school experiences. Using multiple approaches, including matched controls, statistical adjustments, and before–after comparisons, the book was as comprehensive as possible at the time.

There is now much to add, but relatively little to change. We have continued to monitor the panel's life progress over the years since *Success*'s publication, so that now we are able to examine high school dropout in relation to grade retention. High school dropout persists at epidemic levels in places like Baltimore – for example, 42% of the BSS panel left school without a degree, a figure in line with estimates for other high-poverty cities (*Education Week* 1998). We now can ask: to what extent is grade retention implicated in their dropout? The main reason for revising and updating *Success* is to explore this question. A second reason involves seismic changes in the education policy arena since publication of the first edition. We comment on these first.

The timing of the first edition of *Success* (fall 1994) coincided with the beginning of the current debate over promotion policy. Swings between relaxed promotion standards (e.g., social promotion) and merit-based promotion standards are nothing new, of course (e.g., Larabee 1984; Lawton 1997; Olson 1990; Rothstein 1998), and voices from within the academic community have weighed in all along (e.g., occasions like the symposium on grade retention at the 1991 meeting of the American Educational Research Association, "Retention: Processes and Consequences of a Misguided Practice"). But retention practices burst into the national spotlight when President Clinton proposed ending social promotion in successive State of the Union addresses (1998, 1999). The national response was nothing short of dizzying – Blue Ribbon reports appeared (e.g., American Association of School Administrators 1998; Heubert and Hauser 1999; U.S. Department of Education 1999), school systems scrambled to adopt "get tough" promotion policies (e.g., King and McCormick 1998; Mathews 2000; Toch 1998; White and Johnston 1999; Wildavsky 1999), and the media switched into high gear. A 5-year Lexis-Nexis newspaper search of references to "social promotion" that started in September 1994 (around the time of *Success*'s publication) turned up 431 articles, of which 80% appeared *after* President Clinton's 1998 speech.

With *Success* in the mix, we found ourselves drawn into the debate. Conscientious journalists, we discovered, strive for balance on controversial matters, such as retention. The momentum of the day favored strict enforcement of rigorous promotion standards, but many in the media and the public at large worried about the effect of those standards on children who failed to achieve them. Was grade retention an appropriate response? Critics of retention are easy to find within the scholarly community (e.g., Darling-Hammond 1998; Hauser 1999; Reynolds, Temple, and McCoy 1997), but who will speak for the other side? We are not enthusiasts for holding children back. Still, *Success* did not find unequivocally against retention, so we found ourselves (mis)cast in that role. Because our research as reported in *Success* has not always been treated fairly by our critics (e.g., Shepard, Smith, and Marion 1996), this second edition of *Success* clarifies our position on the educational effectiveness of retention during the primary grades *in the context of recent calls to end social promotion*. We also respond, in an appendix, to technical criticisms directed at the original analyses.

The first edition of *Success* reported that retention did *not* set back children in the BSS panel academically. Instead, in most instances retained children's test scores and marks improved after retention. Moreover, retention was *not* an emotionally scarring experience for these youth, perhaps because it was so common. These conclusions about children's response to retention in the primary and middle grades remain unchanged from the earlier edition (keeping in mind that they apply to a disadvantaged study group and not necessarily to the United States as a whole). Chapter 11, however, which is new and covers the high school years, shows that grade repetition substantially elevates BSS children's dropout risk, even allowing for other differences between retainees and nonretainees, for example, differences involving achievement test levels and family factors.

This evidence on the connection between retention and dropout presents us with something of a conundrum. Retention, so far as we can determine, does not impede BSS children academically or assault their self-esteem in the early years, yet something about the experience apparently weakened repeaters' attachment to school. In presenting this new evidence, this second edition of *Success* tries to fashion a coherent interpretation, one that embraces old *and* new – early positive and then later negative effects of retention.

The first edition followed the study group through the first 8 years of school, the elementary and middle school years for those promoted each year. Mirroring the pattern citywide at the time (Kelly 1989), almost 17% of the BSS panel was held back in first grade, and after 5 years in school 40% had repeated at least one grade. The policy climate then shifted dramatically. Following the national trend (e.g., Lawton 1997; Olson 1990), in the early 90s the Baltimore City Public Schools moved toward a "no fail" promotion policy. As a result, the systemwide retention rate plummeted, from 8.9% in 1990 over grades 1–6 (combined) to 3.0% in 1993 (Bowler 1994). However, members of the BSS panel were entering their ninth year of school (1990) when this policy shift occurred, so their retention experiences were framed by a very different policy context.

The first edition of *Success* assessed one kind of institutional response to a difficult question: when children like those in Baltimore are not keeping up, is it better to hold them back or move them ahead? *Success* examined the experience of first grade, second grade, and third grade repeaters specifically, monitoring their academic progress from the fall of first grade, *before anyone had been held back*, to the end of seventh grade (in the case of repeaters) or eighth grade (in the case of children never retained). This time frame extends 4 to 6 years after children's retention and overlaps their move from elementary school into middle school, which in Baltimore occurs between the fifth and sixth grades.

Those benchmarks are referenced to the 1988/89 school year, 4 years before the group's expected ("on-time") high school graduation in spring 1994. Having continued monitoring these children's academic progress, we now know that just a fourth of the BSS panel graduated on schedule. Some were 1 year or more behind and graduated late. Others gave up and left without a degree. Altogether, it took 7 years for all members of the study group to conclude secondary school. The earliest departure was that of a student who left after 8 years of school with a sixth grade education; the last left after 15 years without a high school degree.

Participants in the BSS all started school together as first graders in fall 1982, but from that point forward they moved along very different educational paths. Chapter 4 sketches the cohort's complicated history of single, double, and even triple retentions, as well as assignments to special education after retention over the first 8 years. This early history deflected many BSS youth from their original graduation timetable, but whether it had the further effect of taking them off the path to eventual graduation could not be explored until now, an omission that has been pointed out in commentary on the first edition (e.g., Dawson 1998b). However, with mode of high school exit known for 92% of the original group, we are able now to pose a key question about dropout in relation to grade retention: does repeating a grade increase dropout risk for BSS youth, as much prior research indicates (e.g., Jimerson 2000), or do the academic benefits of retention documented in the first edition of *Success* carry over to dropout also? Chapter 11 addresses this longer-term issue.

The Beginning School Study is not a narrow study of retention or dropout. Rather, it is a broad-based survey of children's academic and personal development. To our knowledge, it affords a longer and more detailed perspective on retention and dropout than any other research so far available on retention's consequences. And it is focused on a population in which these problems are severe. For research purposes, it is useful to examine "worst cases," those youth who most need help, with the clear understanding that findings for such a group can inform policy for other like groups but do not necessarily generalize to "average" or "advantaged" groups.

We would not expect the causes of retention in suburban or middle-class families necessarily to mimic causes identified in the BSS panel. Nor would we expect consequences to be the same. Repeating a grade in a school where grade retention is common, as in the BSS, is probably a far different emotional experience from being the lone repeater in a school where retentions are more rare. Such contextual differences need to be examined but are beyond the scope of the BSS.

Finally, a few words of thanks are in order. We are indebted first and foremost to the children and families of the BSS who have worked in partnership with us these many years. Without their goodwill and generous cooperation the BSS would not be possible. Members of the BSS panel realize no great personal gain from indulging our intrusions. Certainly they give much more than they receive. But they are part of something important. We hope they realize that and derive a measure of satisfaction from that knowledge – some do, we know. The first edition of *Success* was dedicated to these precious young men and women and their parents. We dedicate the second edition to them also, and especially to the 17 known deceased members of the study group whose lives have been cut tragically short.

Next in line for grateful tribute are the core staff of the BSS. For almost 20 years the work of the BSS has been done "in house" – developing survey instruments; tracking and interviewing respondents; coding, cleaning, checking, and entering data; maintaining the data archive; and, of course, posing questions of the data. This complicated, challenging enterprise has evolved into what is essentially a small, dedicated survey research center. Continuity and competence are key to making it work well, and the core BSS staff has delivered handsomely on both scores. Sona Armenian, Binnie Bailey, Joanne Fennessey, Linda Olson, Anna Stoll, and Mary Ann Zeller make up the current BSS infrastructure. Those six extraordinary women have averaged 14 years of magnificent service to the BSS. Each has a job description, but in practice the division of labor on the BSS is highly fluid. Everyone pitches in when needed and where needed. A special word of thanks is due Anna Stoll for her patience and perseverance in giving order to our scraps of text and seemingly endless changes while helping prepare this manuscript. We are blessed to have such fine friends and colleagues.

Beyond the core, BSS staffing expands and contracts on an "as needed" basis. Included in the mix have been many able graduate and undergraduate research assistants, more than a dozen during the last 2 years alone. One is Nader Kabbani, a Ph.D. candidate in economics while working with the BSS. Nader, who last year completed his doctoral studies, is coauthor of Chapter 11. Another is Nettie Legters, who received her Ph.D. in sociology in 1996 and is now a research scientist at The Center for the Social Organization of Schools, an education research and development center located here at Hopkins. Nettie is coauthor of Chapter 10.

A special debt of gratitude is owed the field operatives and data management staff who worked with us on the age 22–23 Young Adult Survey, used in this edition of *Success* to determine high school completion. More than 20 assistants participated in the effort, which achieved 80% coverage of the original group after 17 years. While Alice Keith and Ken Ruffin were in the field doing interviews and respondent tracking, a small in-office army worked on telephone tracking, telephone interviewing, and data processing – coding, cleaning, entering, and checking.

We also have obligations to acknowledge outside the BSS family. Securing financial support for a project like the BSS is not easy. There is no 20-year "sustaining" award. Rather, we have had to fund the project piecemeal along the way and hope that adequate resources would materialize in time to prevent major gaps. A series of overlapping, multiple-year awards supported the work. Becky Barr, John Rury, Patricia Graham, and Ellen Lagemann at The Spencer Foundation; Lonnie Sherrod, Beatrix Hamburg, and Karen Hein at the Grant Foundation; Nevzar Stacey at The Office of Educational Research and Improvement (OERI); and Bill Bainbridge at the the National Science Foundation (NSF) all were of great help in securing the resources we needed.

Finally, thanks are due our editors at Cambridge University Press. Julia Hough, who helped usher through the first edition of *Success* and arranged for us to "pitch" the second, has been succeeded by Philip Laughlin. We appreciate the help and support both have given.

1

Grade Retention

Lingering Questions

Each spring many thousands of children across the country receive the same dark message: they are failures. These youngsters are to be held back, retained, repeat a grade – all synonyms for failing. According to one national source (U.S. Department of Health and Human Services 2000: 299), 8% of second graders in 1999 were a year behind as a result of kindergarten or first grade retention. Applied to the roughly 7.2 million kindergartners and first graders in fall 1997 (U.S. Department of Education 2000a: 58), an 8% retention rate translates into well over a half million children. Academic difficulties during the early elementary years tend to persist (e.g., Entwisle and Alexander 1989; 1993), so the problems signaled by (and perhaps aggravated by) this setback likely will cast a very long shadow. With so many children involved, this is a matter of grave concern.

The decision to hold children back implies they have fallen short and are not yet ready for work at the next grade level. Unlike many other educational decisions, this one is highly public. The pupil's classmates go on, but the retained child must start over, with new classmates, most of whom are younger, smaller, and brighter. The new teacher knows the child is repeating; so do the new classmates. Furthermore, the judgment of failure is almost never reversed. Most children who repeat a grade will be "off-time" for the rest of their time in school.

Schools use retention to help children who have fallen behind catch up, but does it really help? There are many skeptics, who do not see "catching up," but instead humiliation and harm. Are these apprehensions warranted? Despite strong opinion and much study, the issue is not decided. In the next chapter we review what is known (and believed) about the consequences of retention. First, though, we sketch the dimensions of the problem. There may be disagreement about the pros and cons of retention, but no one disputes its seriousness. We first consider retention rates, then some of its possible "costs."

Falling Behind: The Magnitude of the Problem

Estimates vary, but into the 1990s close to 30% of 12- to 14-year-olds were overage for grade, many no doubt because of earlier retentions (Heubert and Hauser 1999: 150). Next to dropout, failing a grade is probably the most ubiquitous and vexing issue facing school people today. In these days, children can "fail" kindergarten – on the order of 4%–5% do so according to recent national estimates (Karweit 1999: 7; Reaney, West, and Denton 2001; Zill, Loomis, and West 1997) – and in many school systems failing first grade is common.

Astonishing though it is, no authoritative source monitors retention trends on a national level, a result of what Weiss and Gruber (1987) call the "managed irrelevance of federal statistics." The Common Core of Data, the primary set of federal statistics on elementary and secondary education, does not include data on such sensitive matters as retention. "In a delicately balanced political environment...they [the National Center for Education Statistics] have enough trouble getting local districts to categorize grade levels and instructional staff in comparable ways without getting into emotionally laden issues." This leaves a critical void, prompting Hauser (2001: 155) to comment, "I doubt that governments currently make important policy decisions about any other social process with so little sound, basic, descriptive information."

As a consequence, assorted second best options have to do. At the national level, retention rates usually are inferred from annual census data that map the distribution of October school enrollments by age and grade for large, nationally representative samples. Panel surveys like the National Educational Longitudinal Study of 1988 (NELS88) project are a second source for estimating retention rates across the country. Individual school systems and states, of course, also often keep records on retention, but with definitions and the quality of record keeping uneven, it hard to piece together a general picture from local sources.

The Census Bureau regularly monitors children's grade in school in relation to their age. These enrollment data, available since 1966 in the Current Population Survey (CPS) school enrollment supplements, are representative of the civilian noninstitutional U.S. population in the 50 states plus the District of Columbia and can be used to identify children who are in a grade below the modal grade of children their age. They permit educated guesses at overall retention rates, but with no allowance for differences across states or districts in age of school entry, cutoff dates, late starts, and the like, such CPS estimates are best thought of as approximations.

Using these CPS data, Hauser and his colleagues (Hauser 2001; Hauser, Pager, and Simmons 2000; Heubert and Hauser 1999; see also Roderick 1995a) report prevalence estimates for grade retention back to the 1960s. They identify children who are a year or more older than is typical for their grade in school, but retention is not the only reason for being overage for grade (sometimes referred to as "age grade retardation"). Starting school late generates the same pattern, and children assigned to special education classes also often fall off the normal grade progression timetable. And, too, state policies differ. Twelve states, for example, have kindergarten cutoff dates *after* the October reference date used in the CPS; in five others the cutoff is established at the level of school districts (Corman 2001). For these reasons, CPS overage for grade calculations are but a rough guide.

Hauser and his colleagues focus on *changes* in overage enrollments, comparing successive grades between years as opposed to the number or proportion of overage children in a given grade in a given year. Their reports cover roughly three decades for different cohorts of school beginners. For that reason, their many comparisons are hard to summarize. Still, Hauser concludes (2001: 163) that "grade retention is pervasive in American schools." For example, 21% of children ages 6–8 in 1987 were overage for grade according to his calculations. Because being overage could be due to retention, late start, or other considerations, Hauser uses the 21% figure not as an estimate of retention, but as a baseline for anchoring the same children's later experience (a conservative approach). And what happens to this cohort later? At ages 9–11, the percentage overage stands at 28%, and at age 12–14 it is 31% (see pp. 159–161).

Overage enrollments thus increase roughly 10 percentage points over the elementary and middle school years. An indeterminate, but presumably large, fraction of the 21% baseline rate would have to be added onto this figure to gauge the group's retention experience. According to the National Household Education Surveys for 1993 and 1995, about 9% of children who meet the age eligibility cutoff for kindergarten are held out a year by their parents, so-called academic redshirts;[1] another 5%–6% are identified as repeating kindergarten (Zill et al. 1997: 17; see also Meisels 1992). The late starters would show up in CPS data as overage for grade, but not because of retention. In the NHES surveys, then, roughly two-thirds of the overage first grade enrollment traces to delayed kindergarten entry and a third to kindergarten retention.[2]

The percentage of overage first graders rose steadily from the early 1970s through the late 1980s and leveled off thereafter (Hauser 2001: 160). Applying the NHES two-third–one-third divide for delayed entry versus retention to overage 6- to 8-year-olds in 1987, that cohort's cumulative retention through middle school (age 12–14) would be on the order of 17%–18% – that is, Hauser's 21% baseline figure less 14% due to delayed kindergarten entry plus 10% increase from baseline.

The estimates described apply to the country as a whole, but for certain children in certain settings, retention rates are much higher. Hauser's report documents large differences in overage enrollments when comparing Whites, Blacks, and Hispanics, differences that increase over the course of children's schooling. All three groups had roughly similar rates at ages 6–8, but by ages 9–11 minority children were 5 to 10 percentage points above Whites, and the difference increased further at ages 15–17. In recent years, by high school almost half of African-American males are overage for grade as against roughly 30% of Whites (these last figures combine overage enrollments with dropout). Also, boys' retention rates exceed girls' for all racial and ethnic groups.

Analyzing CPS enrollment data for 1979, Bianchi (1984) estimates that in an "average" household (husband–wife family with income above the poverty level, where the wife has a high school education and either does not work outside the family or works part-time) about 18% to 19% of males aged 7 to 15 were enrolled below their modal grade. This estimate is close to Hauser's estimate through middle school for 6- to 8-year-olds in 1987 and close also to the 19.3% overall level of grade retention reported retrospectively by the parents of eighth graders in the NELS88 project, a national longitudinal survey of an eighth grade cohort begun in 1988 (Meisels and Liaw 1993). Retrospective accounts of this sort probably are not completely reliable, but neither is inferring

---

[1] Later-maturing boys are the children most often held out, usually middle class and born in the late months of the calendar year (Graue and DiPerma 2000; Zill et al. 1997).

[2] Another fraction would be children held out on entering first grade, but as 98% of children now attend kindergarten (U.S. Census Bureau 1999), the number of such children must be small.

retention from overage enrollments using CPS data (e.g., Corman 2001). Still, with figures from two such different data sources so well aligned, these estimates probably are reasonable for this period.

In Bianchi's analysis retention rates were about the same for "average household" Whites, African-Americans, and Hispanics, but rates escalated rapidly with other risk factors. For children of high school dropout parents who were living in poverty, the rate was about 50% for males of all three racial/ethnic groups, and around 40% for comparably disadvantaged females. Bianchi's findings reveal that the likelihood of retention differs greatly according to a child's level of family resources, a pattern also seen in later studies. For example, 31.3% of NELS88 eighth graders in the lowest family socioeconomic status (SES) quartile had repeated a grade versus 8.2% in the highest quartile (National Center for Education Statistics 1990: 9).

A like pattern is evident too in more recent data for early retentions specifically. Among second graders in 1999, 5% of those in families above the poverty level repeated either kindergarten or first grade as against 16% of poor children. Likewise, the risk of retention for children of college graduate mothers is less than half that for children whose mothers lack high school degrees: 6% versus 16%. And although in these data differences associated with race/ethnicity are negligible (U.S. Department of Health and Human Services 2000: 299), that is true also of CPS estimates for the earliest grades (e.g., Hauser 2001: 164).

State level sources also afford a sense of overall retention levels. However, as noted, not all states report retention rates and their reporting procedures vary. Thirteen of the 36 states covered in the National Research Council's survey of state practices (Heubert and Hauser 1999: 136–137) collect no retention data at all; others provided figures for two or three grades only; and still others just gave an overall total for all grades. Likewise, 5 of 15 southern and border states covered in a recent Southern Region Education Board (SREB) survey of retention provided figures grade by grade (Denton 2001: 3).

With the understanding that these data are incomplete and may not be strictly comparable (or altogether reliable), Table 1.1 reports state retention levels, by grade. These data are compiled from several sources: Shepard and Smith (1989: 6–7) for the early years; Heubert and Hauser (1999: 137–147) for the 1990s, updated for five southern states with information from Denton (2001: 2). Because the present volume focuses on retention over the elementary and middle school years, Table 1.1

TABLE 1.1. *Percentage of Students Retained in Grade in Selected States, by Grade Level and Year*[a]

	Grade Level:	K	1	2	3	4	5	6	7	8	9
Alabama	90s[b]	4.70	8.03	3.00	2.40	2.17	2.17	3.00	6.70	5.20	12.60
Arizona	79–80	5.20	7.70	4.00	2.40	1.90	1.40	1.30	3.10	2.30	4.40
	85–86	8.00	20.0	8.00	5.00	4.00	4.00	4.00	8.00	7.00	6.00
	90s	1.57	2.33	0.97	0.63	0.43	0.43	1.00	2.50	2.23	5.90
Delaware	79–80	NA[c]	11.40	5.10	2.90	2.40	3.10	2.40	7.90	8.10	13.10
	85–86	5.40	17.20	4.90	2.80	2.30	3.00	3.20	9.60	7.70	15.60
	90s	1.90	5.37	2.17	1.47	0.80	0.83	1.53	3.20	2.03	NA
D.C.	79–80	NA	15.30	10.00	7.20	7.20	6.30	3.10	NA	NA	20.50
	85–86	NA	12.70	8.40	7.40	5.40	4.60	2.80	10.60	6.60	NA
	90s	NA	12.93	9.50	8.13	6.97	5.80	2.93	13.17	14.07	17.00
Florida	79–80	6.10	13.70	7.40	7.00	5.90	4.60	5.50	10.40	8.30	10.20
	85–86	10.50	11.20	4.70	4.50	3.80	2.60	3.50	7.90	5.80	12.10
	90s	3.23	4.28	2.40	1.78	1.28	0.88	4.48	5.45	4.20	13.93
Georgia	79–80	NA	11.00	4.70	3.80	2.80	2.50	2.60	5.30	7.40	13.30
	85–86	8.00	12.40	6.70	7.80	5.20	3.90	5.30	6.70	7.50	18.10
	90s	3.70	4.00	2.40	1.70	1.30	1.10	2.10	2.50	2.10	12.40
Kentucky	79–80	2.30	12.60	5.70	3.40	2.20	1.80	1.90	4.20	3.60	5.80
	85–86	4.00	5.30	4.90	3.00	2.30	1.90	2.70	5.40	3.80	9.60
	90s	NA	NA	NA	NA	1.10	0.75	1.85	2.70	1.75	10.70
Louisiana	90s	8.70	11.80	5.95	5.10	5.40	4.60	8.10	10.80	6.10	15.70
Maryland	79–80	NA	7.60	3.50	3.30	2.50	2.50	1.80	8.50	7.60	8.60
	85–86	NA	NA	NA	NA	NA	NA	NA	NA	NA	NA
	90s	0.93	2.37	1.27	0.80	0.57	0.30	2.30	3.40	2.43	11.87
Mississippi	79–80	NA	15.10	6.90	4.80	5.00	5.60	5.10	13.50	11.10	12.40
	85–86	1.40	16.10	7.00	5.30	5.70	6.00	5.60	11.20	9.30	12.90
	90s	5.03	11.80	6.17	4.97	5.97	6.67	7.83	15.07	12.53	20.53
North Carolina	79–80	4.50	9.80	6.00	4.50	3.20	2.80	3.40	6.80	7.10	14.10
	85–86	6.00	9.30	5.00	5.70	2.70	2.10	8.10	7.90	11.00	13.90
	90s	3.83	5.43	2.98	2.35	1.33	0.93	2.63	3.33	2.48	15.55
Ohio	90s	NA	4.27	1.77	1.37	0.93	0.83	1.77	2.63	2.40	9.53
South Carolina	77–78	NA	8.30	4.40	3.50	2.70	2.60	3.50	3.80	2.60	NA
	90s	NA	6.93	2.83	2.28	1.78	1.90	2.90	3.78	2.70	15.70
Tennessee	79–80	2.40	10.70	5.60	3.90	3.10	3.30	2.80	7.30	5.60	8.50
	85–86	3.90	10.90	5.10	3.90	3.30	3.20	3.20	8.10	6.10	9.60
	96–97	4.30	5.50	2.50	1.80	1.20	1.40	2.70	7.20	5.70	13.40
Texas	90s	1.60	5.90	2.63	1.27	1.10	0.87	1.70	2.80	2.03	17.40
Vermont	90s	1.83	1.90	1.10	0.60	0.47	0.30	0.33	1.50	1.40	4.53
Virginia	79–80	6.20	11.00	6.30	5.30	4.40	4.20	4.20	7.70	12.60	11.50
	85–86	8.30	10.20	4.80	4.20	3.70	2.90	3.40	8.10	9.70	13.90
	90s	5.48	7.43	3.90	3.23	2.73	2.23	3.65	6.58	8.65	13.00
West Virginia	79–80	1.70	10.80	3.40	2.20	1.90	1.80	1.40	3.50	2.50	NA
	85–86	4.40	7.50	3.30	2.70	2.30	2.20	1.80	4.60	2.50	NA
	90's	5.07	5.67	2.63	1.80	1.23	1.23	2.03	3.93	2.87	NA
Wisconsin	96–97	1.20	2.20	1.00	0.50	0.30	0.20	0.60	1.00	0.80	8.50

[a] Figures for 1977–78, 1979–80, and 1985–86 are from Shepard and Smith (1989: 6–7); figures for the 1990s are the average of individual year figures from 1994–95 through 1999–2000 as reported in Huebert and Hauser (1999: 137–147) and Denton (2001: 2).

[b] The 1990s averages are from 1994–95, 1995–96, 1996–97, with the following exceptions: Florida and South Carolina also include 1999–2000; Kentucky excludes 1996–97; Louisiana includes 1995–96 and 1998–99; North Carolina also includes 1998–99 (except for kindergarten); Tennessee and Wisconsin only have 1990s data for 1996–97; Texas includes 1994–95, 1995–96, and 1998–99 (but kindergarten data are missing for 1998–99); and Virginia includes 1994–95 and 1995–96.

[c] NA, not available.

reports figures for grades 1 through 8, with kindergarten and ninth grade (usually the first year of high school) included for comparison. Starting with the 1994–1995 school year, the "90s" entries are the average of the available annual data (usually 3 years; see the table legend). This "smoothing" does no great harm because fluctuations year to year in most localities are not large.[3]

From Table 1.1 we see that retention rates "spike" at certain points in the student career. During the elementary years, the rate generally is highest in first grade, often two or three times rates over grades 2 through 5. And it is impressive that this holds whether rates are high or low in absolute terms (compare Mississippi and Virginia, for example). But it also is the case in most states that levels of first grade retention are much reduced in the 1990s relative to earlier periods, often dramatically so. There are exceptions (e.g., the District of Columbia, South Carolina), but the most striking time trend in Table 1.1 is this broad-based retreat from early grade retention specifically.

In many localities rates begin inching up again in middle school (grades 6–8). Then in ninth grade, the first year of high school in most localities, they soar, often surpassing even the heretofore peak rates from first grade.[4] This holds especially in the 1990s, so the ninth grade trend runs counter to the historic trend for first grade. Ninth grade retention rates generally have not declined over time; indeed, in many places they have increased.

School transitions, and the adjustments they require, we know challenge young people (e.g., Entwisle and Alexander 1989; 1993; Roderick 1995b). Transition shock no doubt helps account for the high rates of retention evident in Table 1.1. for first and ninth grades (a pattern observed by Morris [1993], also), but why the former rates have declined over time and the latter not can only be surmised. Perhaps problems skipped over in the early years later become so severe they can no longer be ignored, or possibly younger children are deemed better prospects for growing out of their problems.

Many critics of retention (e.g., Epstein 1987; Shepard and Smith 1988) object especially to the practice of holding children back in the early grades. For them, Table 1.1 holds much good news. Good news, yes; but far from a sweeping victory, as the grade specific retention rates

---

[3] Table 1.1 does not include states for which data are available only for the earlier periods or are spotty for the elementary and middle grades.

[4] Our table does not cover the remaining years of high school, but the figures for ninth grade generally exceed those for later years as well (e.g., Heubert and Hauser 1999: 138–146).

displayed in Table 1.1 imply high *cumulative* risk of retention across the
student career. And more than that, these statewide figures obscure local
highs and lows. In high-poverty school systems, for instance, it is not
unusual for half the student population to repeat one or more grades
before high school (e.g., Education Week 1998). From all of this it seems
safe to conclude that, despite recent reductions in early retention specifically, retention rates remain high in general and are especially high for
poverty level children and minority youth – so-called at-risk students,
whose academic problems dominate educational policy discussions.

Shepard and Smith (1989: 9) attribute the high rates of retention
that prevailed through the mid- to late 1980s to the education reform
movement ushered in by the 1983 report "A Nation at Risk" (National
Commission on Excellence in Education 1983). Although widely credited with prompting the "excellence movement" of the 1980s, this report
probably instead helped crystallize trends already gathering steam. A
"swelling chorus of complaints" about social promotion in the public
schools extends back at least to the 1970s (Larabee 1984; for historical
perspective, see Rothstein 1998) and so predates the commission's work.

The Excellence Commission focused its recommendations on a
narrow set of policy options, such as the "New Basics" high school curriculum and higher educational standards. In consequence, "social promotion" declined for a time, as presumably is reflected in the high "baseline" retention figures in Table 1.1. But the educational reform movement
is not the only factor behind high retention rates. Large demographic
shifts in the school-age population no doubt also have played a role.
In 1980 about 74% of U.S. children age 18 and under were classified as
non-Hispanic White. By 1999 this percentage had shrunk to 65%, and
projections to 2020 anticipate a further decline to 55%. Non-Hispanic
Blacks, by way of comparison, made up 9.3% of youth age 18 and under
in 1980, increased to 10.5% in 1999, and are projected to rise to 12.2%
by 2020. The trend for Hispanic youth (any race) is more dramatic still.
Their share of the total increased from 5.7% in 1980 to 10.8% in 1999 and
is projected to soar to 17.2% by 2020 (U.S. Department of Health and
Human Services 2000: 20).

Minority group youngsters who are poor are at great risk of school
failure (e.g., Kaufman, Bradby, and Owings 1992), so over the next few
decades rates of retention may rise considerably above current levels
if the momentum to limit social promotion continues. As reviewed,
retention rates in many localities already are quite high and "tighten-
ing up" policies could well drive them higher still. By one estimate, for

example, two-thirds of Los Angeles's 1.1. million children were reading below grade level in 1999 (Sahagun 1999). Is it practical or wise to hold back so many youngsters? How can marginal students who have experienced only failure be shielded from further failure? For many of these youth enforcing rigid standards will backfire: they will be encouraged to drop out, to act out, or to do both (McDill, Natriello, and Pallas 1986; Pallas, Natriello, and McDill 1987). Poor, inner city minority youth are those whose promotion prospects are most in jeopardy. For many of them flunking a grade could well shape life chances and incur costs for years to come. The next section reviews some of these possible costs.

Some Costs of Retention, in Dollars and Otherwise

Although retention is commonplace, its costs and benefits are not easily calculated. Some costs are clear-cut, but others are hard to assess because firm evidence is lacking. One obvious consequence of grade retention is increased educational expenditure. The extra year of schooling demanded of repeaters was estimated in the mid-1980s to add about $10 billion to the nation's school bill, on the basis of the then average annual per pupil expenditure of $4,051 and a national annual retention rate of 6% (yielding 2.4 million repeaters per year: Center for Policy Research in Education 1990; see also Dyer and Binkney 1995). The 1985/86 figure for per pupil expenditures (based on enrollments, not attendance) would be just over $5,000 in 1998/99 dollars, but expenditures per pupil today are higher still (a bit under $6,400: U.S. Department of Education 2000a: 187). Additionally, repeaters often receive extra services, including special education services – for example, 8.5% of children age 5–18 with no disabilities were identified as repeaters in 1995 versus just over a third of those with a learning disability (U.S. Department of Education 1997: 54). If $10 billion was a reasonable estimate for 1985, then almost certainly the cost associated with repeaters' "extra" year now is well beyond $10 billion – retention rates remain high, per pupil expenditures are up, and extra services are more costly. Retaining up to half the children in a district one or more times by the fifth year of elementary school is roughly equivalent to increasing its elementary school population by 10%, and the associated costs almost certainly exceed 10%.

One cost especially hard to calculate is a deferred one: school discontinuation. Failing a grade in school is a major risk factor for high school dropout, increasing dropout odds in many studies two- and threefold (e.g., Jimerson 2000). High school dropout entails severe costs. To cite but one example, in 1999 a high school diploma or general equivalency diploma (GED) conferred a wage premium of about a third, comparing dropouts in the 25–34 age range with comparably aged high school graduates (U.S. Department of Education 2001: 137–139). This sizable 1-year differential implies much larger differences over a lifetime – on the order of $100,000 according to one estimate, even after adjusting for related disadvantages that would depress dropouts' earnings for other reasons (McDill et al. 1986). Being behind in school is one of the strongest predictors of dropout even when other risk factors such as minority status and poverty background are taken into account (Grissom and Shepard 1989; Rumberger 1995; Rumberger and Larson 1998; Temple, Reynolds, and Ou 2000). Indeed, connections between dropout and early retention specifically are documented in several sources (Cairns, Cairns, and Neckerman 1989; Ensminger and Slusarcick 1992; Lloyd 1978; and Stroup and Robins 1972; Temple, Reynolds, and Ou 2000), including the BSS (e.g., Alexander, Entwisle, and Horsey 1997; Alexander, Entwisle, and Kabbani 2001).

Retention affects life success after high school in other ways as well. For example, Royce, Darlington, and Murray (1983: 444–445) report that, compared to similar students who had not repeated a grade, repeaters were more likely later to be unemployed or not seeking work, to be living on public assistance, or to be in prison. Here too the retention–dropout linkage no doubt is relevant, as about half the prison population and half of welfare recipients lack high school degrees (Educational Testing Service 1995; National Research Council 1993). The excess costs for teaching students who repeat a year is thus in actuality only a small fraction of the long-term costs to the student and to society.

Beyond costs calculated in dollars, there also may be psychological costs involving self-esteem and personal happiness. These costs are borne by both children and their families – parents because dreams for their children are compromised, and children because they grow to see themselves as failures or misfits. Teachers and parents worry a great deal about the socioemotional consequences of children's being off-time in school, and with good reason. Repeating a grade seems to increase children's adjustment problems in school (Kellam, Branch, Agrawal, and Ensminger 1975), perhaps because it disrupts peer relations. When children move from grade to grade they generally keep the same peers, but retention separates children from their peers. Evidence indicates that school performance deteriorates when peer groups are disrupted (Felner and Adan 1988; Felner, Ginter, and Primavera 1982).

Does retaining pupils in grade accomplish enough good to warrant the risks and costs it entails? No one knows. Despite extensive study and strong opinions, the jury is still out.

Retention: Solution or Problem?

When children fail to master the curriculum at an acceptable level of proficiency, there are at least three courses of action. The first is to alter policies so students will not have to be held back: redesign schooling so everyone can be promoted. But promoting children who fall short of pre-scribed standards (e.g., social promotion) is now out of favor (American Federation of Teachers 1997; U.S. Department of Education 1999), and many children, unfortunately, still fall short. In the context of the recent debate over social promotion versus rigorous promotion standards, it is interesting that retention is less common in many other countries, even developed countries whose educational systems are seen as equal to or better than our own. Though coverage is spotty (and reliability hard to assess), recent figures on grade repetition at the primary and secondary levels for industrial and industrializing countries in Europe and Asia all are single digit, mostly in the vicinity of 1%–3% (e.g., UNESCO 2000: Table 5; World Bank 2001: Table 2.13). And in most places these low levels of grade retention extend back at least to the 1960s (i.e., Haddad 1979; Lockheed and Verspoor 1991: 12 and Table A-11). Thus far, though, the option of promoting everyone has not proved practical on a broad scale here in the United States.

Another possibility is for students to make up ground by attending summer school. As an alternative to retention, summer remediation has considerable appeal and programs have proliferated in recent years (e.g., Abercrombie 1999; Gewertz 2000; Stenvall 2001). However, for reasons not well understood, summer programs at the elementary level are not successful in making up for academic deficiencies (Cooper, Charlton, Valentine, and Muhlenbruck 2000; Entwisle, Alexander, and Olson 2000a; Heyns 1987) and certainly have not eliminated the need for retention. The experience from Chicago's ambitious "Summer Bridge" program is that about half the children who fail to meet promotion standards are able to advance to the next grade level after summer school and other interventions (Chicago Public Schools 1998; Roderick, Bryk, Jacob, Easton, and Allensworth 1999). Half is an impressive figure, but it still leaves many students behind. Results elsewhere typically are no better and sometimes are much worse. In Cincinnati, for example, only about

10% of children assigned to a summer remediation program after first grade achieved satisfactory levels of reading achievement and advanced to second grade; the other 90% had to repeat first grade anyway (Mueller 1989).

The third solution when performance is below standard is for youngsters to repeat the school year. As reviewed earlier, this course of action is far more common in the United States than most people probably realize. In many high-poverty school systems retention rates over the primary grades approach 50%. Baltimore, the site of our study, is one such community.

Repeating a Grade: The Fairness Issue

Popular sentiment and probably most practitioners would have youngsters repeat a year rather than pass them along ill prepared for the work that lies ahead (e.g., Byrnes 1989; Byrnes and Yamamoto 1986; Lombardi, Odell, and Novotny 1990; Tomchin and Impara 1992). According to a Public Agenda survey (2000), 66% of public school parents would approve (strongly or somewhat) the school's recommendation to hold their child back if he/she failed to meet academic standards after attending summer school, and 77% of respondents to a recent Gallup poll (2001) agree that students should be required to pass a standardized test in order to be promoted to the next grade. As to professional sentiment, Smith and Shepard (1988: 330) find a strong achievement orientation among kindergarten teachers: "Teachers believe ... the pupil career should be driven by competence or readiness rather than by social promotion and ... for the most part, they act according to these beliefs."

Is this unreasonable? According to the American Federation of Teachers (1997: 1) promoting children who clearly are not prepared sets them up for further failure and poses challenges for teachers, who then must instruct children with widely varying competencies and motivation. Their report describes social promotion as

an insidious practice that hides school failure and creates problems for everyone – for kids who are deluded into thinking they have learned the skills to be successful or get the message that achievement doesn't count; for teachers who must face students who know that teachers wield no credible authority to demand hard work; for the business community and colleges that must spend millions of dollars on remediation; and for society that must deal with a growing proportion of uneducated citizens, unprepared to contribute productively to the economic and civic life of the nation.

Even if a bit overstated, this indictment hardly reflects a mean-spirited desire to penalize those who fail to make the grade. Yet according to much commentary on the topic, harm is the actual, if unintended, result.

The "mean-spirited" idea subsumes two themes. The first is "effectiveness," the surface concern. Sometimes this expands to "cost effectiveness," but whether cast in bookkeeping terms or not, educational interventions are expected to do more good than harm, and preferably at least some good and no harm. Most research on retention takes this perspective, if only implicitly: if retained children are worse off later than if they had been passed along, then the intervention is judged unsuccessful or ineffective.[5] And if this deficit could reasonably have been anticipated by those responsible for the decision, then mean-spirited would seem an apt characterization.

But with "harm" and "good" on the table, we also need to ask "to whom" and "for whom." This takes us to the second theme, which involves "fairness" or "equity" issues. Schools in the modern era shoulder many responsibilities. Helping children of poverty background who enter school poorly prepared is one of those. "Compensatory education," after all, exists for a reason. One particularly compelling study (Hart and Risley 1995: 76) finds that 3-year-olds in professional families have a more extensive working vocabulary than do adults in welfare families!

Despite many exceptions, as a group poor children and disadvantaged minority children already are behind when they begin school (e.g., West, Denton, and Germino-Hausken 2000). And barring a mid-course correction, the prognosis is that over time they will fall further and further back, mainly because of hardships outside school (e.g., Entwisle, Alexander, and Olson 1997; Frymier 1992; 1997). For such children to do well in school can be a Herculean struggle, and schools must be meticulous in serving their needs.

Impressive progress has been made over the years in furthering equal opportunity for the less advantaged. To mention but one example, African-American and White rates of high school dropout (e.g., Hauser, Pager, and Simmons 2001) and high school completion (Day and

---

[5] We suppose it should also be stipulated that there are no advantages accruing to other classes of students large enough or important enough to justify the harm to some. Research evaluations rarely consider such tradeoffs, but they are commonplace in the real world, and somehow to resolve them is one of the heavy burdens of education administration. For relevant comment, see Natriello (1998).

Curry 1998) are closer now than ever before in U.S. history.[6] Vigilance
still is needed, though. Even if most teachers rate children strictly
in terms of classroom performance, there is always the possibility of
so-called institutionalized discrimination – that is, practices taken for
granted as right and proper that can have the effect of denying opportunities to poor and minority youngsters. In the minds of some, retention
is one of these practices. According to Smith and Shepard (1987: 133),
retention and homogeneous grouping by ability "[help] advantaged
groups, [create] further barriers for the disadvantaged, and [promote]
segregation and stratification."

Such concerns are longstanding (see, e.g., Abidin, Golladay, and
Howerton 1971) and of course are not peculiar to the practice of
retention. In fact, the potential for unfairness is present whenever instructional and organizational interventions separate students from one
another on the basis of skill or achievement level and then treat them differently thereafter. Because academic and social disadvantage overlap,
minority and disadvantaged youngsters almost always rank lower than
Whites and advantaged youth on so-called merit selection criteria, and
so lag behind under such systems. To mention some of the more obvious examples, minority and/or disadvantaged children are assigned in
disproportionate numbers to special education classes, to low-ability instructional groups, and to general or vocational tracks at the secondary
level; they are underrepresented in programs for the gifted and talented
and in admission to select colleges and universities; and they are more
likely to be held back, the focus of our interest here.

Some critics view merit criteria as either unnecessary or inappropri-
ate, because using them has the effect of perpetuating historic inequali-
ties, and of legitimating them under a veneer of "equal opportunity."
Even though it may be an unintended consequence of well-intentioned
procedures, relying on merit criteria tends to relegate minority and
disadvantaged youth to the bottom rung of most education ladders.

"Meritocrats" and their "cognitive elite" first cousins (e.g., Henry
1994; Herrnstein and Murray 1994) view these same selection criteria
as necessary and appropriate. Although they may regret that minorities
and the disadvantaged fall at the low end, such an outcome is viewed
as society's failing, not a reason to compromise academic standards. In
fact, the argument goes, merit standards serve all children's interests,

---

[6] Patterson Research Institute (1999) affords a good overview of progress made in the
education arena, and of challenges that remain.

because they channel youth into the education "slots" best suited to their talent and aptitude. Put differently, this view holds that most children will make better use of their potential under merit-based sorting than they would under any reasonable alternative.

The weak line here is "their potential." Transactional notions of development are absent from many of these arguments. Human development, whether involving growth of the brain or skill as a dancer in adolescence, is very much a *product* of the interactions between humans and their institutional contexts. "Merit standards" suffer from the drawback of being static and one-sided. They assess a student with respect to final standards at one point in time. This assessment may or may not reflect their potential.

This particular debate will continue for many years to come.[7] Equity concerns almost always hover in the background when educational practices are being scrutinized, especially for practices involving a remediation component. Under such circumstances, questions of "effectiveness" take on added significance. If retention hurts rather than helps, this fact needs to be known. As Shepard and Smith (1988: 142) say, "Special placements require evidence of effectiveness ... good intentions are not sufficient." The reason is straightforward: an intervention that has good consequences for its recipients is not likely to be deemed unfair. Fairness and effectiveness thus are joined.

The analyses presented in this volume speak most directly to the question of effectiveness. In the narrow context of program evaluation, this sort of separation is possible, but whether a particular practice is good or wise is much more complicated. Some of these broader questions surrounding retention are addressed in the concluding chapter.

---

[7] For overview and comment in the context of so-called high stakes testing, see Madaus and Clarke (2001) and Natriello and Pallas (2001). For discussion of the conceptual and value underpinnings of the debate, see Husén (1976), Miller (1976), Roemer (2000), and Sen (2000).

2

Research on Grade Repetition

Strong Opinions, Weak Evidence

> The evidence is quite clear and nearly unequivocal that the achieve-
> ment and adjustment of retained children are no better – and in most
> instances are worse – than those of comparable children who are pro-
> moted. Retention is one part of the current reform packages that does not
> work.
>
> (Smith and Shepard 1987: 134)

> The evidence is extensive and unequivocal. It includes test scores, sur-
> veys, personality and emotional adjustment measures, case studies –
> everything from elaborate statistical analyses to asking students how
> they feel. Almost everything points in the same direction – retention is
> an extremely harmful practice.
>
> (House 1989: 210)

> Those who continue to retain pupils at grade level do so despite cumula-
> tive research evidence that the potential for negative effects consistently
> outweighs positive outcomes ... the burden of proof legitimately falls on
> proponents of retention plans to show there is compelling logic indicating
> success of their plans where so many other plans have failed.
>
> (Holmes and Matthews 1984: 232)

These are the voices, and the sentiment, most often encountered when
the results of research on grade retention are distilled for general con-
sumption. The judgments quoted reflect the point of view that prevailed
in academic circles in the wake of the Excellence Commission's "back to
basics" call for rigorous enforcement of high academic standards. And
though recent stocktaking in the literature generally is more balanced
(see, for example, Dawson 1998a; Jimerson 2000; Karweit 1992; Tanner

16

and Galis 1997; Thompson and Kolb 1999; Woodward and Kimmey 1997), some of the voices that most command attention (e.g., Darling-Hammond 1998; Hauser 1999; Reynolds, Temple, and McCoy 1997) would be hard to distinguish from those of the 1980s.

Are such sweeping conclusions really warranted? The body of evidence in fact is far less compelling than one would suppose from evaluations like those quoted. The most frequent finding across studies is that repeaters and nonrepeaters do not differ significantly on "in school" criteria – test scores, marks, and measures of affect or attitude.[1] Jimerson's review (2000) is especially useful here because he covers recent studies, those conducted during the 1990s. For socioemotional outcomes (e.g., attitudes toward self and school) his review assesses 146 analyses (derived from 19 studies). The retainee–promoted difference fails to attain significance in 125 (86%). For performance measures (test scores and marks), his review covers 163 analyses of which 84 comparisons (51%) fail to attain significance – a slight majority. Still, many more of these comparisons favor promotion than favor retention, so if we use a sign test (e.g., is the direction of results more often positive or negative?) promotion wins. This same pattern holds in earlier reviews, also (e.g., Holmes 1989).

But such a scorecard approach to weighing the evidence is problematic. Consider how the analyses presented in the first edition of this volume fare in Jimerson's review (2000). His tally of BSS results for achievement outcomes has 44 significant differences favoring promotion and just 1 favoring retention (along with 35 that are nonsignificant). Reviewing his compilation reveals that the BSS accounts for nearly half the comparisons in the entire review. Moreover, the 44–1 BSS "vote" in favor of promotion is among the most pronounced skews across all 19 studies. Yet Jimerson's narrative says the BSS is one of four studies that reflect favorably on grade retention's effectiveness. How can this be? The answer is simple, but not discernible in his totals: for most of the 44 comparisons in which BSS repeaters fall short, *they are not as far behind their classmates after retention as they had been before.* This seems to us the most reasonable standard for weighing retention's effectiveness, but it is certain that most readers of Jimerson's review will miss the distinction and remember only the string of "minuses" his summary table assigns to our work.

---

[1] Results for high school dropout as the criterion are different, as these studies generally report large, significant differences favoring promotion (e.g., Jimerson 2000).

There are other issues involving "standards," too. Many of the studies covered in the various reviews are methodologically weak, an opinion that is not ours alone. For example, Reynolds (1992: 3), whose own research with a panel of low-income Chicago children does *not* find in favor of retention, offers the following commentary on Holmes's literature review (1989). Reynolds begins by noting that just 25 of the 63 studies in Holmes's meta-analysis use matching or statistical adjustments to evaluate retention's effects, further that just 16 of those match on students' prior achievements, and finally that just 4 of the 63 match "on attributes that are consistently found to be predictive of the decision to retain, including prior achievement, sex and socioeconomic status." Reynolds fails to note that one of the four studies employing all these controls finds positive effects for retention (i.e., Peterson, DeGracie, and Ayabe 1987), but he does say that the literature covered by Holmes "hardly constitutes conclusive evidence for or against retention." Similar sentiments are expressed by Karweit (1992: 1117): "The lack of high-quality studies severely limits what can be said about the effects of grade retention. Problems in research design, specification of the basis for comparison, treatments being compared, and limited time frames for comparison all detract from the quality of the research."

At issue here is "quality control" (Harvard Education Letter 1986). One serious failing is that many studies do not follow a comparison group of nonretained youngsters. If only repeaters are followed, a drop in their performance after retention could reflect a general decline in performance with age that would be seen for any group, whether retained or not (e.g., Simmons and Blyth 1987). On average, *all* students' liking for school tends to decrease with age (e.g., Epstein and McPartland 1976; Harvard Education Letter 1992b), so how retention affects children's liking of school can be determined only if comparable children who are not retained are also followed. Also, many studies examine students only *after* retention occurs, so if retained students have a lower effort level or lower feelings of competence than other students, it could be that they displayed these same characteristics before retention. Without knowing repeaters' preretention status, it is impossible to know whether retention has affected them or not.

In light of considerations like these, one has to wonder how much faith to place in a simple tally of favorable and unfavorable results. The sections that follow take up some of these issues in more detail.

Negative Findings Overstated; Positive Findings Neglected

Setting aside for now the results presented in the first edition of this volume, at least four persuasive studies in the corpus of contemporary retention research find positive effects of retention on achievement outcomes: the Texas studies conducted by Dworkin and colleagues (Dworkin, Lorence, Toenjes, Hill, Perez, and Thomas 1999b; Lorence, Dworkin, Toenjes, and Hill 2002); Karweit (1999); Peterson and associates (1987); and Pierson and Connell (1992). Additionally, some studies report positive effects on attitudes and behaviors (e.g., Gottfredson, Fink, and Graham 1994; Pianta, Tietbohl, and Bennett 1997; Reynolds 1992). Moreover, findings in general are more mixed than is generally appreciated. Consider again Holmes's literature review, often invoked as though it lined up unequivocally against retention.[2] The evidence he presents in fact is mixed. He divides studies into two groups: those that report same-age comparisons and those that report same-grade comparisons (some studies report results both ways). Results differ depending on which perspective is used.

Same-age comparisons evaluate the performance of repeaters against that of children of the same age who have not been held back, for example, second grade repeaters against their promoted peers at the end of third grade. It would be strange indeed to find second grade retainees performing at the level of third graders after 2 years in second grade, yet that is what is required to achieve parity in same-age comparisons. Comparing repeaters with children who have been exposed to a more advanced curriculum puts them at a decided disadvantage, and a same-age frame of reference almost preordains results that favor promotion.

Same-grade comparisons evaluate repeaters' performance against that of their classmates finishing the grade for the first time. This approach gives repeaters the advantage of having gone through the curriculum twice (the intended "treatment") and of an extra year's seasoning, including an extra year of maturity. Results under a same-grade framing, which Karweit (1999) argues and Shepard (2000) acknowledges probably is the more appropriate frame of reference for evaluating retention's effectiveness, often favor retention. According to Karweit (1999: 43–44): "We pay specific attention to the same-grade comparisons

---

[2] Holmes's own words encourage this, but his excess of enthusiasm has not gone unchallenged. One astute reviewer of his meta-analysis accuses Holmes of "glaring mismeasurements and misinterpretations"; see Wilson 1990.

because these are the comparisons that are probably most relevant to teachers and parents. That is, parents and teachers are probably most interested in how the retained child does in comparison to his class-mates given the retention, not to his former classmates in another grade." Wilson (1990: 229) is more blunt: "No proponent of retention (in his or her right mind) has ever claimed that retention in grade will result in the child's learning the next year's curriculum. The correct contrast is the equal-grade contrast, which compares students with a reference group at the same-grade level."

Holmes's review covers 10 studies that use the same-grade approach. These report 107 comparisons for 1 year post retention and 41 com-parisons for 3+ years post retention. The achievement test advantage accruing to retention in the first year averages 0.25 standard deviation (sd). At 3+ years post retention the difference is essentially zero. Across studies, then, same-grade benefits appear short-term, a 1-year boost possibly attributable to test-wiseness (i.e., a result of taking the same test over). However, there are two studies (providing 30 comparisons for the first year) with results consistently favoring retention, and for them advantage accruing to retention remains a robust 0.73 sd 3+ years afterward. Moreover, in another section of his review, Holmes looks in detail at nine studies published since 1980 that report positive effects for retention. His intent is to discern commonalities, and Holmes finds some. In most of the nine retention was combined with supplemental services (sometimes referred to as "retention plus") and the subject pro-file was atypical – for example, middle class repeaters with relatively high preretention achievement scores.

Given the preceding, it hardly seems fair to say that the evidence lines up consistently and unequivocally against retention. And this is before considering individual projects. To illustrate the diverse approaches that have been brought to bear on the question, we shortly will review four studies that find in favor of retention, all but one postdating Holmes's stocktaking (the exception is Peterson et al. 1987). First, though, we ex-pand on the same-age versus same-grade frame of reference distinction just introduced, as it is critical for a proper understanding of this litera-ture (including the analyses presented in this volume).

Meaningful Comparisons: Same-Age; Same-Grade

Evaluating the effects of retention requires tracking the same students over time, and the means by which comparison groups are formed is crucial. Same-grade studies evaluate retained pupils against their new classmates; same-age studies evaluate retainees against promoted members of their original class at some later point – for instance, how do retained pupils fare after 2 years in first grade compared with their original, promoted classmates, who would be finishing second grade? Same-grade comparisons are useful for deciding whether an extra year in a grade raises children to grade level expectation (which presumably is what motivates the intervention), whereas same-age comparisons set a high standard: for example, how can children who have seen only the first grade curriculum be expected to perform on the same level as children who have seen both a first and a second grade curriculum?

Such problems notwithstanding, both types of comparisons are needed: under a traditional grade organization it is impossible to have retained and nonretained youngsters be of the same age *and* in the same grade. Figure 2.1 illustrates the two approaches. It tracks two successive cohorts of school beginners for 3 years. In this example, all members of cohort 1 start out together as first graders (point A). At year's end most of the cohort move up to second grade (point C), but some are held back and hence in the second year still are first graders (point B). Between the second and third years the study group continues to spread out. By the third year most first grade repeaters have joined some second grade repeaters in second grade (point D), while their "on time" peers have moved into third grade (point E). Meanwhile, in the second year a new

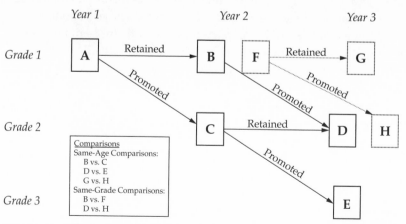

FIGURE 2.1. Illustration of same-age and same-grade comparisons involving retainees in the early primary grades. Solid lines: members of cohort 1; dotted lines: members of cohort 2.

beginning cohort starts its journey. In Year 2, these "new" first graders from cohort 2 (point F) are joined by repeaters from cohort 1 (point B). In Year 3, some members of cohort 2 still are in first grade (point G), but those who advance to second grade (point H) are assigned to classes with first and second grade repeaters from the first cohort (point D).

The picture gets more complicated still as time goes on, but the snapshot in Figure 2.1 is sufficient to set up the contrasts of interest. Point B locates first grade retainees from the first cohort at the end of their repeated grade. To see how they are faring relative to their original cohortmates, we would compare their performance against that of children at point C – this is a same-age comparison. The corresponding comparison 2 years post retention involves points D and E. These youngsters are the same age but have just finished grades 2 and 3, respectively.

Same-grade comparisons can be made two ways. One would be at points B and F in Figure 2.1, where first grade repeaters from cohort 1 are evaluated at the end of their repeated year against their new grademates from cohort 2, who have just gone through first grade for the first time. Another such comparison, at the end of second grade, points D and H, carries the comparison a year beyond retention for first grade repeaters from the first cohort. In both instances, retainees are compared with their new classmates, who are a year or so younger but at the same grade level. A second strategy for making same-grade comparisons is to evaluate retainees' performance at the end of a particular grade against that of their original cohortmates a year earlier, when they successfully finished the same grade. In Figure 2.1, one such comparison would evaluate repeaters at point B against the to-be-promoted subset at point A. This is the type of same-grade comparison made in the present research, as the experience of a single cohort is examined over time.

Same-age and same-grade comparisons afford complementary perspectives on retention. Same-age comparisons may tilt results against retention because the agemates are at different grade levels and the promoted group has been exposed to more of the elementary school curriculum. Same-grade comparisons may favor retention because the retained youngsters have advantages: being older than their grademates, having gone through the curriculum twice, possibly receiving special remedial efforts, and perhaps being test-wise if the same evaluation instrument is used repeatedly. But with the exception of "test-wiseness," these advantages are intended and reflect the logic of retention. The idea is to give children a chance to catch up – the so-called gift of time – and the period required to reach this goal should not be the only factor weighing on the merits of the practice. If repeating a year raises performance to the requisite standard and children thereafter progress comparably with those who are able to meet that standard in just 1 year, then repeating has fulfilled its purpose. Of course, there also are reasons why the extra year may work against repeaters: if their new teachers harbor doubts about repeaters' abilities or their new classmates tease them, then the second time through a grade could well prove a long and difficult year.

Arguments pro and con are easy to construct. Much harder is to procure solid evidence that tilts the scales, authoritatively, toward one or the other. The answer, in fact, is not yet in. Many seemingly authoritative voices tell us that they have the answer, which is that retention does not have the intended effect. In our view, more balance is needed. Toward that end, the next section describes several studies that run counter to these voices of authority.

Research Indicating Positive Effects of Retention

1. Peterson and colleagues (1987) evaluate the experience of first, second, and third grade repeaters in a sample of children attending public schools in Mesa, Arizona. The question for them is whether retained children do better in reading, language, and math after 4 years of schooling than do children not retained. In the Mesa school system retainees get special remedial assistance – a "retention plus" intervention. Their project, which began in 1981, includes all children held back that year for whom California Achievement Test (CAT) data were available in at least one subject over the 4-year period.[3] The number of students is not exactly the same in every achievement domain, but the analysis includes about 65 first grade retainees, 26 second grade retainees, and 14 third grade retainees.

To create a basis of comparison, matched samples of promoted youngsters were identified at each grade level. Criteria used in the matching include information on the pupils' sex, ethnicity, age, and reading, math, and language scores from the spring 1981 CAT administration, with good correspondence achieved between retained and promoted subsamples on all matching criteria. Such extensive matching – several test domains along with student demographic characteristics – is uncommon.

[3] Children who have complete records closely approximate the characteristics of those lost from the analysis as a result of gaps in the testing series.

Peterson and coworkers' analysis is straightforward. They present CAT means and standard deviations for each year, from spring 1981 through spring 1984, separately for retainees and matched controls. This mode of presentation allows both same-age and same-grade comparisons.[4]

At the end of the repeated grade, children held back are ahead of their former classmates at the same point in time (B versus C from Figure 2.1, for example). These same-age advantages diminish in subsequent years, however, and by the third year the achievement differences are no longer significant. Even so, there is no indication in these data that retained students are falling behind their promoted peers.

In same-grade comparisons significant advantages again are found for retainees at the end of their repeated grade, most notably for those held back in first grade. That is to say, retainees' scores at the end of their second time through first grade are higher than their promoted grademates' had been when they finished first grade the previous year – the B versus A comparison of Figure 2.1.

This particular comparison is potentially misleading, however, because the "matched" first grade students who were promoted were "matched" partly on the basis of their poor performance on the CAT battery in the spring of that year. If retained pupils advance at all during the repeated year, as would be expected, their gains necessarily would outdistance those of their matched classmates, as the latter had no opportunity to register improvement – that is, they were selected for study partly on the basis of their (low) spring 1981 CAT scores. The appearance of a repeated year advantage in this instance is a same-grade artifact that follows from the mechanics of the matching procedure.[5] However, Peterson and associates' results also show small advantages for repeaters when they finish the second and third grades compared to their promoted classmates at the end of their second and third grades. The advantages of repeating a grade thus persist for 2 or 3 years, and

[4] Their use of the normal curve metric is a minor problem, as this causes a different "fulcrum" to be used for the various comparison groups (e.g., the performance of retained first graders is scaled relative to the distribution of first graders, whereas that of second graders is referenced to other second graders). It would obviously be useful to know whether retainees are doing better or worse than promoted youngsters at some specified time after retention, and normal score equivalents do not inform that particular comparison. Since the various CAT batteries are vertically calibrated, it would have been a simple matter to report raw score means as well. These use a common metric across grade levels and would have informed such questions.

[5] Mantzicopoulos and Morrison (1992) also report significant same-grade differences favoring repeaters in the repeated year, but again this is largely a consequence of the way the comparisons were structured.

these comparisons, unlike those for the baseline year, probably are meaningful.

This study, then, shows some positive consequences of retention. Same-grade advantages are found for retainees for several years, and same-age comparisons indicate improved relative performance in the repeated year. Peterson and coworkers consider the finding that the remaining same-age comparisons show retainees performing at about the same level as their matched-control agemates a negative showing for retention. Since the later testing levels of retainee and comparison groups were not significantly different, it cannot be said that retention accomplished anything useful in these instances.

This is typical of how findings of "no difference" are treated in the literature, but for retainees just to be holding their own may be an accomplishment. Much hinges on what *would have happened* if these children had not been held back and given the opportunity to consolidate their skills. The logic of matched controls presumes to simulate that reality, but is the simulation believable? Under a social promotion regimen would we really expect repeaters' postretention achievement profile to mimic that of their poorly performing but promoted matched peers? The very fact that retainees were designated for retention and the controls were not suggests that retained children's difficulties were more severe in ways not reflected in the matching. It is impossible to match retained and promoted students on all relevant factors – the promoted group, for example, may be more mature, have fewer family problems, or be less aggressive than the held-back group.

Under a social promotion policy, retained youngsters may have fallen further and further behind, as skill deficiencies, poor work habits, low self-esteem, and other characteristics continued to hinder their progress. If this is the expectation, then to find children who have been held back performing more or less on par with their classmates 3 years afterward would be a positive showing. This scenario is addressed in Karweit's study, described next.

2. Karweit (1999) examines retentions in grades K–3 for children in the Prospects longitudinal first grade cohort ($N = 9,240$). The group's educational progress was tracked from 1991 to 1994 and sample coverage is national. Almost 20% of the panel registered a retention over this period, half of them in first grade (which we saw in Table 1.1. generally is the modal grade of retention at the elementary level).

Karweit's analysis examines reading and math achievement as assessed in fall of first grade (fall 1991), spring 1992, spring 1993, and spring 1994. She too reports both same-age and same-grade comparisons, and from several perspectives: retained versus all promoted, retained versus all promoted after adjusting statistically for background differences, retained versus a low-performing promoted comparison group.

Her same-age comparisons show no benefit or harm that accrues to retention – the achievement gap separating repeaters and promoted children is about the same after retention as it was prior to the former's being held back. As mentioned, a finding of "no difference" is common in the retention literature. Karweit's same-grade comparisons, on the other hand, favor retention, even though repeaters' scores in every instance lag behind those of the comparison children. How can this be favorable for retention? It is favorable because before their retention repeaters were even further behind. In the year prior to their retention, to-be repeaters were scoring on average 1.21 sd's behind to-be promoted children in reading comprehension, vocabulary, and math. At the end of retainees' repeated year, the deficit average was down to 0.38 sd, and though it increased gradually thereafter, at 3 years post retention it stood at 0.55 sd, still well below repeaters' preretention shortfall.

On the basis of these and other results from her analysis, Karweit (1999: 43–44) concludes as follows:

Retention appears to be a catching up year that benefits children 2 or 3 years afterwards. These results ... are somewhat at odds with the verdict on retention offered by the educational research community over the last 25 years. Why might this be the case? The primary methodological difference between this study and prior studies is the ability in the present study to make comparisons of retained students' performance to non-retained children before, during and after retention. . . . In most cases, studies have looked at the achievement differentials at the end of the year of retention, concluded that retained students were still behind, and therefore concluded that retention was not effective. Even studies that look longitudinally at the effect of retention stress that retention is not effective because the gap between retained and promoted starts to widen after the retained year. However, even with the widening gap, the gap between retained and promoted children after retention is not as large as it was before retention.

Karweit's "before–after" frame of reference is uncommon in retention studies. Before being held back, repeaters trail so far behind promoted children that the "boost" provided by an extra year in grade is not enough for them to catch up. But "catching up" is not the only standard. For several years after retention these children manage to perform at a level closer to that of the promoted group than before their retentions, and in that sense retention can be said to have helped them.

3. Pierson and Connell (1992) compare achievement scores and attitudes across four groups: repeaters ($N = 74$), a matched-ability comparison group ($N = 69$), a random sampling of students ($N = 60$), and – this is the interesting comparison – a group of children who were socially promoted ($N = 35$). Their research covers children in grades 3 through 6 in two upstate New York school districts, one urban, one rural. The socially promoted group is small, but its inclusion affords a rare comparison – these youngsters were identified in school records as having an "unearned promotion" or were recommended by their teachers for retention but were promoted anyway.

Here is what Pierson and Connell (1992: 305–306) say about their results:

> It appears that whereas retention is not a cure-all for below grade-level academic performance, students whose academic performance suggests they should be retained, and who are retained, perform better 2 or more years later than students with comparable performance who are promoted... the findings support the use of retention as a potentially effective remediation for academic difficulty in the early elementary grades... early academic difficulties tend to persist over the course of elementary school and whereas retention does not eliminate these difficulties, social promotion may exacerbate them.

"Some help" would seem an apt summary of their results.

4. During the late 1990s, events in the state of Texas commanded considerable attention in education policy circles because of dramatic, across-the-board achievement gains on the state's customized test, the Texas Assessment of Academic Skills (TAAS). Dubbed the "Texas Miracle," achievement results from the Lone Star state initially were greeted with much enthusiasm (e.g., Grissmer and Flanagan 1998), but there followed a second wave of mainly skeptical reaction, in which the psychometric properties of the TAAS were probed and TAAS gains compared against gains on the National Assessment of Educational Progress (NAEP) and other nationally normed tests (e.g., Haney 2000; Klein, Hamilton, McCaffrey, and Stecher 2000; McNeil and Valenzuela 2001). The original lofty claims have not stood up well under scrutiny, raising doubts in the minds of many and leading to much confusion (compare, for example, Greene 2000, with Schrag 2000).

Of most immediate relevance is that the statewide testing program in Texas provides the benchmarking for an evaluation of grade retention on a scale perhaps never before attempted. The TAAS is a criterion-referenced assessment device, designed to gauge children's mastery of local curricular objectives. According to statewide figures for 1996–97 reported by the Sociology of Education Research Group at the University of Houston (Dworkin et al. 1999b), 1.2% of all children in grades 3–7 were held back that year (16,530 children) compared with 3.2% of those with TAAS reading scores below the pass level of 70 (6,685 children). That is just shy of a threefold difference in the odds of retention. Nevertheless, state policy at the time restricted the use of TAAS performance in promotion–retention decisions, such that more than 200,000 students with scores below expectation advanced to the next grade and almost 10,000 with TAAS scores above expectation were held back.

The fact that so many children in Texas are promoted despite scoring below grade level expectation on the TAAS is the opening used by the Texas research team to structure their evaluation. Using these children as a socially promoted comparison group, they look to see how repeaters fare across successive years – before being held back, after completing the repeated year, and for several years post retention.

Their most encompassing analysis evaluates the performance of children who were third graders in 1994 ($N = 32,151$, including 815 repeaters) who also had TAAS reading scores in 1995, 1996, 1997, and 1998. The analyses include both same-grade and same-age comparisons. Because repeaters score below the promoted comparison group at baseline, the "out year" comparisons also are adjusted statistically for initial TAAS scores and sociodemographic characteristics.[6]

The results of this evaluation are quite striking: the many comparisons *all* favor retention. Repeaters' TAAS scores after 2 years in third grade exceed those of the socially promoted group after 1 year in third grade; repeaters' gains continue to outpace the socially promoted pupils' gains over the years after third grade; repeaters' TAAS average reaches 70 sooner; and statistical adjustments increase all these advantages. Moreover, the pattern is the same when the analyses are performed for White, African-American, and Hispanic children separately; when a subset of the promoted group is selected out whose baseline scores, as a group, are comparable to the baseline scores of repeaters; when replicated on later cohorts (for whom fewer years of data are available); when the requirement that excludes children from the analysis with incomplete testing data is relaxed (to check on possible selection biases); and when the researchers look specifically at children who were held back later, after being promoted out of third grade despite failing TAAS scores.

---

[6] All children included in their analysis scored below 70, but repeaters' average was 7.1 points lower, just below a half standard deviation.

Here is what Dworkin and associates (1999b) have to say about this clean sweep: "These ... analyses reveal no evidence that retention in third grade leads to negative academic consequences among elementary students in Texas. Overall findings suggest that retaining students who fail the TAAS helps Texas students pass the TAAS more quickly than does the practice of social promotion" (p. 16); and "the findings among each of the cohorts demonstrate that retention does not harm the academic performance of students. Indeed the results strongly support the converse in that retention enables students more time to obtain reading skills necessary for success in school. All students are helped by retention regardless of their ethnic or racial status" (p. 37); and, commenting on the results of checking done to probe possible methodological skews, including practice or test-wiseness effects, "the reported higher scores ... observed among retained students at the end of the repeated grade likely reflect genuine academic achievement rather than results due to methodological artifacts" (p. 38; see also Lorence et al. 2002).

By now it will be no surprise that this work and the integrity of its conclusions have been criticized (e.g., Hauser 2001; Shepard 2000), often in terms similar to those directed at the claims of a Texas Miracle discussed previously – the same testing data are used, after all. We cannot resolve all such disputes, but at least it should be noted that the Texas research team has been sensitive to these concerns. Their main report (Dworkin et al. 1999b) comments specifically on several alternative interpretations: regression toward the mean (this would not account for repeaters' continued favorable showing after the repeated year), practice effects (repeaters do not take the identical test, but a psychometrically equivalent version), and selection bias (checked by including children with missing test scores in the analysis). And in separate reports the research team assesses the psychometric properties of the TAAS (Dworkin et al.,1999a) and reports on interventions statewide that are intended to help shore up repeaters' skills – retention plus interventions (Hill et al. 1999).

Technical problems in evaluating retention's effectiveness are hardly peculiar to the Texas research, of course. All the studies just reviewed no doubt are flawed in some ways, as shortfall from the ideal is a given in researching this difficult topic. And, too, there are recent studies not covered that favor promotion over retention (e.g., Jimerson, Carlson, Rotert, Egeland, and Sroufe 1997; McCoy and Reynolds 1999). Our selective rendering of the literature is not intended to declare victory for retention – such a declaration would be unwarranted, as this volume will make clear. Rather, it is to point out that the existing literature is mixed and not one-sided, a point worth making because so many stocktakings lack balance. A second purpose is to establish our reason for revisiting the issue, with new data and a research design that precludes some of the more serious challenges to achieving clarity. Some of these challenges have been mentioned already. Additional ones are discussed in the next sections.

The Matching Strategy and Its Problems

Beyond the same-grade–same-age issue for framing comparisons, there are further complications. For example, to make a fair comparison of a retained group with a nonretained group, the groups should be about equal in terms of ability test results and other relevant qualities before retention occurs. This is a large order because promoted children who test at the same level as retained children are not likely to be in other ways the same: if they were the same in all relevant respects, they presumably would also be retained. For example, those who are low in ability but nevertheless promoted may do well because they try hard or because they are more emotionally mature. Equating the two groups only in terms of ability or achievement test scores does not provide a fair comparison, because the later success of promoted students could be due to other qualities, not to their being spared the burden of retention.

It is hard to separate effects of retention from effects of other problems that lead children to be retained. The most powerful approach would be to list all children whose performance puts them "at risk" for retention and then randomly place them into two groups: one group to be retained and another group to be promoted. Then the two groups would be equivalent (within sampling fluctuations) with respect to risk factors that prompt a retention decision. If the promoted group is doing better than the repeaters in the years after retention, and if the difference is too large to be due to chance, we then could conclude that retention had an adverse effect. This conclusion is justified because other likely sources of uneven performance would be equated in the two groups by random assignment and so should not contribute to *group differences* in performance.[7]

---

[7] However, these very same factors could, and probably would, contribute to individual differences in performance within groups.

Random assignment, though, is not a viable strategy because parents or schools would not be willing to have a child pass or fail a grade at the toss of a coin, even for purposes of a scientific experiment (see Harvard Education Letter 1986: 3, on the impracticality of this approach). Also, human subjects review boards and most investigators would demur for ethical reasons. One alternative is to identify children who were designated for retention but who for some reason were moved ahead anyway. The Pierson–Connell study (1992) described earlier is an example, but this kind of research design is not generally possible. The more usual approach is to identify the complicating factors that cloud comparisons and then somehow "adjust" for their influence, either by matching repeaters and promoted children with similar risk profiles or, better, by using statistical methods. As a practical matter, there is no way to begin except to compare retained and promoted groups that are *not* equivalent.

The matching approach tries to approximate the kinds of groups that would result from random assignment. That is, after retainees are identified, the investigator selects a comparison group from the (larger) pool of promoted children who are similar to their retained classmates. This kind of "matched control" framework is common but is a poor choice. A group of "at-risk but promoted" children will never be matched perfectly to a group of retained children, and the matching operation vitiates the assumptions made by statistical tests. Even with a large group from which to select, it is impossible to match children on more than a very few characteristics at a time, and by selecting on some factors one is almost bound to bias the groups on other factors. It would be hard, for example, to match children exactly on age, sex, ethnic group, parents' socioeconomic status, and test performance, even with a pool of several hundred youngsters, and matching on these criteria does not match students on teachers' marks, family size, peer popularity, and many other potentially critical factors not specified or perhaps not even known. No matter how extensive the matching, there can be no guarantee that all relevant risk factors have been covered and that some "unmatched" difference is not responsible for differences found later between promoted and nonpromoted students.

The situation is also far from ideal when statistical adjustments are used to achieve fair comparisons, but compared to case-by-case matching, statistical equating generally is preferred. It can accommodate more potentially confounding variables, and it gives estimates of the relative strength of other influences besides retention on group differences. Still, something relevant may be left out, and this fundamental dilemma has no sure solution.

Other Weaknesses in Prior Studies

The available evidence on retention has weaknesses beyond those involving the nature of comparison groups. Much of the literature is dated, as many studies are now more than a half-century old. In light of demographic shifts and changes in school organization and curriculum over the last few decades, the current relevance of these older studies is suspect. A contemporary urban school with a high minority enrollment and a 40% retention rate is far different from a 1950s school with no minority students and a 5% retention rate.

Another serious problem is that many retention studies are unpublished. Only 20 of the 63 studies reviewed by Holmes (1989) were published. The others were unpublished dissertations, M.A. theses, and the like. Importantly, published research has likely gone through a refereeing process in which researchers in the same field examine it and decide whether or not it merits publication. Jimerson's (2000) review of studies conducted during the 1990s includes only published sources. As a result the yield is rather small – just 19 studies – but in evaluating retention or any other practice, the scientific quality of the research is central. Retention has not been as thoroughly investigated as many suppose.

Sampling – how study subjects are selected – too often is a weakness in retention research. Rarely does research on retention use representative, or even especially diverse, samples. Years ago Jackson (1975: 628) mentioned the "failure to sample from a population large and diverse enough to allow broad generalization" as a weakness that future studies should try to correct. And though Jackson's advice remains sound some 25+ years later, most often it is honored in the breech.

Research based on the NELS88 project (e.g., Meisels and Liaw 1993; Schneider, Stevenson, and Link 1994) is national in scope and representative but illustrates another pitfall. It contains only retrospective accounts of children's retention over the elementary years. Children in eighth grade or higher recall their elementary school promotion patterns with all the conscious and unconscious editing of experience that such retrospective reports entail. Parents likewise filter such recollections.

Other nationally representative panels (e.g., Prospects, Early Childhood Longitudinal Study [ECLS]) provide excellent coverage of the early grades but have only recently been launched so they cannot address longer-term consequences. Finally, a handful of other local studies like the BSS cover the primary grades and span many years (e.g., Brooks-Gunn, Guo, and Furstenberg 1993; Cairns and Cairns 1994; Ensminger and Slusarcick 1992; Temple, Reynolds, and Ou 2000). These projects are not nationally representative but are extremely valuable. But unlike the BSS these are convenience samples, homogeneous in composition (e.g., all low-income and/or all African-American) without broad coverage of outcomes. These are serious limitations – none fatal perhaps, but certainly leaving room for additional inquiry.

Most evaluations of retention involving performance and affective outcomes such as self-esteem or future hopes are short term, extending but a semester or two after children are held back. What happens during the child's repeated year may be unlike what happens in subsequent years (the child is going through the curriculum for the second time and adjusting to the new peer group), so a short follow-up will not give a full reading of retention's impact. For example, what about youngsters retained in first grade who later reach puberty before their grademates? They may have made a satisfactory adjustment earlier but at the adolescent transition be conspicuous because of their off-time status. Of course, there could be long-term positive consequences as well. Repeating might reduce the need for special education services later or lead to better reading proficiency in high school.

The linkage between early retention and later dropout is one area in which evaluation necessarily is long-term. Many studies establish that retention in the early grades is associated with elevated risk of dropout, but whether the link is causal is less certain (the question is taken up in Chapter 11). Clearly the longer-term consequences of retention could be different from, and possibly more important than, the immediate consequences.

Finally, most studies consider retention from a limited vantage point, focusing either on children's academic performance or on some aspect of their socioemotional adjustment, but not on both. Cognitive and affective development go hand in hand, though, and retention could affect both children's intellectual growth and their socioemotional functioning. Some evidence, for example, suggests that repeaters have fewer friends than children not held back (Harvard Education Letter 1986), and that condition could impair their self-esteem or undermine their parents' confidence in them. Either outcome would undercut their school performance. But there are countervailing possibilities, too. Children who are held back could get better marks in school as they repeat a grade, and this could draw out their academic potential. Not all such questions can be answered in this book. It nevertheless is a step forward that we are able to examine, for the same group of children and with a unified approach, the three areas of development that have commanded the most attention in retention research – school performance, as reflected in achievement test scores and report card marks; socioemotional adjustment; and high school dropout.

3

Retainees in the "Beginning School Study"

The purpose of this book is to address some of the questions about retention raised in the first two chapters, using information from the Beginning School Study (BSS) for guidance. The BSS commenced in fall 1982, when members of the study group were just beginning first grade. Evaluating the consequences of retention is the book's primary objective, but along the way we also provide a risk factor profile of repeaters in the BSS, sketch the complex retention patterns that have framed the group's experience over the elementary and middle school years, and describe how retention intersects other aspects of "administrative sorting" during this time, including assignment to special education classes, ability group placements for instruction in reading, and curricular placements in middle school. The broader system of educational tracking within which retention is embedded typically is neglected in research on retention. This oversight is serious because retention is more often than not linked to these various placements and interventions in children's experience. If retention causes children to be placed in low reading groups and that placement is ignored, any effects of retention could just as well be effects of low group placement.

The BSS, which is ongoing still, was not designed specifically to study retention. Rather, as a long-term study of young children's academic and socioemotional development, it was undertaken to see what helps or hinders typical urban youth as they go through school. It began in first grade in order to shed light on the beginning school transition, to determine how adjustment problems then affect children's later development. This broad sweep, it turns out, also is extremely useful for exploring retention's consequences.

This book evaluates consequences of grade retention prior to high school for repeaters' school performance and socioemotional adjustment and also its longer-term consequences for high school dropout. When BSS children started first grade, no one knew who would fall behind, but many did. The Baltimore public school system mainly follows a K–5, 6–8 grade organization, so the 8 in-school years over which retentions are monitored in this volume coincide with the end of middle school for children who are "on-time." But being held back throws repeaters "off-schedule," so at the end of 8 years they are not finishing middle school. About half the BSS cohort was in this situation. Unlike their on-time peers, they took 9 years or more to make it into high school, and some dropped out before then.

The BSS contains information on the academic performance and personal development of retainees and nonretainees before and after retention. The data were obtained directly from retained children and their promoted classmates, directly from teachers and parents, and from school system records. That is to say, no proxy sources are used. Thus a rich store of data is available for studying retention, and because of the project's unusually long duration, the impact of retention can be traced over many years.

The Sample

A stratified random sample of just under 800 students was selected from the pool of children entering first grade in Baltimore City Public Schools in 1982 (hereafter BCPS). The 20 schools selected for inclusion in the study were chosen on a random basis from strata defined by the school's integration status (i.e., "mostly White," "mostly African-American," "racially integrated") and by community socioeconomic level (i.e., "blue-collar," "white-collar") (see Table 3.1). After recruiting the schools so selected into the project, children then were sampled. Using kindergarten rosters from the previous year, samples were drawn in all 20 schools over the summer before first grade; then in early fall, new first grade registrants were sampled. The summer sampling allowed us to obtain parental consent before the start of the school year (a practical necessity, as our goal was to complete fall interviewing before first report cards were issued); the fall supplementation maintained representativeness by adding children who attended kindergarten elsewhere or had skipped kindergarten altogether (about 10% of the group). The sampling included all first grade classrooms in the 20 schools.

TABLE 3.1. *Socioeconomic and Racial Classification of Schools in the Beginning School Study Sample*

Community Type	Predominantly African-American		Integrated		Predominantly White		Total
	No. of Schools	Av. Parent Education (Years)	No. of Schools	Av. Parent Education (Years)	No. of Schools	Av. Parent Education (Years)	
Blue collar	5	11.6	4	10.9	5	10.6	14
White collar	1	12.8	4	14.2	1	12.7	6
Total	6		8		6		20

Note: On the basis of data on entire first grade enrollments, African-American children in the integrated schools ranged from 13% to 85%, with an average for the eight schools of 45%. Figures based on the BSS sample range from 12% to 97%, averaging 51%. Data on parents' educational level are from the parent interviews conducted summer through early fall 1982.

A particular strength of this sampling plan is that it yields a nonvolunteer study group. Parents did not volunteer their children or otherwise secure their admission to the study, but when approached, 97% of those selected agreed to participate. Without random sampling, as in most other studies of retention, the schools and parents studied may be especially concerned about retention and its consequences, or more concerned than other parents with their children's schooling. This kind of selection bias is a serious concern. If parents of retained children recruit themselves and their children into a study, or if a principal volunteers the school as a study site, there may be biases in terms of the attention that parents and schools devote to retention and to retainees: they may be unusually aware of the problems retention breeds or know exactly which children have been retained, whereas in other schools where retention is not a focus of attention, retained children may be much less visible. Parents who volunteer their children for educational studies also are likely to be more concerned about their children's educational progress and therefore more motivated to do things to help their children than other parents.

Though randomly drawn, the BSS sample intentionally overrepresents Whites and higher-SES youngsters with respect to the Baltimore city school population – the random sampling was "stratified," not "simple." The sample is 55% African-American as against 77% of the city system enrollment at the time the project commenced (U.S. Census Bureau 1983). A simple random sample of Baltimore children in 1982 would have yielded too few well-off students and too few White students to permit SES comparisons and racial or ethnic comparisons.

The sampling strategy employed maintains representativeness, while guaranteeing adequate coverage of the two major racial groups enrolled in Baltimore schools and the full range of SES levels.[1]

Despite oversampling Whites and upper-SES school settings, the BSS beginning school cohort still exemplifies the "high-risk" profile expected of children attending public schools in a high-poverty, deindustrializing city. Two-thirds qualified for subsidized meals at school during the elementary years (the same percentage as citywide at the time), 40% of their mothers lacked high school degrees, and 44% of the sample children were in solo-parent households as first graders.

The BSS first grade cohort thus consists of a large, diverse, representative, nonvolunteer sample of "typical" children attending public schools in a high-poverty city. The majority are African-American, but a large number are White. Many are in low-income families, but a significant fraction are not. Low-income, urban, minority children are at highest risk of being off-time in school and figure prominently in policy discussions. The BSS sample ought to provide a solid foundation for drawing conclusions about effects of retention for the children most typically held back. These conclusions, of course, are specific to Baltimore, but circumstances there ought to be at least broadly similar to those in other high-poverty, large city school systems.

Strengths and Weaknesses of the BSS for Studying Retention

The BSS data and design provide a strong foundation for trying to understand the impact of retention in our study children's lives. The data are longitudinal, so we know these children's histories from a point before any was retained. The students' preretention status on many characteristics – achievement level, classroom deportment, self-regard, and others – can be assessed. Also, their parents' and teachers' views of them before they were retained are known, a matter of great importance, since children who are retained typically have academic or adjustment problems that *predate* retention. Failure to take account of preexisting problems could cloud comparisons with nonretained children, giving a false picture of retention's impact. Beginning the study at the start of

---

[1] As mentioned, during the early 1980s around 77% of the population in the city public schools was African-American. By 1999, this had increased to 87.2%, with another 11.3% White (Maryland State Department of Education 2000: 8). Other minorities make up less than 2% of the BCPS enrollment.

first grade or even earlier, before anyone has been held back, is an important safeguard against misconstruing some children's long-standing academic and adjustment problems as consequences of retention.

It also is important that coverage of the panel's experience extend several grades beyond the repeated year. We said earlier that the repeated year is a special one in many ways. Only after the repeated year is behind them can we judge how students are faring in a "regular" classroom environment. For first grade retainees, we track subsequent performance and adjustment through the completion of seventh grade – 2 years in first grade, plus 1 year in grades 2 through 7. Having an especially long time to study first grade repeaters, and the opportunity to compare them against youngsters held back in second grade or later, allows us to see whether first grade retention differs from retention in later years, as many suspect. Certainly the fact that retention rates typically are higher in first grade than later would seem to suggest so (see Table 1.1).

The year of transition into formal schooling – first grade – carries special pressures and demands. Faring well or poorly at this point has consequences that echo far into the future. In later grades, students have already made various accommodations to the academic routine, and so later retention may have less of an impact. The combination of transition pressures overlaid on a formative stage of schooling sets first grade apart. In addition to examining whether retention has different effects according to the grade in which it occurs, we can pose questions about the scheduling of retention and about how retention ties in with other interventions, for example, special education.

Our analysis plan also is different from that used in most prior retention research in that we rely mainly on statistical adjustments to make "fair" comparisons between retainees and other children, rather than matching cases one-for-one to form comparison groups. This strategy preserves the representativeness of the sampling base and ideally also prevents some of the problems discussed earlier in connection with matched comparison groups. We make several kinds of comparisons, rather than relying on just one. The quality of the baseline information and the size of the BSS sample are sufficient to permit the necessary statistical adjustments, and the over-time data allow us to consider retention's possible effects from several vantage points.

Finally, and perhaps most important, the BSS data allow retention's academic consequences, socioemotional consequences, and consequences for high school dropout to be examined together. We examine children's gains on standardized tests and their report card marks. Teachers' marks are certainly related to test performance, but they also capture other aspects of the child's performance, such as degree of effort expended, ability to solve problems independently, tendencies to work consistently toward a goal and to cooperate with others in a group, and the like.

In terms of socioemotional outcomes, retainees' reaction to retention is assessed in terms of their academic "sense of self" and their future expectations with respect to schooling. If retention is as punishing for children as many fear, this reaction should be detectable in children's ideas about themselves and their future prospects. Many questions about self-regard and hopes for the future were asked in individual interviews with children both before and after they were held back. We therefore can look specifically for changes in outlook that surround the retention experience.

The data are from school records, from many one-on-one interviews with BSS children, and from self-administered interviews in the case of their teachers and most of their parents (parents were interviewed individually upon request). We have talked directly with the students involved and have done so many times over the years. Having available test scores and report card marks for 8 years allows us to cover children's academic progress all through the elementary grades and well into middle school. From pupil interviews we can monitor changes in repeaters' thinking over this same period, and their self-reports of dropout extend coverage into the years beyond high school. This uncommonly long and broad sweep embraces virtually the entirety of these children's schooling and overlaps four school transitions – into first grade, from elementary into middle school, into high school, and out of high school.

The BSS project has some weaknesses, too, however. For one, there are issues that cannot be addressed with the BSS data, at least not as fully as we would want. Probably the main shortcoming is that we have not done detailed classroom observation. Consequently, we can comment on pupil–teacher interactions and retainees' relations with their classmates only in terms of what they have told us. Survey respondents may not always be candid or forthcoming, especially when they are being queried about potentially sensitive issues. Also, problems can be undetected, either because they are not covered in the interview or because questions have not been framed properly. Then, too, some matters simply do not lend themselves to a survey format, because they are too nuanced, are too sensitive, or involve issues of which the respondents may not even be aware.

In the BSS, the risk of deliberate distortion probably is slight. We did not set out to study retention and none of our queries was cast in those terms. Children were selected for participation in the study because they started first grade in the fall of 1982, not because they were repeaters. Likewise, our questioning had little to do with retention. When exploring children's self-attitudes, feelings about school, and the like, questions were asked of everyone and none dealt with retention per se. The same is true of questions posed of parents and teachers. That some youngsters were repeaters and others not never was an issue in any of our fieldwork, so participation in the study should not have heightened sensitivity to the subject. To the extent that concerns about retention can be addressed this way, the BSS should be a good source.

A second area of concern involves problems encountered in implementing our research design. The analyses we present extend over many years and use data from many sources. To illustrate, a total of 12 pupil interviews were conducted between fall 1982 when the BSS commenced and spring 1990 (Project Year 8). During the same time, parents were interviewed on eight occasions. Our procedures generally have worked well – for example, through the group's eighth school year almost 80% of the original sample was still participating in the project and coverage on the Young Adult Survey used to identify dropouts also is 80% (that survey was administered over an 18-month period in 1998/99; equivalently, at age 22–23). Nevertheless, information from all sources is not available each year. The testing data, for example, are from the school system's regular testing schedule. Scores are missing for children absent on the testing days or not tested because they moved between schools. Similarly, not all parents and children were interviewed each time we ventured into the field (mainly because of difficulty in locating them), and not all teachers consented to participate in the study as respondents (although all granted us access to the BSS pupils in their classes for in-school interviewing).

Gaps in coverage thus are a concern throughout, especially for the many children who transferred out of the BCPS during the 8 "in school" years covered in this volume. In Chapter 4, in which movement up the grade structure and through the school system is plotted in detail, we see that some 40% of the study group had left Baltimore's public schools by the end of Project Year 8. For most, there are no school record data after they left the BCPS; interview coverage for them and their parents is uneven, too. Problems that result from these missing data and sample attrition are taken up in Chapter 4.

Another concern is that school record data on grade level progressions are sketchy or unreliable for some children. Fifteen children, in fact, had to be excluded from the entire investigation because we could not track them well enough with school records to be certain what happened to them. The inability to track these children and other problems of incomplete data alerted us to an important issue not acknowledged in previous studies of retention: the sorting of children during the first few years of school places many of those with the most severe problems outside normal record-keeping procedures. Some with severe family problems move frequently from one school to another, and as a result their records are lost or misplaced. Testing data may be missing for them as a result of absenteeism, and often children assigned to special education are exempted from standardized testing altogether.

These children would be completely overlooked in conventional studies of retention or, for that matter, in most research on schooling because students typically are sampled by grade rather than by cohort. That is fine if "grade" is the intended organizing frame, but not if the goal is capture of an age cohort's experience. Grade sampling misses children who are off-time because of retention and may miss children who are off-track because of placement in special education classes. These children, as a consequence, are not studied as part of their age cohort, and that omission gives a false or skewed reading of the cohort's experience. BSS sampling, in contrast, covers the total potential population of children who began school at the same time – the age cohort of beginning first graders in fall 1982.

Another drawback is that our data on parent's economic standing are not as detailed as we would like. Coverage of students' social and demographic characteristics is important for describing "who is retained," and also for making statistical adjustments when trying to isolate effects of retention from possible confounding influences. From parent interviews we have data on education level and family type (e.g., whether two parents or one parent is in residence), but to cover economic well-being we rely mainly on school records pertaining to eligibility for reduced price school meals. This criterion places parents in crude low-/not-low-income categories. Other aspects of family circumstance, such as regularity of income, total amount of income, depth and duration of poverty spells, or family welfare benefits, are not known.[2]

Also, we know little about special services provided for children before, during, or after their retention year. During the years at issue there was no citywide program of supplemental services for repeaters, but individual teachers, and perhaps even schools, no doubt took note of their situation. We know a bit about repeaters' reading group placements and receipt of remedial instruction in math and reading, but little else. Consequently, our analysis can say little about "retention plus" initiatives. This is unfortunate, as retention with supplementation generally seems to work better than simple recycling or grade repetition.

Plan of the Book

Chapter 4 charts children's movement through the school system during the elementary and middle school years, with particular attention to the separation of retainees from their original cohortmates. Sample attrition also is examined in this chapter. In Chapter 5 we look to see exactly who the BSS retainees are, in terms of family background, demographic characteristics, and school "readiness" problems. Then, in Chapters 6, 7, and 8 we consider how retention affects school performance, as reflected in achievement test scores and teacher-assigned report card marks. In Chapter 9 possible stigmatizing effects of retention are examined, using children's responses to questions posed in individual interviews. The first of these was fielded in the fall of first grade, before issuance of first quarter report cards. Chapter 10 then describes how retention ties in with other forms of "administrative sorting," including assignment to special education classes, group placements for reading instruction in first grade, and middle school curricular assignments. High school dropout occupies the last analysis chapter (Chapter 11), using data on high school completion up to 5 years beyond the group's expected graduation in spring 1994.

The 17 years covered in this volume overlap virtually the entirety of the BSS cohort's schooling, tracing progress from age 6, when they

---

[2] We decided not to inquire about income or welfare status, fearing that such inquiries would discourage some parents from participating in the study.

started first grade in fall 1982, into young adulthood at age 22–23. The long time frame afforded by the BSS is useful for understanding both the dropout dynamic and the way grade retention fits into the picture. The concluding chapter then steps back from all these details to reflect broadly on the findings presented and their possible implications for policy and practice.

4

Children's Pathways through the Elementary and Middle School Years

Retention+

Repeating a grade in elementary school is commonplace. Indeed, often for minority and disadvantaged youngsters in high-poverty school systems it is the rule rather than the exception. Yet, as noted in Chapter 1, the picture is sketchy because the best national data cover overage and underage enrollments, not grade retention per se. Other sources either rely on retrospective accounts (e.g., the NELS88 survey of eighth graders and their parents) or do not follow children long enough to provide a complete picture (e.g., the Prospects and ECLS projects). This leaves a void that at present only local panel studies like the BSS can fill. These afford a glimpse of what is happening "real time" in the lives of children as they progress through the elementary grades.

This chapter plots the BSS cohort's history of retentions over the first 8 years of their schooling. For children who remain on schedule, this time frame covers all of elementary and middle school. However, many children are thrown off-schedule because of retention and other complications and so do not move into or out of middle school "on-time." One consequence is that their transition between levels of schooling is delayed. Most retainees are not with their age peers or with their entering cohort when they advance from elementary to middle school or from middle school to high school. Problems integrating with their new classmates in the year when they are retained and again when they make transitions between schools could add to the adjustment challenges that attend such school changes even under ordinary circumstances (Eccles and Midgley 1989; Roderick 1995a; Simmons and Blyth 1987).

We also describe how retention ties in with other "sorting" or "tracking" experiences over this period, including assignment into, and sometimes out of, special education classes. Provision of special education services through "pull-out" programs for retained children in regular classrooms are considered, too. In Baltimore, these programs provide instruction in math and/or reading. The link between retention and special education is of particular interest because many children are assigned to special education *after* being held back (Barnett, Clarizio, and Payette 1996; McLeskey and Grizzle 1992). These youngsters very likely have especially severe problems, academic and/or emotional, and so the special education connection may be important for understanding how retention works. If these children are the "worst cases," not keeping track of them could be a serious oversight when attempting to evaluate retention's role in repeaters' academic success and school adjustment. Grade acceleration after retention – midyear promotion and skipping of grades between years – also are examined, although in a more limited way. These irregularities too would be easy to miss in a cross-sectional or retrospective study.

The main purpose of this chapter is to trace children's promotion histories in light of administrative sorting. This sorting includes transfers between Baltimore schools and also out of the system. School (and residential) moves are important in their own right, as these impose heavy burdens on young children, with serious academic consequences (e.g., Alexander, Entwisle, and Dauber 1996; Astone and McLanahan 1994; Rumberger and Larson 1998; Swanson and Schneider 1999; Temple and Reynolds 1999; Wood, Halfon, Scarlata, Newacheck, and Nissim 1993). But sample attrition is another reason for examining transfers. As mentioned in the previous chapter, for many children we lack data over the entire 8-year period covered in this volume, and the consequences of this lack have to be weighed carefully. Most attrition from the BSS panel is due to transfer out of the BCPS. Examining school moves allows us to see how many children leave, who they are (selective sample loss), and whether the sample's representativeness is compromised as a result.

Children's Promotion Histories: E Unum Pluribus?

Children in the BSS all began first grade in the fall of 1982. From that point forward, their school careers diverged along many paths. Some of this complexity is conveyed in Figure 4.1, which maps the schedule of children's grade level progress over 8 years. Intersecting columns and rows highlight on-time and off-time patterns. The figure also shows movement out of the school system, a major source of sample attrition.

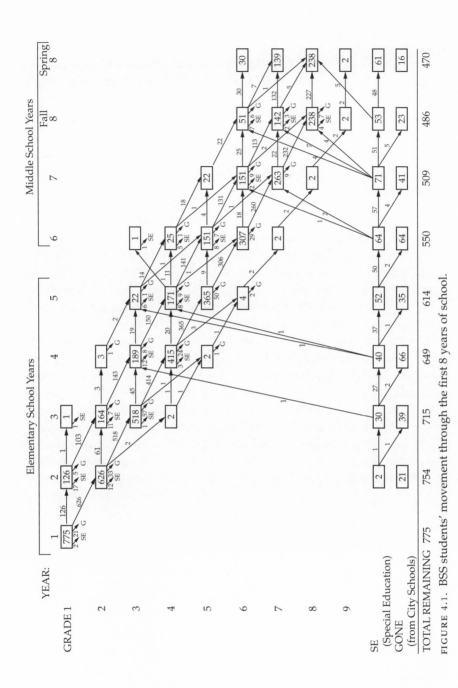

FIGURE 4.1. BSS students' movement through the first 8 years of school.

47

Although initially we sampled 790 fall 1982 beginning first graders, only 775 are covered here. Fifteen are excluded because of gaps in the record of annual grade assignments that could not be filled from other sources or because inconsistencies could not be reconciled.[1] To keep the display manageable, Figure 4.1 tracks fall-to-fall placements. Midyear gaps are filled in later.[2]

Educational Sorting in the Elementary Grades

Figure 4.1 is the main record of the BSS cohort's history of administrative sorting. It spans the elementary grades – in most schools grades 1 through 5 – and middle school, grades 6, 7, and 8. The "775" entry in the first cell locates all members of the cohort as first graders in fall 1982. The arrows plot subsequent movement, with the "SE" trail indicating assignment to separate special education (SE) classes. These assignments are made during the school year and refer to classes in the spring of that year. Some SE children eventually return to regular classes, but not until after at least a year in special education.[3] The G trail identifies transfer out of the Baltimore City Public School (BCPS) system (*G* means "gone from the BCPS"). The timing of out-transfer is determined from school records.

The main path from Year 1 to Year 2 is from first to second grade, with 626 children remaining "on schedule" at this point. The 126 students who are still in first grade in the fall of the second year are first grade repeaters, as is one of the two children assigned to special education classes in the first year. The total retention rate for the first year is just

[1] Other records were problematic also, either incomplete or internally inconsistent in some way. In the absence of indications otherwise, an orderly promotion history was assumed (e.g., a spring code for a given year was missing, but the previous fall code was one grade level behind the subsequent fall code). This resolved most complications.
[2] Many midyear reassignments involve special education students. Special education classes usually include pupils from all grades. In BCPS records sometimes a grade level is indicated, sometimes not. Figure 4.1 does not report grade levels for children while they are in special education classes. This circumvents the problem of inconsistent administrative treatment but obscures to some degree the overlap between retention and special education: that is, the retention experience of students who are placed in special education before being retained is not displayed. However, most special education assignments occur after at least one retention, so this is minor. All retentions are covered in the text, whether they occur before or after special education assignment.
[3] In Figure 4.1, children receiving special education out of regular classes are included in the tally for their grade level. During the 8-year period, 144 children received such services at some point, 60 in Year 1, 59 in Year 2.

over 16% (127 of the 775 students in the sample).[4] This is the highest grade-specific rate of first retention for any year; correspondingly, it yields the largest single group of retainees.

Sixty-one children are identified as second grade repeaters in Year 3 (not shown are 7 repeaters assigned to special education classes at the end of the year). They are joined in second grade by 103 first grade repeaters, promoted after 2 years in first grade. One other first grade repeater was held back again in the third year and so is identified in the third column as a double retainee (still in first grade). Other first grade repeaters (13.4% of the original 127) have been moved into special education classes. In comparison, just 12 of 626 Year 2 second graders (under 2%) were in special education in Year 3. The connection between retention and special education apparently is established early.

The third year yields the panel's first "skips": two children who had been second graders in Year 2 are identified in Year 3 as fourth graders. The cohort thus is spreading out. After 3 years its members are dispersed across four grade levels and many are in special education. At the same time, and despite this dispersion, most of the cohort is in second (164) or third (518) grade in Year 3. The 518 who remain on schedule through 3 years constitute 72% of the 715 children still in city schools at this point, or 67% of the original sample of 775 (60 children had left the city system by the fall of Year 3).[5]

Between the third and fourth years the group spreads further. Only 415 children are fourth graders in the fourth year. This is 54% of the original total, or 64% of the 649 sample members still in the BCPS through Year 4 (66 more left city schools between Years 3 and 4). Of the various off-time possibilities, 45 involve children who repeated third grade in the fourth year (2 other third grade repeaters were assigned to special education before the third year). In the figure, the 45 third grade repeaters not in special education are joined by 143 first and second grade

---

[4] Identifying the sample of retained students in Figure 4.1 is complicated by the timing of special education assignment. A horizontal line between boxes across 2 years identifies most repeaters, but students assigned to special education in the spring of the year (before being retained) are included in the special education category at the bottom of Figure 4.1. Their grade placement after the assignment is not displayed. The numbers in the upper section of the figure thus somewhat undercount retentions. The complete tally of retainees, year by year, is as follows: first grade, 127; second grade, 68; third grade, 47; fourth grade, 21; fifth grade, 10; sixth grade, 22; and seventh grade, 22.

[5] Children who left the BCPS are not included in Figure 4.1 after their departure even if they later returned. We know of 12 such youngsters, but their school records may not be reliable – 6 of the 12 appear to have returned for just one semester.

retainees, who in the fourth year have made it to third grade. In addition, 3 children still are in second grade at this point (double repeaters), and 13 more have moved into special education (11 second grade retainees, 1 on-time third grader, and 1 child who after three tries is still in first grade). Meanwhile, a single child has moved into third grade out of special education.

By the fifth year the sample of students still in BCPS ($N = 614$) is under 80% of the original cohort. Three hundred sixty-five of them are in fifth grade (60% of the total); 171 are in fourth grade, including 20 fourth grade repeaters. There also are 22 double retainees at this point, and the number of special education students, at 52, is up 12 from the previous year (this despite the return of 2 pupils to regular classrooms and the departure of 1 from the school system). Most of these new special education assignees had been retained previously (i.e., they were already a year behind in the fourth year).

All told, the cohort's off-time rate through 5 years (the typical elementary school span in the Baltimore school system) is on the order of 40%. Though these children all entered the system together, after 5 years those still in city schools are spread across four grades and many are in special education classes. Another 161 (21%) have left the system.

This dispersion of students is striking and is revealed only by monitoring prospectively the grade level progressions of a well-defined cohort. Such detailed tracking is rare in educational research. A cross-sectional survey of children in a particular grade level, or even a longitudinal study of a selective panel, almost certainly would miss the complicated history of retainees and probably also many special education students. A simple tally of repeaters by grade almost certainly will underestimate both the number and the consequences of the administrative sortings that occur in the first few years of school.

Educational Sorting over the Middle School Years

During Years 6, 7, and 8, middle school years in most Baltimore schools, many BSS children still are finishing elementary school.[6] Figure 4.1 uses fall grade placements to identify children's standing over the first

---

[6] The most common grade-span arrangement in the BCPS is the typical middle school structure. At the end of fifth grade, 84% of those still in the BCPS were in schools that went through fifth grade (479 of 569). Another 7% attended elementary schools with just third, fourth, and fifth grades. Other grade spans represented in the panel include Pre-K–6, K–6, K–8, 4–6, Pre-K–8, and 1–6. At the end of eighth grade 88% (415 of 469)

7 years, but Year 8 is characterized by an exceptional volume of within-year movement, so for that year fall and spring placements are given separately.

Each year more children fall behind: there are 9 fifth grade repeaters in Year 6, 18 sixth grade repeaters in Year 7, and 22 seventh grade repeaters in Year 8.[7] Though these figures generally are lower than those for the elementary grades, the case base also has dwindled. There were only 263 seventh graders in Year 7, for example, and so the 22 retainees that year constitute 8% of the eligible pool, still a significant fraction.

We also see a large jump in the number of double retentions over this period, especially among sixth graders in Year 7. There are 151 children that year who had already repeated one grade. In the fall of Year 8, 25 of them still are in sixth grade, representing a 17% retention rate in a group already retained once. Although only 2 students are assigned to special education classes for the first time in the seventh year, 13 new special education assignments, 7 of whom are double retainees, are made in the eighth year.

The jump in retentions toward the end of middle school probably reflects teachers' reluctance to pass children along to the next level of schooling whom they deem unready. The high rates of middle school retention seen here may be intended to shield struggling students from the pressures of high school, but one consequence is that many children will still be in middle school, or barely into high school, when they reach the legal dropout age. In the BSS, the average age of never-retained students on entering ninth grade is 14 years, 5 months; students retained once would average 15 years, 5 months; those retained twice would be 16. This is relevant because the legal school-leaving age in Maryland is 16, and getting a court decision on chronic truants can take nine months or more. Effectively, then, most repeaters would have little trouble dropping out, if they chose to, before high school.

During these years we also see the first significant outflow from special education: 3 at the end of Year 6, 15 in the spring of Year 7, and 5 in the spring of Year 8. Although all 5 students who leave special education in Year 8 are placed in eighth grade, those moved back into regular classes at the end of Year 7 are dispersed across three grade levels. Four

were in middle schools that spanned sixth through eighth grades. The others attended schools with five other patterns: 6–9, 7–8, 7–9, K–8, and Pre-K–8.
[7] These are the figures reported in Figure 4.1, but they leave out children assigned to special education classes in a given year. The actual fifth, sixth, and seventh grade retention totals are 10, 22, and 22, respectively.

are placed in eighth grade and hence are back on schedule. Another 4 are put in sixth grade, the equivalent of double retention because they are 2 years behind schedule; the remaining 7 are back 1 year—they are in seventh grade in Year 8.

These reassignments probably reflect a desire to get children back into regular classes before high school, but they leave many still behind: 12 of the 23 children moved out of special education classes during the middle school years remain off-time. Too, most children in special education in Year 7 remain there in Year 8 (51 of 71, with 5 others leaving the system), so the placement of children back into regular classes is highly selective.

A similar organizational imperative probably is behind the modest number of "skips" seen among former retainees during the middle school years. There are seven of these altogether, five of which have children returning to their regular grade levels (the other two involve double retainees, who remain one grade behind). In contrast, all six of the skips registered in elementary school involved on-time children, and hence genuine acceleration.

In middle school, then, the volume of sorting activity increases generally: more children are held back; some previously held back are moved up; and for the first time, appreciable numbers of children return to regular classrooms from special education. Since high school begins in ninth grade, all this activity very likely anticipates that upcoming transition. The intent, no doubt, is to shield some children from pressures they cannot handle, and to "normalize" the situation of those able to hold their own. That these actions are triggered by an impending school transition illustrates how organization considerations structure the sorting process.

Finally, outflow continues from city schools during the middle school years, with a particularly large loss at the transition into middle school. The 64 who leave between the fifth and sixth years constitute 10% of the 614 children still in city schools at the time. Included in this group are two of the four Year 5 sixth graders, the only accelerated children in the cohort at that point.

Middle schools have larger catchment areas than elementary and so often lack the sense of community that characterizes the latter. Many parents worry about their children's traveling long distances outside the neighborhood, and White parents in particular often are concerned about sending their children to a school with a larger minority enrollment. For these reasons, a jump in out-transfers around the time of the middle school transition is not surprising. But departures continue, and by the end of Year 8 the BSS enrollment in city schools is down to 470. This is 144 less than the Year 5 total, a loss of almost one-fourth over the middle school years. Looking back to first grade, the cumulative out-transfer is nearly 40% (and beyond the total involved, we will see shortly that the outflow is socially patterned, as some categories of children leave in greater numbers than others).

Just over half (238) the 470 youngsters still in city schools at this point are at grade level. Thirty-six percent (169 of 470) are behind one or more grades, and 13% (61) are in special education. Of the original 775 who began first grade in fall 1982, only 30% (238 of 775) have moved ahead smoothly, in the sense of staying on schedule for 8 years in the same school system.

Educational Sorting in Relief: First Grade Retainees and Year 8 Seventh Graders

Figure 4.1 depicts numerous retentions, but much more than that, it also reveals some of the extraordinary complexity of the underlying process. Retention happens in a larger context of administrative sorting, and Figure 4.1 makes this vivid (additional aspects of administrative sorting are taken up in Chapter 10).

There are 127 first grade repeaters identified in Figure 4.1 (the 126 students who are in first grade in Year 2 plus 1 of the 2 students assigned to special education in Year 1). Just over one-fourth of these children (34 of the 127) had smooth promotion histories after repeating the year. These 34 were promoted in each of Years 3 through 8 and were never assigned to special education classes. Another 16 also were promoted each year but received special education "pull-out" instruction in math and/or reading at some time along the way. This accounts for about 40% of first grade repeaters; the others encountered many additional complications.

Forty-nine, or over a third of the total, were retained a second time, 3 had triple retentions, and 58 were assigned to special education classes at some point (4 in separate special education schools). Further, most double repeaters actually are "triples," in that 30 of them also were placed in special education classes and another 7 received pull-out services from regular classrooms. That amounts to 76% of double retainees receiving special education services, 61% in separate classes. And special education assignments were high for the other first grade repeaters, too, as 56% received some services (20% who received pull-out from regular classes; 36% in special education classes). Altogether, 81 of 127 first grade retainees, or 64%, received some special education services during these 8 years. By way of comparison, just 9% (40 of 458) of never-retained youngsters did so; most (35 of the 40) received pull-out instruction from regular classes. Other studies also find high levels of special education assignment after retention (Barnett et al. 1996; McLeskey and Grizzle 1992), including the Chicago Longitudinal Study (CLS) (e.g., Temple, Ou, and Helevy 2001), a single-city, long-term panel much like the BSS. In the CLS 10.5% of nonrepeaters were assigned to special education at some point over grades K–8 compared to around 30% of repeaters (personal communication, Arthur Reynolds and Suh-Ruu Ou).

Erratic grade-level progressions further complicated these repeaters' promotion histories: 17 experienced midyear promotions, 12 experienced double promotions, 1 was put back a grade during the school year, and another was put back a grade over a summer break. Despite all this, by the beginning of Year 8, only 9 of the 127 were at grade level. Children assigned to special education classes also tend to stay there: for example, of the 42 first grade retainees placed in special education classes who were in city schools all 8 years, 38 still were in special education at the end of Year 8.

The situation of seventh graders at the beginning of Year 8 affords another perspective on this administrative sorting. There are 179 such youngsters (only 142 show up in the main body of Figure 4.1; the other 37 entered special education classes before the start of Year 8). All are 1 year behind, but seventh grade retentions account for just 22 of the total (12%). The others are in seventh grade a year late as a result of earlier detours, often much earlier. For 55, it is the legacy of being held back in first grade, 42 others repeated second grade, and 59 were held back in grades 3 through 6. In addition, 37 had been in special education classes, 61 received special education services out of regular classes, and 19 had been held back twice (along with a skip at some point, preventing their falling 2 years behind.)

Review of "Pathways" Through the First 8 Years of School

In the ideal, children's journey through the elementary and middle school years ought to be uneventful – an orderly progression up the grade structure. But the promotion histories reviewed in this chapter give the lie to any such benign imagery. Instead, "disorderly" promotion histories dominate the cohort's experience. Numerous sorting interventions encountered along the way put many children off-time and often off track, such that *only a minority of the cohort moves smoothly through the grade structure over the 8-year period covered.* In most studies, this complicated history is hidden from view and its implications submerged. This is a particular risk in research that samples students by grade level (e.g., the NELS88 project or like studies keyed to high school students). Children in the same grade may be in the same place at the same time, but it is certain not all arrived by the same route – as an example, witness the experience of BSS seventh graders in Year 8.

Special education is one such submerged experience. Here we see that placement in special education is rare before retention has been tried, but once made such assignments tend to be permanent. The exceptions generally are toward the end of middle school, probably in anticipation of high school (the frequency of skips among former retainees also picks up in these years, probably for the same reason).

Finally, Figure 4.1 shows another reality of life in Baltimore's public schools – the loss of pupils from the system. We have focused thus far on sorting *within* schools – falling behind through retention and assignment to special education. Sorting *between school systems* also has implications, though, and in the next section we consider how this exodus of children from the BCPS complicates the picture.

School Transfers and Sample Attrition

After 8 years just 60% of the BSS cohort remains in city schools. And this outflow of students, it turns out, is decidedly nonrandom: 52% with no retentions left during this period versus 29% of first grade repeaters. In Chapter 3 we mentioned that out-transfer is a major source of sample attrition. This overlap of attrition with retention commands attention for procedural as well as substantive reasons.

On the substantive side, school transfers complicate children's academic adjustment, and transfers during the early primary grades may be especially disruptive (e.g., Ingersoll, Scamman, and Eckerling 1989). In addition to the 40% of the cohort that left the city school system, others transferred between city schools within the BCPS. This story of "children in motion" from the vantage point of our study group, told in detail elsewhere (Alexander et al. 1996), is reproduced in Table 4.1 from that report. It covers the first 5 years of the cohort's schooling (the elementary years in most city schools), distinguishing among within-year

TABLE 4.1. *Tally of School Moves on an Annual Basis: Within the Baltimore City System and Outside the System*

	Year 1	Year 2	Year 3	Year 4	Year 5
No. in BCPS in the fall	767	745	693	631	605
Stayers (through the following fall)[a]	663	616	547	520	524
Within-year transfers	64	68	65	57	50
Between-year (summer) transfers[a]	34	31	41	35	–
Transfers outside city system	22	52	62	26	37
Total moves	120	151	168	118	87
Percentage who move[b]	13.6	17.3	21.1	17.6	13.4

[a] Except in Year 5, when moves are tracked only through the spring.
[b] Percentage who move in a given year is calculated as 1 − (No. of stayers/No. in BCPS).

transfers, summer transfers, and transfers out of the BCPS.[8] "Stayers" are children in the same school from one fall to the next.

The total volume of school relocations is summarized in the last row. Between 13.4% and 21.1% of children who start a year in city schools transfer between schools during the year. Of children who remain in city schools the entire time, 21.5% register one transfer, 13.4% two transfers, and 5.6% three or more transfers. Another 26% (199) leave city schools during this 5-year period (see Table 4.1, row 5) and so are known to have moved at least once. All told, probably two-thirds of the cohort changes schools during the elementary years.

This total is split into two quite distinct migration streams: Whites and higher-SES children tend to leave the city system ("Exiters"); African-Americans and lower-SES children tend to relocate within it. The contrasts are dramatic: 71% of the Exiters are White; 79% of those with two or more transfers within the system are African-American (the African-American percentage in the original cohort is 55%). Similarly, though a large fraction (46%) of the Exiters qualify for subsidized meals at school (putting them near or below the federal poverty level), 88% of multiple movers within the system are on meal subsidy. Over time, then, the cohort's BCPS enrollment becomes increasingly disadvantaged, and within the BCPS disadvantaged youth are the most mobile.

[8] Table 4.1 covers 767 children, 8 fewer than Figure 4.1. These exclusions are due to problems with information on school moves in the school system records.

Over the 5 years covered in Table 4.1, the cohort collectively attended 112 different schools *just within the BCPS,* and an unknown additional number of schools outside the BCPS. For the first 2 years of the BSS project only students who remained in the original 20 schools were tracked; beginning in Year 4 coverage was extended to all children still in the BCPS. Because of this, the retention histories of children who stayed in Baltimore public schools are reasonably complete.[9]

The situation of children who moved out of the BCPS is more complicated. Cohort tracking was extended beyond Baltimore and to private schools in Baltimore beginning in Project Year 6. Since then, many "lost cases" have been recovered, but mainly for pupil and parent interview data. School record information is available only from the BCPS. Of the 775 children who constitute the "core" analysis sample for this volume, 307, or 40%, were out of BCPS schools by the fall of 1990 ("Year 8" in terms of our study design). BCPS data identify 21% of the Exiters and 53% of the Stayers as retainees. This is a large difference, but children's retention status is known from school records only while they were in city schools, and undoubtedly some Exiters were held back outside the BCPS.

Children who leave the city schools are disproportionately White and relatively well-to-do (and have good readiness skills), so lower levels of retention would be expected for them. Still, it is a stretch to think all Exiters progressed smoothly after leaving city schools. Missed retentions outside the BCPS likely exaggerate the difference in retention rates between Stayers and Exiters, and Stayers' having a greater presence in the analysis also could distort comparisons later.

To check on missed retentions and their possible implications, we compared BCPS school record data against retrospective self-reports obtained from 636 youngsters in interviews conducted in the spring of 1991 (Project Year 10). For 92% of the 636, the two sources agree on retention status; however, 4.6% ($N = 29$) report no retention when school records indicate otherwise, and 3.5% ($N = 22$) report a retention when none is indicated in BCPS records. The discrepancies are a small fraction of the total and practically offsetting in the aggregate, but the 22 self-identified repeaters could be retentions missed after children left the

---

[9] However, some children "retrieved" in Year 4 are missing pupil and parent interviews from the early years. Coverage of various data sources also is uneven for other reasons – for example, no parent or child interviews were conducted in the third year, and no child interviews were conducted in the fifth year. These complications are discussed more fully as data are introduced for particular analyses.

TABLE 4.2. *Comparision of Full Sample, Stayers, and Exiters on Background Characteristics and Early Academic Performance Measures at Point of School Entry*[a]

	Percentage Female[b]	Percentage African-American	Average Mother's Education	Average Father's Education	Percentage No Meal Subsidy	Average CAT-M Score	Average CAT-R Score	Average Math Mark	Average Reading Mark
Full sample	50.1	54.4	11.6	12.1	33.1	293.1	281.2	2.2	1.9
	(775)	(775)	(731)	(489)	(699)	(684)	(666)	(695)	(695)
1. Never retained	56.6	48.5	12.4	12.8	47.0	304.6	290.8	2.6	2.2
	(458)	(458)	(431)	(306)	(389)	(408)	(396)	(418)	(418)
2. Retained	42.9	63.1	10.6	10.9	15.5	276.1	267.1	1.8	1.5
	(317)	(317)	(300)	(183)	(310)	(276)	(270)	(277)	(277)
3. Difference (1–2)	13.7	14.6	1.8	1.9	31.5	28.5	23.7	0.8	0.7
Stayers	50.8	68.5	11.3	11.6	24.6	290.2	279.3	2.1	1.8
	(486)	(486)	(456)	(326)	(483)	(443)	(432)	(446)	(446)
1. Never retained	60.9	68.3	12.2	12.3	38.8	304.6	292.5	2.6	2.2
	(230)	(230)	(214)	(169)	(227)	(215)	(208)	(218)	(218)
2. Retained	41.8	68.8	10.5	10.8	12.1	276.6	267.0	1.8	1.5
	(256)	(256)	(242)	(157)	(256)	(228)	(224)	(228)	(228)
3. Difference (1–2)	19.1	0.5	1.7	1.5	26.7	28.0	25.5	0.8	0.7
Exiters	51.2	30.1	12.3	13.1	51.9	298.5	284.6	2.4	2.0
	(289)	(289)	(275)	(163)	(216)	(241)	(234)	(249)	(249)
1. Never retained	52.2	28.5	12.6	13.4	58.6	304.7	288.8	2.6	2.2
	(228)	(228)	(217)	(137)	(162)	(193)	(188)	(200)	(200)
2. Retained	47.5	39.3	11.1	11.6	31.5	273.5	267.7	1.8	1.4
	(61)	(61)	(58)	(26)	(54)	(48)	(46)	(49)	(49)
3. Difference (1–2)	4.7	10.8	1.5	1.8	25.1	31.2	21.1	0.8	0.8

[a] All four performance measures are from the fall or first quarter of first grade.
[b] Numbers in parentheses are sample sizes.

BCPS, our main concern.[10] However, considering just those who left the BCPS at some point and did not return (178 of the 636, or 28%), agreement with school reports also is 92%. These would be the most problematic cases in terms of missing retention data because there is no school record information on them after they left. Just 12 of the 178 report a retention not indicated in BCPS data; 3 others (1.7%) contradict school records by reporting no retentions.

There is no sure way of knowing which reports are the more accurate – school records can be wrong, but so can recalled reports, especially when sensitive issues are involved. All in all, it appears not many retentions have been missed, and this is reassuring. But we also need to consider whether children who left the BCPS differ in other ways that might distort retained–never-retained comparisons. Most Exiters are missing report card marks and test scores for at least some of the upper grades, for example, and the credibility of later academic comparisons thus could hinge on what these checks reveal.

Table 4.2 presents comparisons of Exiters and Stayers on background characteristics (family and personal) and school performance measures from early in first grade. The entire sample is covered in the top panel, which gives summary descriptive statistics separately for retainees and never-retained children. Girls, for example, constitute 57% of the never-retained group versus 43% of repeaters. The second panel describes Stayers – children in city schools all 8 years. Data coverage is best for them, and so they are overrepresented in the analyses reported in later chapters. Since our wish would be to have all children represented in these analyses, the central concern here is how the Stayers compare to the full sample – are they similar or dissimilar?

The third panel reports data for the Exiters. Their social profile is quite different from that of the Stayers (compare panels 2 and 3). Two-thirds of the Stayers are African-American, three-fourths receive subsidized meals at school, and the average Stayer parent (both mother and father) is a high school dropout. Exiters are much more advantaged in these respects: 70% are White, only about half receive subsidized meals, and the average Exiter parent has had some college.

---

[10] Disagreement on the year of retention is greater, but even at this level of detail the two sources align reasonably well. Where school records and self-reports both indicate a retention ($N = 241$), 66% agree exactly on the year and another 15% are 1 year apart. The 44 other discrepancies almost all involve self-reported retentions that are more recent than in school records. This could be a memory problem or reporting of second retentions when first retentions were intended.

Exiters also have stronger academic readiness skills as beginning first graders. In the rightmost entries, they average a bit above Stayers on all four academic measures.[11] These comparisons all favor Exiters, but this differentiation along academic lines is much less pronounced than differentiation in terms of family and personal background characteristics. The 8-point difference on the CAT quantitative subtest corresponds to about a fourth of a standard deviation (samplewide), whereas the 5-point difference on the verbal subtest is just over 0.10 standard deviation. Differences in first grade report card marks also favor Exiters. Marks are assigned on a 4-point scale, 4 corresponding to "excellent" and 1 corresponding to "unsatisfactory." In math, averages for both groups are a bit above satisfactory (2.1 for Stayers; 2.4 for Exiters), whereas they fall out on either side of satisfactory in reading (1.8 versus 2.0).

These demographic and performance comparisons also are reported separately for repeaters and promoted children in Table 4.2 – rows 1 and 2 in each panel. In these comparisons, children held back at any point through the seventh grade are treated as a single group. We already know, for example, that in the full sample boys constitute a higher percentage of the retained subsample than of the never-retained subsample. Here we see additionally that these retainees include a higher percentage of minority youngsters, of children whose parents have less education, of low-income children, and of children with weak academic skills. These differences, none surprising, are summarized in the fourth row of the "full sample" panel. They are of interest mainly as a frame of reference for judging how selective attrition affects comparisons between repeaters and promoted children.

For a sense of the "after attrition" picture we turn to the second panel of Table 4.2, which reports internal comparisons for Stayers. As expected, there is a large drop in sample size when Stayers are selected for separate consideration (figures in parentheses). Gender and race are especially useful as benchmarks, as these are known for everyone. Reduced coverage on them reflects attrition due specifically to movement out of the BCPS.[12] The 486 Stayers constitute roughly 60% of the full sample.

The various averages in Table 4.2 often are quite different, comparing Stayers against the full sample; however, and this is quite important,

---

[11] The data sources used in Table 4.2 are described fully later in the volume. California Achievement Test (CAT) scores and report card marks are from school records.

[12] Reduced coverage on other measures can be due to additional sources of attrition (e.g., a single missed interview, absence on the day standardized testing was done).

internal comparisons between retainees and never-retained generally are similar. This holds especially for academic comparisons. For example, in the full sample never-retained children average 0.7 marking unit above retainees in first quarter reading, exactly the same difference as in the subsample of Stayers. The average is higher in the full sample than in the Stayer subsample, but the relative advantage of never-retained over retained is identical. The difference involving math marks is identical, too, and in the CAT subtest comparisons both are very close. These points of comparability are critical, in that selective sample loss apparently does not distort school performance comparisons between retainees and never-retained youngsters.

Comparisons involving personal and family factors – especially racial/ethnic makeup – in some instances do differ. In the full sample 63.1% of retainees are African-American versus 48.5% of the never-retained (the full sample is 54.4% African-American). The difference of almost 15% signals a large overrepresentation of African-American youngsters among retainees. In contrast, among Stayers the African-American percentage is 68% among both retained and never-retained. Hence, looking only at the Stayer subsample, we see no racial imbalance in retentions. The 68% figure is close to the percentage African-American among retainees in the full sample, so we conclude it is the never-retained subsample whose racial composition changes most when Exiters are excluded. It has a much higher percentage of minority youngsters, indicating that Exiters are drawn disproportionately from the pool of never-retained Whites.

Socioeconomic differences (e.g., parents' education and family income level), on the other hand, are minor. The "spread" between retained and never-retained students in the percentage of those not receiving meal subsidies is a bit smaller among Stayers than in the full sample, but both figures are in the same range (i.e., 26.7 versus 31.5), with retainees from poorer families. The comparison for mother's education is quite close, also (a difference of 1.8 years between retained and never-retained in the full sample versus 1.7 years among the Stayers). For father's education the difference is larger (0.4 years), but there is a higher incidence of missing data for father's education, so this is not surprising. The "gender gap" difference (13.7% in the full sample; 19.1% among Stayers) is not great either. Both show boys overrepresented among repeaters.

All in all, these checks are reassuring. Social selection along several dimensions indeed is evident, but only that involving race/ethnicity is especially pronounced. When Whites leave city schools, as they do in large numbers, many other qualities go with them, including their relatively high SES standing and good readiness skills. Selective sample loss along other lines is minor in comparison, and there is virtually no bias or distortion on academic indicators. This parity is most welcome as it permits sound academic comparisons. We turn to those next and include children whenever data are available for them, whether they are Stayers or Exiters.

5

Characteristics and Competencies of Repeaters

Who Is Held Back?

Chapter 4 pulled back the curtain a little on the retention story by revealing some of the twists and turns children encounter along their passage through the elementary and middle school years. We now have a sense of what is happening. To whom it is happening is addressed in the present chapter. What makes retainees different from children who move smoothly through the grade structure, and what distinguishes different kinds of retainees from one another? One comparison is between first grade repeaters and those held back later. First grade retention may be distinctive because of the stress that revolves around entry into school and also because of its being the first decisive time of evaluation. Children retained later have had at least a year of satisfactory performance, which implies a smoother transition experience. Probably, too, those who have made it through first grade are not at the bottom of the test score distribution or the least well adjusted. We also compare retainees who stay on track after repeating a year with children held back twice and/or assigned to special education classes. These children attracted additional administrative attention after being held back. If that is the case, one supposes their problems at school are more acute than those of one-time repeaters, although this remains to be seen.

Who Is Held Back?

We first ask what distinguishes retainees from never-retained children in three areas. First, data on demographics and family background give a social profile of repeaters; second, test scores and report card marks from the fall of first grade give an academic profile; third, nonacademic problems provide a behavior profile. Academic problems at the very beginning of school are the backdrop to retention. They reflect skill deficiencies "carried in" from outside school. For children raised in poverty, as many of the BSS youngsters are, such problems are both common and severe (e.g., Stipek and Ryan 1997; West et al. 2000). Repeaters' social profile thus is backdrop, and their initial academic difficulties a reflection of that backdrop. Deportment is another concern. Conduct marks from first grade report cards, classroom behavior as rated by first grade homeroom teachers, diagnostic evaluations made by kindergarten and first grade teachers, popularity with other children as perceived by teachers, and first grade absenteeism are used to build a school adjustment profile of repeaters. Comparisons for all three areas are reported in Table 5.1.

Repeaters versus Promoted: Demographic Profile

Of the 775 children whose promotion histories while in the BCPS are reasonably complete, 317 were retained at least once through seventh grade; 458 were not.[1] The top panel of Table 5.1 shows the demographic characteristics and family circumstances of these children. This profile is a familiar one – familiar from other studies of repeaters, as well as from more general work on the out-of-school context that puts children "at risk" academically.

The information in Table 5.1 is from school records (gender, race/ethnicity, and eligibility for reduced price meals at school) and from parent interviews (living arrangements and number of siblings). Data about parents' educational level combine information from the first grade interview with that from several later ones.[2]

The table is split into five columns. The first describes characteristics of the entire cohort. The second and third columns report averages for repeaters and promoted children separately; the next columns give the

---

[1] Achievement outcomes, attitudes, and children's experience with educational tracking are monitored over 8 years in this volume, but retentions are monitored only through seventh grade (one-time repeaters take 8 years to complete seventh grade).

[2] The first parent interview ($N = 743$), fielded just before children started first grade, asked about living arrangements, siblings, and the educational level of the parent respondent, 86% of whom were mothers or stepmothers (8% were fathers). In the second, fourth, and sixth years we asked separately about mothers and fathers, permitting gaps from the first year to be filled in. Some of the missing data that remain are due to the many BSS households with no father present (see Table 5.1 for figures from the first year).

difference between those averages, in original scale units in the fourth and in standard deviation units in the fifth.[3]

The sample is nearly evenly divided between males and females (51% female), but the percentage of males in the retained group is higher: 57%, compared with 43% in the never-retained group. Similarly, 63% of retained students are African-American, though African-Americans make up only 54% of the entire sample.[4] These differences involving gender and racial/ethnic composition, both highly significant, are just under 0.3 standard deviation and so would be considered moderately large.

Differences revolving around family socioeconomic status are larger. Eligibility for reduced price meals at school identifies low-income families. According to guidelines for 1984, the period most relevant to our study group, children in a family of four with a yearly income of $12,870 or less could receive free meals; those with income below $18,315 paid a reduced fee. These cutoffs represent 1.3 and 1.85 times the then-applicable federal poverty guidelines, respectively. Fifty-three percent of never-retained students, compared with 85% of retained students, qualify for some subsidy, a difference of 0.67 standard deviation.

Differences involving parents' educational background are also large, with the gap approaching 2 years of schooling, or about 0.7 standard deviation for both mothers and fathers. Beyond being large, these disparities also straddle an important educational divide: the "typical" retainee parent is a high school dropout; the typical parent of a promoted child has at least finished high school. Twenty-five percent of the parents of never-retained children are dropouts, compared with half retained students' fathers (for those whose education level is known) and 56% of their mothers (not in tables).

Since more education is generally associated with higher earnings, this is another sign that never-retained children have more economically advantaged homes. It also probably means that never-retained students' parents understand the educational system better and are better able to provide support and resources at home to reinforce the

[3] The standard deviations reported in the first column (those for all children) are used as the denominators for these last calculations.
[4] We saw in the last chapter that more White than African-American students leave the BCPS over time. These figures could be misleading if many White retentions are missed because they are outside the BCPS catchment area. However, self-reports identify only 14 Exiter retentions after children left the BCPS, and just 10 of those involve Whites. With so few children involved, any distortion must be minor.

TABLE 5.1. *Demographic, Academic, and School Adjustment Profiles of Retained and Never-Retained Students*[a]

	All Children[b]	Retained[c]	Never Retained[a]	Retained vs. Never-Retained	
				Average Difference	Difference in sd Units
Demographic comparisons					
Proportion male	0.49	0.57	0.43	0.14**	0.27
	(0.50)	(0.50)	(0.50)		
Proportion African-American	0.54	0.63	0.48	0.15**	0.29
	(0.50)	(0.48)	(0.50)		
Proportion receiving lunch subsidy	0.67	0.85	0.53	−0.32**	0.67
	(0.47)	(0.36)	(0.50)		
Average mother's education (years)	11.67	10.61	12.40	−1.79**	0.70
	(2.56)	(2.19)	(2.54)		
Average father's education (years)	12.10	10.90	12.82	−1.92**	0.72
	(2.68)	(1.90)	(2.82)		
Proportion in two-parent family	0.53	0.42	0.61	−0.19**	0.39
	(0.50)	(0.49)	(0.49)		
Average number of siblings	1.45	1.62	1.33	0.28**	0.21
	(1.38)	(1.51)	(1.27)		
Academic comparisons					
Average reading mark, first quarter 1982	1.88	1.45	2.17	−0.72**	1.03
	(0.70)	(0.55)	(0.65)		
Average math mark, first quarter 1982	2.25	1.75	2.57	−0.82**	0.98
	(0.84)	(0.71)	(0.76)		
Average CAT-R score, fall 1982	281.16	267.09	290.76	−23.67**	0.58
	(40.62)	(33.75)	(42.13)		

Average CAT-M score, fall 1982	293.11 (31.72)	276.05 (24.00)	304.65 (31.13)	-28.60**	0.90
School adjustment comparisons					
Average number of absences	13.22 (11.35)	16.19 (13.60)	11.22 (9.02)	4.97**	0.44
Average Cooperation–Compliance score	20.72 (3.98)	19.33 (4.71)	21.67 (3.05)	-2.34**	0.59
Average Interest–Participation score	21.98 (5.43)	18.74 (5.07)	24.18 (4.49)	-5.44**	1.00
Average Attention Span–Restlessness score	20.70 (4.03)	18.48 (4.57)	22.21 (2.75)	-3.72**	0.92
Average conduct mark, fall 1982	1.75 (0.43)	1.66 (0.48)	1.81 (0.39)	-0.16**	0.37
MSTOI proportion at risk	0.28 (0.45)	0.49 (0.50)	0.13 (0.34)	0.36**	0.79
Average peer popularity	3.52 (1.13)	3.09 (1.08)	3.81 (1.07)	-0.72**	0.64

[a] Numbers in parentheses are standard deviations.
[b] Sample coverage on all children, except for father's education ($N = 489$) and Maryland Systematic Teacher Observation Inventory (MSTOI) ($N = 559$), varies from 775 to 666.
[c] Sample coverage on retained children, except for father's education ($N = 183$) and MSTOI ($N = 230$), varies from 317 to 270.
[d] Sample coverage on never-retained children, except for father's education ($N = 306$) and MSTOI ($N = 329$), varies from 458 to 389.
** Signifies differences significant at the 0.01 level.

school's agenda (for an overview of differences across socioeconomic and racial/ethnic lines in family practices relevant to school readiness, see Hess and Holloway 1984, Slaughter and Epps 1987; Weston 1989). The educational "boost" that better educated parents provide for their children could be particularly helpful for students who have difficulty handling the first grade curriculum.

Never-retained children have more favorable profiles in terms of family type, as well. As first graders 61% of them are in two-parent families (with either natural parents or stepparents) as against 42% of retained students. Residence in a single-parent household appears to put children at risk academically (e.g., Hetherington, Camara, and Featherman 1983; Zill 1996), although some part of this family type difference no doubt is due to economic strains associated with single parenting (McLanahan and Sandefur 1994). Promoted youngsters also have fewer siblings. This difference is not large, though, as both groups average between one and two siblings (on the relationship of family size to school performance, see Blake 1989).

All in all, the family circumstances and personal characteristics of retained and promoted children are quite different. Girls and Whites are most likely to make it through seventh grade without being held back. Children spared retention also are from families that are better off economically, with parents at least high school graduates, with two parents present, and with fewer other children competing for family resources and parents' attention.

The retained profile is very different. Males, African-Americans, and children receiving reduced price meals at school are overrepresented. Their parents typically lack high school diplomas, most are in single-parent households, and they have more siblings. Numerous other studies yield a like description of repeaters (e.g., Frymier 1997; Hauser 2001; National Center for Education Statistics 1990; Zill et al. 1997), and the risk exposure of such children is not to grade retention only. It is a "high-risk" profile generally – for academic setbacks in the near-term, for a lifetime of struggle over the longer term.

Repeaters versus Promoted Youngsters: Academic Profiles

Repeaters' academic profile at the start of first grade is taken up next. The relevant comparisons in Table 5.1 involve report card marks and test scores. City schools assign four marks in the primary grades: "unsatisfactory," "satisfactory," "good," and "excellent," coded here 1–4.

The averages in Table 5.1 are from the first quarter of first grade and so represent children's first formal academic assessment.

With math marks averaging just above satisfactory (2.25) and reading marks just below satisfactory (1.88) across the entire cohort (second panel), all children, retained and promoted, have room for improvement. Still, some children have more room than others. Retainees' initial math (1.75) and reading (1.45) marks average well below satisfactory; promoted children's are midway between satisfactory and good in math (2.57) and comfortably above satisfactory in reading (2.17). The 0.8 marking unit math difference and the 0.7 marking unit reading difference are both nearly a full standard deviation, quite large by conventional standards.

Retainees' initial achievement test scores also trail far behind. The BCPS administered the California Achievement Test (CAT) battery twice annually, fall and spring, from 1982 (when the study children were just beginning first grade) through the spring of 1988.[5] The averages reported in Table 5.1 are children's first achievement test results. Two subtest averages are reported: Reading Comprehension (CAT-R) and Math Concepts and Applications (CAT-M). Reading and math dominate the curriculum in the primary grades, and these particular areas are included in all versions of the CAT battery designed for first through eighth grades, allowing us to consider achievement trends in the same domains over the entire period covered in this volume. Other CAT subtests do not provide this continuous coverage.[6]

The Reading Comprehension subtest consists of 20 items in the first and second grade versions, 27 items in the third grade version, and 40 items in all later versions. The Math Concepts and Applications test starts out with 36 items, increases to 40 items in second grade, and contains 45 items thereafter.[7] Our displays report scale scores. These

[5] Only spring scores are available for the 1988–89 and 1989–90 school years (Years 7 and 8), the last school years covered in this volume.

[6] These two subtests were also less subject to ceiling constraints in the early years than were some others. For example, around 12% of the sample received the highest possible scores on the Vocabulary and Math Computation subtests in the spring of 1983, whereas only 3% to 4% scored at the top on the CAT-R and CAT-M subtests.

[7] Technical documentation indicates good psychometric properties for the CAT battery. Kuder-Richardson 20 (homogeneity) reliabilities for the entire battery range between 0.83 (beginning of first grade) to 0.92 for tests designed for the first 3 years. The test manual reports fall to spring correlations of 0.69 and 0.81 for the first and second years. The corresponding correlations for the BSS data are 0.64 and 0.77. Test norms (California Achievement Test 1979: 53) show BSS students were 5 points below the norming sample (less than 0.2 standard deviation) when they began first grade.

are vertically calibrated with a common metric across all versions of the test, such that "more than"–"less than" comparisons can be made across grade levels.

Retained and never-retained students' (Table 5.1) CAT averages differ by more than 20 points in both areas. The CAT-M difference is almost a full standard deviation, about the same as the differences in report card marks. The CAT-R disparity is a bit smaller but still large – it favors promoted youngsters by just under 0.6 standard deviation. Moreover, three of the four academic differences – report card marks in both areas and scores on the CAT-M – exceed all differences involving personal and social demographic characteristics.[8]

These large differences in test performance are striking in that they rate children's performance at the beginning of first grade, before anyone has had much experience in school. Marks and test scores thus point to the same conclusion: children who will be retained at some time in elementary or middle school already are far behind academically when they start first grade. That they are challenged by the first grade curriculum is reflected in their report card marks; their test scores reveal serious skill deficits. Hence, upon entering school future retainees in the BSS already are badly disadvantaged.

Repeaters versus Promoted Youngsters: School Adjustment Profiles

Children's school adjustment in nonacademic areas is monitored in their deportment, attendance, and popularity with other students. Children who are frequently absent, have problems with other children, or do not conform easily to the behavioral demands of the classroom are at a disadvantage in school compared with their "well behaved" peers. Such problems signal a poor fit between students and the school environment (e.g., Keogh 1986; Lerner, Lerner, and Zabski 1985). The last comparisons in Table 5.1 show whether retainees, along with their academic problems, also are prone to these kinds of adjustment difficulties.

First grade absence rates are different: never-retained children average just over 11 days absent; retainees, almost 16 absences. A 5-day

---

[8] Elsewhere (Dauber, Alexander, and Entwisle 1993) we examined how these factors affect the likelihood of retention jointly. That assessment, too, finds the academic predictors more discriminating than demographic factors. However, social factors still predict the risk of retention, even among children with comparable testing levels and early marks: boys still are more likely to be held back than are girls; children from low-income families more so than those better off economically.

difference in absences may not seem a great deal, but absences predict school performance (Barcai 1971; Entwisle and Hayduk 1978; Weitzman et al. 1985).

The next three comparisons involve aspects of classroom adjustment as rated by homeroom teachers in the spring of first grade. Fourteen items adapted from the 1976–77 National Survey of Children are used (scale construction and psychometric properties are described in Alexander, Entwisle, and Dauber 1993).[9] The Cooperation–Compliance scale is based on four items that rate students' conformity with rules and acceptable classroom behavior: (1) how they get along with others (whether they fight and tease), (2) whether they lie, (3) whether they lose their temper, or (4) whether they are polite and helpful. Rating categories ranged from "exactly like [this student]" to "not at all like," coded from 1 to 6, with high scores used for more positive qualities. The scale thus has a possible range of 4 to 24. Although most children are evaluated favorably (the overall average is above 20), there is a significant 2-point difference between retained and never-retained children, amounting to almost 0.6 standard deviation. Repeaters thus are judged less cooperative by their first grade teachers *before* they are retained.

The Interest–Participation scale consists of five items that rate students' involvement in, and enthusiasm for, classroom activities: whether they are (1) enthusiastic, (2) cheerful, (3) creative, (4) loners, or (5) afraid of new situations. These items have clear implications for the way students approach their studies. The Interest–Participation scale is significantly related to first grade achievement, reading marks, and math marks (Alexander et al. 1993). Students who are more outgoing, cheerful, and inquisitive perform better in the classroom (alternatively, children who perform better are seen by their teachers as more engaged and better behaved).

In this area, too, students generally are rated favorably by their teachers. The average for the total group is nearly 22 of the 30 possible. Nevertheless, a difference of more than 5 points separates retained and never-retained students: retainees are a full standard deviation below their never-retained peers.

The final classroom adjustment scale, Attention Span–Restlessness, is made up of four items that measure (1) concentration, (2) nervousness,

[9] Here we use teachers' ratings from first grade, but similar ratings were secured in Years 2 and 4, also. Alpha reliability for the three scales ranges from 0.74 for the Attention Span–Restlessness scale to 0.83 for the Cooperation–Compliance scale, and stability correlations across years generally are in the range of 0.3 to 0.5.

(3) maturity, and (4) restlessness. A child rated low on this scale would likely have difficulty keeping pace with the curriculum because of poor concentration or fidgetiness. Children who score higher on this scale also tend to do better on the CAT tests and get higher report card marks (Alexander et al. 1993). Retained and promoted children differ in their Attention Span–Restlessness ratings by almost 4 points, just under a full standard deviation.

These large differences in behavior ratings tell us that teachers view repeaters *prior to their being held back* as not fitting in well with the school routine. They seemingly are not as comfortable in the student role.[10] These three aspects of children's classroom behavior are fairly stable during early elementary school. Also the Interest–Participation and Attention Span–Restlessness scales have continuing relevance for academic performance through at least fourth grade, which is as far into children's schooling as we have pursued the matter (see Alexander et al. 1993).

Conduct marks from report cards, also tallied in Table 5.1, yield a cruder but administratively more important measure of children's classroom deportment. Conduct is rated simply as "satisfactory" (coded 2) or "needs improvement" (coded 1). Retained students again are rated lower than nonretainees (by 0.16 unit or by 0.37 standard deviation).

Another adjustment measure reported in Table 5.1 is taken from the 27-item Maryland Systematic Teacher Observation Inventory (MSTOI),[11] a diagnostic inventory formerly used by the Maryland State Department of Education in the early grades. In the MSTOI teachers evaluate school adjustment in five areas (psychomotor, sensory/perception, language, cognition, affect/motivation), with 5 to 11 items in each area. MSTOI scoring includes an "at-risk" code for youngsters whose total score exceeds a predetermined threshold. That code or "flag" is used in Table 5.1, with children deemed at risk scored 1 and others scored 0. Scores are available for 554 children, mostly ($N = 458$)

[10] Ratings were secured in the spring of the year from first grade homeroom teachers, who in most instances were also subject area instructors. For first grade repeaters, these opinions are no doubt partly behind the retention decisions. However, children held back in second grade and later also score below never-retained children in terms of first grade teachers' evaluations (see the next section). Because ratings from first grade anticipate who will be held back later, the link between poor school adjustment and retention cannot simply be a matter of unfavorable attitudes of retaining teachers.
[11] Validation studies of the MSTOI report correlations ranging from 0.30 to 0.85 with second grade reading achievement (Cooper 1979; Suhorsky and Wall 1978) and a correlation of .33 with third grade reading achievement (Kaufmann 1982).

from kindergarten teachers (the others are from first grade teachers).[12] Future retainees are more likely to be identified on the MSTOI as being at risk for school problems than are never-retained students (49% versus 13%). When just kindergarten teachers' ratings are used, 42% of retainees are identified as at risk versus 11% of the never-retained, so warning signs are present even before first grade.

The final measure in Table 5.1 is the homeroom teacher's rating of children's popularity among classmates. In the spring of the first grade, teachers rated students on a 5-point scale ranging from "least popular" (coded 1) to "most popular" (coded 5). To-be-retained students are rated less popular by about 0.6 standard deviation.

Overview

What does the overall pattern look like? Retained and never-retained students differ in many ways: the demographic differences seen in Table 5.1 are joined by wide disparities in academic performance and in nonacademic criteria that bear on children's school adjustment. The distinctive demographic profile of retainees is important: minority youth, children from lower socioeconomic status (SES) backgrounds, and boys are held back more often.[13] However, much more pronounced is selection on the basis of academics and school adjustment. BSS retained students, like those in the Chicago Longitudinal Study (CLS) sample (Reynolds 1992), fare poorly on *all* measures of early academic standing. In addition, their classroom conduct, "style," and peer relations are rated much less favorably by teachers. They are more often absent from school and even in kindergarten are rated as being at high risk of failure (the MSTOI "warning" designation).

With all this evidence before even one retention decision has been made, rather than a comfortable and successful move into the "student role," future retainees' situation at school is precarious from day one. These children's academic skills when they begin school fall far short, and so they have trouble keeping up with the curriculum. Their social skills and behavior set up further interference. The problems that eventually lead to these children's being held back are foreshadowed in

---

[12] Excluding first grade teachers, the pattern is very much the same.

[13] Minority overrepresentation among retainees can be accounted for almost entirely by their lower family SES. With socioeconomic factors adjusted, African-Americans are no more likely than Whites to be held back (e.g., Dauber et al. 1993).

serious adjustment and academic problems *before* the first day of school –
they are the backdrop to retention, not consequences of retention.

First Grade Repeaters versus Later Repeaters

The previous section establishes that retained and never-retained students differ in many ways relevant to their academic prognosis. Now
we consider heterogeneity *within* the population of repeaters, starting
with children held back in first grade and continuing with those held
back at higher grades (grades 2 through 7).[14]

Do different groups of repeaters have distinctive profiles? Table 5.2
shows that differences involving social demographics are all minor
and nonsignificant. The absence of pronounced "social selection" for
early retention is impressive – there are no differences by gender,
race/ethnicity, or economic level, and those involving mother's education and family composition are all much smaller than differences when
comparing repeaters against never-retained. Minority and economically
disadvantaged youngsters thus do not appear to be held back before
others, even though their rates of retention overall are higher.[15] Clearly,
however, children singled out earliest are the ones struggling most. The
first-quarter math and reading marks of children who will be retained
at the end of first grade are barely above unsatisfactory (at 1.3 and 1.1,
respectively) – 71% receive initial grades of "unsatisfactory" in math;
90% are rated unsatisfactory in reading.

Later retainees also perform marginally at this early point, but with
a math average (barely) above satisfactory (2.03), and a reading average
(1.67) midway between satisfactory and unsatisfactory, their marks are
well above the level of first grade repeaters. Differences between the
averages of early and later retainees (more than half a marking unit on
a 4-point scale) both exceed a full standard deviation.

---

[14] Never-retained children are excluded from these comparisons.

[15] Meisels and Liaw (1993) also compare demographic characteristics of early and late
retainees over the elementary and middle school grades, using retrospective reports
from NELS88. In some of their comparisons, background differences are smaller among
early repeaters than among the later, whereas we find them to be larger. However,
their comparisons contrast children held back in kindergarten through third grade
with those retained in fourth through eighth grades and so are not strictly comparable to those reported in Table 5.2. By *early* we mean first grade repeaters, specifically. Their results do accord with ours, however, in finding much larger differences
across the divide between retained and never-retained than between earlier and later
repeaters.

The test score story is much the same: later retainees outperform first grade retainees on both CAT subtests, and again the differences are large. The 16-point spread in Reading Comprehension is about 0.5 standard deviation; the 19-point gap in Math Concepts, 0.8 standard deviation.

All retainees get off to a shaky start academically, but the children held back earliest are the ones struggling most. First grade repeaters' academic performance is conspicuously bad on the very first evaluations made of them. Later retainees are having problems in first grade, too, but they at least do well enough to be promoted. The scheduling of these youngsters' retentions thus reflects the severity of their early academic problems, such that those lagging furthest behind at the start are held back first.

Perhaps more surprising is that the same pattern holds for indicators of behavioral adjustment. Again, first grade retainees stand out. Except for differences in conduct marks and days absent, their averages are far behind those of children held back in second grade or later. The profile of first grade retainees thus is one of broad-based difficulty. In addition to the academic difficulties already reviewed, teachers see first grade retainees as being less popular with their peers and as behaving in ways that may make it harder for them to respond to the demands of the classroom. First grade repeaters are rated less cooperative, much less invested in classroom activities, more restless, and more easily distracted, scoring almost 2 standard deviations behind never-retained children on classroom behaviors generally recognized as reflecting good school adjustment.

Later retainees do better academically than first grade retainees at the beginning of first grade but still are below the level of the never-retained. The school adjustment indicators give the same impression, as second through seventh grade repeaters are ahead of first grade repeaters but behind never-retained youngsters. Thus, in terms of academic performance or school adjustment, never-retained students fare best, first grade retainees fare worst, and the later retainees are in between.

Single Repeaters versus Multiple Repeaters and Special Education Children

This section considers how children with multiple placements differ from those who manage to make orderly progress after being held back once. Most retainees stay on track after completing their repeated year

TABLE 5.2. *Demographic, Academic, and School Adjustment Profiles of First Grade Retainees and Second through Seventh Grade Retainees*[a]

	All Retainees[b]	Grade 1 Retainees[c]	Combined Grade 2–7 Retainees[d]	Difference between Grade 1 and Grade 2–7	Difference as a Proportion of sd
Demographic comparisons					
Proportion male	0.57	0.57	0.57	0.00	0.00
	(0.50)	(0.50)	(0.50)		
Proportion African-American	0.63	0.63	0.63	0.00	0.00
	(0.48)	(0.49)	(0.48)		
Proportion receiving lunch subsidy	0.85	0.84	0.85	0.01	0.02
	(0.36)	(0.37)	(0.36)		
Average mother's education (years)	10.61	10.77	10.50	0.27	0.12
	(2.19)	(2.12)	(2.24)		
Average father's education (years)	10.90	10.91	10.89	0.02	0.01
	(1.90)	(1.84)	(1.94)		
Proportion in two-parent family	0.42	0.37	0.45	−0.08	0.17
	(0.49)	(0.49)	(0.50)		
Average number of siblings	1.62	1.79	1.50	0.29	0.19
	(1.51)	(1.80)	(1.27)		
Academic comparisons					
Average reading mark, first quarter 1982	1.45	1.10	1.67	−0.57**	1.04
	(0.55)	(0.31)	(0.56)		
Average math mark, first quarter 1982	1.75	1.30	2.03	−0.73**	1.03
	(0.71)	(0.48)	(0.67)		
Average CAT-R score, fall 1982	267.09	257.01	273.60	−16.59**	0.49
	(33.75)	(34.18)	(31.91)		

Average CAT-M score, fall 1982	276.05 (24.00)	264.09 (20.49)	283.62 (23.00)	−19.53**	0.81
School adjustment comparisons					
Average number of absences	16.19 (13.60)	18.20 (15.93)	14.93 (11.78)	3.27	0.24
Average Cooperation–Compliance score	19.33 (4.71)	18.52 (5.15)	19.86 (4.34)	−1.34*	0.29
Average Interest–Participation score	18.74 (5.07)	16.34 (4.61)	20.33 (4.74)	−3.99**	0.79
Average Attention Span–Restlessness score	18.48 (4.57)	16.00 (4.54)	20.13 (3.78)	−4.14**	0.90
Average conduct mark, fall 1982	1.66 (0.48)	1.61 (0.49)	1.69 (0.47)	−0.08	0.16
MSTOI proportion at risk	0.49 (0.50)	0.72 (0.45)	0.34 (0.48)	−0.38**	0.76
Average peer popularity	3.09 (1.08)	2.61 (1.05)	3.39 (0.99)	−0.78**	0.72

[a] Numbers in parentheses are standard deviations.

[b] Sample coverage on all retainees, except for father's education ($N = 183$) and Maryland Systematic Teacher Observation Inventory (MSTOI) ($N = 230$), varies from 317 to 270.

[c] Sample coverage on first grade retainees, except for father's education ($N = 69$) and MSTOI ($N = 89$), varies from 127 to 105.

[d] Sample coverage on combined second through seventh grade retainees, except for father's education ($N = 114$) and MSTOI ($N = 141$), varies from 190 to 163.

** Signifies differences significant at the 0.01 level; * differences significant at the 0.05 level.

TABLE 5.3. *Demographic, Academic, and School Adjustment Profiles of Students Retained Only Once and Those with a Second Retention or Special Education*[a]

	All Retainees[b]	Retained Once[c]	Retained Twice or Special Ed.[d]	Difference between Retained Once and Retained Twice or Special Ed.	Differences as a Proportion of sd
Demographic comparisons					
Proportion male	0.57 (0.50)	0.54 (0.50)	0.62 (0.49)	−0.08	0.16
Proportion African-American	0.63 (0.48)	0.60 (0.49)	0.68 (0.47)	−0.08	0.16
Proportion receiving lunch subsidy	0.85 (0.36)	0.84 (0.37)	0.85 (0.36)	0.01	0.02
Average mother's education (years)	10.61 (2.19)	10.75 (2.36)	10.41 (1.93)	0.34	0.16
Average father's education (years)	10.90 (1.90)	11.05 (2.03)	10.74 (1.75)	0.31	0.16
Proportion in two-parent family	0.42 (0.49)	0.40 (0.49)	0.44 (0.50)	−0.04	0.08
Average number of siblings	1.62 (1.51)	1.53 (1.49)	1.73 (1.54)	−0.19	0.13
Academic comparisons					
Average reading mark, first quarter 1982	1.45 (0.55)	1.59 (0.59)	1.27 (0.45)	0.32**	0.58
Average math mark, first quarter 1982	1.75 (0.71)	1.94 (0.71)	1.50 (0.61)	0.44**	0.62

Average CAT-R score, fall 1982	267.09 (33.75)	272.24 (33.55)	260.04 (32.88)	12.19**	0.36
Average CAT-M score, fall 1982	276.05 (24.00)	280.11 (23.92)	270.11 (22.95)	10.00**	0.42
School adjustment comparisons					
Average number of absences	16.19 (13.60)	15.54 (12.46)	17.09 (15.03)	−1.56	0.11
Average Cooperation–Compliance score	19.33 (4.71)	20.03 (4.36)	18.36 (5.02)	1.66**	0.35
Average Interest–Participation score	18.74 (5.07)	20.04 (4.96)	16.94 (4.68)	3.10**	0.61
Average Attention Span–Restlessness score	18.48 (4.57)	19.72 (3.95)	16.78 (4.82)	2.94**	0.64
Average conduct mark, fall 1982	1.66 (0.48)	1.69 (0.46)	1.61 (0.49)	0.08	0.16
MSTOI proportion at risk	0.49 (0.50)	0.43 (0.50)	0.57 (0.50)	0.14*	0.28
Average peer popularity	3.09 (1.08)	3.37 (1.03)	2.70 (1.03)	0.67**	0.62

[a] Numbers in parentheses are standard deviations.
[b] Sample coverage on all retainees, except for father's education ($N = 183$) and Maryland Systematic Teacher Observation Inventory (MSTOI) ($N = 230$), varies from 317 to 270.
[c] Sample coverage on once-retained children, except for father's education ($N = 94$) and MSTOI ($N = 133$), varies from 184 to 156.
[d] Sample coverage on twice-retained and special education children, except for father's education ($N = 89$) and MSTOI ($N = 91$), varies from 133 to 112.
** Signifies differences significant at the 0.01 level; * signifies differences significant at the 0.05 level.

(58%, or 184 of 317) – they are not retained again or placed in special education. We saw in Chapter 4, though, that many children retained in first grade experience further interventions. The reasons for this now seem clear, because in terms of academics *and* adjustment, these children are much worse off than other repeaters at the start of school. Consistently with this, only 39% (50 of 127) of first grade retainees manage to avoid a second retention and/or assignment to special education.

When comparing single retainees against double retainees and special education children, demographic characteristics are much the same (Table 5.3). None of the differences is statistically significant, and differences involving academics are much larger. Repeaters who later will be held back a second time and/or be assigned to special education earn lower marks than do single retainees at the beginning of first grade, averaging nearly a third of a marking unit above the multiple-problem group in reading and almost half a marking unit higher in math. Both mark differences exceed 0.5 standard deviation – large differences in early school performance among children who are performing poorly altogether. Multiple-problem children also have lower averages in the fall of first grade on both CAT subtests. At around 0.4 standard deviation, these differences too seem noteworthy.

Multiple repeaters and retainees later assigned to special education also give evidence of poor early school adjustment. Teachers view these youngsters as significantly less cooperative, less engaged in their schoolwork, more fidgety, less popular with their peers, and more often as at risk on Maryland Systematic Teacher Observation Inventory (MSTOI) ratings.

Conclusions

Repeaters differ from never-retained children in many ways that bear on their academic prospects; beyond that, different "classes" of retainees can be distinguished from one another on the basis of problems discernible at the very start of school.

Family demographic characteristics, early marks and test scores, and facets of school adjustment in first grade show highly patterned differences before any students have been retained. Contrasts involving academic factors and poor school adjustment are much larger than contrasts defined around family and personal risk factor profiles, yet academics and adjustment have received scant attention in the retention literature. Academic differences that *predate* retention are glossed over, and the broad spectrum of adjustment problems documented here has received virtually no attention.

The logic underlying children's differential treatment by schools is vividly drawn in these contrasting histories: distinctive retention profiles mirror distinctive problem profiles. Retainees as a group have serious problems meeting the standards and expectations that await them at school. Those whose problems are most severe are held back soonest, are often held back a second time, and are more likely than other repeaters to receive special education.

The academic and school adjustment profiles of repeaters reveal a side of this "unjustifiable, discriminatory, noxious policy" (Abidin et al. 1971) that gets short shrift. Children at high risk of retention need help badly. The help that repeating a grade provides is an extra year (or two) to catch up. Whether they in fact do catch up remains to be seen. Having plotted out children's pathways through the elementary and middle school years (Chapter 4) and seen in this chapter who is held back, we are now ready to explore what follows retention, starting with academic consequences.

6

Achievement Scores before and after Retention

We now turn to retention's consequences. This chapter and the next two address consequences in the academic realm: achievement test scores in Chapters 6 and 7; report card marks in Chapter 8. The present chapter provides a detailed description of achievement test patterns. Chapter 7 evaluates retainee–never-retained achievement differences analytically, using statistical models to adjust for possible confounds.

Whether repeating helps or harms children academically is perhaps the single most pressing question in weighing the pros and cons of the practice, yet, as we saw in the first two chapters, the jury is still out. Despite many studies, good research on how retention affects children's school performance is sparse. In the next several chapters, repeaters' postretention performance is evaluated against (1) their own performance profile before retention; (2) the performance of other children whose early academic record was about the same as theirs but who were not held back (the strategy of "matched controls"); (3) the performance of all never-retained children after adjusting statistically for characteristics other than retention that might contribute to differences between the groups; and (4) the performance of other children who will be held back *after* the comparison is made.

This last approach is uncommon. The idea, as an example, is to compare the second grade progress of children held back in first grade against that of children not retained until third grade. Although third grade repeaters have higher first grade test scores than first grade repeaters, they nevertheless are more similar to first grade repeaters in terms of academic and adjustment problems than are nonrepeaters (Chapter 5). Because of these similarities, yet-to-be-retained children's second grade performance may be a better yardstick than the performance of never-to-be-retained children for judging whether first grade repeaters are doing better, worse, or about the same as expected. If first and third grade repeaters are both doing poorly in Year 2 relative to second graders with smooth promotion histories, then something *other* than retention is likely behind repeaters' academic difficulty.

Our data on children's school performance cover 8 years. Retainees spend 2 years in the repeated grade, so we can plot performance profiles through seventh grade for practically everyone (double repeaters are the main exception). The number of retainees is largest in the first 3 years: 127 first-time repeaters in the first year, 68 in the second, and 47 in the third.[1] Because coverage of performance trends *after* retention is longest for them, profiles are presented separately for first, second, and third grade retainees. For fourth through seventh grade repeaters the time line is abbreviated and sample sizes year by year are too small to sustain separate analysis, so these children are grouped together as "late repeaters."

Two never-retained comparison groups also are included in these comparisons. The first consists of all never-retained children; the second is a subset of nonretainees with low first grade spring California Achievement Test (CAT) scores. The latter children ($N = 106$) have early verbal and quantitative CAT scores within 1 standard deviation of the averages of all retainees, a range that encompasses about a fourth of the never-retained subsample. Their CAT Reading Comprehension (CAT-R) average is 326, compared with 312 for retainees and 371 for other never-retained children; their CAT Math Applications and Concepts (CAT-M) average is 327, as against 319 for repeaters and 366 for other nonrepeaters.

Evaluating the later performance of retainees against that of never-retained children with comparable early academic skills involves the logic of matched controls. Chapter 2 reviewed problems with this approach, and here the match itself is not as close as we would like. This is because even with a sample approaching 800, not enough children have first grade CAT scores as low as repeaters'. In the typical study, repeaters are matched with like children from the *same* class or grade level. Achieving good matches can be hard even then, but in the

---

[1] For a local study, these are reasonably large repeater samples (e.g., they compare favorably with those reviewed earlier for Peterson and associates 1987, and Pierson and Connell 1992). And, too, BSS repeaters are typical children, in that they were selected on a random basis without regard to their standing as repeaters.

present instance screening for retentions is over 7 years, not 1. This long time frame redefines the pool eligible for matching. Instead of only repeaters' classmates during the failed year, here the pool consists of children promoted every year through middle school – a more select group.

In one-shot studies probably many candidates for matching are held back at a later point, but these retentions occur after the fact and so are undetected. The academic profile of first grade repeaters is weakest of all, but Chapter 5 established that children held back later also begin school with achievement test scores far below the level of never-retained children's. Because almost half the BSS cohort is held back through middle school, it appears most children with serious academic deficiencies are caught in the retention web at some point. If all children promoted out of first grade were included in the pool for matching, the comparison group would be made up mainly of children held back at later grades. That hardly seems appropriate, but we wonder how often it happens, inadvertently, in other studies that lack the BSS's long time frame and broad coverage.

The restricted pool of eligibles in the present instance limits our ability to match on entry-level achievement scores, and it is one reason why, in later chapters, we mainly rely on statistical adjustments to accomplish fair comparisons. However, despite weak implementation of the matched control logic, there still is value in seeing how children who manage to avoid retention despite low entering scores fare over the long term in relation to repeaters. For that reason, all analyses reported in this volume include "poor performing but promoted" comparisons as one of several frames of reference for judging retention's effectiveness.

The present chapter reports simple comparisons of children's CAT scores through the first 8 years of school. Our main concern is to determine whether retainees' *progress* keeps pace with other children's, as reflected in test score gains or improvement. The statistical analyses performed on these same test data in the next chapter then take other factors into account to clarify whether the descriptive pattern is robust.

Retainees' CAT Gains in the Repeated Grade

Year-by-year test score trajectories for retained and never-retained children (see appendix Table 6.A1) present grade-level *gains* and cumulative *gains* across grade levels to highlight similarities and differences in developmental patterns across the retained–promoted divide. Figures 6.1

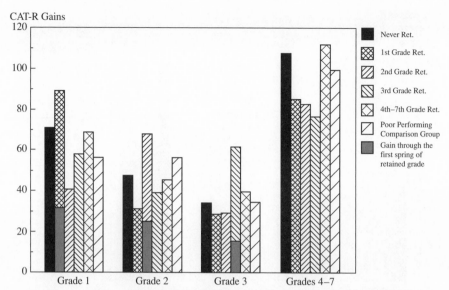

FIGURE 6.1. Gains on the CAT Reading Comprehension test in grades 1 through 7 for first, second, and third grade retainees; for fourth through seventh grade retainees; for all never-retained pupils; and for the poor-performing comparison group. For retained pupils in the year of retention, the first-year component of the grade-level gain is shown below the horizontal divide, the second-year component above the divide.

and 6.2 and Table 6.1 report grade level gains for grades 1, 2, and 3 separately, and for grades 4 through 7 combined. All the figures needed to plot Figures 6.1 and 6.2 are provided in Table 6.1, so the reader can refer to it for details that may be hard to decipher in the figures.[2] Gains relative to children's standing before being held back are the focus, as repeaters almost always start out behind. Whether repeaters perform at the same level as promoted children is taken up later. Here we focus on children's *progress* in relation to their starting point.

Figures 6.1 and 6.2 show how youngsters who repeated a grade compare to those who passed that grade on the first try, including those who repeated some other grade. Except for retainees in the repeated grade,

[2] Gains are computed for all children with scores available at the beginning and end of the interval at issue. These will not always correspond to cross-sectional differences in average scores at the beginning and end points because of differences in case coverage. For example, the first entry in Table 6.1 shows a 31.5-point first grade CAT-R gain for first grade repeaters, based on 104 youngsters. In Table 6.A1, though, first grade repeaters are reported to have fall and spring averages of 257.0 ($N = 106$) and 287.1 ($N = 118$), respectively; their difference is 30.1 points. The approach we use calculates the average individual gain; the second is the difference in Time 1 and Time 2 averages.

CAT-M Gains

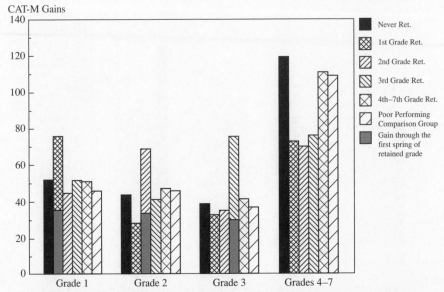

FIGURE 6.2. Gains on the CAT Math Concepts and Applications test in grades 1 through 7 for first, second, and third grade retainees; for fourth through seventh grade retainees; for all never-retained pupils; and for the poor-performing comparison group. For retained pupils in the year of retention, the first-year component of the grade-level gain is shown below the horizontal divide, the second-year component above the divide.

the height of the bars for grades 1, 2, and 3 represents fall-to-spring 1-year gains. For retainees the bar represents a 2-year total gain for the repeated grade, split into a "first year" component (fall to spring of the failed year, below the horizontal divide) and a "second year" component (spring of the failed year to spring of the repeated year, above the horizontal divide). The split within the 2-year period permits same-grade and same-age comparisons in the same display.[3]

---

[3] The second-year component overlaps the summer months between the first and second time through the grade and so credits any summer gains to the repeated year. "High-risk" children generally do not advance much on cognitive tests when school is not in session (e.g., Alexander, Entwisle, and Olson 2001; Entwisle et al. 1997; Heyns 1978), but in this instance combining summer and winter gains for repeaters does alter the picture somewhat. This is because second and third grade repeaters make unusually large strides in the summer after their failed year. Such improvement in their fall testing levels is very likely an artifact of test-wiseness. Retained children take the same version of the CAT battery in the repeated year as in the failed year. The various versions of the CAT battery are grade-specific, so this is not a problem among promoted youngsters. Same-grade comparisons that simply compare spring averages across years (e.g., Mantz-

TABLE 6.1. *Fall to Spring CAT-R and Cat-M Gains over First Grade, Second Grade, Third Grade, Fourth through Seventh Grades Combined, and, for Never-Retained pupils, Fifth through Eighth Grades Combined[a]*

	1st Grade Gain[a]	2d Grade Gain[b]	3d Grade Gain[b]	4th–7th Grade Gain	5th–8th Grade Gain[c]
CAT-R gains					
Year of retention					
1st grade	31.5/57.7	31.6	28.4	85.2	—
	(104)/(70)	(82)	(94)	(57)	
2d grade	40.5	23.4/44.3	29.2	82.9	—
	(59)	(55)/(48)	(48)	(38)	
3d grade	57.8	39.1	16.9/45.0	76.7	—
	(37)	(44)	(35)/(33)	(30)	
4th–7th grade	68.5	45.1	39.6	112.0	—
	(62)	(70)	(64)	(48)	
Never-retained pupils					
All never retained	70.9	47.4	34.3	107.8	99.2
	(387)	(382)	(299)	(201)	(215)
Poor-performing	56.0	56.4	34.5	99.3	93.2
comparison group	(92)	(88)	(72)	(44)	(52)
CAT-M gains					
Year of retention					
1st grade	35.9/40.2	28.3	32.9	72.6	—
	(102)/(69)	(83)	(93)	(55)	
2d grade	45.0	35.1/33.9	35.3	69.6	—
	(58)	(58)/(49)	(49)	(38)	
3d grade	51.9	41.5	32.1/43.3	75.7	—
	(38)	(45)	(35)/(34)	(30)	
4th–7th grade	51.3	47.1	41.2	110.7	—
	(65)	(71)	(64)	(44)	
Never-retained pupils					
All never retained	52.2	44.3	38.9	119.2	102.6
	(396)	(380)	(299)	(200)	(214)
Poor-performing	45.9	46.1	36.9	108.8	90.6
comparison group	(93)	(86)	(72)	(44)	(52)

[a] Numbers in parentheses are sample sizes.

[b] For first, second, and third grade retainees, two gain scores are reported in the year of retention. These separate the 2-year repeated grade gain into its first-year component (fall to spring) and its second-year component (spring to spring). The total 2-year grade-level gain would be the sum of these figures.

[c] Fifth through eighth grade gains are not computed for repeaters.

In every instance save one, retainees' gains during their failed year fall short of every other group's gains that year, including those of children held back in later grades.[4] Their shortfall relative to never-retained youngsters is especially large, however. Consider improvement in reading comprehension (Figure 6.1). First grade repeaters' scores improve, on average, about 32 points, well below the 70-plus-point gain registered by all never-retained children and the 56-point gain achieved by the poor-performing comparison group. Additionally, second grade repeaters' scores improve that year by 40 points, and third grade and fourth to seventh grade retainees' gains, perhaps surprisingly, exceed those of the poor performers. A similar shortfall is seen for first grade repeaters on the CAT-M, and the pattern is repeated for second grade retainees in second grade and for third grade retainees in third grade (although for third grade retainees, shortfall on the Math Concepts and Applications test is small in several comparisons).

Yet-to-be-retained youngsters in grades other than their failed grade also generally gain more than retainees in that grade, but they usually gain less than the never-to-be-retained.[5] Yet-to-be-retained children begin slipping back most noticeably the year *prior to* the year they will fail (second grade repeaters in first grade; third grade repeaters in second grade), so the steep falloff registered in the failed year in most instances continues a progressive slide. Still, retainees stand out most in their failed year – that year their achievement gains lag especially far behind.

The picture changes the second time through the grade, however. In some instances retainees make large gains that year, especially on the CAT-R. These are the bar segments above the horizontal divide in Figure 6.1. The 58-point increase registered by first grade retainees and the 45-point increase registered by third grade retainees during their respective repeated years are both well above their failed-year gains (32 and 17 points, respectively). Second grade retainees' improvement of 44 points also seems large, but a third of this advance (16.7 points) was

icopoulos and Morrison 1992; Peterson et al. 1987) are susceptible to the same distortion. The seasonality of learning is an important topic but cannot be treated thoroughly here. The summer component of achievement gains is clarified later in this chapter, when preretention and postretention gains are compared over the same interval.

[4] The exception involves CAT-M gains (Figure 6.2), in which first grade retainees advance less in second grade than do second grade retainees.

[5] The large gains registered by fourth through seventh grade retainees in the early grades are an exception, but these youngsters are included mainly as another comparison group, and so the "exception" in this instance helps prove the rule.

registered over the summer months and so does not reflect repeated-year progress.[6]

These figures for first and third grade retainees represent impressive strides, and not just when compared with their own meager advances during the year they failed. Their gains on the second try are close to the 1-year gains registered by at least one of the never-retained comparison groups for the same grade even after allowing for summer improvement. Only second grade repeaters fall short in all comparisons.

The pattern for the CAT-M is not quite as favorable for repeaters, but the picture before retention parallels that for the CAT-R. The first time through the grade, children who later will be retained generally advance less than all others. Also, with the exception of second grade retainees, they gain more when repeating the grade than they do the first time through.[7] Third grade repeaters' gain over the repeated year, 43.3 points in Table 6.1, exceeds the gains registered by all other groups in third grade. And even after subtracting the summer component (about 10 points), their 33-point school year gain remains close to that of the comparison group for the same period. However, first and second grade retainees' repeated-year CAT-M gains in most instances fall short of the advances made by others, so the comparisons here are not consistently favorable.

Leaving aside gains made during the summer, which could represent practice effects with the test as well as summer learning unrelated to retention (e.g., Entwisle et al. 1997; 2000a), it is important to note that these 2-year grade-level gains are cumulative and reflect repeaters' assessed competence when they eventually move ahead to the next grade. First grade repeaters, for example, improved their CAT-M performance over first grade by a total of 76 points (35.9 + 40.2). The first grade gains for all other groups ranged between 45 and 52 points. Second grade repeaters' 2-year second grade CAT-M gain of 69 points similarly exceeds the 1-year second grade gains of all other groups, as does the 75-point third grade gain of third grade repeaters when compared with all other groups' gains in third grade.

These 2-year versus 1-year comparisons favor repeaters on the CAT-R as well. Since 2 years of progress is being compared with 1 year, the

---

[6] The same holds for 9 points of third grade repeaters' second-year gain, but for them even a "net" 36-point advance represents good progress. First grade repeaters, in contrast, lost ground over the first summer.

[7] Again, though, if summer gains are subtracted, the improvement is less than indicated in Table 6.1: 2 points for first grade repeaters, 1 point for third grade repeaters.

pattern is perhaps not surprising, but it does imply that after repeating
a grade, retainees are not as far behind as they had been when held
back. The "excess" repeated year gain thus gives the impression that
real progress has been made.

These children make up lost ground in the repeated year – that much
is clear – but how they do it is unclear. Have they merely repeated the
same material or have they had special help?[8] We do not know; however, simply repeating a grade alters children's school experience in important ways even if unaccompanied by targeted remediation efforts.
During the repeated year, retainees are more familiar with the curriculum and with school routines; they are bigger, older, and possibly more
mature than their classmates, advantages that may be especially important in the primary grades; they also often take the same standardized
tests as in the previous year and so may profit from test-wiseness.[9]

Repeating the year gives children in these ways a second chance to
learn skills they failed to master the first time through, and the pattern of
test score gains in Table 6.1 suggests they make up at least some of what
they missed. Even so, retainees have not reached promoted children's
level of performance. Retainees start so far back that even better-than-
average gains still leave them far behind. Nevertheless, some lost ground
has been made up, and that might not have happened had they been
promoted. But does repeating help children keep up once they are back
on track? That question is considered in the next section.

CAT Gains after Retention: Year by Year

The main question about test score gains after retention is whether
progress registered in the repeated year persists. For first, second, and
third grade repeaters, Figures 6.1 and 6.2 plot progress annually through
third grade. After third grade, when all are beyond their repeated year,
we report cumulative totals through the end of seventh grade.

Annual gains in most instances decline over the years, for repeaters
and promoted alike – a developmental pattern seen in other studies
also (e.g., Jencks 1985; Schneider 1980; Stephens 1956).[10] The CAT-R

---

[8] About all that is known is whether they received special education pull-out instruction
in reading or math. Otherwise, the formal curriculum should be the same, although
individual teachers no doubt sometimes make adjustments.

[9] This is what we think is indicated by second and third grade repeaters' unexpected
improvement in the fall of their repeated grade.

[10] Others (e.g., Shepard et al. 1996) view the decline as a feature of the CAT construction
and not a reflection of cognitive development. These contrasting perspectives, and their
implications, are addressed in the appendix at the end of this volume.

gains registered by never-retained children, for example, drop from an average of 71 points over first grade to 47 points over second grade to 34 points over third grade. And after third grade the growth rate continues to slow, as the cumulative fourth through seventh grade increase of 108 points implies an annual average of about 27 points. An orderly drop likewise is evident in the CAT-M pattern. Among the never-retained, annual CAT-M gains fall from 52 points to 39 over grades 1–3 and then to just over 30 points over grades 4 through 7.

Because progress for *all* children slows over time, repeaters' tapering off after retention does not necessarily reflect negatively on the practice. However, among retainees, the pattern is a bit more complicated, and in revealing ways: the single-year gains of yet-to-be-retained children in every instance exceed the single-year gains registered by repeaters after they move back into the normal promotion sequence. For example, third grade retainees gain 39 points on the CAT-R in second grade, and fourth through seventh grade retainees gain 45 points and 40 points in second and third grade, respectively. These *preretention* gains all exceed the *postretention* gains registered by first grade repeaters in second grade (31 points) and by first and second grade repeaters in third grade (28 points and 29 points). The same pattern holds for CAT-M gains, also.

We have seen that the pace of test score improvement slows for everyone moving from lower grades to higher ones. Retainees' gain decline after being held back is consistent with this pattern. Nevertheless, their annual gains after retention consistently fall short of those registered by comparable youngsters – those who have yet to be retained – at the same grade level. From this vantage point, they appear to be experiencing some postretention "backsliding" – that is, their slowdown over this period seems unusually pronounced.[11]

Cumulative gains over grades 4 through 7, displayed in Figures 6.1 and 6.2, support this conclusion. This span of years overlaps the end

[11] Since the comparisons here involve retainees after retention and the yet-to-be retained before retention, the over-time decline seen for everyone is confounded with age differences across groups. In grade-specific comparisons, repeaters are a year ahead of the others and their average increase should be lower for this reason alone. It may have nothing to do with postretention fade. Same-age comparisons beginning in the year after retainees have moved beyond the retained grade point in the same direction, however, as gains prior to retention generally exceed those after it. This is especially the case for CAT-R comparisons. Same-age comparisons are aligned chronologically. To look at retainees after retention, they can be implemented only for Years 3 through 6, as fall CAT scores are not available in Years 7 and 8, and then mainly for comparing grade 4–7 retainees with earlier repeaters. This is more limited than we would like, but it also indicates postretention fade in excess of the general developmental drop in test score gains seen for everyone.

of elementary school and the first 2 years of middle school, and all three early repeater groups lag behind then. On the CAT-M both never-retained groups gain well above 100 points over this interval; on the CAT-R the full never-retained sample also gains more than 100 points, while the poor performers advance 99.3 points. In comparison, the *largest increase* on either subtest posted by first through third grade retainees is first grade repeaters' 85-point gain on the CAT-R. The others range down to 70 points (for second grade repeaters on the CAT-M).

In the *more favorable* of these comparisons first grade repeaters' improvement over grades 4 through 7 falls well short of that registered by both never-retained groups – a shortfall of 23 points relative to all never retained, 14 points relative to the poor performers. These deficits correspond to 0.45 and 0.28 standard deviation (pooled sample), respectively.

In the *less favorable* comparisons second grade repeaters' gains lag even further back, by 50 points against the full sample of never-retained children and almost 40 points against the poor performers. The first difference puts them more than a full standard deviation back; the second about 0.90 standard deviation.

However, these disparities may be exaggerated because of the 1-year "offset" that lines up same-grade comparisons. Since improvement tends to trail off for everyone over time and repeaters are a year older than their grademates, the same-grade format puts retainees at a disadvantage – one that may be developmental and so has nothing to do with retention. Because they were held back previously, their gains across grades 4 through 7 begin and end when they are 1 year older than the corresponding grade-level gains for children with smooth promotion histories. They would make below-average progress for that reason alone.

Consistently with this apprehension, the same-age gains reported for never-retained children in the last columns of Table 6.1 are smaller than the corresponding same-grade figures. These cover grades 5 through 8 for promoted children and so are from the same years as those used in Table 6.1 to calculate repeaters' gains over grades 4 through 7. Three of four never-retained gains over this interval are below 100; just one of the four corresponding figures over grades 4 through 7 is this low. The difference between corresponding never-retained same-grade and same-age 4-year gains ranges from 18 points (among poor performers on the CAT-M) to 6 points (also among poor performers, on the CAT-R).

Same-age comparisons between retained and never-retained youngsters thus do reflect more favorably on retention, but the difference involves the extent to which repeaters lag behind, not whether they have caught up. Even in the more favorable same-age frame of reference retainees fall short, between by about 33 points on the CAT-M (involving second grade repeaters versus all those never retained) and 8 points on the CAT-R (involving first grade repeaters versus poor performers).

Most of the same-age comparisons are closer to 33 points than 8, so regardless of approach we conclude from Table 6.1 that over the postretention period, and for as long as we can monitor their progress, retainees fall further and further behind children who were spared retention. And the time frames at issue are uncommonly long – 6 years beyond the repeated grade for first grade retainees, 4 years beyond for third grade retainees. This period is long enough in both instances that any delayed or lasting benefits of retention almost certainly would be apparent.

A Note on Children Held Back at Higher Grade Levels

Thus far we have said little about children held back in fourth through seventh grades. Too few of them repeat any single grade to examine them separately, and, too, for the combined group the period of follow-up after retention is too short to reflect on consequences of retention. Nevertheless, at the start of school they were performing below the level of children who later have smooth promotion histories (although not below the level of poor performers with smooth promotion histories), so it seems wise to include them as yet another comparison group.

When these children's gains are lined up against those of repeaters held back earlier, the comparisons consistently favor later retainees. In fact, even comparisons with never retained children often favor later retainees. In all but one instance their grade-level gains (including those over grades 4 through 7 combined) surpass those of the poor performers and are close to (and occasionally above) those of all never-retained. The one possible exception is the 8+ -point difference (Table 6.1) on the CAT-M over grades 4 through 7 ($119 - 111 = 8$). However, this comparison, which gives the edge to promoted children, is reversed when the same-age total over grades 5 through 8 is used instead as the basis of comparison.

Combining repeaters from grades 4 through 7 obscures the detail of each group's 2-year "fail–repeat" cycle. Notwithstanding this, it still seems safe to conclude that the situation of later retainees is radically different from that of their counterparts held back earlier: in the early grades they progress at about the same pace as other promoted children; their outcomes during the period that frames their problem years are also favorable (at least in the aggregate); and to the extent that we can comment on what happens to them after retention, that assessment is positive as well. On this basis it is hard to say that retention either helps or harms children held back at higher grade levels: they seem to be doing satisfactorily all along, before, during, and after retention. However, in more detailed comparisons not displayed, in which fourth, fifth, sixth, and seventh grade repeaters' gains are calculated separately, the "failed year dip"–"repeated grade recovery" – seen for the three early repeater groups is evident for them also.

A fail–repeat roller-coaster pattern thus seems to characterize the retention experience generally, but what is most immediately relevant in these comparisons is that early retainees do no better keeping up with later retainees than they do keeping pace with never-retained children. The favorable pattern of CAT gains for later retainees thus is another standard against which early retention can be judged, and again the comparison is unfavorable.

Cumulative Test Score Gains from the Failed Year

CAT gains across grades 4 through 7 give a picture of how well retainees fare after getting back onto the regular promotion schedule. That they have difficulty is clear, but we also see indications of progress in the repeated grade. There thus are countervailing trends at work. Figures 6.3 and 6.4 capture the up and the down. They display cumulative gains for everyone from the fall of first, second, and third grade retainees' failed years to the end of seventh grade. These encompass the period of decline in the failed year, the repeated year "rebound," and the postretention tapering off (the exact figures are reported in Table 6.2).

Tallying progress across the three phases of the retention experience should give a fair reading of how the experience, in its totality, affects repeaters' academic development. Entries in the first column of Table 6.2 also are of interest for another reason, though. Because the baseline for them is the fall of first grade retainees' failed year, they sum gains over the entire interval of our study – from the start of school to the end of seventh grade. Never-retained children advance most

CAT-R

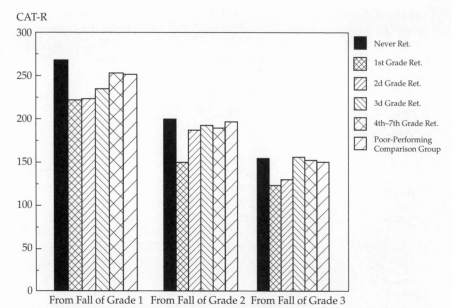

FIGURE 6.3. Cumulative CAT-R gains from fall of grades 1, 2, and 3 to spring of grade 7.

CAT-M

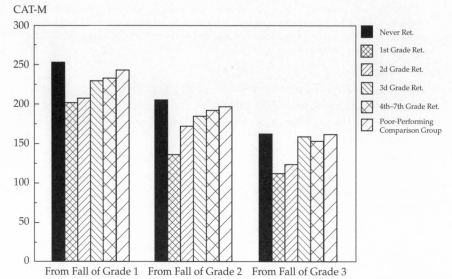

FIGURE 6.4. Cumulative CAT-M gains from fall of grades 1, 2, and 3 to spring of grade 7.

TABLE 6.2. *Cumulative CAT Gains from Fall of Grades 1, 2, and 3 to Spring of Grade 7 for Retained Groups, Never-Retained Pupils, and the Poor-Performing Comparison Group*[a]

	CAT-R			CAT-M		
	From Fall 1st Grade[b]	From Fall 2d Grade[b]	From Fall 3d Grade[b]	From Fall 1st Grade[b]	From Fall 2d Grade[b]	From Fall 3d Grade[b]
Year of retention						
1st grade	**224.4**	149.1	120.4	**202.1**	134.4	108.6
	(53)	(52)	(53)	**(49)**	(48)	(50)
2d grade	225.6	**187.0**	126.0	207.1	**171.1**	120.0
	(35)	**(34)**	(36)	(36)	**(35)**	(35)
3d grade	237.1	192.7	**152.5**	229.1	183.4	**154.4**
	(26)	(31)	**(28)**	(25)	(31)	**(29)**
4th–7th grade	255.5	189.3	148.7	233.1	190.1	149.0
	(44)	(51)	(50)	(44)	(48)	(46)
Never-retained pupils						
All never-retained	271.8	200.8	151.7	252.9	204.8	159.4
	(204)	(222)	(215)	(208)	(220)	(214)
Poor-performing	253.9	196.5	147.5	243.5	195.2	157.2
comparison group	(46)	(51)	(50)	(47)	(51)	(50)

[a] Numbers in parentheses are sample sizes.
[b] Gains for youngsters retained in the baseline grade are in boldface. Because of their repeated year, all retainees require a year more than never-retained pupils to reach the end of seventh grade, so gains are computed over different intervals for retained and never-retained youngsters.

over these years (272 points on the CAT-R; 253 points on the CAT-M); first grade retainees, least (224 points on the CAT-R; 202 points on the CAT-M). All these differences leave first grade repeaters trailing far behind.[12]

The comparison group of poor performers and children retained at the upper grades registers the next largest gains. The two groups are close on the CAT-R (254 versus 256), but on the CAT-M, repeaters' gain over grades 4–7 (233 points) is closer to third grade retainees' (229 points) than to the poor performers' (244 points).

The other retainee groups all lag behind never-retained children. Second grade repeaters are not much ahead of first grade repeaters in

[12] This is despite an extra-year advantage for repeaters (i.e., the interval for retainees spans 8 years, versus 7 years for promoted children).

either area, and both groups fall short of the advances made by third grade retainees. These are small differences in some instances, but the orderliness in these comparisons is striking. Over this 7-year period the rank order of test score gains parallels the scheduling of retention, recapitulating the pattern seen earlier for CAT scores on starting first grade (see Table 6.A1 in the appendix to this chapter).

On the specific question of whether retention helps repeaters, we can see no positive indications for first grade retainees, whose cumulative gains lag far behind almost everyone else's. The situation is much the same for second grade repeaters, whose gains from the autumn of second grade fall short of all others' save those of first grade repeaters. However, they are not as far behind as are first grade repeaters, and possibly more relevant is that their shortfall from second grade on is less than their own shortfall over the entire interval (seen in the previous column). For example, on the CAT-R, second grade repeaters' cumulative gain from the fall of first grade is 28 points shy of the poor performers' gain, whereas the difference when computed from the fall of second grade is less than 10 points. Hence, when never-retained children's exceptional first-year gains are set aside, the comparison for second grade repeaters looks more favorable. They still do not keep pace, but they also are not far behind.

The comparisons reported in the third column, which use third grade repeaters' year of failure as the baseline, are more favorable still. Their cumulative CAT-R gain from the fall of the third grade to the end of the seventh – 152 points – exceeds all others'. Though their margin of advantage in most cases is modest, third grade repeaters keep pace not only with the poor performers and children yet to be held back, but also with the full sample of never-retained youngsters. Such parity seems noteworthy.

Third grade retainees' advance in the quantitative area is not so dramatic, but they lag just 3 points behind the low performers and 5 points behind all never-retained children. Considering the tremendous gaps seen in most other comparisons, these modest differences suggest again some lasting benefits, at least for third grade repeaters.

The many detailed comparisons reviewed thus far establish that considerable detective work is needed to decipher retention's consequences, and even then the signals will not always be clear. Table 6.3, in which CAT gains are calculated preretention and post-, complicates matters further.

TABLE 6.3. *1-Year, 2-Year, and 3-Year CAT Gains, Defined around First, Second, and Third Grade Retainees' Failed Year*[a]

	1-Year Gains through and after Year 1			2-Year Gains through and after Year 2			3-Year Gains through and after Year 3		
	Pre[b]	Post[c]	Post/Pre[d]	Pre[b]	Post[c]	Post/Pre[d]	Pre[b]	Post[c]	Post/Pre[d]
CAT-R									
Year of retention									
1st grade	**31.5**	**54.5**	**1.73**	89.2	60.5	0.68	99.7	86.1	0.86
	(104)	**(71)**		(70)	(82)		(84)	(74)	
2d grade	40.5	23.4	0.58	**62.3**	**52.3**	**0.84**	103.4	91.5	0.88
	(59)	(55)		**(55)**	**(43)**		(49)	(46)	
3d grade	57.8	39.1	0.68	82.8	61.2	0.74	**95.8**	**98.6**	**1.03**
	(37)	(44)		(37)	(33)		**(30)**	**(30)**	
4th–7th grade	68.5	45.1	0.66	106.6	73.5	0.69	136.5	80.2	0.59
	(62)	(70)		(63)	(62)		(56)	(61)	
Never-retained pupils									
All never-retained	70.9	47.4	0.67	121.3	81.5	0.67	157.4	89.4	0.57
	(387)	(382)		(350)	(284)		(274)	(222)	
Poor-performing comparison group	56.0	56.4	1.01	113.0	75.7	0.67	145.1	84.0	0.58
	(92)	(88)		(81)	(70)		(64)	(48)	

CAT-M

Year of retention	Pre[b]	Post[c]	Post/Pre[d]	Pre[b]	Post[c]	Post/Pre[d]	Pre[b]	Post[c]	Post/Pre[d]
1st grade	35.9 (102)	**37.6** **(69)**	**1.05**	76.1 (69)	56.6 (82)	0.74	95.8 (84)	77.1 (73)	0.80
2d grade	45.0 (58)	35.1 (58)	0.78	**72.0** **(57)**	**51.7** **(43)**	**0.72**	103.8 (50)	96.1 (47)	0.93
3d grade	51.9 (38)	41.5 (45)	0.80	86.4 (37)	75.3 (34)	0.87	**102.3** **(29)**	**91.1** **(30)**	**0.89**
4th–7th grade	51.3 (65)	47.1 (71)	0.92	93.7 (67)	73.0 (62)	0.78	120.6 (59)	79.8 (59)	0.66
Never-retained pupils									
All never-retained	52.2 (396)	44.3 (380)	0.85	93.8 (354)	77.2 (283)	0.82	133.4 (283)	93.7 (221)	0.70
Poor-performing comparison group	45.9 (93)	46.1 (86)	1.00	97.1 (76)	80.1 (70)	0.82	127.5 (65)	83.8 (48)	0.66

[a] Numbers in parentheses are sample sizes. Boldface entries identify the retainee reference group for each panel.

[b] The "Pre" entries are from the fall of first grade through the spring of the retainee reference group's failed year. For that panel's reference group, they represent cumulative gains before retention.

[c] The "Post" entries use the fall of the repeated year for that panel's reference group as the baseline, with the gains being computed postretention for as many years as are covered in the preretention interval.

[d] The "Post/Pre" entries are simply the ratio of postretention gains to preretention gains for each panel's reference group. For other groups the calculations give the ratio of gains over the corresponding intervals.

Gains before and after Retention

Children's progress before retention provides still another frame of reference for structuring comparisons. The preretention record for first grade repeaters involves only their failed year. Their gains that year can be evaluated against their 1-year gains during the repeated year, which we already know are sizable. The first panel of Table 6.3 gives these results. The first entry (32) is simply the fall to spring CAT-R increase for the year they are held back. The second entry (54) is the increase, fall to spring, during their second time through the grade. Unlike the intervals used in Figure 6.1 and Table 6.1, change here is monitored over 1 academic year before and after retention, so the gains are directly comparable (i.e., the interval is the same and summer gains are factored out). The third column in Table 6.3 expresses the postretention gain as a proportion of the preretention gain, so we can see which of the two is larger and by how much. More informative, though, are comparisons *across groups*, which indicate whether the change in retainees' rate of progress after retention is greater than, less than, or about the same as other children's over the same period. Are they slowing down more or less than children never held back, or than those held back in other years? The approach is similar to that used by Karweit (1999) with the national Prospects data, as discussed in Chapter 2.

Since the entries for first grade repeaters overlap only the 2-year "dip and recovery" of their repeated grade, the gains themselves do not reveal anything new: first grade repeaters made below-average gains the first year and above-average gains the second. Practically the same figures appear in Table 6.1.,[13] but taking their ratio affords perspective that would be hard to appreciate otherwise. Repeaters' rate of progress from before they are held back seems a reasonable standard against which to judge their progress afterward. When this is done, gains that seem modest in absolute terms in fact can signify rather good progress.

First grade retainees' second year increase on the CAT-M is a case in point. Their 38-point gain that year ranks next to the bottom of that of all groups, but since these children gained even less the first time through the grade, for them a gain of 38 points is a large advance. In fact,

---

[13] The figures are not identical because somewhat different intervals are used in calculating gains for repeaters the second time through the repeated grade. In Table 6.1, the failed-year component is the first year's fall-to-spring gain (31.5 points on the CAT-R), but in order to cover the entire interval, the repeated-year component (54.5 CAT-R points) goes from spring to spring. In Table 6.3, gains are computed fall to spring throughout; in that way the pre- and postretention figures are directly comparable.

at 1.05 times their increase from the previous year, it is the largest *relative* improvement of any group. The poor performers are next, with a post- to preretention ratio of 1.00 – their second-year gain was about the same as their first-year gain. All the other groups gained less over the second year than the first, so their ratios fall below 1.00. At 0.78, second grade repeaters trail off most severely, but the second year for them is their year of failure, so this deficit is not surprising.

First grade repeaters made especially large strides on the CAT-R in the second year. Not only did they gain the most of any group that year, but most others fell off their pace from the previous year. As a result, first grade repeaters' ratio of 1.73 is more than double most other ratios in this panel.

Although these results are not new, the way the comparisons are structured in Table 6.3 shows them in a new light. They reveal differences in the relative pace of improvement, and from this vantage point first grade retainees appear to be making good short-term strides. Comparisons in the next panel line up gains for 2 years pre- and postretention: from the fall of first grade through the spring of second grade for the preretention interval; from the fall of Year 3 (when second grade retainees are repeating second grade) through the spring of Year 4 for the postretention interval. These intervals bracket the retention experience for second grade repeaters.

Again, precisely the same interval is used pre- and postretention, so the gains are directly comparable. On the CAT-R, second grade repeaters make the smallest postretention gains of any group (52 points), which ordinarily would be a negative showing. But the others make much larger strides in Years 1 and 2 than in Years 3 and 4, so their *progress* slows more than that of second grade retainees during this period. In fact, the 0.84 entry for second grade repeaters in the third column indicates they are closest of any group to maintaining their previous rate of gain. The next highest proportion is 0.74 for third grade retainees, with all the rest ranging between 0.67 and 0.69. These figures show second grade retainees do relatively well on the CAT-R for 2 years after retention. The picture is clouded, however, because their ratio for the CAT-M is the lowest (0.72).

For third grade repeaters the signals are more consistently positive. For them, achievement gains over 3 years before their retention are compared to 3 years after (from the fall of their repeated year, Year 4, to the spring of Year 6). On the CAT-R, their gain of 99 points is the largest of any group, and they are the only one whose 3-year gain from Year 4 through Year 6 exceeds that during the 3 previous years (1.03 in the third column). Most of the other ratios, including those of both never-retained groups, are much smaller.

On the CAT-M, third grade repeaters' postretention/preretention ratio (0.89) is not the highest (second grade repeaters' is, at 0.93) but is among the highest. Here again, the ratios for never-retained children fall below those for all others and so repeat the pattern from the 2-year intervals defined around second grade repeaters' retention experience. Never-retained children apparently get a "jump start" in the early grades that puts them far ahead. Retainees never pull even, but they do catch up some. They generally do better afterward than before, and so compared to children with smooth promotion histories they are closer to maintaining a consistent rate of academic progress through the elementary years.[14] Everyone's rate of progress slows, but never-retained children's slows more than retainees'.

Children held back trail behind right from the start and struggle especially in their year of failure. Table 6.3 indicates that the time spent repeating a grade helps these youngsters somewhat, and this pattern is intuitively appealing. It seems repeating allows them to master skills they missed the first time through, and, although delayed, they are better prepared when it is time for them to move on to the next grade. Nevertheless, this retention "boost" still leaves them far behind.

Overview of Performance Trends

To conclude this section, Table 6.4 shows where the several retainee groups stand relative to never-retained children when they begin school, in the spring of their failed year (their "low point"), in the spring of their repeated year (their "high point"), and at the end of seventh grade, which is as far as their school performance is covered in this volume. How retainees fare at these reference points gives a sense of the natural history of the retention experience: academic problems, severe at the outset, worsen until the retention decision is made; some improvement then ensues, both absolutely in the repeated year and, as just seen, relatively in years afterward. But despite the partial recovery, retainees' relative position generally is worse at the end than at the start.

---

[14] We say elementary years here because the longest interval extends through Year 6. All retainees at this point are still in elementary school.

TABLE 6.4. *Differences between Retainee and Never-Retained CAT-R and CAT-M Averages at the Start of First Grade, the End of Each Retainee Group's Failed Year, the End of Each Retainee Group's Repeated Year, and the End of Seventh Grade*[a]

	CAT-R				CAT-M			
	Fall 1st Grade	Spring Failed Year[b]	Spring Repeated Year[c]	Spring 7th Grade	Fall 1st Grade	Spring Failed Year[b]	Spring Repeated Year[c]	Spring 7th Grade
Retained vs. never-retained								
1st grade retainees	(−)33.8 [0.83]	(−)72.7 [1.90]	(−)18.7 [0.49]	(−)82.1 [1.21]	(−)40.5 [1.28]	(−)57.1 [1.77]	(−)16.8 [0.52]	(−)92.7 [1.44]
2d grade retainees	(−)21.2 [0.52]	(−)78.6 [1.82]	(−)37.4 [0.87]	(−)65.1 [0.96]	(−)26.2 [0.83]	(−)43.8 [1.27]	(−)12.8 [0.37]	(−)72.9 [1.13]
3d grade retainees	(−)18.1 [0.44]	(−)80.4 [1.51]	(−)37.3 [0.70]	(−)53.2 [0.78]	(−)24.0 [0.75]	(−)57.8 [1.33]	(−)14.9 [0.34]	(−)50.0 [0.78]
Retained vs. poor-performing comparison group								
1st grade retainees	(−)13.6 [0.33]	(−)39.3 [1.02]	(+)15.1 [0.39]	(−)50.3 [0.74]	(−)17.7 [0.56]	(−)28.3 [0.88]	(+)12.0 [0.37]	(−)66.1 [1.03]
2d grade retainees	(−)1.0 [0.02]	(−)55.2 [1.28]	(−)14.0 [0.32]	(−)33.4 [0.49]	(−)3.4 [0.11]	(−)30.7 [0.89]	(+)0.3 [0.01]	(−)46.3 [0.72]
3d grade retainees	(+)2.3 [0.06]	(−)51.2 [0.96]	(+)8.1 [0.15]	(−)21.4 [0.31]	(−)1.2 [0.04]	(−)28.8 [0.66]	(+)14.1 [0.32]	(−)23.4 [0.36]

a A negative sign in parentheses indicates that the difference favors the never-retained; a positive sign favors the retainee group; figures in brackets express the difference as a fraction of the total sample CAT standard deviation for the grade level at issue.

b Failed-year differences are calculated for first grade retainees at the end of Year 1, for second grade retainees at the end of Year 2, and for third grade retainees at the end of Year 3.

c Repeated-year differences are calculated for first grade retainees at the end of Year 2, for second grade retainees at the end of Year 3, and for third grade retainees at the end of Year 4.

The entries in Table 6.4 are differences between retained and never-retained students' average CAT scores. Since the variance in test performance increases over time, differences are also expressed as proportions of the test score standard deviation for the reference period. This scale conversion can be important because a difference of, say, 10 points is of more concern if scores range between values of 0 and 50 than if they range between 0 and 500: 10 points is a much larger relative gap in the first instance than in the second. Referencing raw score differences to the variation in scores adjusts for increasing spread over time in the range of test scores.

The pattern of signs in Table 6.4 confirms our overall impression. Most signs are negative, indicating that retainees are not doing as well as those never retained and the poor performers. But six positive signs appear for comparisons with the poor performers (youngsters who also began school with relatively low scores), and these are probably the more relevant comparisons. The first column in each testing area shows the now-familiar pecking order. Retainees lag behind badly at the start of school, the more so the sooner they will be held back. And though second and third grade repeaters' scores are close to the level of the poor performers', all three repeater groups trail far behind the full never-retained sample. Their shortfall is larger on the CAT-M, ranging between 0.75 and 1.28 standard deviations, but gaps on the CAT-R are appreciable, too (between 0.44 and 0.83 standard deviation).

Once the school clock begins ticking, to-be-retained children fall even further back. In the spring of their failed years, all three repeater groups lag behind by well over a full standard deviation when compared to the full never-retained sample and by close to a full standard deviation when evaluated against the poor performers. The failed year marks a very low point for all.

On the other hand, if retainees can ever be said to "shine" academically, it is when they finish their repeated year (third column). When compared with the low performers, five of the six entries are positively signed – retainees' scores in those instances are the higher of the two. They still lag behind all never-retained children, but their standing is much improved relative to that just a year earlier (the spring of their failed year), and in most instances also relative to their standing at the start of school.

If performance from that point could be sustained, we would probably count retention a resounding success. Unfortunately, at the end of seventh grade all retainee groups again lag far behind. But even at that, the picture is not altogether unfavorable. Except for first-grade retainees, repeaters are not behind by as many CAT points as they were in the spring of their failed year, and when the differences are expressed in standard deviation units, even first grade repeaters are relatively better off (see the comparison with all never-retained children). Despite a large absolute shortfall, with scores at the end of seventh grade more variable, their relative standing is improved.

The Retention Picture More Fully Considered

The conclusion that there are lasting benefits of retention for retainees at higher grade levels is tentative at this point because complications of the sort discussed in Chapters 1–5 can confound trend comparisons. Sample loss over time and the differences between special education children, double repeaters, and others are examined in this section. Other complications are taken up in Chapter 7, which uses statistical methods to adjust for characteristics of repeaters that might make their later testing patterns different from those of promoted children for reasons other than retention.

The spread of youngsters through the grade structure, into special education classes, and out of the city school system poses complex challenges for our analysis. For most of the years under study we were unable to secure survey and school record data (including test scores) on children who left the BCPS. Even for those who remained in the system, some data may be unavailable. Missing test data are a special concern in tracking cognitive performance before and after retention.

The Beginning School Study was designed to be representative (within the stratifying criteria of its research design) of children who began first grade in the fall of 1982 in Baltimore's public schools. This important feature of the project could be compromised by selective sample attrition and data loss. Chapter 5 showed that those who left Baltimore schools during the course of the study were disproportionately White and well-to-do. Accordingly, what look like changes in performance trajectories could instead reflect differences in the mix of children in the BCPS at different times. For example, our conclusion that test score gains diminish over time, and that gains do not slow as much for retainees as for others, could be artifactual, the result of selective attrition. Indeed, as more never-retained than retained children leave the city system, differential sample loss potentially makes suspect all comparisons across the retained–never-retained divide.

The Stayer–Exiter issue thus needs to be addressed, but other complications not addressed in the main body of this chapter also may have a distorting influence. For example, because first grade repeaters lag so far behind the others, later they are moved into special education classes and held back a second time in large numbers. The situation of special education children is especially complicated. To mention just a few of the characteristics that set them apart, for most or all of the day they are separated from other children in the school, their curriculum is different from the standard one, their classes are ungraded, and the marking distinctions used on their report cards differ in important ways from those used on regular report cards.

First grade retainees seem to fare especially poorly later on, but we need to know whether this deficit means retention in first grade itself is problematic, or whether it appears so only because first grade repeaters' difficulties are so severe. Special education is one such concern; another is double (and triple) retention. Also, the comparisons presented thus far do not adjust for the timing of the second retention of double repeaters. Same-grade comparisons, in consequence, are not properly aligned at the upper grade levels, and this mismatch, too, may affect the seeming advantages and disadvantages associated with retention.

Another potential complication involves the situation of later repeaters. Thus far we have used the performance of retainees held back in grades 4 through 7 mainly as another standard against which to evaluate the performance of children held back earlier. This is sensible from the point of view of our research design, but during the early period these not-yet-retained children would be included in the regularly promoted comparison group with whom retainees are expected to be keeping pace. So, too, for that matter, with second grade repeaters in the first year and third grade repeaters in the first 2 years. It is the difference between a "never retained" comparison group and a "not yet retained" comparison group. Because the former contains fewer poor-performing children than the latter, the approach used in the present volume may tilt comparisons against retention.

All these issues – selective sample attrition and missing test scores, the situation of special education children and of double retainees, and our treatment of children held back at the higher grade levels – are sources of concern. Accordingly, several supplemental analyses were performed to judge their implications:

1. Exiters are excluded throughout so we can see whether their presence in some parts of the analysis and not in others alters the picture.
2. Children assigned to special education classes are excluded. This affects the composition of both retained and never-retained subsamples, but mainly the retained ones, and especially the sample of first grade repeaters (58 of 90 – that is, 64% – of retained special education pupils are first grade repeaters).
3. All fourth through seventh grade retainees are assigned to the never-retained comparison group and also to the poor-performing comparison group if their test scores from the spring of Year 1 meet the criteria for membership. First, second, and third grade retention groups are not affected by this reassignment.
4. Double retainees are excluded.
5. A 2-year "offset" is implemented for double retainees from the time of their second retention. When this is done comparisons can only be made through sixth grade because double repeaters will not finish seventh grade until at least Year 9, which is outside the time frame of this analysis.
6. A final analysis screens on several of these procedural checks at the same time. Only a precious few repeaters survive this screening, but the numbers are sufficient to afford at least a sense of their combined consequences.

All the comparisons reported in the main body of this chapter have been remade with these various exclusions and rearrangements of the data. Never-retained children's grade-level CAT averages are affected very little by any of these procedural checks, including the loss of Exiters at higher grade levels (recall from Chapter 4 that sample attrition was not especially selective along academic lines). Among repeaters the exclusion of special education students has the greatest impact – retainees' CAT averages sometimes are much higher when special education children are omitted. Since achievement gains have been our main focus, the consequence of this exclusion of special education children for various gain comparisons requires careful consideration. This is done in Table 6.5. Special education is the focus, but for completeness several other checks also are reported (additional detail is available in appendix Table 6.A2).

For comparison purposes, Table 6.5 repeats promoted children's gains from Tables 6.2 and 6.3. The corresponding figures for the main

TABLE 6.5. *Comparisons of Cumulative Gains from the Fall of First, Second, and Third Grade Retainees' Failed Year, and Gains Pre- and Postretention when Special Education Children Are Excluded and When Several Exclusions Are Implemented Together*[a]

	1st Grade Retainee Comparisons				2d Grade Retainee Comparisons				3d Grade Retainee Comparisons			
	Gains from Fall 1st Grade to End 7th Grade[b]	1-year Gains through and after Year 1[c]			Gains from Fall 2d Grade to End 7th Grade[b]	2-Year Gains through and after Year 2[c]			Gains from Fall 3d Grade to End 7th Grade[b]	3-Year Gains through and after Year 3[c]		
		Pre	Post	Post/Pre		Pre	Post	Post/Pre		Pre	Post	Post/Pre
CAT-R												
Original retainee figures	224.4 (53)	31.5 (104)	54.5 (71)	1.73	187.0 (34)	62.3 (55)	52.3 (43)	0.84	152.5 (28)	95.8 (30)	98.6 (30)	1.03
Retainee figures excluding special education	239.4 (39)	38.8 (60)	58.9 (43)	1.52	197.4 (26)	63.5 (40)	47.2 (33)	0.74	159.0 (24)	102.4 (25)	100.4 (29)	0.98
Retainee figures with all three exclusions[d]	236.9 (25)	40.6 (27)	44.5 (20)	1.10	200.3 (21)	60.2 (25)	57.9 (25)	0.96	166.8 (18)	114.5 (14)	101.5 (19)	0.89
Original never-retained figures	271.8 (204)	70.9 (387)	47.4 (382)	0.67	200.8 (222)	121.3 (350)	81.5 (284)	0.67	151.7 (215)	157.4 (274)	89.4 (222)	0.57
Original comparison-group figures	253.9 (46)	56.0 (92)	56.4 (88)	1.01	196.5 (51)	113.0 (81)	75.7 (70)	0.67	147.5 (50)	145.1 (64)	84.0 (48)	0.58
CAT-M												
Original retainee figures	202.1 (49)	35.9 (102)	37.6 (69)	1.05	171.1 (35)	72.0 (57)	51.7 (43)	0.72	154.4 (29)	102.3 (29)	91.1 (30)	0.89
Retainee figures excluding special education	211.6 (36)	39.1 (60)	45.0 (42)	1.15	172.1 (28)	73.5 (42)	54.2 (33)	0.74	156.4 (24)	106.6 (25)	91.0 (29)	0.85
Retainee figures with all three exclusions[d]	215.3 (23)	39.4 (27)	43.7 (20)	1.11	167.3 (23)	80.7 (27)	60.0 (25)	0.74	157.3 (19)	110.9 (15)	94.1 (19)	0.85
Original never-retained figures	252.9 (208)	52.2 (396)	44.3 (380)	0.85	204.8 (220)	93.8 (354)	77.2 (283)	0.82	159.4 (214)	133.4 (283)	93.7 (221)	0.70
Original comparison-group figures	243.5 (47)	45.9 (93)	46.1 (86)	1.00	195.2 (51)	97.1 (76)	80.1 (70)	0.82	157.2 (50)	127.5 (65)	83.8 (48)	0.66

[a] Numbers in parentheses are sample sizes.

[b] The "original" gain figures are from Table 6.2.

[c] The "original" "Pre," "Post," and "Post/Pre" figures are from Table 6.3.

[d] For these calculations, Exiters (those who left the BCPS), special education pupils, and double retainees are all excluded.

retainee groups also are reproduced. Two sets of new figures then are reported for retainees: the first excludes special education children from the calculations; the second excludes special education youngsters, double repeaters, and Exiters. This second set of figures indicates what happens to the comparisons when we look just at children in Baltimore city schools the entire period of study, and when complications surrounding special education and double retention are set aside.

For each retainee group and its comparison groups, Table 6.5 reports cumulative gains from the fall of the retained year to the end of seventh grade (as in Table 6.2) and gains for as many years after retention as are available from before retention (i.e., 1 year in the case of first grade retainees, 2 years for second grade retainees, and 3 years for third grade retainees). To detect whether retention is pivotal in altering the pace of test score improvement, we also present the ratio of each group's postretention gain to its preretention gain. For never-retained children, the pace of progress over the same periods is shown.

The first column of figures in Table 6.5 tallies gains from the fall of retainees' failed year to the end of grade 7. The gain for all first grade retainees over this interval is 224 on the CAT-R and 202 on the CAT-M. When repeaters with additional problems (special education, double repeaters, or Exiters) are left out, gains increase 10 to 15 points and so are closer to never-retained children's gains (272 points). Retainees without other problems still fall far short of comparison group children, but the gap for them is smaller, and this is important.

The figures for second and third grade retainees are even more striking, at least on the CAT-R. Just as with first grade repeaters, gains go up appreciably when special education pupils and multiple problem cases are left out. In fact, the new figures are about equal to the gains registered by the never-retained samples. Second grade repeaters' CAT-R gain rises from 187 to 200 when all three exclusions are made. This gain exceeds the poor-performing comparison group's gain over the same interval (at 197) and shows second grade retainees as equal to the full never-retained sample (at 201).

Table 6.5 shows third grade repeaters who do not have added problems as ahead of both never-retained groups on the CAT-R. Indeed, even the modest increases they realize on the CAT-M – just 2 to 3 points – have the effect of pulling third grade repeaters very close to the never-retained groups. They are on a par with the comparison group and only 2 to 3 points shy of the full sample.

On balance, then, the picture for repeaters' cumulative gains from the year of retention forward is favorable when considering just youngsters who manage to stay on track after retention, that is, those for whom a single retention might be the source of school problems. On the other hand, when gains over fixed intervals from before and after retention are compared, as in the postretention/preretention columns of Table 6.5, the results are more mixed. With special education children and others excluded, the ratio of gains from after retention to those from before retention in some instances goes down, not up. This happens when scores increase more over the preretention period than over the postretention period. Sometimes the resulting ratios are a bit more favorable for retention, sometimes for promotion, although most of the changes, in either direction, seem minor.

Summary

These various checks have accomplished several things. For one, there is no indication in any of them that the loss of Exiters over the years distorts comparisons between retainees and those never retained (Table 6.A2). The comparisons are virtually identical whether Exiters are included or excluded. Sample attrition, because it is substantial and highly selective for social factors (e.g., race/ethnicity), probably poses the single greatest procedural threat to a reliable picture of retention's role. That its consequences turn out to be so minor is reassuring.

Other checks sometimes produced large changes. For retainees with uncomplicated promotion histories after being held back, retained–never-retained CAT gaps are much smaller than when all repeaters are used in the comparisons, and cumulative gains over the higher grade levels usually favor repeaters over promoted youngsters. Problems peculiar to special education children and double-retainees thus account for much of the after retention CAT difference between retained and never-retained children, an important clarification.

On the other hand, the pace of progress before and after retention for repeaters with smooth postretention promotion records is not very different from the pace when all retainees are involved. Hence, the favorable indications under this perspective from the main body of this chapter seem to apply pretty much across the board, to all classes of repeaters.

All these comparisons show that retention fails to raise repeaters to the never-retained standard. However, much of the shortfall in retainees' performance relative to that of never-retained children *predates* retention. For gains from the retained year forward, the comparisons sometimes look different. First grade retainees still lag in gains, but second and third grade repeaters' gains mostly are on par with, or above, the gains registered by never-retained children.

In addition, over the postretention period in most instances retainees are *more successful* in maintaining their pace of upward movement than are never-retained youngsters over the same years. Repeaters still usually gained less, but everyone's gains trail off over time, and those of retainees generally do not taper off as much, relative to their earlier pace, as do never-retained children's. Indeed, in some instances they do not trail off at all. Retention thus seems to help repeaters keep pace over the years when others drop back.

This is a detailed, complicated picture already, yet there still are issues to be addressed. The most critical need is to take account of other influences on test performance that might be confounded with retention/nonretention. If, for example, being in a low-income home hinders school performance, we would expect it to do so all along the way. Such other considerations could enlarge or shrink the performance gap, so unless they are allowed for, the details just reviewed could be misleading. More repeaters are from low-income families, more of them are boys, more are African-American, and so on; these factors affect the course of later schooling, quite apart from retention (for an overview of these matters in the BSS, see Entwisle et al. 1997). Performance differences that follow from these other considerations need to be distinguished from effects of retention. This is accomplished in the next chapter, using statistical means to adjust for complicating factors.

Appendix

The following tables provide details alluded to in the main body of this chapter. Table 6.A1 reports CAT-R and CAT-M averages for the several repeater and comparison groups for the fall of first grade and the spring of grades 1 through 7. Table 6.A2 reports the CAT-R and CAT-M averages that were computed to check on attrition bias and the consequences of other procedural decisions (see the section "The retention picture more fully considered").

TABLE 6.A1. *CAT-R and CAT-M Averages for Retained Groups, Never-Retained Pupils, and the Poor-Performing Comparison Group*[a]

	Fall of 1st Grade[b]	End of 1st Grade[c]	End of 2d Grade[c]	End of 3d Grade[c]	End of 4th Grade	End of 5th Grade	End of 6th Grade	End of 7th Grade
CAT-R: reading comprehension average								
Year of retention								
1st grade	257.0	287.1/341.1	358.7	384.7	409.3	440.9	439.7	481.7
	(106)	(118)/(76)	(93)	(97)	(98)	(86)	(77)	(58)
2d grade	269.6	311.5	333.6/374.8	399.9	431.8	454.9	471.3	498.6
	(61)	(65)	(60)/(56)	(50)	(57)	(52)	(48)	(40)
3d grade	272.7	325.6	356.9	369.0/412.1	441.8	478.3	486.1	510.6
	(38)	(43)	(44)	(37)/(35)	(39)	(36)	(34)	(31)
4th–7th grade	277.9	346.0	388.6	448.4	459.6	492.8	502.8	529.3
	(65)	(72)	(72)	(63)	(65)	(72)	(61)	(53)
Never-retained pupils								
All never-retained	290.8	359.8	412.2	449.4	496.0	522.6	542.7	563.8
	(396)	(428)	(389)	(304)	(290)	(291)	(249)	(224)
Poor-performing comparison group	270.6	326.4	388.8	420.2	461.4	481.6	512.6	532.0
	(92)	(106)	(91)	(72)	(70)	(71)	(58)	(52)

CAT-M: Math concepts average

Year of retention								
1st grade	264.1	299.0/339.3	358.9	385.5	412.2	431.3	444.7	465.8
	(107)	(113)/(74)	(97)	(97)	(96)	(86)	(75)	(56)
2d grade	278.4	320.8	350.6/381.6	402.3	432.1	461.6	470.7	485.6
	(62)	(63)	(56)/(56)	(50)	(56)	(51)	(46)	(40)
3d grade	280.6	332.1	368.4	382.4/425.3	445.1	486.3	491.9	508.5
	(38)	(44)	(45)	(36)/(35)	(39)	(36)	(34)	(31)
4th–7th grade	290.1	341.2	385.3	412.4	451.1	484.8	496.6	519.9
	(69)	(71)	(72)	(64)	(64)	(72)	(58)	(49)
Never-retained pupils								
All never-retained	304.6	356.1	394.4	440.2	478.5	511.7	533.3	558.5
	(406)	(425)	(385)	(304)	(289)	(290)	(248)	(223)
Poor-performing comparison group	281.8	327.3	381.3	411.2	454.3	482.2	505.0	531.9
	(93)	(106)	(88)	(72)	(70)	(71)	(58)	(52)

[a] Numbers in parentheses indicate sample size.

[b] All entries except the first are from the spring of the year. The first entry is from the fall of everyone's first grade, in 1982.

[c] For first, second, and third grade retainees, two end-of-grade averages are reported in the year of retention. The first is from the first time through the grade; the second is from the repeated year.

TABLE 6.A2. *Same-Grade CAT Averages, Excluding Exiters, Special Education Students, with Fourth through Seventh Grade Retainees Classified as Never-Retained, Excluding Double Retainees, and with the 2-Year Same-Grade Offset Implemented for Double Retainees*

	CAT-R					CAT-M				
	Fall of 1st Grade	End of 1st Grade	End of 2d Grade	End of 3d Grade	End of 7th Grade	Fall of 1st Grade	End of 1st Grade	End of 2d Grade	End of 3d Grade	End of 7th Grade
1st grade retainees										
1. Full sample	257.0	341.1	358.7	384.7	481.7	264.1	339.3	358.9	385.5	465.8
	(106)	(76)	(93)	(97)	(58)	(107)	(74)	(97)	(97)	(56)
2. Excluding Exiters	256.5	339.9	358.0	382.6	481.7	265.0	338.8	355.5	383.6	465.8
	(81)	(62)	(74)	(78)	(58)	(80)	(60)	(75)	(78)	(56)
3. Excluding special education pupils	259.4	355.9	369.2	410.8	498.7	266.5	350.5	369.4	406.8	480.6
	(61)	(45)	(55)	(54)	(39)	(61)	(44)	(55)	(53)	(37)
4. Excluding twice-retained pupils	260.7	348.7	368.1	396.2	496.7	265.8	345.8	365.0	396.1	474.5
	(67)	(45)	(55)	(56)	(31)	(69)	(44)	(54)	(56)	(30)
5. With 2-year offset for twice-retained pupils	257.0	341.1	361.1	391.6	496.7	264.1	339.0	361.2	394.2	474.5
	(106)	(76)	(94)	(96)	(31)	(107)	(74)	(95)	(94)	(30)
6. 2, 3, and 4 together	265.8	363.6	374.0	416.0	504.6	273.0	358.6	370.3	416.7	489.8
	(27)	(22)	(25)	(25)	(25)	(27)	(22)	(25)	(24)	(23)
2d grade retainees										
1. Full sample	269.6	311.5	374.8	399.9	498.6	278.4	320.8	381.6	402.3	485.6
	(61)	(65)	(56)	(50)	(40)	(62)	(63)	(56)	(50)	(40)
2. Excluding Exiters	269.2	312.5	378.1	399.8	498.6	277.6	316.9	380.6	401.7	485.6
	(47)	(50)	(48)	(44)	(40)	(48)	(48)	(48)	(44)	(40)
3. Excluding special education pupils	272.4	308.9	379.3	407.2	505.6	275.6	319.8	387.2	410.3	488.9
	(41)	(45)	(38)	(35)	(29)	(42)	(43)	(38)	(35)	(30)
4. Excluding twice-retained pupils	271.4	315.0	382.2	410.2	508.3	274.9	326.6	382.3	409.1	484.3
	(44)	(48)	(40)	(37)	(30)	(45)	(46)	(40)	(37)	(31)

	C1	C2	C3	C4	C5	C6	C7	C8	C9	C10
5. With 2-year offset for twice-retained pupils	269.6 (61)	311.5 (65)	374.6 (56)	402.5 (52)	508.3 (30)	278.4 (62)	320.8 (63)	380.1 (56)	406.6 (52)	484.3 (31)
6. 2, 3, and 4 together	272.7 (26)	312.4 (29)	388.0 (27)	416.4 (27)	509.5 (24)	273.7 (27)	320.3 (27)	387.3 (27)	415.7 (27)	485.4 (25)
3d grade retainees										
1. Full sample	272.7 (38)	325.6 (43)	356.9 (44)	412.1 (35)	510.6 (31)	280.6 (38)	332.1 (44)	368.4 (45)	425.4 (45)	508.5 (31)
2. Excluding Exiters	269.5 (29)	326.5 (33)	355.8 (35)	417.7 (29)	510.6 (31)	278.5 (29)	330.5 (34)	361.3 (35)	429.3 (29)	508.5 (31)
3. Excluding special education pupils	272.3 (32)	330.8 (37)	357.1 (39)	416.8 (29)	520.8 (26)	280.4 (33)	333.0 (38)	369.2 (40)	431.9 (29)	514.9 (26)
4. Excluding twice-retained pupils	275.5 (28)	326.6 (34)	357.9 (34)	413.2 (29)	514.3 (24)	280.2 (29)	332.4 (34)	366.8 (35)	426.0 (29)	511.3 (24)
5. With 2-year offset for twice-retained pupils	272.7 (38)	325.6 (43)	356.9 (44)	412.1 (35)	514.3 (24)	280.6 (38)	332.1 (44)	368.4 (45)	425.3 (35)	511.3 (24)
6. 2, 3, and 4 together	268.4 (16)	338.0 (21)	358.1 (22)	428.9 (19)	525.2 (20)	277.5 (18)	330.2 (21)	359.1 (22)	436.4 (19)	517.4 (20)
Never-retained										
1. Full sample	290.8 (396)	359.8 (428)	412.2 (389)	449.4 (304)	563.8 (224)	304.6 (406)	356.1 (425)	394.4 (385)	440.2 (304)	558.5 (223)
2. Excluding Exiters	291.5 (200)	358.9 (214)	411.9 (215)	445.0 (204)	561.8 (214)	304.0 (207)	354.0 (214)	397.6 (215)	437.6 (204)	557.1 (213)
3. Excluding special education pupils	291.0 (392)	360.5 (423)	412.9 (385)	450.3 (301)	564.5 (222)	305.1 (403)	356.7 (420)	400.8 (381)	441.3 (301)	559.7 (221)
4. With 4-7 retained as never-retained	288.9 (461)	357.8 (500)	408.5 (461)	443.9 (368)	557.2 (277)	302.5 (477)	354.0 (496)	397.2 (457)	435.4 (368)	551.5 (272)
5. 2, 3, and 4 together	292.4 (198)	359.7 (211)	411.9 (213)	445.7 (202)	562.5 (212)	304.6 (204)	354.6 (211)	398.0 (213)	438.5 (202)	558.3 (211)

(continued)

115

TABLE 6.A2. *(continued)*

	CAT-R					CAT-M				
	Fall of 1st Grade	End of 1st Grade	End of 2d Grade	End of 3d Grade	End of 7th Grade	Fall of 1st Grade	End of 1st Grade	End of 2d Grade	End of 3d Grade	End of 7th Grade
Poor-performing comparison group										
1. Full sample	270.6	326.4	388.8	420.2	532.0	281.8	327.3	381.3	411.2	531.9
	(92)	(106)	(91)	(72)	(52)	(93)	(106)	(88)	(72)	(52)
2. Excluding Exiters	278.0	325.4	389.3	420.8	531.2	284.8	328.0	382.9	412.5	532.3
	(48)	(54)	(52)	(49)	(51)	(49)	(54)	(52)	(49)	(51)
3. Excluding special education pupils	270.1	326.5	390.3	421.5	532.0	281.7	327.6	382.1	412.7	531.9
	(91)	(105)	(90)	(71)	(52)	(92)	(105)	(87)	(71)	(52)
4. With 4–7 retained as never-retained	269.9	326.5	388.3	419.6	529.0	281.1	326.5	379.7	411.1	524.9
	(113)	(131)	(116)	(96)	(75)	(115)	(131)	(113)	(96)	(75)
5. 2, 3, and 4 together	278.0	325.4	389.3	420.8	531.2	284.8	328.0	382.9	412.5	532.3
	(48)	(54)	(52)	(49)	(51)	(49)	(54)	(52)	(49)	(51)

Note: Numbers in parentheses are sample sizes.

7

Adjusted Achievement Comparisons

*The Need for Controlled Comparisons and
the Multiple-Regression Approach*

The descriptive detail of the last chapter laid out how repeaters' test scores and test score gains compare with promoted children's, as viewed from several vantage points. Such comparisons, however, are a step removed from telling us whether grade retention abets or inhibits children's academic progress because repeaters and promoted children differ in a host of other ways besides their retention status – for example, low family income and weak preretention academic skills. In an evaluation, these factors constitute possible confounds – they, rather than the retention experience, may lead to observed outcome differences. Until they have been addressed we cannot draw firm conclusions about retention's impact.

The strategy of matched controls can be used to isolate effects of retention from other considerations; however, as discussed in Chapter 2, not all alternative explanations can be disposed of under this approach. Our repeater and comparison groups are (roughly) comparable in terms of early testing levels, but retainees and promoted children differ in many other ways not equated by the California Achievement Test (CAT) match. An alternative to creating matched groups is to adjust statistically for characteristics deemed relevant. The statistical approach has the advantage of being able to adjust for more factors than is practical by matching and poses less of a threat to accurate significance levels.

Retainees are disproportionately members of low-income families; they have poorly educated parents; they are often of minority status; and they enter school with weak readiness skills, reflected in low beginning test scores and marks. Children who bear such burdens typically have a difficult time at school whether retained or not. For this reason, some of retainees' later academic problems likely have nothing to do with retention but are the result of risks that are the backdrop to retention.

The demographic factors examined previously are used now to adjust for group differences, along with the child's age in September of first grade. They include race/ethnicity (i.e., African-American versus White), gender, mother's educational level, family income level (as reflected in eligibility for reduced price meals at school), number of siblings, and membership (or nonmembership) in a two-parent household at the start of first grade.[1]

Differences involving academic skills or competence that predate retention also are adjusted for. To-be-retained and never-to-be-retained children's initial CAT averages from the fall of first grade are far apart. The former start out behind, and over time, we have seen, they fall further back until the retention decision is made. This pattern is why many of the descriptive comparisons in Chapter 6 used CAT averages from the fall of the failed year as baseline – differences at that point capture the buildup of academic difficulties that prompt retention. Now we want to adjust for those differences to see whether retainees' standing afterward is better or worse than their standing before, taking into account the fact that retainees began at a lower level.

The statistical method used to implement these adjustments is multiple regression. It adjusts the average difference in CAT gains between retained and promoted youngsters for nonequivalence on other predictors, which in the present application include earlier test scores, along with demographic and family characteristics. We say *gains* because the adjustments include prior levels of the outcome. With Time 1 scores statistically equated, effects of retention (and of the other measures, for that matter) can be thought of as inducing achievement gains or, equivalently, explaining change relative to the baseline assessment.

Retention status is indicated by year of retention – first grade, second, third, and fourth through seventh grades combined. Repeaters' CAT performance is compared against that of all never-retained children and, separately, the never-retained subset who comprise the poor-performing comparison group. *Effects of retention* has a very well-defined meaning under this statistical approach. Grade retention is credited, for good or for bad, with whatever CAT differences continue to be associated with

---

[1] Father's educational level was considered for inclusion as well, but in preliminary analyses this measure made no difference when the others were included. With sample coverage for father's education low ($N = 489$), we decided not to use it.

it after "netting out" or "subtracting off" effects of other differences that distinguish repeaters from the never retained.

The outcome measures in this chapter are spring CAT scores, mainly from the postretention period. These are examined from same-age (Tables 7.1, 7.3, and 7.5) and same-grade (Tables 7.2, 7.4, and 7.6) perspectives. The distinction, at this point a familiar one, hinges on whether performance is aligned chronologically or at grade-level benchmarks. Paired tables summarize the results for each of the three main retainee groups, children held back in first grade (Tables 7.1 and 7.2), second grade (Tables 7.3 and 7.4), and third grade (Tables 7.5 and 7.6).

In each instance, we begin with test score differences as of the fall of retainees' failed year/grade, before their retention. This differential is both a benchmark for comparing shortfalls after retention as well as the preretention differential adjusted for when examining postretention patterns of CAT performance. The remaining columns in these tables present results for spring CAT scores, year by year or grade by grade, for as long as performance is tracked: for same-age comparisons, through the end of Year 8; for the same-grade comparisons, through the end of seventh grade.

For each outcome (grade or year) several regressions phase in the various adjustments being made, allowing us to pinpoint those that are most consequential. In the first panel the only predictor is the child's retention status (whether or not he or she is a repeater), so the CAT differences estimated here are not adjusted for other factors. These initial estimates describe retainees' standing relative to that of never-retained children on the test at issue. In the second panel, CAT performance from the fall of the failed year/grade and the entire set of personal and social demographic controls are added to the analysis. These estimates thus are adjusted for both prior performance *and* demographic factors. Comparing these second estimates to the first entries in a column shows the effects of the statistical adjustments. The last panel introduces additional adjustments for differences in CAT performance associated specifically with special education assignment and double retention. Double retention, special education assignment, and both together in this way are separated from single retentions with no special education.[2] Table entries for this last stage of the analysis estimate the CAT shortfall of

---

[2] Of the 317 retainees covered in these analyses, 184 were neither held back a second time nor assigned to special education; 48 were assigned to special education but not held back a second time; 43 were held back a second time but not put into special education; and 42 were both held back a second time *and* put into special education.

"regular" retainees – those not held back a second time or put into special education classes – compared with that of promoted youngsters.[3]

First Grade Retainees: CAT Shortfall at the Start

Tables 7.1 and 7.2 compare first grade retainees' CAT performance against that of never-retained children. The first column reports scores from the fall of their failed year, which for these retainees is first grade (1982). Subsequent columns report adjusted spring test score differences, beginning in the spring of the failed year (i.e., the first time through the failed grade). These extend in Table 7.1 through the end of Year 8, and in Table 7.2 through the end of seventh grade. The comparisons thus go 6 years beyond first grade retainees' 2-year fail–repeat cycle.

The first entry in Table 7.1 (−33.5) indicates that children to be held back in first grade begin the year with CAT Reading Comprehension (CAT-R) scores some 34 points below the scores of their classmates who later will progress uneventfully through the elementary and middle school years (uneventfully in terms of retention, that is).[4] This is a large, statistically significant difference. Statistical estimates with double asterisks indicate that a difference as large as or larger than the observed one would come about by chance only 1 in 100 times (1%) if the averages

---

[3] We report metric regression coefficients, computed on the basis of pairwise present variance–covariance matrices. The *pairwise present* stipulation is that case inclusion is covariance-specific (i.e., cases are retained in the computation even if they lack the data needed to calculate other covariances). The alternative approach, *listwise present*, screens out cases lacking information on any variable and loses too many cases to be employed. We have compared the two approaches, however, and they yield very similar estimates.

[4] As indicated in the table note, this figure is from an equation in which differences between the other retainee groups and those never retained are also estimated. These figures are −21.5 for second grade repeaters, −18.0 for third grade repeaters, and −13.0 for fourth through seventh grade repeaters. To keep the presentation manageable, these other comparisons are not reported in our tables, but they were included in all analyses. Because of this, the unadjusted differences reported in these tables will differ some from the corresponding unadjusted differences presented in the previous chapter. This happens because somewhat different sets of youngsters are covered in the two approaches. The present computations use test scores of first grade repeaters and never-retained children having fall testing data, which will be the same as reported previously. However, these statistical adjustments also use data for second through seventh grade retainees, which can alter the picture slightly. For example, the corresponding differences computed by simple subtraction from Table 6.A1 are quite close but not identical to those just reported: −33.8 for first grade repeaters (i.e., 290.8 to 257.0), −21.2 for second grade repeaters, −18.1 for third grade repeaters, and −12.9 for fourth through seventh grade repeaters.

were identical in a normal population from which the sample is drawn and the sample is random.[5]

When they are compared with the low-performing comparison group, the fall of first grade difference is much smaller, −13.6 points. In other words, compared with other children with low test scores, retainees show an additional deficit before retention of some 14 CAT points. This difference, too, is significant; it indicates that the comparison group was not comparable initially, something we already knew.

The situation is much the same on the CAT Math Concepts and Applications (CAT-M), reported in the bottom section of the table. The initial retained–never-retained differential is 40 CAT-M points for all promoted youngsters and 17.7 for just the poor performers. Both differences are significant.

Children who will be held back in first grade thus already are behind at the start of the year, before retention. Their shortfall is relatively large and needs to be adjusted for in the remaining analyses.

First Grade Retainees: Same-Age and Same-Grade Comparisons for the Failed Year

From fall to spring of their first time through first grade, retainees' performance relative to promoted children's falls off badly (second column in Table 7.1). When they are compared to all promoted children, the unadjusted differences are about 72 points on the CAT-R and 56 points on the CAT-M. The differences are also large in a comparison with the poor-performer group. The failed year "skid" seen in Chapter 6 thus presents itself again in these regression estimates.

When social demographic factors and CAT scores from the fall of the year are taken into account (second set of results), the retained–never-retained spring difference drops appreciably, especially on the CAT-M. The original difference of 56 points shrinks to 35 points in the comparison with all retainees; against the poor performers, the reduction is from 28 points to 22. In these analyses, then, much of future repeaters' downward trajectory between fall and spring can be attributed to their high-risk profile. The remaining differences, however, show them also to be slipping badly for reasons not covered in the predictor set. The

---

[5] The single asterisk in the tables uses a somewhat less stringent criterion of significance: 1 in 20 times (5%).

TABLE 7.1. *Same-Age Regression-Adjusted CAT Differences: First Grade Retainees vs. Never-Retained Students or the Poor-Performing Comparison Group*

	Fall of Year 1	Spring of Failed Year	Spring of Repeated Year	1 Year Postret (Year 3)	2 Years Postret (Year 4)	3 Years Postret (Year 5)	4 Years Postret (Year 6)	5 Years Postret (Year 7)	6 Years Postret (Year 8)
CAT-R									
With no adjustments[a]									
Ret vs. never-ret	−33.5**	−72.4**	−64.2**	−88.4**	−111.1**	−110.3**	−97.1**	−118.2**	−103.7**
Ret vs. poor-perf comparison group	−13.6**	−39.5**	−47.3**	−58.2**	−73.5**	−68.5**	−63.7**	−81.2**	−69.8**
With fall CAT and demographic adjustments[b]									
Ret vs. never-ret	—	−59.5**	−52.9**	−69.2**	−85.6**	−83.2**	−70.2**	−88.8**	−71.7**
Ret vs. poor-perf comparison group	—	−37.9**	−43.2**	−53.0**	−64.6**	−59.1**	−53.4**	−71.5**	−59.2**
With double-ret and special ed adjustments[c]									
Ret vs. never-ret	—	−49.7**	−42.8**	−53.4**	−57.7**	−50.8**	−34.0**	−55.6**	−46.6**
Ret vs. poor-perf comparison group	—	−27.7	−31.8**	−37.8**	−38.1**	−28.2**	−16.6	−40.0**	−37.4**
Adj R^2									
Ret vs. never-ret[d]	0.09	0.46	0.49	0.52	0.56	0.52	0.46	0.54	0.45
Ret vs. poor-perf comparison group	0.04	0.33	0.38	0.36	0.43	0.43	0.40	0.42	0.30

CAT-M

With no adjustments[a]									
Ret vs. never-ret	−40.0**	−56.4**	−53.6**	−79.9**	−93.1**	−96.6**	−99.1**	−108.6**	−108.3**
Ret vs. poor-perf comparison group	−17.7**	−28.2**	−40.8**	−50.2**	−66.0**	−65.3**	−67.5**	−77.0**	−80.7**
With fall CAT and demographic adjustments[b]									
Ret vs. never-ret	—	−34.6**	−29.6**	−52.7**	−64.0**	−67.4**	−62.9**	−67.6**	−75.1**
Ret vs. poor-perf comparison group	—	−21.5**	−31.5**	−42.8**	−55.2**	−56.7**	−56.9**	−65.1**	−73.6**
With double-ret and special ed adjustments[c]									
Ret vs. never-ret	—	−28.1**	−23.9**	−39.9**	−38.7**	−43.3**	−28.6**	−40.4**	−58.3**
Ret vs. poor-perf comparison group	—	−15.5**	−25.5**	−30.8**	−32.2**	−34.9**	−26.1**	−41.0**	−57.9**
Adj R^2									
Ret vs. never-ret[d]	0.24	0.51	0.55	0.58	0.63	0.54	0.55	0.57	0.53
Ret vs. poor-perf comparison group	0.14	0.37	0.51	0.43	0.55	0.45	0.47	0.44	0.35

[a] These regressions adjust for differences among the several retainee groups and between retainees and those never retained.

[b] Performed after the fall of Year 1, these regressions adjust additionally for CAT scores from the fall of Year 1 and for demographic factors: race/ethnicity, gender, mother's education, lunch subsidy status (eligible or not), number of siblings, age as of the fall of first grade, and living in a two-parent household at the start of first grade.

[c] These regressions adjust additionally for differences associated with special education alone, double retention alone, or both. These analyses are not performed in the fall of Year 1.

[d] R^2 statistics are from the most inclusive equation in each column.

** Signifies differences significant at the 0.01 level.

TABLE 7.2. *Same-Grade Regression-Adjusted CAT Differences: First Grade Retainees vs. Never-Retained Students or the Poor-Performing Comparison Group*

	Fall of 1st Grade	End of 1st Grade	End of 2d Grade	End of 3d Grade	End of 4th Grade	End of 5th Grade	End of 6th Grade	End of 7th Grade
CAT-R								
With no adjustments[a]								
Ret vs. never-ret	−33.5**	−72.4**/−17.6**	−50.9**	−64.6**	−85.2**	−78.3**	−98.9**	−76.0**
Ret vs. poor-perf comparison group	−13.6**	−39.5**/14.4**	−29.8**	−34.7**	−49.2**	−40.3**	−67.9**	−47.4**
With fall CAT and demographic adjustments[b]								
Ret vs. never-ret	—	−59.5**/−2.9	−38.4**	−42.4**	−60.8**	−51.0**	−73.1**	−46.9**
Ret vs. poor-perf comparison group	—	−37.9**/17.8**	−24.7**	−25.5**	−41.4**	−31.5**	−58.5**	−38.0**
With double-ret and special ed adjustments[c]								
Ret vs. never-ret	—	−49.7**/8.9	−25.9**	−17.0*	−28.6**	−14.7	−41.3**	−27.1**
Ret vs. poor-perf comparison group	—	−27.7**/29.7**	−11.8	−0.6	−11.1	−5.4	−27.1**	−16.4
Adj R^2								
Ret vs. never-ret[d]	0.10	0.46/0.30	0.34	0.40	0.46	0.40	0.45	0.36
Ret vs. poor-perf comparison group	0.04	0.33/0.21	0.17	0.26	0.35	0.35	0.39	0.23

CAT-M

With no adjustments[a]								
Ret vs. never-ret	−40.0**	−56.4**/−15.6**	−38.6**	−54.8**	−65.2**	−77.6**	−85.1**	−85.7**
Ret vs. poor-perf comparison group	−17.7**	−28.2**/12.0**	−21.9**	−25.4**	−39.9**	−49.5**	−56.8**	−62.1**
With fall CAT and demographic adjustments[b]								
Ret vs. never-ret	—	−34.6**/7.3*	−14.9**	−26.7**	−38.6**	−47.9**	−48.6**	−50.1**
Ret vs. poor-perf comparison group	—	−21.5**/19.9**	−13.7**	−15.7**	−31.6**	−39.1**	−46.3**	−56.6**
With double-ret and special ed adjustments[c]								
Ret vs. never-ret	—	−28.1**/17.0**	−6.2	−4.7	−14.1*	−16.3*	−20.4**	−34.0**
Ret vs. poor-perf comparison group	—	−15.5**/28.7**	−5.0	5.3	−8.8	−10.0	−22.0**	−40.5**
Adj R^2								
Ret vs. never-ret[d]	0.24	0.51/0.38	0.42	0.48	0.48	0.45	0.51	0.43
Ret vs. poor-perf comparison group	0.14	0.37/0.26	0.29	0.38	0.36	0.41	0.39	0.27

[a] These regressions adjust for differences among the several retainee groups and between retainees and those never retained.

[b] Performed after the fall of first grade, these regressions adjust additionally for CAT scores from the fall of first grade and for demographic factors: race/ethnicity, gender, mother's education, lunch subsidy status (eligible or not), number of siblings, age as of the fall of first grade, and living in a two-parent household at the start of first grade.

[c] These regressions adjust additionally for differences associated with special education alone, double retention alone, or both. These analyses are not performed in the fall of first grade.

[d] R^2 statistics are from the most inclusive equation in each column.

** Signifies differences significant at the 0.01 level; * differences significant at the 0.05 level.

adjustments are not nearly so impressive for the CAT-R, but a noteworthy drop still appears in the comparison with all promoted youngsters.

CAT-R changes are more impressive when adjustments are made for
special education and double retention in the third set of estimates. Then
retainees' shortfall drops from 60 points to 50 when they are compared
with all promoted youngsters, and from 38 points to 28 when they are
compared with the poor-performing promoted group. The remaining
differences are a little over two-thirds the size of the original disparities,
before any adjustments are made. Reductions in the quantitative area are
comparable. Hence, a portion of first grade repeaters' shortfall at year's
end reflects the especially severe problems of children later assigned to
special education and/or held back twice. Special education youngsters,
for example, average 21 points below the others on the CAT-R (not
shown in table).

Whether the problems peculiar to double retention and special education should be separated out in this way is arguable, but first grade
retainees' performance relative to that of others falls off sharply during
the year even apart from these further complications. This decline adds
to large initial differences, so at year's end the CAT averages of held back
children are far below those of their promoted classmates. Some of this
shortfall (about a third) is traceable to difficulties already apparent in
repeaters' test scores from the fall of first grade, to demographic risk factors,[6] and to the severe problems of children who will later experience
multiple retentions and/or be placed in special education, but about
two-thirds is not. Our statistics indicate these children are not keeping
up, and their teachers no doubt see this also. Their performance slips
from bad to worse, and that decline must affect the decision to hold them
back. The consequences of that decision are addressed next, with short-
term consequences, evaluated at the end of the repeated year, taken up
first.

First Grade Retainees: The Repeated Year

The picture for first grade repeaters after the second time through the
grade is mixed (column 3, Table 7.1). Compared with all promoted children, they make up a little ground, but just a little. Before adjustments,
retainees are 64 points lower on the CAT-R and 54 points lower on the

---

[6] Analyses not shown indicate that early testing levels are the major factor here. Socioeconomic differences play only a minor role with preretention test scores in the equation.

CAT-M. These are large differences, but smaller than those registered a year earlier, when it was decided to hold these children back. At that time, they fell 72 points short on the CAT-R and 56 points short on the CAT-M.

The statistical adjustments reduce these differences further, by about a third in the verbal area and by more than half in the quantitative. More relevant, though, are comparisons *across the corresponding adjusted estimates* at different benchmarks. Retainees' CAT shortfall at the end of the repeated year is less than it had been a year earlier, when they were held back, but not dramatically so. The gap relative to all promoted children has narrowed from 50 points on the CAT-R to 43 points, and from 28 points on the CAT-M to 24. A little progress is indicated in these instances, but against the poor-performing group there is none. Instead, after 2 years in grade repeaters are relatively further behind than at the end of their failed year.

At issue to this point are same-age comparisons. These compare repeaters' achievement levels on finishing first grade with those of never-retained children on finishing second grade, and the results are contradictory.[7] When a same-grade format is used, the pattern is more consistent and rather different. These comparisons are reported in Table 7.2, which parallels Table 7.1, except CAT scores are compared at grade level benchmarks. Retainees' spring scores from the second year, when they are finishing first grade, are compared with promoted children's scores from the previous year, when they too are finishing first grade. On repeating a grade, retainees are folded in with a new set of classmates, children with whom they probably will be compared for the rest of their school career. The same-grade framework approximates how retainees are faring in this new classroom context.

When end-of-first-grade scores are compared, the retainee–promoted gap is much smaller. On the CAT-R they pull up from 72 points behind to just 18 points behind; on the CAT-M they move up from

---

[7] These contradictions come about because the poor-performing comparison group makes above-average gains in the second year, exceeding even those registered by the full never-retained sample. It may be that some of these children's poor first-year scores were unusually low and hence give a false reading of their levels of competence. This phenomenon, known as *regression toward the mean*, is common when focusing on changes at the high and low extremes. If this is behind retainees' unfavorable comparison with the poor performers, then not much should be made of it. The regression phenomenon occurs for statistical and other reasons that have no bearing on the efficacy of retention. Larabee (1984) explores this regression phenomenon in some detail in his study of promotion practices.

56 points back to 16 points back (compare entries on each side of the vertical divide at the top of the table). These *unadjusted* same-grade comparisons look good, and when the comparisons are adjusted for risk factors that affect test performance apart from retention, they become more favorable still. Indeed, when all adjustments are made, retainees score about 17 points *above* promoted children on the CAT-M. This advantage is a first for retainees. Retainees' scores also surpass the poor-performing comparison group's in every instance, reaching almost 30 points on both CAT subtests when all statistical adjustments are made.

The same-grade regression pattern thus evidences the same dip–recovery retention cycle described in Chapter 6. When first grade repeaters move to second grade, they are performing at a level much closer to that of their classmates than they had before, and after adjustments are made for other factors that damp scores, retainees are performing at a level ahead of their classmates'. In other words, when we allow for the level where children started, and for disadvantages such as low family income, being held back seems to confer a benefit.[8]

First Grade Retainees after Retention

First grade repeaters take 2 years to finish first grade, so it is not until the spring of Year 3 that we see how repeaters fare after getting a bit of distance from the experience. Table 7.1 summarizes their progress relative to that of never-retained children year by year for 6 years after first grade. Table 7.2 uses the same-grade format, so its comparisons extend through seventh grade. The two perspectives are entirely consonant: first grade repeaters begin slipping as soon as they get beyond their repeated year/grade, and after just a few years they are far behind again.

The Year 8 comparisons in Table 7.1 show retainees averaging more than 100 points below all never-retained children on the CAT-R and almost 70 points below the poor-performing comparison group. These enormous differences amount to 1.3 standard deviations and 1.1

---

[8] However, the comparison also "builds in" an advantage for repeaters, at least against comparison group youngsters, whose end of first grade scores have no opportunity to improve from their level as of spring of first grade – it is the same "matching artifact" discussed in Chapter 2, when we reviewed the Peterson and colleagues (1987) data. As an indication of retention's effectiveness, this poses problems; as a descriptive statement, the comparison is unproblematic. Repeaters' scores in fact are much closer to their new classmates'; more than that, when statistical adjustments are made, they are ahead.

standard deviations, respectively. Retainees' relative standing falls off sharply even when adjustments are made for demographic factors and beginning test scores. On the CAT-R they fall from 53 points behind in the spring of their repeated year to 69 points behind a year later. On the CAT-M the drop is from 30 points to 53 points. These comparisons evaluate repeaters against all promoted children, but the picture is much the same when viewed against poor performers' scores.

In practically every instance the gap in CAT averages is bigger at the end of Years 4 through 8 (or equivalently, Years 2 through 6 post-retention) than at the end of retainees' repeated year. The deficits all are large, and they remain large in the last panel too, after adjusting for the especially poor performance of special education children and double repeaters.

First grade repeaters thus generally are worse off after retention than in the spring of their failed year. This holds under the same-grade perspective (Table 7.2), also. In these comparisons, retainees at the time of the comparison have had one more year of schooling than promoted children, but even this edge does not prevent them from regressing badly once back on the regular promotion schedule. Indeed, in only a year the advances registered while repeating first grade evaporate. At the end of second grade, first grade retainees remain a bit ahead of where they had been at the end of their failed grade (see the figures to the left of the slashes in column 2), but not by much, and even these modest gains do not hold up long.

By fourth grade the (unadjusted) gaps separating retainees' performance from promoted children's are again large, and they remain large even after demographic and first grade CAT adjustments. On the CAT-M, the disparities increase grade by grade, peaking in seventh grade at 50 points against all never-retained youngsters and 57 points against the poor performers. Though somewhat more favorable, in the CAT-R results too retainees lag far behind in seventh grade, by 38 points and 47 points, depending on the frame of reference.

Only in the last set of estimates – those that isolate one-time repeaters – are there indications of lasting benefit. Most same-grade differences in the elementary years (through fifth grade) are much smaller than in the spring of the failed year, and most of these are not significant. By sixth and seventh grade, though, even one-time repeaters are behind on the CAT-M, and they also have slipped some on the CAT-R (although not to where they had been in first grade).

Summary: First Grade Retainees

Throughout the 6-year postretention period, first grade retainees' scores fall well below expectation when evaluated against the performance of children with similar sociodemographic characteristics and with similar test scores before retention. Not only do they trail badly, but they trail by a larger margin after being held back than before. Their improved academic performance during the repeated year is not sustained, so over the long term, first grade repeaters appear not to be helped by retention.

Second and Third Grade Repeaters

Analyses similar to those just reviewed for first grade repeaters are reported for second grade retainees (Tables 7.3 and 7.4) and third grade retainees (Tables 7.5 and 7.6). To distinguish effects of retention from the consequences of children's prior academic experience, our approach again looks forward from the fall of the failed grade.[9]

The first columns in these tables indicate that retainees trail far behind at the start of their failed year. We saw in Chapter 6 that children held back in second and third grades also lag behind in the fall of first grade, but not by as much as first grade repeaters. What emerges clearly now is that they also fall further back over the ensuing years. They may have started out a bit ahead of first grade repeaters, but by the time they are retained, their relative standing is no better than, and possibly worse than, that of first grade retainees when they were held back. None of this reflects consequences of retention, though. Adjusting for testing patterns only at the time of school entry, as we did for first grade repeaters, would miss this downward trend after starting school. The shortfall over first grade for second grade retainees, and over first and second grades for third grade retainees, would show up as consequences of retention.

---

[9] In these tables, unlike those already reviewed for first grade repeaters, entries in the corresponding same-grade and same-age comparisons differ even in the first couple of columns because for second and third grade retainees, a same-grade "offset" is required in all comparisons. By the fall of second grade, first grade repeaters have already been held back, so their fall scores for the first analysis are from the third year (when they are going into second grade). In Table 7.1, the baseline score is from the fall of first grade, before any retentions. Hence there is no difference between averages from the "fall of first grade" and averages from the "fall of Year 1." The differences in the first couple of columns comparing results in Tables 7.3 and 7.4, and in Tables 7.5 and 7.6, are slight, but that they are different at all reflects the same-grade offset for children held back before the grade at issue.

Entries in the second column of Table 7.3 for second grade repeaters and in the second column of Table 7.5 for third grade repeaters reflect the now familiar failed-year pattern. Retainees start the year badly behind and end it back further still. Second grade repeaters, for example, go from 60 points behind in the fall to 82 points behind in the spring (Table 7.3). All entries in the second column are negative and most are sizable. The adjusted figures add that their preretention shortfall is well above expectation even allowing for repeaters' risk profile.

It is a consistent picture to this point – consistent with that seen for first grade repeaters and consistent with the descriptive plots reviewed in Chapter 6. Now what of the period after retention – is that parallel, also? Same-age results for second grade repeaters (Table 7.3) are taken up first.

The unadjusted trends look unfavorable, but matters change when adjustments are made for demographic characteristics and baseline CAT level. On the CAT-R, retainees are never again as badly off as when they fail second grade (an adjusted deficit of 57 points). Their standing instead holds close to the level achieved after repeating the grade (−44 points, adjusted). CAT-M results are a bit different, though, with gaps after retention in most instances larger than those before retention, even for the adjusted figures. Except for Year 8, though, they are not much larger.

Our review thus far focuses on scale-score deficits before and after retention. A somewhat different calibration is needed to appreciate changes in repeaters' relative standing. When the tendency for test scores to increase over time is taken into consideration, the somewhat favorable picture for second grade retainees becomes even more favorable. Recall that when scores become more variable, as does the CAT distribution as children age, a smaller difference can signify relative improvement. To illustrate, the second grade adjusted CAT-R difference of 57 points in Table 7.3 is about 1.2 standard deviations, a very large shortfall. In Year 8 the difference is 50.2 points, a bit smaller than previously, but not dramatically so. However, over the intervening 5 years the CAT-R standard deviation for the full sample (promoted and retained combined) has increased from 47.3 points to 79.7 points, so the 50.2-point difference toward the end of middle school is about 0.63 standard deviation. When looked at this way, retainees' progress is more impressive, because almost every difference after retention reflects improved *relative* standing for repeaters.

TABLE 7.3. *Same-Age Regression-Adjusted CAT Differences: Second Grade Retainees vs. Never-Retained Students or the Poor-Performing Comparison Group*

	Fall of Year 2	End of Failed year	Spring of Repeated Year	1 Year Postret (Year 4)	2 Years Postret (Year 5)	3 Years Postret (Year 6)	4 Years Postret (Year 7)	5 Years Postret (Year 8)
CAT-R								
With no adjustments[a]								
Ret vs. never-ret	−60.1**	−82.1**	−75.0**	−93.4**	−89.1**	−86.9**	−89.6**	−96.0**
Ret vs. poor-perf comparison group	−31.2**	−60.7**	−43.7**	−57.4**	−47.3**	−52.7**	−52.0**	−57.8**
With fall CAT and demographic adjustments[b]								
Ret vs. never-ret	—	−57.1**	−43.7**	−48.8**	−47.6**	−46.2**	−48.2**	−50.2**
Ret vs. poor-perf comparison group	—	−49.5**	−34.7**	−40.2**	−33.5**	−39.7**	−40.1**	−46.6**
With double-ret and special ed adjustments[c]								
Ret vs. never-ret	—	−52.0**	−34.7**	−32.9**	−28.7**	−24.8	−28.1*	−35.8**
Ret vs. poor-perf comparison group	—	−43.9**	−26.3**	−25.9**	−16.0	−18.6	−21.5	−34.2**
Adj R^2								
Ret vs. never-ret[d]	0.33	0.57	0.57	0.64	0.55	0.49	0.54	0.48
Ret vs. poor-perf comparison group	0.26	0.43	0.37	0.46	0.43	0.39	0.40	0.30
CAT-M								
With no adjustments[a]								
Ret vs. never-ret	−43.0**	−51.8**	−58.7**	−74.1**	−78.2**	−69.5**	−85.3**	−99.5**

Ret vs. poor-perf comparison group	−24.7**	−35.6**	−28.4**	−48.5**	−46.9**	−38.6**	−53.0**	−67.3**
With fall CAT and demographic adjustments[b]								
Ret vs. never-ret	—	−23.7**	−27.6**	−35.6**	−41.7**	−30.0**	−38.8**	−59.3**
Ret vs. poor-perf comparison group	—	−18.4**	−16.2**	−28.8**	−30.8**	−18.2	−32.9**	−55.2**
With double-ret and special ed adjustments[c]								
Ret vs. never-ret	—	−20.5**	−19.5**	−19.7**	−26.6**	−5.8	−22.4**	−48.7**
Ret vs. poor-perf comparison group	—	−15.4**	−9.4	−15.7*	−18.5*	−1.0	−20.1**	−46.0**
Adj R^2								
Ret vs. never-ret[d]	0.31	0.65	0.63	0.72	0.61	0.62	0.61	0.57
Ret vs. poor-perf comparison group	0.31	0.57	0.44	0.59	0.50	0.50	0.46	0.36

[a] These regressions adjust for differences among the several retainee groups and between retainees and those never retained.

[b] Performed after the fall of Year 2, these regressions adjust additionally for CAT scores from the fall of Year 2 and for demographic factors: race/ethnicity, gender, mother's education, lunch subsidy status (eligible or not), number of siblings, age as of the fall of first grade, and living in a two-parent household at the start of first grade.

[c] These regressions adjust additionally for differences associated with special education alone, double retention alone, or both. These analyses are not performed in the fall of Year 2.

[d] R^2 statistics are from the most inclusive equation in each column.

** Signifies differences significant at the 0.01 level; * differences significant at the 0.05 level.

TABLE 7.4. *Same-Grade Regression-Adjusted CAT Differences: Second Grade Retainees vs. Never-Retained Students or the Poor-Performing Comparison Group*

	Fall of 2d Grade	Spring of 2d Grade	End of 3d Grade	End of 4th Grade	End of 5th Grade	End of 6th Grade	End of 7th Grade
CAT-R							
With no adjustments[a]							
Ret vs. never-ret	−57.8**	−80.0**/−37.6**	−48.0**	−63.0**	−68.4**	−70.6**	−65.9**
Ret vs. poor-perf comparison group	−26.8**	−56.8**/−15.2*	−19.1*	−27.0**	−29.3**	−38.9**	−34.5**
With fall CAT and demographic adjustments[b]							
Ret vs. never-ret	—	−54.4**/−11.6*	−11.5	−21.9*	−27.4**	−27.7**	−21.4*
Ret vs. poor-perf comparison group	—	−45.4**/−3.4	−3.6	−14.1	−15.9	−22.7	−20.1
With double-ret and special ed adjustments[c]							
Ret vs. never-ret	—	−49.0**/−4.4	3.8	−2.4	−5.7	−9.0	−10.1
Ret vs. poor-perf comparison group	—	−40.1**/3.3	10.7	3.1	5.3	−4.9	−8.4
Adj R^2							
Ret vs. never-ret[d]	0.20	0.52/0.46	0.48	0.53	0.45	0.50	0.41
Ret vs. poor-perf comparison group	0.09	0.36/0.27	0.29	0.36	0.36	0.40	0.25
CAT-M							
With no adjustments[a]							
Ret vs. never-ret	−41.4**	−49.8**/−18.1**	−36.7**	−45.6**	−49.3**	−61.9**	−74.8**

134

Ret vs. poor-perf comparison group	−21.2**	−31.8**/−0.6	−8.4	−20.6**	−26.5*	−33.0**	−47.8**
With fall CAT and demographic adjustments[b]							
Ret vs. never-ret	—	−22.4**/8.8*	−3.6	−8.0	−12.7	−19.2*	−35.6**
Ret vs. poor-perf comparison group	—	−16.0**/14.1*	7.4	−1.8	−2.7	−11.8	−38.4**
With double-ret and special ed adjustments[c]							
Ret vs. never-ret	—	−19.8**/12.5*	8.4	4.9	4.1	−4.6	−27.3**
Ret vs. poor-perf comparison group	—	−13.8**/17.3**	17.7**	8.9	11.3	−0.9	−30.0**
Adj R^2							
Ret vs. never-ret[d]	0.17	0.60/0.54	0.57	0.62	0.53	0.58	0.47
Ret vs. poor-perf comparison group	0.07	0.51/0.40	0.43	0.45	0.45	0.46	0.28

[a] These regressions adjust for differences among the several retainee groups and between retainees and those never retained.

[b] Performed after the fall of second grade, these regressions adjust additionally for CAT scores from the fall of second grade and for demographic factors: race/ethnicity, gender, mother's education, lunch subsidy status (eligible or not), number of siblings, age as of the fall of first grade, and living in a two-parent household at the start of first grade.

[c] These regressions adjust additionally for differences associated with special education alone, double retention alone, or both. These analyses are not performed in the fall of second grade.

[d] R^2 statistics are from the most inclusive equation in each column.

** Signifies differences significant at the 0.01 level; * differences significant at the 0.05 level.

TABLE 7.5. *Same-Age Regression-Adjusted CAT Differences: Third Grade Retainees vs. Never-Retained Students or the Poor-Performing Comparison Group*

	Fall of Year 3	Spring of Failed Year	Spring of Repeated Year	1 Year Postret (Year 5)	2 Years Postret (Year 6)	3 Years Postret (Year 7)	4 Years Postret (Year 8)
CAT-R							
With no adjustments[a]							
Ret. vs. never-ret	−68.0**	−79.8**	−81.0**	−77.8**	−60.0**	−73.3**	−85.9**
Ret vs. poor-perf comparison group	−37.0**	−49.1**	−45.4**	−37.0**	−27.4*	−36.2**	−45.8**
With fall CAT and demographic adjustments[b]							
Ret vs. never-ret	—	−34.7**	−25.1**	−21.3*	−7.9	−17.3	−22.9
Ret vs. poor-perf comparison group	—	−28.6**	−22.4*	−16.6	−9.7	−14.7	−23.8
With double-ret and special ed adjustments[c]							
Ret vs. never-ret	—	−28.4**	−15.9	−13.9	1.1	−9.7	−16.0
Ret vs. poor-perf comparison group	—	−23.3**	−14.9	−10.3	−1.1	−8.4	−18.5
Adj R^2							
Ret vs. never-ret[d]	0.41	0.66	0.67	0.60	0.53	0.58	0.54
Ret vs. poor-perf comparison group	0.29	0.51	0.51	0.46	0.41	0.42	0.35
CAT-M							
With no adjustments[a]							
Ret vs. never-ret	−48.6**	−56.4**	−50.3**	−64.1**	−42.3**	−62.7**	−77.1**

Ret vs. poor-perf comparison group	−20.4**	−27.3**	−25.7**	−33.5**	−12.7	−30.4**	−43.1**
With fall CAT and demographic adjustments[b]							
Ret vs. never-ret	—	−13.6**	−6.7	−18.8*	9.2	−7.2	−26.3**
Ret vs. poor-perf comparison group	—	−11.2*	−9.6	−16.5*	7.8	−9.1	−26.7**
With double-ret and special ed adjustments[c]							
Ret vs. never-ret	—	−10.6*	0.4	−12.4	17.1*	−2.9	−21.6
Ret vs. poor-perf comparison group	—	−8.8	−3.6	−11.1	14.3	−5.9	−22.0
Adj R^2							
Ret vs. never-ret[d]	0.42	0.75	0.74	0.67	0.66	0.64	0.62
Ret vs. poor-perf comparison group	0.30	0.60	0.63	0.53	0.56	0.51	0.41

[a] These regressions adjust for differences among the several retainee groups and between retainees and those never retained.

[b] Performed after the fall of Year 3, these regressions adjust additionally for CAT scores from the fall of Year 3 and for demographic factors: race/ethnicity, gender, mother's education, lunch subsidy status (eligible or not), number of siblings, age as of the fall of first grade, and living in a two-parent household at the start of first grade.

[c] These regressions adjust additionally for differences associated with special education alone, double retention alone, or both. These analyses are not performed in the fall of Year 3.

[d] R^2 statistics are from the most inclusive equation in each column.

** Signifies differences significant at the 0.01 level; * differences significant at the 0.05 level.

TABLE 7.6. Same-Grade Regression-Adjusted CAT Differences: Third Grade Retainees vs. Never-Retained Students or the Poor-Performing Comparison Group

	Fall of 3d Grade	End of 3d Grade	End of 4th Grade	End of 5th Grade	End of 6th Grade	End of 7th Grade
CAT-R						
With no adjustments[a]						
Ret vs. never-ret	−68.6**	−81.0**/−35.6**	−51.8**	−42.7**	−54.8**	−54.9**
Ret vs. poor-perf comparison group	−37.2**	−50.2**/−7.0	−16.6	−4.7	−23.3	−22.0
With fall CAT and demographic adjustments[b]						
Ret vs. never-ret	—	−31.2**/15.6*	4.7	15.0	0.2	−0.2
Ret vs. poor-perf comparison group	—	−23.7**/21.6**	7.9	17.9	2.4	−2.3
With double-ret and special ed adjustments[c]						
Ret vs. never-ret	—	−24.9**/21.7**	8.4	20.7*	4.3	2.5
Ret vs. poor-perf comparison group	—	−18.1*/27.1**	11.0	23.3*	6.3	1.0
Adj R^2						
Ret vs. never-ret[d]	0.26	0.62/0.60	0.61	0.52	0.52	0.46
Ret vs. poor-perf comparison group	0.09	0.52/0.49	0.46	0.40	0.41	0.29
CAT-M						
With no adjustments[a]						
Ret vs. never-ret	−48.9**	−57.4**/−13.3	−31.3**	−23.5*	−39.7**	−51.5**

Ret vs. poor-perf comparison group	−20.5**	−28.1/14.5*	−6.9	3.5	−10.6	−23.2*
With fall CAT and demographic adjustments[b]						
Ret vs. never-ret	—	−12.7/31.1**	10.9	20.7**	7.8	−3.1
Ret vs. poor-perf comparison group	—	−11.2/31.5**	8.2	20.3*	6.6	−10.1
With double-ret and special ed adjustments[c]						
Ret vs. never-ret	—	−9.7/34.9**	14.4*	25.4**	10.4	0.5
Ret vs. poor-perf comparison group	—	−8.3/35.2**	12.0	24.8**	9.0	−5.9
Adj R^2						
Ret vs. never-ret[d]	0.28	0.72/0.70	0.60	0.55	0.55	0.50
Ret vs. poor-perf comparison group	0.09	0.59/0.57	0.45	0.45	0.40	0.31

[a] These regressions adjust for differences among the several retainee groups and between retainees and those never retained.

[b] Performed after the fall of third grade, these regressions adjust additionally for CAT scores from the fall of third grade and for demographic factors: race/ethnicity, gender, mother's education, lunch subsidy status (eligible or not), number of siblings, age as of the fall of first grade, and living in a two-parent household at the start of first grade.

[c] These regressions adjust additionally for differences associated with special education alone, double retention alone, or both. These analyses are not performed in the fall of third grade.

[d] R^2 statistics are from the most inclusive equation in each column.

** Signifies differences significant at the 0.01 level; * differences significant at the 0.05 level.

Improved standing is evident for the same-grade comparisons, also (Table 7.4). In fact, in the fully adjusted figures second grade repeaters perform either on a par with (CAT-R) or above (CAT-M) their new classmates at the end of their repeated year. As now seems typical, their standing trails off again later, but in about half the postretention comparisons in which retainees' averages fall below those of promoted youngsters the difference is too small to be significant. And though retainees do lag significantly in the other comparisons, the disparities in those instances are less than they were before retention (seventh grade CAT-M comparisons are an exception). Hence, second grade retainees' relative standing generally improves after retention.

For third grade retainees, trends are even more favorable. On the CAT-R, none of the adjusted same-age disparities (Table 7.5) after retention is as large as any of the benchmark disparities, that is, fall of third grade, spring of the failed year, spring of the repeated year. Adjusted same-age differences on the CAT-M are small throughout, with several nonsignificant (spring of the repeated year, Year 6, and Year 7; see Table 7.5). Hence, for several years after retention, retainees in these comparisons are doing better than previously relative to promoted children. And again, since scores get more variable over time, retainees are faring even better in relative terms.

Same-grade comparisons (Table 7.6) for third grade repeaters continue this favorable showing. After adjusting for CAT scores and background factors, they are significantly *ahead* of their new classmates in the repeated year, and their advantage increases when additional adjustments are made for special education and double retention. And later, when retainees have moved beyond third grade, their adjusted CAT averages never fall significantly below those of promoted youngsters.

These children still trail far behind when judged by the unadjusted comparisons, and we must bear this in mind. In the years after retention, though, performance deficits can be traced almost entirely to circumstances other than retention, including poor readiness skills at the start of school, slower progress in the early grades, and other risk factors. When allowance is made for academic problems associated with these risks, repeaters are doing about as well as everyone else. Our best guess is that the CAT performance of third grade repeaters is better in fourth, fifth, sixth, and seventh grades than it would have been had they not been held back: that is, retention likely has helped them.

Retention and Test Performance: Taking Stock

We now return to the question posed at the outset: does retention help or harm children academically? We have examined the issue from several angles – comparing different groups of repeaters with one another, with children not retained (including a low-performing promoted group), with themselves over time, and with others of the same age or grade level – by looking at descriptive trends and, in a more analytic mode, using statistical adjustments. For all these comparisons, verbal and quantitative performance have been examined in parallel over many years. There is much to digest.

The clearest patterns involve the backdrop to retention, not its consequences: yet-to-be-retained children are performing far below the standard of never-to-be-retained children at the start of first grade, and those furthest behind are retained the earliest.

First grade repeaters are furthest back on these initial CAT assessments, and later many of them are assigned to special education classes and/or held back a second time. Children held back in second grade and beyond also enter school with low scores, but not as low as those of first grade repeaters. They are passed along, but over the first, second, and, in the case of third grade retainees, third grade, they fall further back, such that the shortfall of each group is most pronounced during its failed year. We saw this in Chapter 6 by comparing repeaters' gains through their year of retention (whether second or third) with those of children who move smoothly through the system, and it is evident in the regression patterns, also.

The competencies tapped in these tests are important to the early elementary curriculum, so the problems they reveal are real and severe, a fact often slighted by critics of retention. These children need help. Repeating a year surely is not the ideal, but it does seem to help some, especially in the short term: during the repeated year all retainees make up ground. These advances are most apparent in same-grade comparisons, which simulate the classroom context repeaters experience after retention. However, advances are apparent in same-age comparisons also for second and third grade repeaters with their original classmates, now a grade ahead.

If the standard of success is that repeating a grade will halt retainees' downward slide, help them catch up somewhat, help them do better than would be predicted from their prior academic record, and enable them to perform at a level closer to grade level when they move up to the next grade, then retention's showing, on balance, is favorable. This certainly holds for retentions after first grade, and even first grade repeaters appear to realize near-term benefits in the form of a quite substantial repeated year rebound.

Unfortunately, our comparisons do not illuminate what it is about retainees' experience during the repeated year that accounts for this success. In Baltimore schools at the time there were no supplemental programs designed specifically to help repeaters, although some teachers no doubt made special efforts for them. The most obvious inferences are that working on the same curriculum a second time enables repeaters to master some of what they missed the first time and that retaking the same tests helps them show what they have learned.

Has retention transformed these struggling children into academic stars? Absolutely not, but when allowance is made for their problems before retention, they are doing better than would be predicted. In fact, our estimates suggest that had it not been for their prior difficulties, in many instances they would be performing close to, and occasionally even ahead of, their new classmates. But retainees continue to suffer from their early difficulties, which retention does not erase. Most repeaters never catch up once they have fallen behind, but for many the free-fall is slowed, possibly even stopped, as appears to be the case for second and third grade repeaters. In the concluding chapter we attempt to weigh the benefits of grade repetition against possible alternatives (e.g., mandatory summer school for children who are behind at year's end). Now, though, the issue is more narrowly focused – how effective is grade retention?

Short of raising repeaters to the level of their promoted agemates – a goal that we argued in Chapter 2 probably is not realistic – our results to this point reflect favorably on retention. Children who are not too far behind to begin with are the ones helped most. It buys them the time to mobilize their resources and to master some of the skills they apparently did not acquire the first time through the grade. Once second and third grade repeaters get back on track, they pretty well hold their own. On the other hand, children who are struggling the most – first grade repeaters and those destined for special education and/or a second retention – are helped very little. Retention's effectiveness varies inversely with its scheduling and the severity of children's problems, helping first graders least and third graders most. Indeed, even though we have not explored the situation of fourth through seventh grade repeaters in detail, they appear to be having the least difficulty all along the way.

But achievement test scores are not the only consideration, and we need to withhold judgment pending examination of other possible consequences. Report card marks are evaluated next to round out coverage of retention's implications for BSS children's school performance. After that, evidence on stigmatization is examined. The concluding chapters address retention's tie in with other forms of educational tracking and high school dropout.

8

Academic Performance as Judged by Teachers

Report Card Marks before and after Retention

This chapter examines report card marks in math and reading. Math and reading dominate the curriculum in the primary grades and are the building blocks for most other academic subjects. For that reason they have special relevance for the way children come to think of themselves in their academic role (a topic taken up in Chapter 9). Marks also are integral to the social relations of schooling. Not all children are aware of how they rank on standardized tests like the California Achievement Test (CAT) battery, but everyone in a classroom knows who is getting high marks and who is getting low ones. Invidious distinctions crop up around the marks teachers assign, and getting a low mark can be hurtful. Children work for good marks; they and their parents understand their meaning. Marks, moreover, are the centerpiece of children's cumulative academic record, and in that way early marking patterns shadow children throughout their schooling. For these reasons we view marks not as mere supplement to achievement scores, but as a coequal and complementary assessment of academic progress.

Retained children, we saw in the last chapter, were unable to keep up before being held back, but their test performance improved during the repeated year, and many repeaters after retention continued to do better relative to their classmates. These successes are important, but whether children fully appreciate them is dubious. Feedback about test scores is hard to decipher and often reaches children indirectly or not at all. Report card marks, on the other hand, are readily understood and are much more public than test scores. By design, marks provide direct feedback from teachers to children on the quality of their performance, so successes registered in report card marks carry great weight.

Marks thus are important because they evaluate children's performance in the classroom *and* because they send signals. For marks,
though, unlike test scores, there are no particular age-graded benchmarks against which to judge children's standing.[1] Marks are best compared at grade level, because there children are being rated against the
same curriculum and in the same classroom context. Accordingly, in this
chapter marks are evaluated only from the same-grade perspective.

We first plot marking trends from first through seventh grade. After
reviewing these trends, regression-adjusted estimates are presented to
determine whether retainees' marks are better or worse after being held
back than would be predicted on the basis of preretention achievement
levels and sociodemographic characteristics. As before, we evaluate the
performance of first, second, and third grade retainees separately, comparing their marks with those of (1) all promoted children, (2) the poor-
performing yet promoted subsample, and (3) fourth through seventh
grade repeaters combined.

Report Card Marks before and after Retention:
More Indications of Success

Table 8.1 lines up same-grade comparisons of report card marks, starting
with the fall of first grade and at the end of every grade thereafter.[2] For
the retained grade, they are reported from the initial time through the
grade, when students are earmarked for retention, and from when the
grade is repeated.[3]

The situation in middle school is different from that in the primary
grades in ways that affect our procedures. In middle school children
do not all take the same courses and not all courses run the full year.
English is part of the regular middle grades curriculum, whereas reading
is remedial (e.g., children who fail the state's functional reading test are
obliged to take reading in sixth grade). Some children take only reading,
some take only English, and some take both. Taking one math course is

[1] Level of schooling may be relevant, though, as children's school performance tends to
spiral downward over the course of their schooling (e.g., Roderick 1995a; Simmons and
Blyth 1987).
[2] In middle school, some of these may be one-semester courses, and so marks would be
from midyear, rather than from year's end. The scheduling of middle school courses is
described later in this chapter.
[3] Retainees' entries in columns beyond their repeated grade reflect a same-grade offset;
for example, their seventh grade averages are from Year 8, whereas never-retained
children's are from Year 7.

TABLE 8.1. *Average Reading and Math Report Card Marks from First through Seventh Grade for Retained Groups, Never-Retained Pupils, and the Poor-Performing Comparison Group*[a]

	Fall of 1st Grade[b]	End of 1st Grade[b]	End of 2d Grade[b]	End of 3d Grade	End of 4th Grade	End of 5th Grade	End of 6th Grade	End of 7th Grade
Average reading mark								
Year of retention								
1st grade	1.1	1.0/1.9	1.9	1.8	1.9	2.1	1.9	1.9
	(106)	(105)/(84)	(105)	(93)	(86)	(90)	(74)	(89)
2d grade	1.5	1.7	1.2/2.2	2.0	1.9	2.2	2.0	2.0
	(61)	(62)	(53)/(60)	(55)	(55)	(50)	(49)	(54)
3d grade	1.6	2.1	1.9	1.3/1.8	1.9	2.0	1.9	2.1
	(42)	(43)	(41)	(40)/(36)	(34)	(34)	(33)	(35)
4th–7th grades	1.9	2.2	2.3	2.0	2.0	2.2	1.9	1.9
	(68)	(68)	(60)	(70)	(64)	(57)	(67)	(68)
Never-retained pupils								
All never-retained	2.2	2.7	2.7	2.7	2.6	2.8	2.6	2.6
	(418)	(414)	(358)	(331)	(295)	(254)	(234)	(234)
Poor-performing comparison group	1.9	2.2	2.2	2.2	2.1	2.3	2.4	2.4
	(98)	(98)	(80)	(78)	(69)	(60)	(54)	(55)

Average math mark

Year of retention								
1st grade	1.3 (105)	1.3/2.2 (104)/(84)	1.9 (107)	1.9 (92)	1.9 (85)	2.1 (90)	1.8 (74)	1.9 (89)
2d grade	1.8 (62)	2.0 (62)	1.6/2.3 (53)/(60)	2.1 (55)	2.1 (56)	2.2 (52)	1.7 (49)	1.8 (54)
3d grade	2.1 (43)	2.6 (43)	2.1 (41)	1.6/2.3 (42)/(36)	2.2 (34)	2.1 (34)	2.2 (33)	1.9 (35)
4th–7th grades	2.2 (67)	2.5 (68)	2.4 (60)	2.1 (70)	2.1 (65)	2.1 (61)	1.9 (67)	1.6 (68)
Never-retained pupils								
All never-retained	2.6 (418)	3.0 (412)	2.8 (358)	2.7 (333)	2.6 (294)	2.8 (255)	2.5 (235)	2.3 (234)
Poor-performing comparison group	2.4 (98)	2.6 (98)	2.5 (80)	2.2 (77)	2.2 (69)	2.4 (60)	2.2 (54)	1.9 (55)

[a] All marks are on a scale from 1 (unsatisfactory) to 4 (excellent). All entries except those in the first column are from the final quarter of the year. The first-column entries are from the fall of first grade, in 1982. Numbers in parentheses are sample sizes.

[b] For first, second, and third grade retainees, two end-of-grade averages are reported. The first is from the first time through the grade; the second is from the repeated year.

the norm, but its nature varies. Many sixth graders take remedial math – courses with titles like Special Education Math and Supplementary Remedial Math; others take the regular sixth grade math program; others take advanced courses (e.g., Advanced Academic Math and Prealgebra).

In this chapter only marks are examined, without regard to whether they are obtained in remedial, regular, or advanced courses. Marks embody the feedback children receive from their teachers, and our purpose is to determine whether these signals are positive or negative. Middle school course-taking patterns are scrutinized in Chapter 10 to see whether repeaters are tracked differently, an important concern in its own right.

The middle school marking system uses percentages, whereas letter grades are assigned in elementary school: E(xcellent), G(ood), S(atisfactory), and U(nsatisfactory) (assigned values 4–1, respectively). To align marking distinctions across levels of schooling, middle school percentiles are collapsed into four categories, scoring 90% through 100% as 4, 80% through 89% as 3, 70% through 79% as 2, and below 70% as 1. This roughly parallels the primary-grade distinctions, allowing us to plot marks all 7 years with a common scale.

Fourth quarter marks (at year's end) generally are used, but for one-semester middle school courses they can be from the second quarter.[4] At the elementary level, fourth-quarter marks are used throughout, so the last evaluation received is used at both levels of schooling.

Finally, there is the matter of whether to use reading or English marks in middle school. At the elementary level, reading is the focus, so reading marks are used from middle school when available. There are 200 children with reading marks in Year 6, 357 in Year 7, and 300 in Year 8. English marks are used for children who lack reading marks. This increases coverage in Year 6 to 293, in Year 7 to 458, and in Year 8 to 470.

Sample coverage for Year 6 is low but is a consequence of the cohort's promotion timetable. In Year 6 most repeaters are still in elementary school (exceptions are children held back for the first time in sixth or seventh grade) and so are not yet taking English. With elementary school reading marks added in, as in our tables, sixth grade case coverage increases to 491.[5]

---

[4] End-of-year marks, end-of-semester marks, and marks from the final quarter all yield averages that are virtually interchangeable.

[5] Coverage in Year 7 is a concern, also. Only double repeaters would be in elementary school then, but because of administrative problems in procuring records that year,

As we saw for CAT scores, retainees' early marks tend to be low and aligned with the eventual scheduling of their retentions (Table 8.1). First grade repeaters' marks from the fall of first grade are lowest, more than a full marking unit behind never-retained children's marks in both reading and math. In fact, their math average lags a full marking unit behind even the poor-performing comparison group's. The samplewide standard deviations for reading and math marks are 0.7 and 0.8, respectively, so these disparities are large whether considered in absolute terms or relative to the overall variability in marks.

Second and third grade repeaters also have lower entering marks than do never-retained children, and in three of four instances they are lower also than those of the poor-performing comparison group. This orderliness is striking, and another indication that the timing of retention is tied to the severity of children's academic difficulties: the earlier the retention, the greater the first grade mark gap between retained and never-retained students.

All retainees start out behind, but those held back earliest trail furthest back. First grade repeaters' marks start out so low there is barely any room for them to fall further, yet they do fall: their spring reading average of 1.0 and their spring math average of 1.3 are the two lowest entries in Table 8.1. Note that a reading average of 1.0 indicates that every first grade repeater fails reading at year's end.

Other repeaters' marks improve somewhat from fall to spring of first grade. Second grade repeaters' progress over the year is modest (only a fifth of a marking unit in both instances), but they at least are moving in the right direction. After first grade, though, their marks also decline, falling to 1.2 in reading and 1.6 in math by the spring of second grade. Both averages are below those from the start of first grade, and well below the second-year averages of children not held back until third grade or later.

A similar pattern is evident for third grade repeaters and for children held back in the fourth through seventh grades – their mark averages go up before dropping back. Our format does not pinpoint the year of retention for the combined group, but their general trend is consistent with that for the others.

This backsliding apparently triggers the decision to retain. Teachers and administrators, it seems, resort to retention when children's

many were missed. Just 49 double retainees are covered in Year 7, compared with 69 in Year 6 and 71 in Year 8. Possible implications of this lack are addressed later, when marking trends are reviewed.

performance slips from bad to worse: in the year of their retention, the marks of first, second, and third grade repeaters all trail those of every other group. But as many marginal performers are moved along for several years before being held back, it appears the decision is not made lightly.

Looking ahead, it is hard to be optimistic about retained children's future prospects. Certainly their experience through the year of their failure gives little cause for optimism. Another relevant trend line apparent in Table 8.1 also does not augur well for repeaters' future prospects. Promoted children's marks also decline over time, and especially in middle school (and then later again in high school), a pattern seen in other studies as well (e.g., Roderick 1995a; Simmons and Blyth 1987). Hence, even if repeaters, after making it through the failed year, were to parallel the later performance of promoted youngsters, they still would be headed down, not up.

With the experience of promoted children a frame of reference for anticipating repeaters' future, their record over this period bears scrutiny. Except for a noticeable jump in fifth grade,[6] promoted children's marks generally do not change much over the elementary grades – usually only on the order of 0.1 marking unit across years. This stability ends abruptly in middle school, though. Marks decline then, and not just when viewed against the relatively high marks from fifth grade. In both reading and math for all never-retained children and in math for the poor performers not a single sixth or seventh grade average is above *any* spring average from the first through fourth grades.

The transition from elementary to middle school challenges children generally, and performance typically dips (Eccles and Midgley 1990; Harvard Education Letter 1992b). What is important for our purposes is that even the most successful BSS children – those spared retention – are struggling at this point.

And what are the implications of this downward drift in marks for retainees? Before retention their marks are dropping, as are promoted children's. Neither trend suggests retainees' marks will improve after retention, yet improve they do. The relevant figures at the end of retainees' repeated year are those to the right of the slash marks in Table 8.1. Juxtaposing children's failing marks at the time of their retentions against their marks on finishing the grade highlights a dramatic repeated year "rebound." In math, the three main repeater groups have

---

[6] Fifth grade is the end of elementary school, so this "up-tick" may be the school's way of wishing them well.

marks well above satisfactory at the end of their repeated grade, whereas the previous year their marks hover midway between unsatisfactory and satisfactory. First grade repeaters' marks improve 0.9 marking unit on average; second and third grade repeaters' marks improve 0.7 unit.

For other groups, the largest spring-to-spring changes in marks during these years are 0.3 unit, and these are *declines*: fourth through seventh grade retainees' math average drops from 2.4 to 2.1 between second and third grades; poor performers' math average falls from 2.5 to 2.2 over the same period. Retainees' mark improvement on repeating a grade thus not only is exceptionally large, but moves against the downward tide that appears to envelop other children.

Their marks improve, and the previous chapter shows improvement in their test scores also, so it is unlikely teachers are simply being easy on repeaters. When the time comes for these children to move on, teachers are rating their school performance much more favorably, and closer to the levels achieved by their new classmates. Positive feedback of this sort has been rare in repeaters' experience to this point, and we suspect many of them (and their parents) are buoyed by it.

After this encouraging picture, do these children's successes continue when they move up to the next grade and encounter a new curriculum? Are they able to keep up because of retention, or are the new challenges too difficult? The indications in Table 8.1 are mixed. Retainees' performance drops off a bit when they start a new grade, but since promoted children's marks also fall off in the upper grades, repeaters' decline does not necessarily reflect retention's lasting influence. In fact, retainees' middle school marks remain close to their marks over the later years of elementary school, whereas those of their promoted peers are lower.[7]

After retainees finish their repeated grade, their marks generally hover around satisfactory for the rest of elementary school and into the middle grades. First grade repeaters' marks drop just below 2.0; those of second and third grade repeaters average a bit above 2.0. And later, their sixth and seventh grade marks are about the same as in elementary school. At 2.0 in reading and slightly lower in math, neither average is at the level of promoted children, but retainees' marks then are closer to promoted children's than before retention, closer even than at the

---

[7] There are two exceptions to this pattern. The first involves fifth grade marks, which we have seen are high for everyone. Retainees' middle school marks in most instances are below their fifth grade marks, but this is true for promoted youngsters, too. Also, second grade repeaters' math marks consistently fall below their averages from the second through fourth grades.

"high point" of their repeated year.[8] The main exception involves comparisons with the poor-performing promoted group in reading, whose marks improve slightly in middle school.

In sum, retainees' marks after retention remain marginal (right around satisfactory). On the one hand, they continue to lag behind promoted children's, and their performance trails off some after the repeated year. On the other hand, they register noteworthy improvement during the repeated year and though their marks do taper off later, the decline is not peculiar to repeaters. In fact, in most instances repeaters' marks do not drop quite as much as promoted children's, and even after a postretention "dip" they remain ahead of their preretention position. It is a mixed picture, but one with some decidedly favorable elements. Whether these reflect actual benefits of retention is taken up in the next section.

Regression-Adjusted Comparisons of Same-Grade Marks

In this section we adjust marking patterns for prior achievement levels and for children's demographic characteristics. As in Chapter 7, multiple regression is used to implement these adjustments. The analyses are set up as before, except that this time only same-grade regressions are estimated. Regression-adjusted differences are reported for first, second, and third grade repeaters separately, beginning with marks from the fall of each's respective failed year. For first grade repeaters the analysis extends 6 years postretention; for third grade repeaters the after retention interval is 4 years.

We begin in Table 8.2 with adjusted and unadjusted differences for first grade retainees, but we are mainly interested in mark disparities

---

[8] We were concerned that this favorable showing for retainees in middle school might be misleading because of missing elementary school records from Year 7. Most double repeaters are still in elementary school in Year 7, and because of the way same-grade comparisons are structured (i.e., the 1-year offset), this would mainly affect figures for sixth grade. However, as best we can determine, sparse coverage of double retainees in sixth grade does not change the picture at all. We checked this by recalculating the sixth grade averages using the larger of the fifth or seventh grade subsamples as the sixth grade base for double repeaters (e.g., for first grade repeaters in math, the number of double retainees used in computing the new average is 42, as opposed to the 26 for whom marks actually are in hand; we assume that these 42 would have the same average as observed for the 26). None of these new averages differs by as much as 0.1 marking unit from those reported in Table 8.1, and since the averages in Table 8.1 are rounded to one decimal place, the recomputed entries are identical to those reported.

after adjustments are made for test scores from the fall of the failed year and for personal and social demographic characteristics. Difficulties peculiar to double repeaters and children in special education also are adjusted for in a separate stage of the analysis. These adjusted differences give the clearest reading of how "regular," one-time retainees are faring.

In both reading and math, repeaters' initial marks lag far behind all promoted children's and those of the poor-performing comparison group, by more than a full standard deviation in the first instance. Why this shaky start? It cannot be determined from Table 8.2, but with the marking gap widening fall to spring, it clearly goes beyond initial "settling in" problems. Even after statistical adjustments, at year's end retainees' marks remain more than a full unit behind promoted children's (see entries to the left of the slashes in the second column).[9]

It is a gloomy picture to this point, but what happens to these youngsters during their second try at first grade? Do their marks improve, or do they remain near the lowest level possible? The unadjusted figures to the right of the slashes in the End of First Grade column compare first grade repeaters' marks on finishing first grade with those of promoted youngsters from the previous year, when they too were finishing first grade (i.e., Year 2 marks in the first instance versus Year 1 marks in the second). Retainees' averages in these comparisons are from 0.36 to 0.78 marking unit back, so problems remain. However, in each instance the shortfall is much less than it was the first time through the grade (fall or spring). Additionally, in the adjusted comparisons three of the disparities are too small to be considered reliable (and the fourth, at 0.29 marking unit, is less than half the [adjusted] gap from before retention).

There is no indication here that retainees' marks suffer because they are held back. Indeed, the opposite is true: at the end of first grade these children perform at about the same level as others once allowance is made for their prior difficulties. This is a much better picture than the previous one and is pretty much the same through the rest of elementary school and into middle school.

---

[9] Marks get more variable over time just as test scores do, but the increase is not so great. Partly this is because the middle school percentage metric is collapsed into four categories so as to parallel marking distinctions from the primary grades. And, too, marks often are "curved" or otherwise subject to grading norms. That practice also limits their variability. The fall of first grade reading standard deviation is 0.82; in spring of seventh grade it is 0.90; and all but one from the intervening years fall between these values. The corresponding figures for math marks are 0.81 and 0.92, and in math all the others are in between.

TABLE 8.2. *Same-Grade Regression-Adjusted Mark Differences: First Grade Retainees vs. Never-Retained Students or the Poor-Performing Comparison Group*

	Fall of 1st Grade	End of 1st Grade	End of 2d Grade	End of 3d Grade	End of 4th Grade	End of 5th Grade	End of 6th Grade	End of 7th Grade
Reading marks								
With no adjustments[a]								
Ret vs. never-ret	−1.04**	−1.68**/−0.78**	−0.81**	−0.84**	−0.68**	−0.61**	−0.59**	−0.61**
Ret vs. poor-perf comparison group	−0.79**	−1.25**/−0.36**	−0.34**	−0.41**	−0.21	−0.09	−0.34*	−0.39**
With fall CAT and demographic adjustments[b]								
Ret vs. never-ret	−0.82**	−1.41**/−0.46**	−0.47**	−0.46**	−0.27**	−0.22**	−0.43**	−0.37**
Ret vs. poor-perf comparison group	−0.74**	−1.23**/−0.28**	−0.25**	−0.31**	−0.13	0.01	−0.29*	−0.30*
With double-ret and special ed adjustments[c]								
Ret vs. never-ret	−0.76**	−1.36**/−0.29**	−0.38**	−0.34**	−0.18	−0.23	−0.38**	−0.42**
Ret vs. poor-perf comparison group	−0.69**	−1.18**/−0.13	−0.16	−0.19	−0.04	0.00	−0.24	−0.36*
Adj R^2[d]								
Ret vs. never-ret	0.41	0.55/0.34	0.32	0.34	0.35	0.29	0.22	0.18
Ret vs. poor-perf comparison group	0.31	0.55/0.14	0.11	0.08	0.02	0.05	0.17	0.07

Math marks

With no adjustments[a]								
Ret vs. never-ret	−1.25**	−1.67**/−0.71**	−0.85**	−0.77**	−0.64**	−0.65**	−0.61**	−0.39**
Ret vs. poor-perf comparison group	−1.10**	−1.38**/−0.44**	−0.50**	−0.32**	−0.26*	−0.21	−0.32*	−0.01
With fall CAT and demographic adjustments[b]								
Ret vs. never-ret	−0.85**	−1.22**/−0.23**	−0.48**	−0.31**	−0.18	−0.23	−0.41**	−0.11
Ret vs. poor-perf comparison group	−0.91**	−1.22**/−0.25*	−0.39**	−0.20	−0.16	−0.18	−0.31**	−0.04
With double-ret and special ed adjustments[c]								
Ret vs. never-ret	−0.74**	−1.12**/−0.09	−0.38**	−0.18	−0.07	−0.19	−0.41**	−0.25
Ret vs. poor-perf comparison group	−0.83**	−1.12**/−0.11	−0.33**	−0.08	−0.07	−0.16	−0.32*	−0.09
Adj R^2[d]								
Ret vs. never-ret	0.42	0.57/0.36	0.24	0.26	0.22	0.19	0.19	0.15
Ret vs. poor-perf comparison group	0.41	0.56/0.22	0.11	0.06	0.02	0.00	0.14	0.10

[a] These regressions adjust for differences among the several retainee groups and between retainees and those never retained.

[b] These regressions adjust additionally for CAT scores from the fall of first grade and for demographic factors: race/ethnicity, gender, mother's education, lunch subsidy status (eligible or not), number of siblings, age as of the fall of first grade, and living in a two-parent household at the start of first grade.

[c] These regressions adjust additionally for differences associated with special education alone, double retention alone, and both combined.

[d] R^2 statistics are from the most inclusive equation in each column.

** Signifies differences significant at the 0.01 level; * differences significant at the 0.05 level.

In the unadjusted comparisons, retainees' averages most years are on the order of 0.6 to 0.7 marking unit behind those of all never-retained children (7 of the 12 figures are in this range) and 0.2 to 0.3 marking unit behind those of the poor performers (several of which are not significant). These are "raw" differences, and retainees' standing improves when adjusted for problems that predate retention. In Table 8.2 only half the adjusted comparisons with all promoted youngsters are large enough to be considered reliable – those on the order of 0.3 to 0.4 marking unit. Against those of the poor performers, only 3 of 12 differences are significant.

Most troubling about these figures is that differences that are significant appear mainly in the middle school years, sixth and seventh grades (five of the eight middle school differences are significant). Though still far ahead of where they had been before retention, repeaters' middle school marks nevertheless have slipped a notch from the later years of elementary school. The more challenging middle school curriculum and the less supportive middle school environment may be taking a toll on these children, who otherwise have been doing reasonably well since repeating. In the previous section, where we reviewed simple mark trends, repeaters' marks appeared to be holding up better than most other children's in middle school. That is not the case in Table 8.2, though.

The picture for second and third grade repeaters is more consistently favorable (Tables 8.3 and 8.4). Their failed grade dip-and-recovery cycle parallels that of first grade repeaters. They start the year behind and at year's end both groups lag even further behind. This dip in most comparisons leaves them a full marking unit back, whereas the recovery at the end of their repeated year shows them vastly improved. In the most favorable comparisons they draw even with promoted children (in three of the four unadjusted comparisons with the poor performers), but even in the least favorable comparisons they are much closer to the promoted standard than during the failed year. And when adjustments are made for prior test scores, and the like, not a single one of the repeated-year disparities between retained and promoted children is significant (and in six of the eight, the direction favors retainees). In contrast, all the unadjusted comparisons from the failed year show retainees significantly behind promoted children.

The story is much the same beyond the repeated year through seventh grade. In most instances retainees trail promoted children by about 0.5 to 0.7 marking unit. These unadjusted differentials, all significant, reflect real shortfall; nevertheless, in every case the shortfall is less than before retention and generally not much above the repeated year differential. Against those of poor performers, the mark gaps are small and most (15 of 18) not significant. However, again some slippage during the middle grades is evident: two of the significant differences are from sixth grade, and some of the other middle school comparisons, though not significant, are large enough to catch the eye (those in the 0.24 to 0.26 range). After adjustments are made for testing levels from before retention and for other risk factors, second and third grade retainees' marks lag significantly behind in only 2 of 36 comparisons. Rather than lagging far behind, their adjusted marks are about on par with promoted children's all throughout the postretention period.

For all three retainee groups, then, marks improve in the postretention period, absolutely and relatively to those of their promoted classmates. Retainees' test scores also receive a limited boost as a result of retention (Chapter 7), so the picture with respect to retention's academic consequences is basically positive for both test scores and marks. This conclusion – that retention helps repeaters learn more and do better in school than they would otherwise – accords with most practitioners' intuition (e.g., Smith and Shepard 1988; Tomchin and Impara 1992) but flies in the face of much commentary on the issue. The next chapter examines how retainees' attitudes respond to the experience, but before moving on, we want to reflect on the lessons learned to this point, for it appears that being retained is not entirely, and perhaps not even preponderantly, a negative experience for this group of mainly disadvantaged urban school children.

Retention and School Performance: What Have We Learned?

We now have examined test scores and marks from many vantage points in trying to fathom retention's academic consequences. Along the way we also have pointed out obstacles to securing credible evidence on the issue. Some complications, such as retainees' academic difficulties before they are held back and problems arising from selective sample loss, are obvious. Others, as whether special education children and multiple repeaters are included or excluded from the evaluation, are more subtle. In a typical cohort of children attending public school in cities such as Baltimore, a great many children will experience one or another of these "treatments," yet most studies of retention make no mention of how multiple retentions and special education are handled. In our judgment, it makes sense to focus on children who are held back a

TABLE 8.3. *Same-Grade Regression-Adjusted Mark Differences: Second Grade Retainees vs. Never-Retained Students or the Poor-Performing Comparison Group*

	Fall of 2d Grade	End of 2d Grade	End of 3d Grade	End of 4th Grade	End of 5th Grade	End of 6th Grade	End of 7th Grade
Reading marks							
With no adjustments[a]							
Ret vs. never-ret	−1.18**	−1.44**/−0.52**	−0.68**	−0.78**	−0.53**	−0.53**	−0.48**
Ret vs. poor-perf comparison group	−0.64**	−0.98**/−0.04	−0.23	−0.26*	−0.01	−0.26	−0.26
With fall CAT and demographic adjustments[b]							
Ret vs. never-ret	−0.56**	−0.83**/0.08	−0.13	−0.20	0.00	−0.33*	−0.16
Ret vs. poor-perf comparison group	−0.43**	−0.76**/0.15	−0.10	−0.16	0.08	−0.18	−0.14
With double-ret and special ed adjustments[c]							
Ret vs. never-ret	−0.48**	−0.79**/0.12	−0.07	−0.15	−0.01	−0.29	−0.19
Ret vs. poor-perf comparison group	−0.37**	−0.73**/0.19	−0.04	−0.11	0.08	−0.14	−0.17
Adj R^2							
Ret vs. never-ret[d]	0.48	0.54/0.43	0.38	0.39	0.32	0.23	0.18
Ret vs. poor-perf comparison group	0.20	0.33/0.16	0.08	0.02	0.02	0.17	0.06

Math marks

With no adjustments[a]						
Ret vs. never-ret	−0.88**	−1.20**/−0.49**	−0.61**	−0.53**	−0.56**	−0.83**	−0.53**
Ret vs. poor-perf comparison group	−0.63**	−0.85**/−0.12	−0.15	−0.12	−0.12	−0.50**	−0.12
With fall CAT and demographic adjustments[b]						
Ret vs. never-ret	−0.45**	−0.73**/−0.03	−0.10	0.01	−0.08	−0.52**	−0.12
Ret vs. poor-perf comparison group	−0.42**	−0.64**/0.06	0.05	0.03	0.01	−0.35*	0.00
With double-ret and special ed adjustments[c]						
Ret vs. never-ret	−0.43**	−0.68**/0.01	−0.05	0.04	−0.07	−0.50**	−0.22
Ret vs. poor-perf comparison group	−0.42**	−0.62**/0.08	0.09	0.07	0.02	−0.35*	−0.07
Adj R^2						
Ret vs. never-ret[d]	0.32	0.37/0.29	0.30	0.27	0.23	0.23	0.18
Ret vs. poor-perf comparison group	0.18	0.22/0.13	0.09	0.03	0.01	0.16	0.09

[a] These regressions adjust for differences among the several retainee groups and between retainees and those never retained.

[b] These regressions adjust additionally for CAT scores from the fall of second grade and for demographic factors: race/ethnicity, gender, mother's education, lunch subsidy status (eligible or not), number of siblings, age as of the fall of first grade, and living in a two-parent household at the start of first grade.

[c] These regressions adjust additionally for differences associated with special education alone, double retention alone, and both combined.

[d] R^2 statistics are from the most inclusive equation in each column.

** Signifies differences significant at the 0.01 level; * differences significant at the 0.05 level.

TABLE 8.4. *Same-Grade Regression-Adjusted Mark Differences: Third Grade Retainees vs. Never-Retained Students or the Poor-Performing Comparison Group*

	Fall of 3d Grade	End of 3d Grade	End of 4th Grade	End of 5th Grade	End of 6th Grade	End of 7th Grade
Reading marks						
With no adjustments[a]						
Ret vs. never-ret	−1.19**	−1.45**/−0.80**	−0.71**	−0.76**	−0.67**	−0.44*
Ret vs. poor-perf comparison group	−0.77**	−0.95**/−0.36**	−0.22	−0.24	−0.39*	−0.24
With fall CAT and demographic adjustments[b]						
Ret vs. never-ret	−0.65**	−0.79**/−0.14	−0.05	−0.11	−0.41*	−0.16
Ret vs. poor-perf comparison group	−0.56**	−0.76**/−0.17	−0.05	−0.07	−0.29	−0.14
With double-ret and special ed adjustments[c]						
Ret vs. never-ret	−0.63**	−0.78**/−0.15	−0.02	−0.10	−0.28	−0.13
Ret vs. poor-perf comparison group	−0.54**	−0.74**/−0.17	−0.02	−0.05	−0.17	−0.12
Adj R^2						
Ret vs. never-ret[d]	0.44	0.46/0.41	0.40	0.37	0.23	0.21
Ret vs. poor-perf comparison group	0.23	0.21/0.12	0.04	0.06	0.17	0.06

Math marks

With no adjustments[a]					
Ret vs. never-ret	−1.02**	−1.13**/−0.32*	−0.38*	−0.62**	−0.29	−0.39*
Ret vs. poor-perf comparison group	−0.50**	−0.64**/0.13	0.01	−0.18	0.01	−0.01
With fall CAT and demographic adjustments[b]					
Ret vs. never-ret	−0.46**	−0.56**/0.24	0.20	−0.07	0.07	0.05
Ret vs. poor-perf comparison group	−0.34**	−0.50**/0.25	0.13	−0.08	0.12	0.16
With double-ret and special ed adjustments[c]					
Ret vs. never-ret	−0.45**	−0.55**/0.25	0.23	−0.03	0.15	0.00
Ret vs. poor-perf comparison group	−0.34**	−0.48**/0.27	0.17	−0.03	0.21	0.13
Adj R^2					
Ret vs. never-ret[d]	0.39	0.38/0.31	0.26	0.25	0.25	0.17
Ret vs. poor-perf comparison group	0.19	0.10/0.06	0.02	0.01	0.14	0.09

[a] These regressions adjust for differences among the several retainee groups and between retainees and those never retained.

[b] These regressions adjust additionally for CAT scores from the fall of third grade and for demographic factors: race/ethnicity, gender, mother's education, lunch subsidy status (eligible or not), number of siblings, age as of the fall of first grade, and living in a two-parent household at the start of first grade.

[c] These regressions adjust additionally for differences associated with special education alone, double retention alone, and both combined.

[d] R^2 statistics are from the most inclusive equation in each column.

** Signifies differences significant at the 0.01 level; * differences significant at the 0.05 level.

year and then get back on track, as approximated in the "fully adjusted" statistical analyses. Others will favor evaluating consequences for all repeaters, and for that reason test score differences and mark differences without adjustments for special education and double retention are reported also. It turns out, though, that results are not radically different under the two approaches, especially for report card marks.

When using test scores to compare retainees with others, there are additional complications. We have used only tests for which ceiling limits are adequate. Tests that are too easy will affect promoted children's performance more than retainees' and so understate retainees' shortfall. We rarely see the issue addressed in the literature, but evaluations that neglect the ceiling issue may be seriously flawed.

Distorting tendencies can work in both directions, though. For example, younger children typically make greater strides than older ones on tests like the California Achievement Test (CAT). This phenomenon of decelerating gains has nothing to do with retention, yet it would be easy to misread it as a poor showing for retention. It would have been so misread, for example, if we had compared just retainees' gains after retention with those from before. The declining growth rate also affects same-grade comparisons, which compare older retainees' performance against that of younger children who have been promoted.

Determining what constitutes success is another challenge – what is the appropriate standard or criterion? For retention to be deemed effective must repeaters be raised to promoted children's level of performance? If that standard is too high, then is it sufficient for them to perform at the level of promoted youngsters who are similar to them (i.e., a finding of "no difference" in matched control studies); or must they score ahead of such children? Does narrowing the gap constitute a positive showing, even if it still leaves repeaters behind? In repeaters' preretention trajectory they fall further and further back before being retained. If that pattern holds generally, then for the gap to remain unchanged after retention would be an accomplishment. Or perhaps if retainees simply make better progress after being held back than they had been making before, is that a positive showing?

There are many reasonable standards, and too often commentary on retention fails to define the one or ones being used. If retention is to raise repeaters to the level of promoted children and keep them there for the rest of their school career, then the evidence in these chapters is unequivocal: retention does not work. But this standard requires that retention effectively redress *all* these children's problems, including those traceable to circumstances outside school. Does anyone really think retention is the solution to the school difficulties of poor-performing, disadvantaged children? That is *not* the standard implicit in matched control evaluations, which ask whether repeaters are keeping up with (or surpassing) other poor-performing children, none of whom may be doing particularly well academically. The criterion is whether they are doing "better than expected," although that level may be far below what we would want for them.

The analyses in these three chapters present evidence relevant to all these criteria for judging retention's effectiveness, including the most stringent. The picture for all save the one requiring parity is basically positive.

First grade repeaters' test performance did not improve in the long run, but otherwise even their profiles generally favored retention. During their repeated year, all three retainee groups drew closer than they had been before to the performance level of promoted children, and for second and third grade retainees at least part of these gains were sustained for as long as we were able to track them (through seventh grade in these same-grade comparisons). In no instance did these youngsters actually reach the performance level of promoted children, but they often were close in comparisons with the poor performers (gauging repeaters' standing postretention relative to that of classmates they join after being held back).

The indications were even more favorable when adjustments were made for testing levels prior to retention and for other risk factors that complicate repeaters' school adjustment. These adjusted comparisons indicate whether retainees' test scores relative to those of promoted children are better or worse than expected in light of preexisting conditions. Often retainees' scores were not significantly below those of promoted children in these comparisons: indeed sometimes they were ahead; almost always they were closer than they had been before retention. To be clear, the issue here is not whether retention "fixes" these children's problems. Controlled comparisons, rather, ask whether retainees after retention are doing better or worse than other academically challenged children who have not been held back. These comparisons provide our best evidence about retention's effects, and from them we conclude that it often helps children.

Test scores and marks afford complementary perspectives on retention. It turns out that the way they are affected by retention is complementary, too. Test scores show that repeaters learn more; marks show that this enhanced learning is rewarded in the classroom. The 2-year dip-and-recovery pattern seen for test scores is evident also in retainees' marks. Their marks go from bad to worse until they are held back, but on repeating the grade they improve – not to the level of promoted children, but still to a higher level than before.

This pattern is clear and is replicated in the experience of all three repeater groups. Our evidence, unfortunately, sheds little light on the underlying dynamic and so leaves many questions still in need of answer. Teachers no doubt feel uneasy about holding children back twice, especially in the same grade, so it is possible they shade their standards for repeaters. This is unlikely the entire explanation, though, because many children are held back twice. More important, the testing data confirm that after retention these children in fact know more of what is expected of them, so it seems likely their academic performance actually has improved.

After the repeated year all three retainee groups come close to keeping pace. Their actual marks are comparatively low, but their adjusted marks are usually either equal to (in the case of all promoted children) or ahead of (in the case of the poor-performing comparison group) those of other children. The mark trends are favorable throughout, even more so than those for test scores.

Retained children never shine academically, but they "get by," whereas before retention they were losing ground. For retention to be helpful does not require that marginal and below-marginal students be transformed into academic superstars; just to be keeping up with others is an accomplishment for children who previously knew only failure.

Academic consequences of retention are not the only considerations, of course; there is concern, too, about the possible stigma of retention, and then later about whether repeating of a grade disposes children to leave school early. Even if retention helped children academically, we would still worry whether it assaulted their sense of self or pushed them out of school without a degree. But the evidence just reviewed on retention's positive contributions to repeaters' school performance suggests there are countervailing forces at play. In school systems like the one being studied, where retention rates are high, retainees probably do not attract much attention; there is anonymity as well as strength in numbers that may shelter their self-esteem. At the same time, these youngsters are getting positive signals from their teachers in the form of improved marks. Assuming this positive feedback registers with children, it ought to mitigate emotional repercussions of retention and strengthen attachment to school, especially later on, after the failure itself has faded into the background.

The pattern of improved marks after retention has implications for the stigma issue, but certainly it is not the only consideration. Class-mates may tease repeaters, teachers may communicate their doubts in other ways, and children in such a situation still may feel self-conscious despite their new-found success. For these reasons and others like them, the issue needs to be addressed directly – inferring children's reactions from marking trends is too great a remove.

9

The Stigma of Retention

This chapter deals with possible stigmatizing effects of retention, exploring children's reactions to the experience of retention by way of interview data secured directly from them. It is important to know whether practices intended to help children are harmful instead. One such apprehension about retention – that it sets children back academically – turns out to be mainly unfounded. Another apprehension is that children are scarred emotionally by retention, and this may be the case even if they are better off academically.

Retainees are conspicuous. Their failure is public. Parents, classmates, and teachers all know who repeaters are. Teachers and parents may not be as blunt in communicating their feelings as are classmates, but if parents doubt repeaters' abilities or if teachers resent having them in their classes, children likely sense such feelings. Most BSS repeaters, in line with retention rates nationally, are held back in grades 1 through 3. In these years children's sense of self and academic self-image are just taking form (see, e.g., Stipek 1984; Weisz and Cameron 1985). At this life stage, when children's personal resources are frail, difficulties in relationships with others carry special weight.

BSS children were initially interviewed during the first quarter of first grade,[1] and then again in the spring, between third-quarter and fourth-quarter report cards. In subsequent years individual interviews were conducted in fall and spring (Years 2, 4, 6, 7, and 8).[2]

[1] Their ages when they began school ranged from 5 years, 8 months to 6 years, 8 months. Children repeating first grade when the project commenced were excluded.

[2] In Years 2 and 4 spring reports are used when available. In Years 6 and 8 self-image questions were posed only in the fall; in Year 6 locus of control was not measured at all;

No direct questions about retention per se were posed in these interviews, but they contain a great deal of information about these children's attitudes toward school, about themselves, and about how well they expect to do academically. If retention shakes children's self-confidence or colors their thinking, this effect should be revealed in their ideas about self and school.

First grade repeaters are the main focus in this chapter. They are by far the largest group, they were the youngest when held back, their academic problems are the most severe, and their situations are the most complicated and disorderly (i.e., they more often than other retainees are put into special education or are held back a second time). For these reasons, first grade repeaters would seem prime candidates for emotional suffering. Procedural considerations also dictate this focus. Because interviews were not conducted in Year 3, first graders are the only repeater group for whom the fail–repeat cycle can be monitored in the same detailed way used for test scores and marks. Interviews from Years 1 and 2 cover their failed and repeated years; their later thinking is captured in interviews conducted in Year 4 and beyond. No fieldwork was carried out in the third year, and this hiatus leaves critical gaps in the case of second and third grade repeaters: for example, Year 3 is the repeated year for second grade repeaters and the failed year for third grade repeaters.

The missing interview years (Years 3 and 5 – and, in practical terms, Year 7, too, as too few interviews were done that year to be used) also preclude constructing same-grade comparisons in a consistent way across repeater groups. For that reason, this chapter reports same-age comparisons only. We favor same-grade comparisons for reasons already discussed and prefer doing both. However, for children's attitudes curriculum coverage is not particularly an issue – it is not likely that children who have been through third grade should *for that reason* think better or worse of school and of their academic prospects than do second graders. Reference group theory and theories of reflected appraisal (Goethals 1987; Richer 1976; Ruble 1982; Suls 1993) point to the immediate classroom context as weighing most heavily on children's thinking. After retention, repeaters and promoted children who are the same age will be in different grades, and their attitudes will form in reaction to

in Year 8 it was measured in fall only; and in Year 7 sample coverage is sparse, as that year only off-time sixth graders were interviewed (for that reason Year 7 data are used only in a supplementary way).

their surroundings. Still, to know that repeaters are more upbeat, or less so, after their retention compared to other children of the same age informs the issue even if we cannot align their views on a grade-level basis.

First Grade Repeaters' Thinking in the Failed Year, the Repeated Year, and Afterward

Academic Self-Image

Does retention shake children's self-confidence? First grade repeaters' attitude averages are plotted in Figures 9.1–9.5 against those for all pro-moted children and those for the comparison group of poor performers (exact values are given in Tables 9.A1 through 9.A5 in the chapter appendix; values for second grade repeaters, third grade repeaters, and the combined group of fourth through seventh grade repeaters also are reported there). Repeaters do have negative ideas about themselves, but *these predate retention*. The plots begin with Year 1, before retention. First grade retainees' scores are lowest on each measure. Consider the pattern in Figure 9.1, which presents average scores on a scale that ranks children's academic self-image. Children were asked how "good" or "bad"

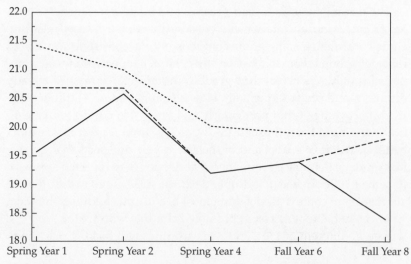

FIGURE 9.1. Academic self-esteem averages for first grade retainees (—), never-retained pupils (··), and the poor-performing comparison group (---)

they are at reading, writing, arithmetic, learning new things quickly, and being a good student, with response options ranging from very good (5) to very bad (1). The score is the sum of children's responses to these five items, and so can range from 5 to 25 (alpha reliability averages 0.59 across years).

Scale averages are skewed high overall. Most are about 20 points, equivalent to a self-assessment of "good" on each of the five items. Within years (and even between years), most differences among groups are not large. In Year 1, the full sample of never-retained children has the highest average, 21.4, followed by never-retained poor performers.[3] First grade retainees are lowest: their 19.6 average is nearly 2 points behind the average of never-retained children and more than a full point behind the poor performers' average. This gap of 2 points, the largest difference seen, is about 0.67 standard deviation.

Earlier we saw that first grade retainees test poorly, receive low marks, and have other problems at the start of first grade. It is likely that these children realize they are not doing well and that classroom dynamics reflect this also. Seeing children at the very beginning of their school career burdened by self-doubt is a serious matter, but at this stage grade retention is not the issue. Problems before children are held back, even if rooted in classroom experience as these probably are, constitute the *backdrop to retention*.

Most studies do not establish children's preretention status this way and so have no anchor for evaluating children's postretention status. Here we see that first grade repeaters' academic self-assessment in Year 2 is *higher* than it was in first grade, not lower. Their academic self-image increases by 1 point between spring Year 1 and spring Year 2, the largest increase registered by any group (see Table 9.A1).[4] In contrast, the Year 2 average for the never-retained group is 0.4 point *below* their Year 1 average (the largest drop registered by any group), while the comparison group average is unchanged.

Improvement in repeaters' feelings about themselves in the student role implies retention cannot be only a burden. These children's marks and test scores improve markedly when they go through the grade for a

[3] In Table 9.A1 we see additionally that third grade repeaters and fourth through seventh grade repeaters start out with self-esteem averages close to those of the poor-performing comparison group.
[4] The next-largest increase – that is, 0.3 point – is registered by second grade repeaters; the finding seems anomalous because this is the year they are held back.

second time, and this improvement apparently sends a positive signal. It is key to note that first grade repeaters' average is still below promoted children's, however, so without a preretention baseline this favorable showing would be misread.

Moreover, favorable signs are not limited to self-image. On all the measures examined in this chapter, first grade repeaters' averages start out lower than promoted children's and in most instances show the greatest upward movement between Years 1 and 2. This improvement mimics changes in their academic standing as seen in previous chapters.

The remaining columns of Figure 9.1 reveal that retainees' self-image scores go down after first grade, in Years 4, 6, and 8. In Year 4 their average is well below that in Year 2 and even lower than in first grade, which was initially the lowest of any group.

The repeated year "boost" thus is short-lived, so one possibility is that problems surrounding retention finally catch up with these children. But the experiences of other children over the same interval suggest another interpretation, because all children's self-confidence in the academic area drops over time, not just repeaters' (e.g., Eccles and Midgley 1990; Stipek 1984; Weisz and Cameron 1985). In fact, every group is lower in Year 4 than in Year 2 (see Table 9.A1, as well as Figure 9.1), and first grade repeaters' decline is about midrange, not exaggerated as it might be if retention were a dominant consideration.

Over the longer interval from Year 1 to Year 4 first grade repeaters fall back about 0.4 point, the smallest net decline of any group (second grade repeaters are closest, at 0.5 point). By way of comparison, the never-retained Year 4 average is 1.4 points below their Year 1 average and never-retained poor performers' average is 1.5 points below. First grade repeaters' level of academic self-regard thus holds up better than other children's. This positive pattern continues in Year 6, when averages are not much different from those of Year 4. In Year 8, however, scores fall sharply, down a full point from Year 6 (18.4 versus 19.4). During this period promoted youngsters' averages have either increased slightly (i.e., the poor performers') or held steady (the full never-retained sample's).

This sharp fall in self-assessments between Years 6 and 8 leaves first grade repeaters 1.2 points *behind* their score from the spring of first grade, the time of retention. But never-retained children also are further back at this point, and some of the other retained groups have dropped off even more than first grade repeaters (third grade retainees and the combined group of fourth through seventh grade repeaters are almost 2 points back; see Table 9.A1).

The picture, if not mixed, at least is complicated, and by Year 8 first grade retainees' improved standing relative to promoted children's has evaporated. Recall, though, that these comparisons are not grade aligned. We said previously that this might not be a fatal limitation when examining attitudes, and this seems likely grade by grade. But *crossing levels of schooling*, as these comparisons do, may be more serious. In Year 6, first grade repeaters still are in elementary school, most in fifth grade; those held back twice are in fourth grade. Their ideas about the self at this point are still relatively favorable, at least compared with those of never-retained children, who in Year 6 already moved to middle school. By Year 8, though, first grade repeaters too have reached middle school, and at that point their self-confidence slips badly, relative to that of others and to their own position from before middle school.[5]

Middle school is at least 5 years beyond first grade retainees' repeated year, and it seems unreasonable to blame retention for problems that arise so much later. Other research shows that the middle school transition challenges children generally (Eccles, Lord, and Midgley 1991), and previous chapters establish that retainees had difficulty sustaining academic advances from the elementary years into middle school. The Year 8 drop in academic self-evaluation thus aligns with academic performance trends seen previously, suggesting that much of the shoring up that follows retention in elementary school is overwhelmed by middle school's heightened demands.[6]

In middle school curricular tracking becomes more formal and rigid, and retainees, as seen in the next chapter, tend to be relegated to low-level, remedial courses. Children may not be harmed by retention academically or socioemotionally in the short term, but we suspect that it does not equip them to keep up over the long term when they move into middle school and possibly again later, when they make the transition to high school (e.g., Roderick 1995a).

---

[5] And relative also to those of most other repeaters; the tables in the appendix to this chapter show this.

[6] As mentioned, we also interviewed children in Year 7 who were just entering middle school, including 63 first grade repeaters. Their Year 7 average on the academic self-esteem scale is 18.6, just a bit above their Year 8 average, and well below the figure from Year 6. The dropoff for them seen in Figure 9.1 thus does seem to be a middle-grades phenomenon, documented in Simmons and Blyth (1987) and in reports of Eccles and her colleagues (1984; 1989; 1990; 1991).

Expectations for Marks in Reading and Math

Other attitudinal data, beginning with children's expectations for their marks, mirror the general pattern for self-image. Expectations for upcoming report card marks are specific and reflect academic self-confidence. Children who expect to do better in school generally do (Alexander, Entwisle, and Bedinger 1994; Entwisle and Hayduk 1982). Figures 9.2 and 9.3 report spring expectations for reading and math marks, when in one-on-one interviews children were asked to guess their upcoming marks at year's end.

Expectations are coded in the same way as marks, with values 4 to 1 assigned, respectively, to mark expectations of excellent, good, satisfactory, and unsatisfactory.[7] All Year 1 mark expectation averages are above 3, most well above (see Figures 9.2 and 9.3; also Tables 9.A2 and 9.A3); that corresponds to an average expectation of better than "good," at a time when marks themselves are averaging midway between satisfactory and good (e.g., across the entire cohort, the average fourth-quarter Year 1 reading mark is 2.4). Optimism thus is pervasive, a pattern seen in other studies, too (e.g., Entwisle and Hayduk 1978). First grade retainees expect the lowest marks in both areas (3.0 in reading and 3.2 in math), but the marks they receive are lower still. We saw in Chapter 8 that every one of them fails reading at year's end, and their marks in math are not much better, averaging 1.3. In comparison, never-retained children average 2.7 and 3.0 in reading and math, respectively, so their expectations (3.4 in both areas) are more closely aligned with their actual performance. The expectation–performance gap is large for everyone, but it is much greater among repeaters.

Whether such elevated expectations are good or bad is not clear (see Alexander, Entwisle, and Bedinger 1994; Entwisle and Hayduk 1978). Here, however, the question is whether children's expectations, despite their high skew, are colored by retention. First grade repeaters have the lowest initial expectations, and never-retained children the highest, paralleling the pattern of their marks. What happens to repeaters' confidence *after* being singled out as failures?

[7] In Years 1, 2, and 4 we asked about expectations in reading. In Year 6, when some children were still in elementary school and some were in middle school, we asked about expectations in "reading/English." In Year 8 we asked separately about expectations in reading and English. When a response is not available for reading, the English expectation is used, collapsed to the elementary school metric. This parallels the procedure used for marks in middle school.

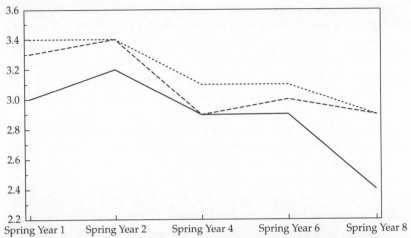

FIGURE 9.2. Average reading mark expectations for first grade retainees (—), never-retained pupils (··), and the poor-performing comparison group (---).

Contrary to what might be predicted, first grade repeaters' performance expectations in Year 2 are not lower. Rather, they either increase (by 0.2 point in reading) or hold steady (in math). These are not dramatic changes, but they exceed never-retained children's (both groups). Promoted youngsters' math expectations do not fall off during this interval, but Table 9.A3 shows modest Year 2 declines among some of the other repeater groups.

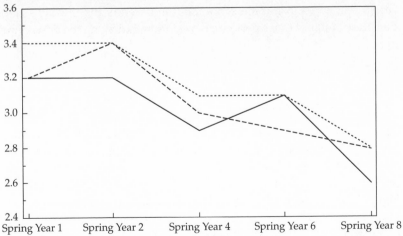

FIGURE 9.3. Average math mark expectations for first grade retainees (—), never-retained pupils (··), and the poor-performing comparison group (---).

Beyond Year 2, expectations trail off for everyone, probably because children become more adept at processing mark feedback and begin to appreciate that their expectations and marks are misaligned (e.g., Nicholls 1978; Parsons and Ruble 1977; Stipek 1984). In Years 4 through 8 children's expectations range mostly between satisfactory and good, still high, but considerably closer to their actual marks than in Years 1 and 2.

First grade repeaters' expectations drop along with everyone else's but hold up better than most, at least through Year 6. In both reading and math, their Year 6 averages are the closest of any group to their Year 1 level, with a net decline of just 0.1 unit (2.9 versus 3.0) in reading and 0.1 unit (3.1 versus 3.2) in math, compared to declines of 0.3 unit for all never-retained children and the poor-performing comparison group. None of these differences is large, but first grade repeaters' expectations hold up at least as well as other children's, and perhaps a bit better. This pattern up through grade 6 is hard to reconcile with a view of the retention experience as a hovering dark cloud.

The picture in Year 8 looks quite different, however, and resembles academic self-regard. First grade repeaters' expectations drop sharply between Years 6 and 8 by about half a marking unit in each area. These declines are the largest registered by any group over this period – for example, never-retained children's expectations dip only from 0.1 to 0.3 point. As a result, first grade repeaters' and promoted youngsters' expectations in Year 8 are both about 0.6 marking unit behind their respective Year 1 levels. Whatever "advantage" repeaters might have had through Year 6 dissipates in middle school, but apparently the middle school transition, and not the experience of retention, is driving the downward trend.

Satisfaction with School

Two items measure satisfaction with school. One asks whether children find school work "dull" (coded 1) or "interesting" (coded 2). The other asks whether they "like school a lot" (coded 3), "think it's just OK" (coded 2), or "don't like it much at all" (coded 1). The measure used in Figure 9.4 is the sum of spring scores on these two items, so values can range from 2 to 5, with higher values reflecting more favorable sentiment (detailed results are reported in Table 9.A4).

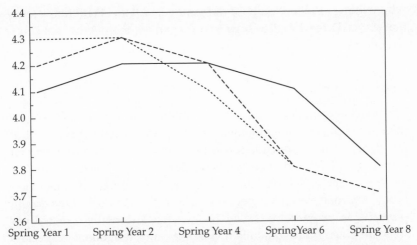

FIGURE 9.4. School satisfaction averages for first grade retainees (—), never-retained pupils (--), and the poor-performing comparison group (---).

All the Year 1 averages are in the 4.0 range (out of a possible 5.0), but first grade repeaters, at 4.1, again start out lowest. Their average is 0.1 unit below that of the poor performers and 0.2 unit below that of the full sample of never-retained children. With the standard deviation (samplewide) for this two-item scale 0.9 unit, the spread in averages across groups is small, and smaller than for other measures already reviewed.

First grade repeaters' average school satisfaction is a bit higher in Year 2 (by 0.1 unit), as are most of the other indicators. In Years 4 and 6 liking of school drops for all students, but the decline is smaller among first grade repeaters than among others. As a result, in Year 6 their average is the highest. The changes themselves are trivially small, but during the later years of elementary school, first grade repeaters say they like school more than any of the other groups.

Between Years 6 and 8 school satisfaction scores continue to drop, with all below 4.0 and with first grade repeaters falling back 0.3. This is the largest decline for them and again it overlaps their elementary-to-middle-school transition, a pattern evident in other studies, also (Blumenfeld, Pintrich, Meece, and Wessels 1982; Epstein and McPartland 1976). Even so, the other groups' liking for school continues to slip as well, and their earlier, steeper falloff leaves both promoted groups in Year 8 a little below first grade retainees. As a result, in middle school liking of school is about the same regardless of children's reten-tion status. These data thus suggest no negative consequences specific to retention.

Sense of Control

The final measure examined in this chapter ranks children according to their sense of control – whether they tend to attribute events that af-fect them mainly to outside forces (an external orientation) or to their own actions (an internal one). Often referred to as *locus of control* (Rot-ter 1966), such scales are intended to measure feelings of personal ef-ficacy. Internally oriented persons tend to be more self-directed and proactive in response to challenges, whereas externally oriented per-sons are given more to fatalism, passivity, and resignation, especially in the face of adversity. Of most immediate relevance, internally driven proactivity appears to carry over to academic striving, giving internally oriented children a modest edge over others (e.g., Coleman et al. 1966; Gottfried 1985; Stipek and Weisz 1981). Though different from the other kinds of attitudes considered in this chapter, sense of control is no less relevant. If retention impairs children's sense of personal efficacy, this is a serious consequence. If retention increases feelings of impotence or powerlessness, from there would be a short step to psychological disengagement. Does being held back prompt a sense of fatalism, as might be suspected?

When the BSS began, suitable scales to measure control feelings in 5-year-olds in the inner city were not extant. The measure used in Figure 9.5 is cobbled together from portions of two scales designed for use with young middle class children, the Stanford Preschool Internal–External Scale (Mischel, Zeiss, and Zeiss 1974) and the Crandall Intellec-tual Achievement Responsibility Questionnaire (Crandall, Katkovsky, and Crandall 1965). The Stanford scale is designed to rate children in terms of their general internal–external orientation – that is, whether events occur as a result of the children's own action (internal control) or as a result of external forces (external control). All items use a paired-choice format. The following is a sample item:

> When you are happy, are you happy (a) because somebody was nice to you, or (b) because you did something fun?

Response (b) is the internal response. The original scale is balanced between good outcome questions and bad outcome questions, but of

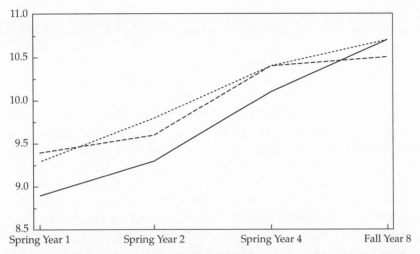

FIGURE 9.5. Locus-of-control averages for first grade retainees (—), never-retained pupils (··), and the poor-performing comparison group (---)

the six items used in our interviews, only the three positive ones proved adequate psychometrically.

The Crandall scale rates children in terms of their internal–external orientation specifically in the academic domain. The original scale consists of 34 items, again forced choice. We use three positive items from this scale, too, again because of their superior psychometric properties. Wording was altered in minor ways to make items more intelligible. For example, in the original item *solve* was used rather than *put . . . together*.

> If you put a puzzle together quickly, is that (a) because it wasn't a very hard puzzle, or (b) because you worked on it carefully?

Response (b) is the internal option.

The six questions (three from each scale) were asked in the fall and spring of Years 1, 2, and 4, and in the fall of Year 8.[8] Internal options are scored 2 and external ones are scored 1, so scores can range from 6 to 12. Reliability coefficients for the scale constructions hover around 0.50, lower than we would prefer, but serviceable. Spring averages are reported in Figure 9.5 when available (see Table 9.A5 also, for the detailed comparisons).

[8] Year 6 data are not available on this measure.

As has been true throughout, first grade repeaters start out lowest. Their Year 1 average internal control self-rating in Figure 9.5 is 8.9; promoted children have averages of 9.3 and 9.4. This puts first grade repeaters about half a point below never-retained children, roughly a third of a standard deviation.[9]

Averages in Year 2 are substantially higher than in Year 1, as first grade repeaters' increase along with everyone else's (by about 0.4 point). Not shown in the displays, though, are some details of first graders' experience that makes their pattern distinctive. Their fall average in the second year, as they begin their repeated grade, is lower, not higher, than their average from the previous spring.[10] Hence, the gain in first grade retainees' feelings of internal control by the end of their repeated year in fact represents a turnaround for them – their sense of control had decreased by about half a point from fall of first grade. Scores of two other groups also decline over this period (by 0.1 point), but the other groups either held steady or rose modestly.

The experience of failure apparently does compromise children's self-confidence temporarily, but they rebound by the spring of their repeated year and from that point forward scores track modestly upward, paralleling those of most other groups. In fact, in Year 8 first grade repeaters' average of 10.7 is 0.2 point above that of the comparison group of poor performers and is the same as that of the full never-retained sample. Their Year 8 average is not the highest, but neither is it the lowest.

These favorable indications involving locus of control are consistent with the trends for general academic self-regard, specific performance expectations in reading and math, and general liking of school. Improvement after retention is evident for each measure, and for most children this improvement is at least maintained into Year 8. Still, the Year 8 picture is mixed because several measures drop sharply that year for repeaters.

For retention in first, second, and third grades to explain problems first detectable in Year 8 means that problems originating in the retention experience would be delayed until then. To us, this sequence seems unlikely. Children's immediate reaction in all the attitudinal areas is

---

[9] In the fall of first grade, first grade repeaters' average was 9.1, a bit higher than the spring figure reported in Table 9.5. They are the only group whose average dropped from fall to spring. Academic difficulties that year apparently inclined them to more of an external orientation.

[10] Their decline from the spring of Year 1 to fall of Year 2 is 0.3 point, from 8.9 to 8.6. This is the largest decline over the interval.

positive, just as it is for academics. The later problems suggested by these trend comparisons most likely involve pressures peculiar to the middle school environment and the challenges faced by marginal students at that point in their schooling.[11]

Retention and Children's Thinking: Regression-Adjusted Comparisons

The trends involving affective measures are consistent, but by now we know not to read too much into simple trends. As before, retained and promoted children differ a priori in many ways, as the Year 1 comparisons in Figures 9.1 to 9.5 show so clearly. First grade repeaters *before being held back* rank at the bottom on all five sense-of-self and attitudinal measures.

Beyond Year 1, preexisting differences, including those grounded in children's early academic difficulties, are confounded with the retention experience. Simply comparing averages makes no allowance for these differences. Just as for test scores and marks, initial differences between repeaters and nonrepeaters need to be allowed for. Still, it is unlikely such adjustments will be as consequential here as previously because repeaters (at least those held back in first grade, who thus far have been our main concern) do not have especially negative or self-critical attitudes after retention, even in the simple trend comparisons. There are no negative indications to begin with as there were with the academic indicators, so instead of guarding against exaggerating retention's adverse effects, the checks here are used more to ensure an accurate reading of children's initial status. Also, attitudes are not as reliably measured or as stable as test scores or marks over time; nor are they as highly confounded with other potential risk factors. For example, Year 8 CAT-R performance is correlated 0.40 with mother's education, 0.39 with the

---

[11] As has been the case throughout this volume, we need to be careful that trend comparisons reflect real changes in children's thinking and are not artifactual, the results of changes in sample composition over time. As a check, all the averages reported in this section were recomputed using only children for whom data are available in Year 8. Most of these are youngsters who remain in Baltimore City Public Schools the entire period of this study, and for them data coverage is reasonably complete. This restriction reduces group sizes in the early years by 50% to 65%, but despite this shrinkage, most of the averages change very little. And when changes do occur, they tend to sharpen the contrasts just reviewed, not weaken them. For instance, in several tables, the Year 1 averages for first and second grade repeaters are a bit lower than those reported here, whereas most of the others do not change. This puts repeaters even further back at the beginning, making their later progress even more impressive.

family income indicator, and 0.50 with CAT-R performance from the fall of first grade. The last reflects stability or continuity in performance trends over time (for all children, repeaters and promoted). Correlations involving the Year 8 measure of academic self-esteem are generally much smaller: 0.10 with mother's education and 0.07 with family income; 0.11 with fall first grade CAT-R; and only 0.12 with the counterpart Year 1 measure, the last representing stability over time.

Almost all the correlations of retention with self-esteem are statistically significant, so children's ideas about the self indeed are socially patterned, reflect their abilities, and are somewhat stable over time.[12] Still, as is typical for affective measures generally, none is especially large, and except for race/ethnicity, all are much smaller than the corresponding associations involving CAT performance. Because of the modest overlap between measures of attitude and preretention controls, the statistical adjustments probably will not alter the picture much.

In making these statistical adjustments, we again need to allow for the lack of pupil interview data from Year 3, which complicates matters for second and third grade repeaters especially. For third grade repeaters there is no baseline measure from their failed year, and for second grade repeaters the repeated year part of the fail–repeat cycle cannot be examined. Nothing can be done about the repeated year gap for second grade retainees, but for third grade repeaters data from Year 2 are used as a preretention baseline. For both groups the postretention period is well covered.

Baseline data from the year of retention are used when available to adjust for conditions up to the time of retention. As before, adjustments also are made for demographic factors, including family income level and gender, and CAT performance from the fall of the failed year. Preretention attitudes are used as further controls – the first year measure for first grade repeaters, the second year measure for second and third grade repeaters (the latter because a third year measure is not available).

---

[12] That we see any correlation between Year 1 and Year 8 expressions of academic self-esteem is noteworthy, given the length of the interval and the modest reliability of the measures. Over-time stability in children's ideas about self increases as they get older. The Year 8 measure correlates 0.12 with the Year 1 measure, 0.22 with that in Year 2, 0.29 with the Year 4 measure, and 0.45 with that in Year 6. This pattern also holds for most of the measures considered in this chapter. There are two important implications: first, children's sense of self becomes more stable as they mature (in Year 8, most are age 14); second, and conversely, their ideas about self are more malleable, and hence more susceptible to influence, during the early formative years. This is one reason for being especially interested in young children's reactions to retention.

Apart from these additional Time 1 controls, the statistical procedures in this chapter parallel those used in Chapters 7 and 8. The statistics reported are metric regression coefficients that estimate average differences between retained and promoted youngsters, other factors being equal.[13]

Academic Self-Esteem

Table 9.1 covers academic self-esteem, with separate columns for outcomes in Years 1, 2, 4, 6, and 8. Within years, differences are reported separately for first, second, and third grade repeaters.[14]

The first estimates are from regression equations that yield average scale score differences between the retention groups, identical to properly weighted differences that could be derived from Table 9.A1. For first grade repeaters in first grade, these initial differences are quite large, exceeding a full scale point in both never-retained comparisons. The question then is what happens when these large initial differences are adjusted for children's demographic characteristics and entry-level CAT performance (the second pair of entries), and for the compounding of children's later problems (i.e., double retention and/or special education placement)? With these adjustments, the differences shrink by about a third to a half (Table 9.1), and that for poor performers slips to nonsignificance. But even after adjustments, first grade retainees' academic self-regard still lags behind all promoted youngsters', even with adjustments for special education assignments and the experience of double retainees.[15]

In Year 2 retention's consequences for first grade repeaters should appear, but in the second year their academic self-image is like that of other children their age (i.e., their original classmates' responses from the same interview cycle). None of the differences is statistically significant and all are quite small. This pattern is at odds with the widely held notion that repeaters' sense of self is compromised by the stigma of

---

[13] The tables also report levels of explained variance (the R^2 statistics at the bottom of each column) for the most inclusive equations. Most are in the vicinity of 0.10 or less, indicating that variance in these attitudes is not well explained by the set of predictors being used. This is typical in studies of attitude and personality development involving young children.

[14] Differences between fourth through seventh grade repeaters and never-retained children are not reported but were included in the analysis.

[15] In contrast to those in the academic area, the adjustments here are not of great consequence.

TABLE 9.1. *Regression-Adjusted Self-Esteem Differences: First, Second, and Third Grade Retainees vs. Never-Retained Students or the Poor-Performing Comparison Group*

	Spring Year 1[a]	Spring Year 2		Spring Year 4			Fall Year 6			Fall Year 8		
	First Grade ret	First Grade ret	Second Grade ret	First Grade ret	Second Grade ret	Third Grade ret	First Grade ret	Second Grade ret	Third Grade ret	First Grade ret	Second Grade ret	Third Grade ret
With no adjustments[b]												
Ret vs. never-ret	−1.79**	−0.45	−0.79*	−0.71*	−0.51	−0.55	−0.42	−0.84	−0.48	−1.42**	−0.91	−0.94
Ret vs. poor-perf comparison group	−1.11**	−0.13	−0.46	−0.01	0.21	0.15	0.10	−0.24	0.06	−1.14**	−0.63	−0.69
With fall CAT and demographic adjustments[c]												
Ret vs. never-ret	−1.14**	−0.06	0.12	−0.32	0.22	0.40	−0.24	−0.41	0.02	−1.31**	−0.65	−0.30
Ret vs. poor-perf comparison group	−0.57	0.19	0.41	0.42	1.09*	1.07*	0.43	0.55	0.73	−0.85	−0.14	0.03
With baseline measure adjustments[d]												
Ret vs. never-ret	—	0.20	—	−0.18	0.19	0.34	−0.08	−0.43	−0.04	−1.24**	−0.67	−0.33
Ret vs. poor-perf comparison group	—	0.32	—	0.49	0.99*	0.98	0.52	0.47	0.65	−0.81	−0.20	−0.02

With double-ret and special ed adjustments[e]

Ret vs. never-ret	−1.22**	0.42	0.24	−0.26	0.06	0.27	−0.36	−0.66	−0.23	−1.59**	−0.97	−0.50
Ret vs. poor-perf comparison group	−0.47	0.49	0.52	0.60	1.01*	0.97	0.51	0.45	0.58	−0.90	−0.29	−0.08

Adj R^2

Ret vs. never-ret[f]	0.10	0.16	0.13	0.07	0.14	0.15	0.12	0.16	0.15	0.14	0.17	0.18
Ret vs. poor-perf comparison group	0.09	0.16	0.15	0.08	0.17	0.18	0.12	0.18	0.17	0.13	0.16	0.17

[a] In Year 1 only first grade contrasts are reported; in Year 2 separate analyses are performed for first and second grade repeaters, using the moving baseline controls appropriate for each; from Year 4 through Year 8, separate analyses are performed for first, second, and third grade repeaters, using the moving baseline controls appropriate for each.

[b] These regressions adjust for differences among the several retainee groups and between retainees and those never retained.

[c] These regressions adjust additionally for CAT scores from the fall of the appropriate baseline year and for demographic factors: race/ethnicity, gender, mother's education, lunch subsidy status (eligible or not), number of siblings, age as of the fall of first grade, and living in a two-parent household at the start of first grade.

[d] These regressions adjust additionally for self-esteem scores from the appropriate baseline year. For first and second grade repeaters, in the baseline year these are the outcome measures and are not used as controls (indicated by a dash in table body).

[e] These regressions adjust additionally for differences associated with special education alone, double retention alone, and both combined.

[f] R^2 statistics are for the most inclusive equation in each column.

** Signifies differences significant at the .01 level; * differences significant at the .05 level.

retention but agrees with other studies (e.g., Pierson and Connell 1992; Reynolds 1992).

Prior research on retention, in fact, often reports equivalence for repeaters and promoted children on academic and attitudinal outcomes (see Chapter 2). This equivalence usually is interpreted as showing that retention does not help, but retainee attitudes that are no different from those of promoted children are a positive finding: either concerns about stigmatizing effects are exaggerated, or negative effects are offset by other experiences that help sustain children's sense of self. In either event, the net effect is neutral.

Examining scores only after retention will give a misleading or incomplete picture, as was pointed out in Chapter 2. Retainees' scores before they were held back show that the Year 2 pattern of "no difference" is a substantial improvement over Year 1, because these repeaters' scores lagged far behind promoted children's. Over-time comparisons afford a key perspective because, as shown here, retention precedes improvement in retainees' self-regard and their scores rise to match those of other children.

Most differences in Years 4 and 6 fall short of significance. In Year 8, though, first grade repeaters again lag behind, with differences relative to all promoted children not explained by preretention factors. The adjusted difference against the poor performers is large, but the sample sizes in Year 8 are too small for a difference of this magnitude (almost a full point) to be statistically significant. Still, the drop is suggestive.

The adjusted comparisons in Table 9.1 are the best evidence from the BSS archive on the existence of stigma. These comparisons bear out the descriptive trends: first grade repeaters' academic sense of self, which is depressed in first grade, reflects difficulties that preceded retention. During the repeated year, their self-confidence improves, so their attitudes about the self rise to roughly the same level as other children's, a level they sustain throughout the remaining elementary years. Scores drop off again in Year 8, the first middle school assessment of repeaters' self-attitudes.

The second panel gives comparisons for second grade repeaters; the third panel gives them for third grade repeaters. There are few significant differences even before making adjustments, and most often the adjusted comparisons favor repeaters when differences are large enough to be statistically reliable (e.g., entries in the spring Year 4 panel). However, these repeater groups too evidence slippage in Year 8, so the setback at the middle school transition is broad-based.

Other Outcomes

The same basic story that describes self-image is retold for the other attitudinal measures: reading and math mark expectations in Tables 9.2 and 9.3, school satisfaction in Table 9.4, and locus of control in Table 9.5. In all these analyses, most of the significant differences involve first grade repeaters and are not especially numerous. Significant differences almost always exist in Year 1, before retention, and then do not appear again until Year 8, when repeaters are in middle school. Before adjustments, first grade retainees lag behind all promoted children in reading expectations, math expectations, and locus of control (differences involving the school satisfaction measure are insignificant throughout). This evidence is troubling, because it reveals how demographic factors and entering testing levels, over which children have no control, can compromise children's self-confidence.

For mark expectations, differences involving first grade repeaters again become significant in Year 8 and generally remain so even after statistical adjustments (including an adjustment for first grade mark expectations). Hence, the middle school setback is most apparent in attitudinal measures that relate to academics (i.e., self-esteem and mark expectations), and among first grade repeaters specifically. For second and third grade repeaters, significant positive differences are more numerous than are negative differences, and these positive differences begin to appear when preretention statistical adjustments are phased in.

Conclusions

These results give little reason to think retention imposes an emotional burden on second and third grade repeaters; however, the strongest evidence in these assessments is for first grade repeaters. They are the largest repeater group and the only repeater group whose failed and repeated years are both covered. This completeness is strategically important, because these children's low standing in their failed year, before retention, reveals their improvement in the repeated year.

We earlier argued that first grade repeaters, who are the youngest and furthest behind at the time of their retention, are those most likely to suffer emotionally from the experience. The results seem to agree: the only negative indications in the many reported comparisons involve first graders. But these negative signs do not appear until Year 8 and

TABLE 9.2. *Regression-Adjusted Reading Expectation Differences: First, Second, and Third Grade Retainees vs. Never-Retained Students or the Poor-Performing Comparison Group*

	Spring Year 1[a]	Spring Year 2		Spring Year 4			Spring Year 6			Spring Year 8		
	First Grade ret	First Grade ret	Second Grade ret	First Grade ret	Second Grade ret	Third Grade ret	First Grade ret	Second Grade ret	Third Grade ret	First Grade ret	Second Grade ret	Third Grade ret
With no adjustments[b]												
Ret vs. never-ret	−0.36**	−0.16	−0.28**	−0.14	−0.21	−0.20	−0.20	−0.22	−0.36*	−0.48**	−0.33*	−0.39*
Ret vs. poor-perf comparison group	−0.22	−0.10	−0.22	0.04	−0.02	−0.02	−0.09	−0.12	−0.24	−0.41**	−0.24	−0.30
With full CAT and demographic adjustments[c]												
Ret vs. never-ret	−0.23*	−0.09	−0.11	0.04	0.15	0.19	−0.17	−0.15	−0.13	−0.33**	−0.13	−0.18
Ret vs. poor-perf comparison group	−0.13	−0.04	−0.10	0.15	0.23	0.27	−0.04	−0.01	−0.03	−0.28*	−0.08	−0.11
With baseline measure adjustments[d]												
Ret vs. never-ret	—	−0.06	—	0.06	0.17	0.20	−0.15	−0.14	−0.13	−0.33**	−0.12	−0.17
Ret vs. poor-perf comparison group	—	−0.03	—	0.17	0.24	0.27	−0.03	0.00	−0.03	−0.28*	−0.07	−0.11

With double-ret and special ed adjustments[e]

Ret vs. never-ret	−0.18	0.05	−0.04	0.09	0.16	0.21	−0.11	−0.12	−0.11	−0.49**	−0.23	−0.20
Ret vs. poor-perf comparison group	−0.08	0.05	−0.05	0.21	0.24	0.28	0.04	0.03	−0.01	−0.36**	−0.12	−0.10

Adj R^2

Ret vs. never-ret[f]	0.07	0.10	0.10	0.08	0.13	0.13	0.06	0.06	0.09	0.18	0.20	0.20
Ret vs. poor-perf comparison group	0.07	0.11	0.10	0.09	0.15	0.15	0.05	0.06	0.11	0.17	0.19	0.19

[a] In Year 1 only first grade contrasts are reported; in Year 2 separate analyses are performed for first and second grade repeaters, using the moving baseline controls appropriate for each; from Year 4 through Year 8, separate analyses are performed for first, second, and third grade repeaters, using the moving baseline controls appropriate for each.

[b] These regressions adjust for differences among the several retainee groups and between retainees and those never retained.

[c] These regressions adjust additionally for CAT scores from the fall of the appropriate baseline year and for demographic factors: race/ethnicity, gender, mother's education, lunch subsidy status (eligible or not), number of siblings, age as of the fall of first grade, and living in a two-parent household at the start of first grade.

[d] These regressions adjust additionally for mark expectations from the appropriate baseline year.

[e] These regressions adjust additionally for differences associated with special education alone, double retention alone, and both combined.

[f] R^2 statistics are for the most inclusive equation in each column.

** Signifies differences significant at the .01 level; * differences significant at the .05 level.

TABLE 9.3. *Regression-Adjusted Math Mark Expectation Differences: First, Second, and Third Grade Retainees vs. Never-Retained Students or the Poor-Performing Comparison Group*

	Spring Year 1[a]	Spring Year 2		Spring Year 4			Spring Year 6			Spring Year 8		
	First Grade ret	First Grade ret	Second Grade ret	First Grade ret	Second Grade ret	Third Grade ret	First Grade ret	Second Grade ret	Third Grade ret	First Grade ret	Second Grade ret	Third Grade ret
With no adjustments[b]												
Ret vs. never-ret	−0.27**	−0.19*	−0.02	−0.24*	−0.17	0.09	0.00	−0.16	−0.04	−0.25*	−0.16	−0.29
Ret vs. poor-perf comparison group	−0.08	−0.24*	−0.07	−0.11	−0.04	0.19	0.15	0.00	0.11	−0.17	−0.08	−0.21
With fall CAT and demographic adjustments[c]												
Ret vs. never-ret	−0.15	−0.17	0.18	0.05	0.18	0.45**	0.11	−0.06	0.20	−0.16	−0.07	−0.11
Ret vs. poor-perf comparison group	0.00	−0.22	0.08	0.07	0.25	0.40*	0.25	0.16	0.30	−0.07	0.05	−0.03
With baseline measure adjustments[d]												
Ret vs. never-ret	—	−0.14	—	0.06	0.15	0.46**	0.12	−0.09	0.21	−0.16	−0.10	−0.09
Ret vs. poor-perf comparison group	—	−0.22	—	0.07	0.24	0.43*	0.25	0.14	0.33*	−0.07	0.04	0.00

With double-ret and special ed adjustments[e]

Ret vs. never-ret	−0.11	−0.14	0.18	−0.02	0.10	0.43*	0.11	−0.09	0.23	−0.33*	−0.21	−0.14
Ret vs. poor-perf comparison group	0.06	−0.23	0.07	0.02	0.22	0.41*	0.27	0.17	0.35*	−0.15	0.00	−0.01

Adj R^2

Ret vs. never-ret[f]	0.04	0.05	0.06	0.09	0.12	0.12	0.07	0.08	0.10	0.09	0.11	0.12
Ret vs. poor-perf comparison group	0.05	0.06	0.06	0.10	0.14	0.14	0.09	0.11	0.15	0.09	0.10	0.12

[a] In Year 1 only first grade contrasts are reported; in Year 2 separate analyses are performed for each; from Year 4 through Year 8, separate analyses are performed for first, second, and third grade repeaters, using the moving baseline controls appropriate for each.

[b] These regressions adjust for differences among the several retainee groups and between retainees and those never retained.

[c] These regressions adjust additionally for CAT scores from the fall of the appropriate baseline year and for demographic factors: race/ethnicity, gender, mother's education, lunch subsidy status (eligible or not), number of siblings, age as of the fall of first grade, and living in a two-parent household at the start of first grade.

[d] These regressions adjust additionally for mark expectations from the appropriate baseline year. For first and second grade repeaters, in the baseline year these are the outcome measures, so they are not used as controls (indicated by a dash in the table body).

[e] These regressions adjust additionally for differences associated with special education alone, double retention alone, and both combined.

[f] R^2 statistics are for the most inclusive equation in each column.

** Signifies differences significant at the .01 level; * differences significant at the .05 level.

TABLE 9.4. *Regression-Adjusted School Satisfaction Differences: First, Second, and Third Grade Retainees vs. Never-Retained Students or the Poor-Performing Comparison Group*

	Spring Year 1[a]	Spring Year 2		Spring Year 4			Spring Year 6			Spring Year 8		
	First Grade ret	First Grade ret	Second Grade ret	First Grade ret	Second Grade ret	Third Grade ret	First Grade ret	Second Grade ret	Third Grade ret	First Grade ret	Second Grade ret	Third Grade ret
With no adjustments[b]												
Ret vs. never-ret	−0.16	−0.12	−0.09	0.06	0.19	−0.01	0.23	0.15	−0.05	0.12	0.14	0.02
Ret vs. poor-perf comparison group	−0.07	−0.08	−0.05	−0.01	0.11	−0.08	0.26	0.19	0.00	0.06	0.08	−0.04
With fall CAT and demographic adjustments[c]												
Ret vs. never-ret	−0.09	−0.08	0.02	0.00	0.12	−0.10	0.26	0.11	−0.06	0.04	0.01	0.00
Ret vs. poor-perf comparison group	−0.03	−0.07	0.02	−0.03	0.10	−0.14	0.29	0.22	0.03	0.03	0.01	−0.01

	1	2	3	4	5	6	7	8	9	10	11	12
With baseline measure adjustments[d]												
Ret vs. never-ret	—	−0.06	—	0.01	0.11	−0.15	0.28*	0.11	−0.09	0.04	0.01	0.00
Ret vs. poor-perf comparison group	—	−0.06	—	−0.02	0.09	−0.18	0.30*	0.22	0.00	0.03	0.01	−0.02
With double-ret and special ed adjustments[c]												
Ret vs. never-ret	−0.12	−0.07	0.00	0.04	0.13	−0.12	0.21	0.07	−0.10	−0.02	−0.02	−0.01
Ret vs. poor-perf comparison group	−0.03	−0.07	0.01	−0.01	0.10	−0.17	0.25	0.20	0.00	0.00	−0.01	−0.03
Adj R^2												
Ret vs. never-ret[f]	0.03	0.10	0.04	0.08	0.10	0.10	0.06	0.05	0.05	0.05	0.05	0.05
Ret vs. poor-perf comparison group	0.03	0.10	0.04	0.08	0.11	0.11	0.07	0.06	0.06	0.05	0.05	0.05

[a] In Year 1 only first grade contrasts are reported; in Year 2 separate analyses are performed for first and second grade repeaters, using the moving baseline controls appropriate for each; from Year 4 through Year 8, separate analyses are performed for first, second, and third grade repeaters, using the moving baseline controls appropriate for each.

[b] These regressions adjust for differences among the several retainee groups and between retainees and those never retained.

[c] These regressions adjust additionally for CAT scores from the fall of the appropriate baseline year and for demographic factors: race/ethnicity, gender, mother's education, lunch subsidy status (eligible or not), number of siblings, age as of the fall of first grade, and living in a two-parent household at the start of first grade.

[d] These regressions adjust additionally for satisfaction scores from the appropriate baseline year. For first and second grade repeaters, in the baseline year these are the outcome measures, so they are not used as controls (indicated by a dash in the table body).

[e] These regressions adjust additionally for differences associated with special education alone, double retention alone, and both combined.

[f] R^2 statistics are for the most inclusive equation in each column.

* Signifies differences significant at the .05 level.

TABLE 9.5. *Regression-Adjusted Locus-of-Control Differences: First, Second, and Third Grade Retainees vs. Never-Retained Students or the Poor-Performing Comparison Group*

	Spring Year 1[a]	Spring Year 2		Spring Year 4			Fall Year 8		
	First Grade ret	First Grade ret	Second Grade ret	First Grade ret	Second Grade ret	Third Grade ret	First Grade ret	Second Grade ret	Third Grade ret
With no adjustments[b]									
Ret vs. never-ret	−0.45*	−0.45*	−0.33	−0.29	−0.28	−0.23	−0.02	0.29	0.29
Ret vs. poor-perf comparison group	−0.53*	−0.34	−0.21	−0.28	−0.27	−0.23	0.11	0.40	0.41
With fall CAT and demographic adjustments[c]									
Ret vs. never-ret	−0.34	−0.23	−0.17	−0.18	−0.30	−0.28	0.03	0.21	0.26
Ret vs. poor-perf comparison group	−0.46	−0.25	−0.22	−0.24	−0.34	−0.31	0.08	0.28	0.32
With baseline measure adjustments[d]									
Ret vs. never-ret	—	−0.09	—	−0.10	−0.25	−0.30	0.01	0.22	0.26
Ret vs. poor-perf comparison group	—	−0.06	—	−0.13	−0.28	−0.38	0.06	0.29	0.31

With double-ret and special ed adjustments[e]									
Ret vs. never-ret	−0.38	−0.05	−0.15	0.11	−0.12	−0.25	−0.03	0.19	0.23
Ret vs. poor-perf comparison group	−0.50	−0.04	−0.22	−0.02	−0.20	−0.35	0.03	0.27	0.30
Adj R²									
Ret vs. never-ret[f]	0.04	0.21	0.05	0.13	0.18	0.18	0.05	0.04	0.05
Ret vs. poor-perf comparison group	0.04	0.22	0.07	0.13	0.18	0.19	0.06	0.06	0.06

[a] In Year 1 only first grade contrasts are reported; in Year 2 separate analyses are performed for first and second grade repeaters, using the moving baseline controls appropriate for each; in Years 4 and 8, separate analyses are performed for first, second, and third grade repeaters, using the moving baseline controls appropriate for each.

[b] These regressions adjust for differences among the several retainee groups and between retainees and those never retained.

[c] These regressions adjust additionally for CAT scores from the fall of the appropriate baseline year and for demographic factors: race/ethnicity, gender, mother's education, lunch subsidy status (eligible or not), number of siblings, age as of the fall of first grade, and living in a two-parent household at the start of first grade.

[d] These regressions adjust additionally for locus-of-control scores from the appropriate baseline year. For first and second grade repeaters, in the baseline year these are the outcome measures, so they are not used as controls (indicated by a dash in the table body).

[e] These regressions adjust additionally for differences associated with special education alone, double retention alone, and both combined.

[f] R^2 statistics are for the most inclusive equation in each column.

* Signifies differences significant at the .05 level.

seem to be better explained by the challenge of middle school transition than by the fact of retention, so far back in the past.

Does retention stigmatize children and harm them emotionally? Indication of any such consequences is absent. Instead, children's attitudes about themselves and about academics improve after retention, especially while they are repeating the failed grade. This pattern of improvement in children's affective profile dovetails with the signs of academic improvement associated with repeating a year (Chapters 6, 7, and 8).

The pattern also dovetails with findings of other research. A prospective study of Philadelphia first graders with comparison and non-promoted groups like those in the present study also found children's self-concepts higher in their repeated year, with averages across groups indistinguishable (Finlayson 1977). Another study of inner-city Chicago children finds positive effects on attitudes through fourth grade (Reynolds 1992), and Pierson and Connell (1992) find no differences in comparisons of retained and matched-control students involving general self-worth and perceived cognitive competence among children from upstate New York.[16] These findings generally accord with reference-group ideas (Goethals 1987; Richer 1976) about how images of the self form in relation to comparisons with nearby individuals. Retained pupils, for a year at least, have an advantage over their classmates in terms of chronological age and previous experience with the curriculum, and their performance improves, relatively with respect to their classmates and absolutely with respect to their own prior status. Apparently these sources of positive feedback have the effect of shoring up their attitudes toward self and school. This conclusion is at odds with much critical commentary on the practice of retention and with studies that ignore children's preretention status.

Appendix

This appendix provides the tables that correspond to Figures 9.1 to 9.5. The figures display trends only for first grade repeaters and never-retained children. The tables include these groups, as well as second grade, third grade, and fourth through seventh grade repeaters.

---

[16] Third through sixth grade repeaters did score lower on perceived competence in comparison with a random sample of promoted children, however.

TABLE 9.A1. *Academic Self-Esteem Averages for Retained Groups, Never-Retained Pupils, and the Poor-Performing Comparison Group*

	Spring Year 1	Spring Year 2	Spring Year 4	Fall Year 6	Fall Year 8
Year of retention					
1st grade	19.6	20.6	19.2	19.4	18.4
	(111)	(89)	(101)	(92)	(80)
2d grade	19.9	20.2	19.4	19.1	19.0
	(63)	(53)	(58)	(58)	(54)
3d grade	20.8	20.5	19.4	19.4	18.9
	(41)	(41)	(37)	(36)	(33)
4th–7th grade	20.8	20.9	18.6	18.8	18.9
	(69)	(61)	(67)	(66)	(61)
Never-retained pupils					
All never-retained	21.4	21.0	20.0	19.9	19.9
	(421)	(358)	(295)	(231)	(215)
Poor-performing comparison group	20.7	20.7	19.2	19.4	19.8
	(102)	(80)	(68)	(55)	(51)

TABLE 9.A2. *Average Reading Mark Expectations for Retained Groups, Never-Retained Pupils, and the Poor-Performing Comparison Group*

	Spring Year 1	Spring Year 2	Spring Year 4	Spring Year 6	Spring Year 8
Year of retention					
1st grade	3.0	3.2	2.9	2.9	2.4
	(114)	(89)	(96)	(89)	(69)
2d grade	3.3	3.1	2.9	2.9	2.6
	(63)	(54)	(54)	(52)	(44)
3d grade	3.3	3.2	2.9	2.7	2.5
	(43)	(42)	(33)	(35)	(31)
4th–7th grade	3.3	3.4	2.8	2.8	2.5
	(70)	(61)	(65)	(59)	(49)
Never-retained pupils					
All never-retained	3.4	3.4	3.1	3.1	2.9
	(428)	(361)	(287)	(228)	(205)
Poor-performing comparison group	3.3	3.4	2.9	3.0	2.9
	(103)	(80)	(67)	(52)	(50)

On the Success of Failure

TABLE 9.A3. *Average Math Mark Expectations for Retained Groups,
Never-Retained Pupils, and the Poor-Performing Comparison Group*

	Spring Year 1	Spring Year 2	Spring Year 4	Spring Year 6	Spring Year 8
Year of retention					
1st grade	3.2	3.2	2.9	3.1	2.6
	(114)	(89)	(96)	(89)	(68)
2d grade	3.4	3.3	3.0	2.9	2.7
	(63)	(54)	(54)	(52)	(44)
3d grade	3.2	3.2	3.2	3.0	2.6
	(43)	(42)	(32)	(35)	(31)
4th–7th grade	3.5	3.4	2.8	2.7	2.5
	(70)	(61)	(65)	(59)	(49)
Never-retained pupils					
All never-retained	3.4	3.4	3.1	3.1	2.8
	(428)	(361)	(287)	(228)	(204)
Poor-performing comparison group	3.2	3.4	3.0	2.9	2.8
	(103)	(80)	(67)	(52)	(50)

TABLE 9.A4. *School Satisfaction Averages for Retained Groups, Never-Retained
Pupils, and the Poor-Performing Comparison Group*

	Spring Year 1	Spring Year 2	Spring Year 4	Spring Year 6	Spring Year 8
Year of retention					
1st grade	4.1	4.2	4.2	4.1	3.8
	(112)	(89)	(101)	(92)	(69)
2d grade	4.2	4.2	4.3	4.0	3.8
	(63)	(53)	(58)	(54)	(44)
3d grade	4.3	4.4	4.1	3.8	3.7
	(42)	(41)	(37)	(36)	(32)
4th–7th grade	4.4	4.5	4.1	3.9	3.7
	(69)	(61)	(67)	(63)	(50)
Never-retained pupils					
All never-retained	4.3	4.3	4.1	3.8	3.7
	(422)	(357)	(295)	(231)	(209)
Poor-performing comparison group	4.2	4.3	4.2	3.8	3.7
	(103)	(79)	(68)	(53)	(50)

TABLE 9.A5. *Locus-of-Control Averages for Retained Groups, Never-Retained Pupils, and the Poor-Performing Comparison Group*

	Spring Year 1	Spring Year 2	Spring Year 4	Fall Year 8
Year of retention				
1st grade	8.9	9.3	10.1	10.7
	(111)	(89)	(101)	(80)
2d grade	8.9	9.5	10.1	11.0
	(63)	(53)	(58)	(52)
3d grade	9.2	9.8	10.2	11.0
	(42)	(41)	(37)	(33)
4th–7th grade	9.2	9.9	10.6	11.1
	(69)	(60)	(67)	(61)
Never-retained pupils				
All never-retained	9.3	9.8	10.4	10.7
	(420)	(356)	(293)	(215)
Poor-performing comparison group	9.4	9.6	10.4	10.5
	(102)	(79)	(68)	(51)

10

Retention in the Broader Context of Elementary and Middle School Tracking

To this point in our excursion grade retention has mainly positive effects.[1] It bolsters children's academic skills and self-confidence, the first almost certainly implicated in the second. But we have yet to consider an important facet of the retention experience: how retention overlaps other administrative placements. This concern arises because retention is a form of "educational tracking" that causes children to be off-time. They are older than their classmates and have been separated from their cohort.

Curiously, the literature on retention has been almost silent on the way retention ties in with other "sorting and selecting" arrangements used by schools, even though placement of children in special education and in low-level instructional groups occurs more often for retainees. Even less is known about closed doors later, in middle school and beyond, when formal tracking begins in earnest (an exception is the study by Stevenson, Schiller, and Schneider (1994), which finds evidence of such constraints using the National Educational Longitudinal Study of 1988 (NELS88) data; other relevant studies are from the BSS: Alexander and Entwisle 1996; Dauber, Alexander, and Entwisle 1996). We say *curiously* because retention is an organizational and administrative intervention, yet research and commentary on the practice rarely take an organizational perspective (e.g., Sørensen 1970; 1987). If they did, the parallels between retention and other forms of tracking would be hard to miss (e.g., Alexander, Entwisle, and Legters 1998).

---

[1] Nettie Legters is coauthor of this chapter.

Retention, like other placements, is a form of educational tracking in that it places children in an instructional setting thought to afford them their best chance of keeping up. Tracking in its most generic sense matches educational delivery to students' presumed needs. All forms of tracking have legitimate educational objectives; however, all are subject to the same concerns that swirl around grade retention, as discussed in the first chapter: selections or placements may not be fair; the education provided in "low" tracks may be inferior to that provided in "high" tracks; and children consigned to low tracks may be looked down upon and denied opportunities (i.e., the stigma issue). These themes – selection, reduced learning opportunities, and stigma – are intrinsic to all kinds of educational sorting.[2] Practices merit careful scrutiny when they set some children apart from others, treat them differently, and confer on them organizational identities that may have pejorative connotations. Furthermore, when such placements overlap, they may have countervailing or interactive effects. A student who has been retained, for example, may be excluded from higher tracks later.

In this chapter we examine ways that different aspects of educational sorting articulate over the course of children's early schooling. To our knowledge no such description exists at present, and even the most basic information is lacking. For example, we do not know of a single evaluation of retention using a strategy that matches retainees with comparison youngsters in terms of prior track placements. This piecemeal approach to studying educational sorting is potentially a serious mistake. By examining sorting mechanisms separately, the consequences of retention obviously could be over- or underestimated, misconstrued, or missed altogether, depending on how different practices intersect retention and affect students.

Tracking practices are not isolated in students' lives. In the case of retention, children held back are not just "repeaters," even if researchers choose to look at them from that vantage point alone. In elementary school they also are likely to be in low reading groups or special education classes, or to be receiving special education services in pull-out programs. In middle school they may be taking remedial courses while their schoolmates are in regular or advanced ones. All along the way there are multiple facets of tracking in operation. We know, for example,

---

[2] In Chapter 1 we discussed some of the literature on retention. For an overview on grouping/tracking from an educational stratification/tracking perspective see Dougherty (1996), Murphy and Hallinger (1989), and Oakes and coworkers (1992). On special education, see Carrier (1986); and Richardson (2000).

that all first grade repeaters in the BSS failed reading that year. It is reasonable to expect that most were reading below grade level and assigned to low reading instructional groups before being retained. How will those assignments bear on future achievement?

Experiences such as these could magnify retention's consequences. But effects also could be offsetting if children's placements turn out to be "cross-cutting." Low-level instructional groups, for example, are not populated by repeaters only. Teachers use reading groups mainly to help with classroom management, and typically three or four groups are designated regardless of children's ability levels (Dreeben 1984; Hallinan and Sørensen 1983). When this is the case, at some point many children with perfectly satisfactory academic records may find themselves in low reading groups. For that matter, some repeaters may not be tracked low in other areas. When large numbers of children are retained in first grade, this selection implies that students in second grade may have higher ability, on average, than was true in first grade – the class makeup or mix is different, yet some children still must populate the "low" second grade group. Other BSS research shows that these patterns linked to retention affect assignments of nonretained children (Entwisle et al. 1997).

Isolating retention from other types of tracking means that it will be faulted for problems that may originate elsewhere. As already seen, many of retainees' problems predate retention, as may low track assignment. Also, as discussed in Chapters 4 and 5, many repeaters are moved into special education classes after being held back, and many are held back a second time. With low ability groups, special education, and multiple retentions all in the mix, it is hard to single out a particular intervention as the source of children's problems. But if only retention is considered, it will be the one faulted.

And, too, by ignoring the broader *system* of tracking, we miss altogether the consequences of retention for children's schooling that play themselves out within that system. For example, early retention could close off opportunities in the middle grades, when formal tracking into different kinds of courses begins. Perhaps because of lingering questions about their abilities, retainees are channeled into remedial or low-level courses, even though they may be able to handle a more challenging curriculum. In this way retention could limit children's educational prospects even as it helped their performance in the near term.

Recent studies of curriculum tracking in high school typically find considerable movement across tracks, with much movement upward (i.e., into higher-level courses) as well as downward (e.g., Hallinan 1996; Lucas 1999), a seemingly more open system than prevailed earlier (i.e., Rosenbaum 1976).[3] Still, course placements are linked across the high school years (e.g., Lucas 1999; Stevenson et al. 1994), and it is likely that children's placements prior to high school are constraining as well. This topic has yet to be explored in depth (exceptions include Dreeben 1984; Eder 1986; Gamoran 1989; 1992; Hallinan 1992).

In this chapter we examine the set of organizational pathways within which retention is embedded by profiling children's encounters with educational tracking across the elementary and middle school years. These pathways are created by administrative interventions that sort and select children for different treatment as they move up the education ladder.

The chapter has three sections. The first focuses on first grade, when all children are acclimating to the school routine and when those who will repeat first grade suffer their "setback." Children's reading-group placements, reading instructional level, special education placements, and retention are considered. The second section examines reading placements across the elementary and middle school years. Reading is central to the curriculum in the primary grades and is the subject used most often to group children at the elementary level. During the early through mid-1980s, more than 90% of schools nationally used within-class ability grouping for reading in first grade, about the same percentage as in the BSS – 48 of 50. Grouping for math is less common; it is used in only about 25% of schools in first grade (McPartland, Coldiron, and Braddock 1987).

The third section compares repeaters' sixth and seventh grade placements in their academic subjects – English/reading, math, and foreign language. We stop with seventh grade because by middle school repeaters are at least a year behind, so their seventh grade is the eighth project year. In most school systems the curriculum begins to differentiate in middle school when tracking as commonly understood begins. In math, advanced students may take prealgebra, while others still are working on number skills; in the language curriculum, high-level students often take a foreign language and are working on literary criticism and creative writing, while children in lower-level classes are limited to remedial reading, rules of grammar, vocabulary building, and the like.

---

[3] Tracking may be less rigid nowadays than previously, as many schools have moved away from across-the-board curricular concentrations in favor of more flexible programs (e.g., Harvard Education Letter 1992a; 1992c).

Until middle school, children's options de jure remain open even if they have fallen behind; it is still possible to catch up, and retention presumably encourages that potential. But often in middle school and beyond, catching up is no longer even theoretically possible. Children placed in general math will not take calculus in 12th grade; nor will children taking functional reading later be able to enroll in advanced-placement English literature. Doors are irrevocably closed, because the curriculum is sequenced and differentiated. Many college preparatory courses in high school have prerequisites, and so in a very literal sense access to them often is determined years earlier (e.g., Oakes 1988 and 1989/1990). But although formal tracking may not begin until the middle grades, earlier forms of "hidden tracking," such as retention, also put students on different pathways (e.g., Alexander and Entwisle 1996; Alexander et al. 1998; Dauber et al. 1996).

Tracking in First Grade

In first grade children first encounter educational sorting. Experiences then set the tone for everything that follows. Children begin to acquire "pupil identities" and an organizational history that will stay with them as long as they remain in school. For many children, but especially re-peaters, these first encounters have a decidedly negative cast. To gain perspective on repeaters' tracking experiences, promoted youngsters (both groups) are also covered.

Reading group placements are available from first grade teachers for 615 children in the fall and 622 in the spring.[4] Report cards provide reading instructional levels; information on retention and special education services is taken from BCPS central records. For each placement children's standing is either "low" or "not low." In the case of reading group placements, "low" means being in the teacher's lowest group. Our intent is to monitor placements that might put students at a disadvantage and possibly be stigmatizing, and the lowest placements should send the clearest signals. Hence, a child in the third of three groups is classified as low, whereas one in the third of four is not. Consistent with practices nationally (e.g., Dreeben 1984; Hallinan and Sørensen 1983), most children (501 of the 615 in the fall) are in classes with three or four groups (47 are in classes with two groups, 34 are in classes with five groups, and 33 are in ungrouped classes).

[4] These data are from teacher questionnaires administered in first grade. Fifty-one of 57 homeroom teachers, most of whom also were subject-area instructors, responded.

For reading instructional level we classify as *low* children who are reading below grade level in a given quarter.[5] Reading level is not itself part of the tracking system, but it plays a role in screening for placements.[6] According to BCPS guidelines at the time, *satisfactory* is the highest permissible mark for children reading one grade below expectation, and reading two or more levels below is the standard for "failure." *Good* is reserved for children reading at expectation, and *excellent* readers should be one or more levels above expectation with at least 90% mastery.[7] Official policy is clear: reading marks ought to reflect reading level.

Special education placements are recorded in the spring of the year and usually indicate assignments for the next school year. Our tallies combine pull-out services from regular classrooms (these provide supplemental instruction in reading or math) with assignment to self-contained special education classes. This approach casts a wider net than in Chapter 4, in which only separate class assignments were counted in plotting children's "pathways" through the grade structure.

More than 70% of first grade repeaters are in low first grade reading groups (fall and spring), and slightly more than 90% are reading below grade level at year's end. Additionally, some 20% (26 of 127) are placed in special education at that point. These figures compare with 20% of all children in low reading groups, 23% reading below grade level, and 7% in special education. Such statistics are sobering. Most first grade repeaters receive first-quarter reading marks of "unsatisfactory" (Chapter 5), and all of them receive failing marks at year's end (Chapter 8). We now see that even before being held back, most are in low-ability instructional groups and a sizable minority are designated for special education services. These low placements reflect the classroom management side of academic difficulties. They are both symptom

---

[5] This classification does not necessarily mean they are reading below *expectation*. Children at the beginning of the year generally are not expected to be reading at grade level. In the BCPS, the average expectation for children's reading level in the first quarter of first grade is beyond beginning preprimer; children reading at the primer level are above average.

[6] It also affects instruction. Barr and Dreeben (1983) found large differences in the first grade basal readers used in three Chicago area school districts. The readers differed in number and difficulty of words introduced, and this difference influenced the number of words learned during the year. In addition, teachers paced their coverage of materials differently as a function of ability-group level and reading level.

[7] At the end of first grade, children in the BCPS are expected to be reading either in the second half of a level-1 book or in the first half of a level-2 book.

and signal, the latter in the form of organizational identities children bear in addition to the repeater label.

But these identities are not the exclusive province of repeaters. Only a few never-retained children (16) are earmarked for special education services in first grade, but a sizable minority are in low-instructional groups (16% in the fall; 10% in the spring) and 9% are reading below grade level at year's end. The percentages are higher still for all children promoted at the end of Year 1, which includes children held back in Years 2 through 7 (this expanded group would be the frame of reference in a typical study of grade retention): 20% low fall reading placements, 12% low spring placements, 14% reading below grade level, and 6% assigned to special education.

These last figures for all children not held back at the end of grade 1 give balance to the data on first grade repeaters. As a group their tracking experiences in Year 1 are extreme; as individuals, their experience is not all that exceptional.[8] Many promoted children, even some who make it through middle school without being held back, are in precisely the same circumstances as repeaters in first grade.

Table 10.1 shows how these several placements combine in children's experience. Each row represents a distinctive combination defined by children's reading group placements (low or not low, fall and spring) and spring instructional level (below or at grade level). The X's signify low placement. The number of children in each pattern is indicated in the left-hand column, along with the percentage that this low placement represents of the entire group $(N = 543)$.[9] To fill out the description, for each configuration we also report the number of children assigned to special education at year's end. Tallies by children's retention status (Year 1, grades 2 through 7; never retained; and comparison group) are reported to the right of the patterns.

Most children – 340 of the 543, or 63% – have no low placements; they are not in low reading groups either quarter and at year's end are reading at grade level or higher. Ten of the 340 (3%) are designated for special education services, but this assignment is less common (percentagewise) in the no-low-placement group than in most others. It is striking too that not 1 of the 340 is a first grade repeater (see the right-side

---

[8] At least not when placements are treated singly. There are substantial differences in placement *patterns,* as seen next.

[9] The figure covers only children with information on all the tracking measures. The largest loss (137 youngsters) involves reading-group placements (including the 33 children in classes in which small groups are not used).

TABLE 10.1. *First-Year Tracking Patterns*[a]

No. with Pattern	Low-Reading Group (Fall)	Low Reading Level (Spring)	Low-Reading Group (Spring)	No. in Special Education	1st Grade Retainees	2d–7th Grade Retainees	Never-Retained	Poor-Performing Comparison Group[b]
340 (63)[c]	—	—	—	10	0 (0)	79 (57)	261 (79)	46 (62)
75 (14)	X	X	X	15	57 (75)	11 (8)	7 (2)	3 (4)
46 (8)	—	X	—	3	13 (17)	19 (14)	14 (4)	7 (9)
37 (7)	X	—	X	4	0 (0)	12 (9)	25 (8)	10 (14)
26 (5)	X	X	—	4	1 (1)	10 (7)	15 (5)	6 (8)
12 (2)	X	—	—	0	2 (3)	5 (4)	5 (2)	1 (1)
4 (1)	—	—	X	0	0 (0)	2 (1)	2 (1)	1 (1)
3 (1)	—	X	X	1	3 (4)	0 (0)	0 (0)	0 (0)
Total 543				76		138	329	74

[a] Numbers in parentheses are percentages, going down columns. X identifies placements in pattern; dashes indicate not part of pattern. Looking across rows, the *No. with pattern* sample size corresponds to the sum of the 1st grade retainees, 2d–7th grade retainees, and never-retained groups.

[b] The poor-performing comparison group youngsters are a subset of the never-retained group.

[c] Percentages in column sum to 101 as a result of rounding.

205

distributions), and that 79% of never-retained children fall into this "no low" group.[10]

In contrast, first grade repeaters' placements are concentrated at the other extreme. Three-fourths (57 of 76) have all low placements and so constitute 76% of the children with this profile. If placements were random with respect to retention status, 14% would be expected in the all-low group (76 of 543); 15 also are special education designates. Eighteen of the 19 remaining first grade retainees are reading below grade level, so even those spared other low-track placements repeat the grade with a blemished record. Just 1 of the 76 first grade repeaters covered in Table 10.1 is reading at grade level at year's end.

The exceptional nature of first grade repeaters' tracking also is evident when viewed against the placements of children held back later in grades 2 through 7. The 138 second through seventh grade retainees are just about a fourth of the table total. This fraction matches almost exactly their percentage in the group spared all low placements ($79/340 = 23\%$), so in that respect their first-year experience is unexceptional, and clearly better than that of first grade repeaters. At the other extreme, only 8% (11 children) are in the all-low pattern. Low across-the-board placements in first grade are uncommon among children held back later, but they are not spared low placements altogether. To the contrary, they are a bit above expectation in most other low-pattern groupings, but this group's situation is decidedly more negative than that of never-retained children (including the poor-performing comparison group).

There generally are a few more comparison-group children with low placements than expected, but no dramatic concentrations, and they are conspicuously underrepresented in the all-low-placement pattern, making up just 4% of it. In contrast to most first grade repeaters, the comparison group children manage somehow to get by despite low entering test scores (albeit not as low as first grade repeaters'). They experience low-track placements somewhat more often than do all never-retained children (e.g., 62% are in the no-low-placement group compared with 79% of the latter), but their placement pattern is more favorable than that of children retained in grades 2 through 7, and vastly better than that of first grade repeaters. These tracking patterns thus reflect an orderliness across groups similar to that seen in earlier chapters for academic and adjustment difficulties in first grade.

[10] Figures for the comparison group and later repeaters are 62% and 57%, respectively.

To summarize: first grade retainees' placement profile in their year of failure is exceptional. These children are not just repeaters: most also are in low-reading groups, almost all read below grade level at year's end, and a sizable minority are headed for special education. Comparison by comparison, repeaters much more often show a *pattern* of consistently low placements. The signals, all predating retention, are loud and clear and aligned with retainees' academic and school adjustment difficulties.

First grade repeaters' first-year tracking experiences in these ways place them outside the mainstream; nevertheless, many promoted children also experience some form of low placement during the year – about a fifth (21%) of never-retained children and almost two-fifths (40%) of the comparison group experience at least one low placement. These sizable percentages remind us that educational sorting in first grade also gives many promoted children reason to question their competence. For that matter, a fifth (16 of 76) of first grade repeaters are not in low reading groups at the end of first grade or targeted for special education, so mixed signals are sent both ways.

The main message thus far is that repeaters' placement profiles put them more often and more consistently at the low end of the several first grade tracks. It is important, though, that many promoted children are placed low, too. Even though tracking experiences in first grade are not usually labeled as such, nor are all kinds of tracking acknowledged, the consequences of early de facto tracking may be as serious as, or more serious than, those of tracking for older children. These early decisions are made at a life stage when judgments about ability are much less reliable than later. They launch children into achievement trajectories that determine how much they are exposed to in the basic areas of reading and arithmetic.

Tracking across the Elementary Grades into Middle School: Placements in Reading/English

In this section we examine children's standing in reading and English through elementary school into the first year of middle school (sixth grade). Children who are held back are especially challenged in reading because, as we saw, first grade repeaters are placed disproportionately in low-reading groups in first grade and few read at grade level when they finish the year. Here we consider whether their standing changes over the years that follow, as indicated by reading instructional levels in the spring of Years 1 and 2 (their fail–repeat cycle), through the spring of fifth grade (for most, the last year of elementary school),[11] and finally by the level of sixth grade class assignments (the first year of middle school) in reading/English.

Reading level tracks children's proficiency and structures the instructional process in many ways. To some extent it even proxies for children's reading-group placements. Correspondence between the two is far from perfect, but in first grade only 10% of youngsters reading at grade level are in low-reading groups, versus 57% of children reading below grade level. Among the never retained, the figures are 9% and 27%. Seventy-eight percent of the 77 first grade repeaters reading below grade level also are in low-reading groups, whereas the sole retainee reading at grade level is not.

In middle school, distinctions are drawn among remedial, regular, and advanced classes, so we can look more directly at curriculum tracking. In the BCPS, reading is remedial in middle school. These courses mostly are special education classes, with titles like Developmental Reading, Remedial Reading, Supplementary Reading Resource, and English with Reading/Writing Emphasis. English is the "regular" track (e.g., English, Level 1 or Level 2; English, Grade 6). The school system also offers an advanced English program for children who qualify (e.g., have passed the school system's proficiency tests, score above grade level on standardized tests, receive grades of 80 or above in all subjects). Course titles in the advanced program include English Grade 6 – Enriched and English Grade 6 – Advanced Academic.

Children in remedial classes work on basic reading skills, whereas those in advanced classes study "characterization, literary devices, and authors' purposes"; "essays of comparison and contrast, interviews, rudimentary research skills and business letter writing"; and "writing in a variety of genres and some lower level skills of debate and defense" (excerpted from BCPS course descriptions). Enriched courses are available in all middle schools; the advanced academic program is available in 11 of the city's 27 middle schools (two of which are magnet schools with citywide enrollments).

---

[11] Here, as in the previous section, the distinction is between those reading below grade level and those reading at or above grade level. For first grade repeaters, reading at grade level in the second year means they are in a level-1 reader; for all others the standard is level 2. The criterion thus is grade-specific. This system seems appropriate, but still, the standard is different, and this difference must be kept in mind. By fifth grade, the comparisons are offset for all elementary school repeaters, as under a same-grade approach. All children are rated at the end of fifth grade, regardless of how long they took to get to that point.

Children who are taking reading or English courses identified as special education (e.g., Special Education (SE) Language Arts, Grade 6) are considered in the "low track." Regular or advanced courses are classified as "not low" in the coding used in this section. The vast majority of children, whether retained or not – some 85% overall and 99% of first grade repeaters – are enrolled in low-level reading/English classes in sixth grade. Many, though, take two language-arts courses in sixth grade, a common practice in middle school (see Epstein and Maclver 1990). Moreover, the two courses do not always fall on the same side of the divide between low and not low. That variability complicates matters. For example, 200 sixth graders take both reading and regular or advanced English (153 in regular English courses, 47 in advanced courses). It is true that 85% of the children followed into sixth grade take low-level courses that year, but if instead children are classified according to their highest-level course, the "low" percentage would be 56%.

Our interest in this volume is to understand the experience of repeaters, and for that reason we give close scrutiny to remedial placements especially. The advanced curriculum in middle school has very little relevance for repeaters. Almost all children enrolled in advanced courses are from the never-retained pool: 3 of the 108 are first grade repeaters; 12 others are repeaters from Years 2 through 5. Repeaters' sixth grade standing altogether is not good. Only 1 of 92 first grade retainees and 2 of 115 second through fifth grade repeaters are *not* in remedial reading/English. Among the never-retained (29%) and comparison-group children (14%), the percentages are higher.[12] It seems that repeating a grade in elementary school virtually guarantees remedial placement at the beginning of middle school. At the same time, such placements are high – in the 70% range – for promoted children, too.

We know that most first grade repeaters are reading below grade level when they fail first grade. In Table 10.2 we see that after repeating the year, many are reading at grade level: a decline from more than 90% reading below grade level in the first year to 35% in the second year. Unfortunately, usually this improvement is not maintained, and by fifth grade more than 60% again are reading below grade level.

Many second through fifth grade repeaters also read below grade level in elementary school, but their percentages are far lower than those

---

[12] Using enrollment in a nonremedial course (whether regular or advanced) as the criterion yields the following: 28.3% of first grade repeaters, 46.9% of second through fifth grade repeaters, 73.2% of never-retained children, and 50.9% of comparison-group children.

TABLE 10.2. *Percentage of Students Reading below Grade Level in Elementary School*[a]

	1st Grade Retainees	2d–5th Grade Retainees	Never-Retained	Poor-Performing Comparison Group[b]
Spring Year 1	90.4	30.2	9.2	21.4
	(104)	(129)	(411)	(98)
Spring Year 2	35.0	35.3	2.0	2.6
	(80)	(116)	(351)	(77)
Spring 3d grade	52.2	31.0	5.8	10.3
	(90)	(126)	(312)	(78)
Spring 4th grade	54.9	37.8	9.7	23.5
	(82)	(111)	(288)	(68)
Spring 5th grade	62.5	38.7	9.7	15.0
	(56)	(93)	(247)	(60)

[a] Numbers in parentheses are sample sizes.
[b] The poor-performing comparison group youngsters are a subset of the never-retained group.

of first grade retainees, hovering in the 30% to 35% range most years, peaking at 39% just before the middle school transition. Among the never retained, in contrast, 10% or less read below grade level, and even in the comparison group percentages peak in the low 20s. In fifth grade, for example, just 15% of the comparison children read below grade level, compared with 63% of first grade retainees and 39% of repeaters held back after first grade.

These large differences in children's competencies at the time of the middle school transition almost certainly close doors for them later. To look for such consequences, Table 10.3 organizes reading/English configurations from first through sixth grade.[13] Of the many such configurations, the six largest patterns account for most children. These are presented in descending order by size. For completeness, the less-populated patterns are also displayed, but the largest of these includes just 8 youngsters (3% of the total).

The most common profile, covering 44% of the total, involves children reading at grade level all through elementary school yet placed in low-level middle school reading/English.[14] The majority of children are in remedial reading/English in sixth grade, regardless of their reading

[13] In Table 10.3, placements and reading instructional levels are grade appropriate throughout, even for double retainees. For these youngsters, sixth grade reading/English courses reflect their Year 8 enrollments.
[14] However, about 62% of the 136 took nonremedial English courses at the same time.

TABLE 10.3. *Tracking Patterns from First Grade through Sixth Grade*[a]

No. with Pattern[b]	Low Reading Level (Spring Yr. 1)	Low Reading Level (Spring Yr. 2)	Low Reading Level (Spring gr. 5)	Low Read/Eng. Course (gr. 6)	1st Grade Retainees	2d–5th Grade Retainees	Never-Retained	Poor-Performing Comparison Group[c]
136 (44)	—	—	—	X	1 (3)	25 (37)	94 (53)	18 (47)
54 (17)	—	—	—	—	0 (0)	1 (1)	51 (29)	3 (8)
29 (9)	—	—	X	X	3 (8)	16 (24)	8 (4)	3 (8)
28 (9)	X	—	—	X	9 (23)	4 (6)	13 (7)	9 (24)
20 (6)	X	X	X	X	13 (33)	3 (4)	4 (2)	2 (5)
15 (5)	X	X	X	X	10 (26)	4 (6)	0 (0)	0 (0)
8 (3)	—	X	—	X	0 (0)	7 (10)	1 (1)	1 (3)
6 (2)	—	X	X	X	1 (3)	4 (6)	0 (0)	0 (0)
5 (2)	X	X	—	X	1 (3)	4 (6)	0 (0)	0 (0)
3 (1)	—	—	X	—	0 (0)	0 (0)	3 (2)	0 (0)
2 (1)	X	—	—	—	1 (3)	0 (0)	1 (1)	0 (0)
2 (1)	—	X	—	—	0 (0)	0 (0)	2 (1)	1 (3)
1 (0)	X	—	X	—	0 (0)	0 (0)	1 (1)	1 (3)
Total 309					39	68	178	39

[a] Numbers in parentheses are percentages, going down columns. X identifies low placements in pattern; dashes indicate not part of pattern.

[b] All children are covered in these pattern totals, so they characterize the experience of the entire cohort. However, children held back for the first time in middle school (sixth or seventh grade) are not included in the right-side subgroup totals. Hence, the left- and right-side row totals will not always be equal.

[c] The poor-performing comparison group youngsters are a subset of the never-retained group. Looking across rows, the *No. with pattern* sample size corresponds to the sum of the 1st grade retainees, 2d–5th grade retainees, and never-retained groups.

211

proficiency in fifth grade. Nevertheless, reading level still plays a role in sixth grade placements because a fourth of fifth graders reading at grade level are spared low-level sixth grade reading/English placements versus 6% of fifth graders reading below grade level.

The next largest pattern involves children with unblemished placements over the entire interval (17%). They are reading at least at grade level through fifth grade and in sixth grade are placed in regular or advanced English. Among this group five of six are taking advanced English and about the same number read above grade level in fifth grade. The other relatively large patterns (15 to 30) all involve multiple low placements, including the one that has all low placements.

The several student groups are distributed much differently across these six largest patterns.[15] Only one of the children spared all low placements is a repeater, whereas more than a fourth of never-retained children fall into this pattern. Another 53% of the never retained are in the group placed low in middle school reading/English despite reading at grade level all through elementary school (also the modal pattern among second through fifth grade repeaters and the comparison group). Eighty-one percent of the never-retained group thus can be accounted for by just these two patterns. Over half the comparison group also falls into these two patterns of low placement, and another 24% is in the pattern that picks up on these children's first-year difficulties (i.e., below-grade reading in Year 1 and low middle school placement). There is not another "problem pattern" that includes even 10% of the never-retained or comparison group.

Repeaters' situation is radically different. Most of them, including practically all first grade repeaters, are in patterns with multiple low placements. More than a fourth (26%) of first grade retainees are placed low on every occasion; another 33% are low every year except the second, reflecting their "boost" from repeating first grade. Their next most numerous pattern (at 23%, but just nine children) involves those reading below grade level only in Year 1, with low placements in middle school. There are thus some first grade repeaters who maintain their reading skills after first grade, but they are a minority.

Repeaters in the second through fifth grades fare a bit better, but their profiles still indicate many more low placements than do those of

---

[15] Children not held back until middle school are included in the left-side pattern tallies in Table 10.3 ($N = 309$), but not in the right-side group comparisons. This is why the subgroup pattern totals sometimes are less than the *No. with pattern* total in the first column.

the promoted children. More than a third read at grade level at each elementary school benchmark,[16] so their only low placement does not occur until middle school. Almost a fourth (24%) read below grade level for the first time in fifth grade, and the rest are scattered widely over other multiple low-placement patterns, including 6% in the pattern with all low placements. Although some of these youngsters appear to be doing satisfactorily until middle school, most show problems that overlap levels of schooling.

Not just repeaters are tracked low in middle school, though: most students, regardless of retention status, are placed in remedial sixth grade reading/English. Low middle school placements are much more common among former repeaters, of course, but this pattern can be understood largely in terms of their continuing problems with reading. Apart from those few first grade repeaters who recover somewhat while repeating, most read below grade level at every benchmark in Table 10.3, and practically all are below grade level at the time of their transition to middle school. These youngsters are overrepresented in low-track classes, but their standing as repeaters is not likely responsible: 20 of the 24 never-retained children reading below grade level in fifth grade also wind up in remedial sixth grade reading/English.

Tracking in Middle School: Reading/English, Math, and Foreign Language

In middle school academic subjects often are tracked, and within tracks classes often are grouped by ability level (e.g., Epstein and Maclver 1990). In this section, we examine children's placements in sixth and seventh grade reading/English and math and foreign language enrollments. Middle school English and math placements no doubt affect placements in these same subjects later, and foreign language study also sometimes serves as a filter for program screening in high school (e.g., Alexander and Cook 1982; Rosenbaum 1976). But despite this, not much research has examined continuities in track placements across levels of schooling (e.g., Gamoran 1989; Hallinan 1992; Stevenson et al. 1994), and none to our knowledge (outside the BSS) begins in the early primary grades. Still, lack of prerequisite courses in middle school almost certainly limits options later.

[16] By fifth grade all these youngsters have been held back at least once, so the pattern for all of them is grade-adjusted. They have had the benefit of an extra year to get to grade level.

Almost all repeaters take remedial reading/English in both sixth and seventh grades. Hardly any are in high-level English. As expected, remedial placements are also more common in the comparison group than overall (86% versus 71% in sixth grade). Most never-retained youngsters are in the remedial program, too, but their percentages are below those of repeaters.

Despite these large disproportionalities, the largest differences in retained and never-retained placements occur outside the remedial program. In sixth grade, 38% of never-retained middle schoolers and 16% of the comparison group take high-level English. The corresponding figures for seventh grade are 33% and 20%. For all practical purposes, these classes are beyond the reach of elementary school retainees. Is this unfair? Possibly, but the groups also differ in preparation and qualifications. Hardly any first grade repeaters read at grade level at the end of fifth grade, and this certainly bears on sixth grade placements. For example, three-fourths of never-retained children and half of comparison group children in high-level sixth grade English read *above* grade level in fifth grade.

Differences in children's fifth grade CAT-R performance are similarly large. In the spring of fifth grade, first grade retainees average 441 on the CAT-R. The corresponding figures for promoted children $(N = 86)$ and those in the comparison group $(N = 8)$ in high-level sixth grade English are 571 and 549, respectively. The lowest-scoring advanced English student is 28 points above retainees' CAT-R average, and only 2 of 127 first grade repeaters have scores above the averages of either never-retained group. The 130-point gap separating repeaters from the never retained exceeds 2 standard deviations, and the 108-point gap separating them from comparison group children is in the vicinity of 1.6 standard deviations. These huge disparities show that first grade repeaters do not match other children's qualifications for high-level middle school coursework. Are first grade retainees denied opportunities when they enter middle school simply because of their status as repeaters? The answer seems to be no. Their history as repeaters is not at issue here so much as their poor academic skills at the beginning of middle school.

The same trends appear in the other areas covered in Table 10.4. Fewer children overall fall outside the regular math curriculum, but among those who do, mainly repeaters take lower-level courses (most of which are special education classes), whereas promoted children primarily take upper-level courses. In both sixth and seventh grades, about half of first grade repeaters are tracked low in math (49% and 56%,

TABLE 10.4. *Placements in High-Level and Low-Level Sixth and Seventh Grade Courses (in Percentages)*[a]

	1st Grade Retainees	2d–5th Grade Retainees	Never-Retained	Poor-Performing Comparison Group[b]
Sixth grade				
Reading, % low	98.9	98.3	71.4	86.2
	(92)	(115)	(245)	(58)
English, % high	3.3	10.4	37.9	15.8
	(92)	(115)	(235)	(57)
Math, % low	48.9	27.8	6.3	5.3
	(92)	(115)	(237)	(57)
Math, % high	3.3	3.5	23.6	5.3
	(92)	(115)	(237)	(57)
% taking a foreign language	9.7	17.4	55.7	24.6
	(92)	(115)	(237)	(57)
Seventh grade				
Reading, % low	100.0	95.3	70.3	83.9
	(81)	(107)	(236)	(56)
English, % high	3.7	4.7	33.1	19.6
	(81)	(106)	(236)	(56)
Math, % low	55.6	21.5	4.7	5.4
	(81)	(107)	(236)	(56)
Math, % high	0.0	0.9	28.0	14.3
	(81)	(107)	(236)	(56)
% taking a foreign language	12.3	36.4	66.9	55.4
	(81)	(107)	(236)	(56)

[a] Numbers in parentheses are sample sizes.
[b] The poor-performing comparison group youngsters are a subset of the never-retained group.

respectively), as are about a fourth of second through fifth grade retainees. The corresponding never-retained figures range between 4% and 6%, so they are about as rare in remedial courses as repeaters are in high-level courses.

At the other end of the scale, in the sixth and seventh grades about a fourth of the never-retained group are in upper-level math. This sizable minority exceeds levels realized by any other groups. Just as does the English curriculum, then, the high-level middle school math program seems beyond the reach of elementary school retainees.

Disparities involving foreign language study are less pronounced, but the figures favor those never retained. About 10% to 12% of first grade repeaters study a foreign language each year, the only high-level area in which they number above 5%. The never-retained figures, at 56% in sixth grade and 67% in seventh grade, are much higher, though, and the comparison group and second through fifth grade repeaters fall between.

These parallels in middle school course assignments are not simply coincidence children with strong academic records in one area tend to be strong in others too. However, administrative considerations also play a role. Some schools use "block scheduling" in making class assignments. Under this arrangement, children move together as a group from class to class throughout the day, with the effect that children are placed in the same track level across academic courses. In sixth grade, for example, 94% of those in low-level math also are in low-level reading/English; 88% of those in high-level math also are in high-level English. Foreign language enrollments also align with other placements. In sixth grade, 92% of children enrolled in remedial math do not take a foreign language, whereas 83% of those in advanced math do. For high- (91%) and low-level (78%) English, the same holds true.

Overlap in middle school placements is thus substantial. To illustrate this overlap more clearly, along with exactly where repeaters fit in, Table 10.5 shows placement profiles. These patterns reveal whether sixth and seventh grade placements in reading/English, math, and foreign language are low or not. Also shown are the number of children receiving special education services each year and the number held back in middle school.

Again, most patterns are sparsely populated. Only six apply to as many as 20 children; these encompass 89% of the total in the table (354 of 400). These common patterns warrant particular attention, but the others help fill out the picture. In fact, 33 different curricular configurations describe BSS youngsters' middle school experience.[17] The 14 displayed in Table 10.5 apply to 1% or more of the study group. These configurations overlay additional distinctions involving special education placement and middle school retention, not to mention children's early history of tracking, which follows them into the middle grades from elementary school. It is a much more complicated picture than generally appreciated.

The most heavily populated patterns show significant parallels across student groups. The largest pattern involves low reading/English with

---

[17] There would be many more than 33 patterns if we also distinguished high-level placements in English and math from regular-level courses.

TABLE 10.5. *Middle School Tracking*[a]

No. with Pattern[b]	Low Rdg/Eng Grade 6	Low Math Grade 6	No Foreign Language Grade 6	Low Rdg/Eng Grade 7	Low Math Grade 7	No Foreign Language Grade 7	No. in Spec. Ed. Grade 6	No. in Spec. Ed. Grade 7	6th or 7th Grade ret	1st Grade Retainees	2d–5th Grade Retainees	Never Retained	Poor-perf. Comparison group[c]
105 (26)	X	—	X	X	—	X	7	5	15	24 (33)	28 (30)	44 (22)	17 (37)
68 (17)	X	—	X	X	—	—	4	3	14	2 (3)	24 (26)	31 (16)	12 (26)
61 (15)	X	X	X	X	X	X	52	47	4	36 (50)	16 (17)	6 (3)	1 (2)
56 (14)	X	—	—	X	—	—	1	0	10	4 (6)	8 (9)	38 (19)	4 (9)
44 (11)	—	—	—	—	—	—	1	0	1	0 (0)	1 (1)	42 (21)	3 (7)
20 (5)	X	—	X	X	—	X	0	3	0	2 (3)	5 (5)	10 (5)	0 (0)
9 (2)	X	X	X	X	—	X	5	4	0	1 (1)	6 (6)	2 (1)	1 (2)
7 (2)	X	—	—	—	—	—	0	0	0	0 (0)	1 (1)	6 (3)	1 (2)
7 (2)	X	—	X	—	—	—	0	0	0	0 (0)	1 (1)	6 (3)	3 (7)
6 (2)	X	—	X	X	X	X	1	1	0	2 (3)	3 (3)	1 (0)	3 (7)
6 (2)	—	—	—	X	—	—	0	0	0	1 (1)	0 (0)	5 (3)	1 (2)
4 (1)	—	—	X	—	X	X	0	0	0	0 (0)	0 (0)	4 (2)	1 (2)
4 (1)	—	—	—	—	—	—	0	0	0	0 (0)	0 (0)	4 (2)	1 (2)
3 (1)	X	—	X	—	—	X	0	0	2	0 (0)	1 (1)	1 (0)	0 (0)
Total 400							70	60	49	72	94	200	46

[a] Numbers in parentheses are percentages, going down columns. X identifies low placements in pattern; dashes indicate not part of pattern.

[b] All children are covered in these pattern totals, so they characterize the experience of the entire cohort. Children held back for the first time in middle school (sixth or seventh grade) not included in the right-side subgroup totals. Hence, the left- and right-side row totals will not always be equal.

[c] The poor-performing comparison group youngsters are a subset of the never-retained group. Looking across rows, the No. with *pattern* sample size correspond to the sum of the 1st grade retainees, 2d–5th grade retainees, and Never-retained groups.

no foreign language both years, along with regular or advanced math. In a strictly empirical sense, this is the "regular" middle school curriculum for our study youngsters: regardless of what else they might be doing in the English program, a fourth of the entire study group take remedial reading, do not take a foreign language, and are in a nonremedial math sequence. This configuration is more than a third larger than the next largest pattern and includes many youngsters from each group (including first grade repeaters). Included are a fifth of the never-retained students, about a third of children held back after first grade, and roughly a third of the comparison group. Considering how divergent placement patterns have been thus far, this degree of overlap is unusual. If there is a middle school "melting pot," this is it.

Another 68 children have the same pattern, except that in seventh grade they begin a foreign language. For many youngsters, then, selection for foreign language study occurs in seventh grade. This pattern, too, is relatively "open," at least for all but first grade repeaters. Sixteen percent of never-retained children are in it, along with 26% each of second through fifth grade repeaters and the comparison group.

Relatively large percentages of these same groups also appear in the pattern with low placements only in reading/English both years (the fourth largest pattern, $N = 56$). Nineteen percent of the never retained and 9% each of the comparison group children and of those held back after first grade are in this group. These children begin foreign language study in sixth grade and are never in low-track math. The percentages in this pattern favor never-retained children somewhat.

The never retained more often take a foreign language and begin it earlier; nevertheless, overall the disparities are not large. These three patterns account for substantial common ground in middle school placements, which enroll roughly one-half to two-thirds of never-retained children and of those held back in elementary school after first grade.[18]

But although in this comparison many elementary school repeaters "blend in," few of them are first grade repeaters, whose single largest middle school pattern involves across-the-board low placements both years. Accounting for 15% of the total, this pattern is the third largest in Table 10.5. Half of the first grade retainees have low placements across the board (36 of 72), and they constitute 59% of its membership. Another 26% are children held back in grades 2 through 5. First grade repeaters,

---

[18] We note, too, that not many children in these three groups are in special education (although they do account for 39 of 49 children held back in sixth and seventh grades).

with their long history of academic difficulties, have problems that continue into middle school, because 52 of the 61 children in this all-low pattern also receive special education services in sixth grade and 47 do so in seventh.

Compare these figures against those for the no-low pattern. Forty-four children have this profile, 11% of the total. Just 1 of these is an elementary school retainee; 42 are never retained.[19]

Disproportionalities at the extremes are pronounced: hardly any of the "low-end" children are drawn from the never-retained pool; conversely, only one of the "high-end" children is from the retained pool. In these details, retained and promoted children's middle school tracking patterns are radically different. These two patterns account for about a fourth of the total (11% in the no-low pattern; 15% in the all-low pattern), so the numbers involved are far from negligible. Still, for most youngsters other than first grade repeaters, middle school tracking patterns overlap substantially. Had the various dimensions of tracking been examined individually, as they usually are, this would have been missed.

Tracking and Retention: Some Concluding Thoughts

This chapter has examined retention from the perspective of educational tracking. Tracking is an administrative device for placing together students deemed to have like needs and/or competencies. Tracking takes many forms, and its use is widespread. Our present "sampling" includes retention, reading-group placements in first grade, reading instructional level all through the primary grades (a proxy for grouping as well as a measure of children's competencies), special education placements, and middle school placements in three core subjects linked to college preparatory curricula later on. Each type of track has legitimate educational objectives, yet each also raises concerns: does it meet its objectives, does it burden children, perhaps in ways often not even recognized? The fairness and effectiveness of tracking have been questioned, especially for low-track youngsters.

How these sundry placements intersect has been our main concern. In every comparison retainees are overrepresented in the lowest educational slots and never-retained children are more often spared low

[19] The group subtotals in Table 10.5 do not sum to the full-row total in this instance because children held back for the first time in sixth or seventh grade are not displayed separately. The 54 such youngsters are dispersed across many patterns, including some not displayed in the chart.

placements. This tracking emerges in first grade, before anyone has been held back, and continues through middle school, after all primary grade retentions. That the lines are so rigidly drawn is part of the reality of retention: in middle school most *first grade* repeaters are on separate tracks from their classmates. Their situation is the most extreme, however, in that middle school tracking patterns are not especially distinctive for repeaters held back after first grade.

The variety and complexity of tracking profiles seen in this chapter are submerged in most retention research, hidden from view. Rigid tracking is most severe in the case of first grade repeaters, who consistently fall behind their classmates: their track placements are low before their retention and remain so afterward; their skill levels in middle school continue to lag far behind everyone else's, so they continue to be tracked low.

An important concern is whether being held back in elementary school closes doors for children when they get to middle school. If not shut, the doors certainly are not opened wide: almost all first grade repeaters take remedial reading in sixth and seventh grades, about half take low-level math, and only about 10% study a foreign language, a much lower percentage than in any other group. Clearly, many first grade repeaters have consistently low placements and few others do, so early retention appears to throw up daunting barriers.

But retention is not the only problem, and because its early consequences appear helpful, it may not be implicated at all. These children already have severe difficulties in first grade, before anyone is held back. Their placements for instruction in reading are consistently low, and most of them are assigned to special education at some point. The initial academic and adjustment difficulties of first grade repeaters are extreme and continue all through elementary school.

Under such circumstances exactly what is behind first grade repeaters' low middle school placements is hard to determine. Negative consequences usually attributed to retention could instead result from other placements that exercise a stronger pull on children's daily experience, such as special education or ability-group assignments. Consequences likely magnify when children's placements are consistently low, across different dimensions of tracking and across years.

The effectiveness of educational programs is evaluated nonexperimentally by comparing the later experiences of children who are alike in all relevant respects save exposure to the "treatment" at issue, in this case, retention. These first grade repeaters have so many more problems than other children that a rigorous implementation of this logic of comparison may not be possible. Most studies typically do not match on factors *prior to* retention or on children's track placements, so the kinds of comparisons made in this chapter ordinarily are not even attempted. Retention is highly confounded with other low placements and with prior academic difficulties, so the power of statistical adjustments like those used in the present volume is greatly diminished.

The tracking patterns reviewed in this chapter are a sobering reminder that definitive answers may not always be possible. However, not all repeaters' problems and placements are as extreme as those of first grade retainees. Indeed, middle school patterns for later repeaters and promoted youngsters are highly varied, with considerable overlap between retained and nonretained students. This may be one reason why the later consequences of repeating a grade, with whatever problems attend it, for these youngsters are relatively minor or muted.

Effects of sorting practices early in children's school careers clearly are more complicated than generally appreciated. To help distinguish these complications, research is badly needed on educational tracking as it exists prior to middle school. It is, in fact, a comprehensive system of interventions. Research on *parts* of the system – on retention alone, or special education, ability grouping, or curriculum tracking alone – will be inadequate for two reasons: (1) the effects of the tracks not taken into account will be mistakenly attributed to retention and/or (2) these treatments may interact.

We need to know whether the overlap of retention with these other tracking mechanisms aggravates or cushions problems surrounding retention. Consider, for example, how within-class ability grouping affects repeaters and complicates the task of assigning responsibility for their problems. Same-grade comparisons after retention – the frame of reference that we have argued is most appropriate and that tends to yield more favorable results for retention – typically find repeaters lagging behind their grademates. They may not be as far behind as before, but they lag behind, and for critics of retention this is an indictment of the practice. But although all these children may be in the same grade, we have seen in this chapter that they are not all receiving the same education. Those consigned to low-ability groups are exposed to a different curriculum, move along at a different pace, perhaps are slighted by their teachers, and for those reasons learn less (e.g., Barr and Dreeben 1983; Dougherty 1996; Oakes, Gamoran, and Page 1992; Pallas, Entwisle, Alexander, and Stluka 1994). Accumulated across years, such consequences could well be substantial, but should they be construed as effects of retention, or do they instead reflect denied learning opportunities due to children's poor academic standing? It is a difficult question, and any simple answer – the kind that tends to dominate discussion of controversial topics – is likely to be too simple.

This chapter's glimpse of elementary and middle school tracking reveals that retention is not an isolated experience, easily separated from other aspects of children's schooling. Rather, it is one of a complex set of administrative interventions, all designed to treat – and channel – students in different ways. It is a complicated picture. Furthermore, our other research shows that curriculum tracking is strongly associated with "behavioral" tracking (see Entwisle et al. 1997). Following the lead of Kellam and colleagues (1991; 1994), we discovered that children in various reading groups are characterized by different *behavioral* profiles as well as different achievement profiles. This topic is not one to be explored further here, but the inadvertent tracking by socioemotional status that shadows instructional group tracking is a topic in need of much further research.

11

Dropout in Relation to Grade Retention

To this point we have examined how repeaters fare over the years prior to high school.[1] Critics of grade retention tell us that the experience retards children's academic development and assaults their sense of self, but this appraisal hardly accords with the experience of repeaters in the Beginning School Study (BSS), sketched over the previous several chapters. Repeaters' academic standing after retention generally is better than before, certainly during the repeated year and in many comparisons for several years beyond the repeated grade (although in diminishing measure). Nor do we see great stigma attaching to grade retention. Results differ in minor ways across grade levels, depending on the specific attitudes being assessed, but in the main repeating a grade is associated with improved, not impaired, views of self and school. Even neutral findings would be hard to reconcile with a view of grade retention as a heavy socioemotional burden, and the favorable indications in Chapter 9 make no sense at all if the critics are correct. But if going through the curriculum a second time gives repeaters an academic boost, as seems the case for test scores and marks, then favorable socioemotional consequences make perfectly good sense – indeed they would be expected.

However, there also are troubling signs, which may well have implications later for repeaters' commitment to staying in school. Academic demands escalate in the middle grades (e.g., Eccles et al. 1984; 1991),

---

[1] Nader Kabbani is coauthor of this chapter, which adds to, and borrows liberally from, a series of BSS papers on precursors to dropout, including grade retention: Alexander et al. (1997); Alexander, Entwisle, Dauber, and Kabbani (2000); Alexander, Entwisle, and Kabbani (2001); Alexander et al. (2002); and Entwisle et al. (2000a). The analyses reported in Tables 11.2 and 11.3 appear here for the first time.

and repeaters' marks and test scores begin to trail off at that point. Even though usually they remain above the level where they had been before (relative to nonrepeaters' and their own preretention performance), middle school marks in the barely satisfactory range leave little room to absorb additional setbacks. This makes repeaters' situation precarious. And, too, Chapter 10 established that many repeaters are relegated to remedial courses in middle school, continuing a history of "low-end" educational track placements that very likely will continue into high school.

In Maryland age 16 is the legal age of school leaving. Regularly promoted children are in 10th or 11th grade at that age, well into high school. But most one-time repeaters reach age 16 just when they are beginning high school, and students 2 years behind are still in middle school, with high school still ahead.

The prognosis for high-risk children in the upper grades is not good. Low-income, minority youth in high-poverty school systems leave school at an alarming rate even when they are doing well (e.g., for overview, see Chen, Kaufman, and Frase 1997; Rumberger 1987; 2001, Wagenaar 1987), but their risk compounds when they arrive at high school with a history of poor school performance and low-level track placements (e.g., Alexander et al. 2001; Catterall 1998). This kind of profile holds for many BSS repeaters (e.g., Chapter 5), and it puts them at grave risk of dropout *apart from* their standing as retainees. Does grade retention increase dropout risk *above* this basal level in the BSS given the absence of adverse consequences in other areas of personal development (i.e., academics and attitudes)? In other words, does being a repeater give an *extra* "push," or do positive consequences in the BSS tend to mitigate dropout also?

The dropout rate for BSS repeaters is 67%, much higher than for nonrepeaters. Repeaters, though, have a "high-risk" profile apart from retention, and that clouds the issue. As the Goal 2 Work Group (1993: 18) puts it, "Were these [retained] students . . . more likely to drop out even if they had not been retained?" The panel's query frames this chapter's agenda, but before confronting it, we provide a bit of background.

High School Dropout as a Continuing Concern

Are concerns about high dropout rates exaggerated, as some have argued (e.g., Finn 1987; McLaughlin 1990)? High school completion among 18- to 24-year-olds stood at 84.8% in 1998. Completion figures over the 10 years prior all fell within a percentage point or two of this level, and even as far back as 1972 the *lowest level* of high school completion for youth in this age group was 82.3% (U.S. Department of Education 2000b: 42). These figures all fall short of the 90% national target enunciated by the National Education Goals Panel (e.g., 1999), but with high school completion plateauing at historically high levels, it is tempting to conclude that the need for vigorous efforts at dropout prevention is past. That notion needs to be dispelled.

For one thing, these relatively low levels of high school noncompletion translate into a great many young people without degrees – almost 3.7 million 18- to 24-year-olds in 1998 (U.S. Department of Education 2000b: 18). That is a huge number by any standard, and as a result of well-known imbalances across social lines, the problem hits some youth harder than others: for example, 90% of the non-Hispanic Whites among those 18- to 24-year-olds, but only 81% of non-Hispanic Blacks and 63% of Hispanic youth were in possession of high school credentials (U.S. Department of Education 2000b: 18).

And what of the consequences? For those who fail to finish high school, job prospects in today's high-technology–high-service economy probably are as bleak as they ever have been. Gone are the well-paying manufacturing jobs that not long ago provided steady employment and a comfortable living for much of the blue-collar work force. Dropouts suffer high levels of unemployment and depressed earnings (Markey 1988; U.S. Department of Education 2001: 137–139). To illustrate, in October 2000, 51% of 16- to 24-year-olds who dropped out during the 1999–2000 school year were unemployed, not looking for work, and not in college. The corresponding figure for that year's high school graduates was 11% (U.S. Bureau of Labor Statistics 2001). And in 1999, male dropouts ages 25–34 who worked full-time year-round earned 30% less than their counterparts with high school degrees and general equivalency degrees (GEDs); for female dropouts, the shortfall was comparable, 28% (U.S. Census Bureau 2000: 36–39). Extrapolated over a lifetime's work, a 1-year disparity of this magnitude projects to a huge difference in dropouts' and graduates' cumulative earnings (Mishel and Bernstein 1994; Peng 1985).[2]

---

[2] Moreover, analyses indicate relatively little "ability bias" in the economic returns associated with different levels of educational attainment (e.g., Card 1999; Griliches 1977, McDill et al. 1986). That is, disparities of the sort mentioned appear to follow from differences in level of schooling, and not from academic ability and other factors (e.g., social background) that distinguish dropouts from others.

But the costs associated with dropout are not all monetary; nor are they borne exclusively by those who leave school. There are social costs as well that spread inexorably as the ripples on a pond. Dropouts, for example, make up about half of welfare recipients and a like fraction of the prison population (Educational Testing Service 1995; National Research Council 1993; U.S. House of Representatives 2000). This population incurs huge service expenditures, with huge losses to the U.S. Treasury in terms of taxes forgone. Years ago, Catterall (1987) estimated that high school dropouts from the class of 1981 – a single graduating class – would pay almost $69 *billion* less in taxes over their lifetime than if they had graduated. And for a single dropout class (1985) for a single school district (Los Angeles), he put the cost for *extra* municipal services (e.g., police, health) at $500 million (lifetime).

These figures from the 1980s represent large increases over similar calculations from the early 1970s (Levin 1972) and if carried forward to the present no doubt would be larger still. And beyond such dollar costs, additional costs that are harder to calculate but are no less important are cast in terms of wasted potential, human suffering, and diminished self-regard. Clearly, high school dropout, even at the relatively low levels that have prevailed in recent decades, remains costly – for those who leave school early *and* for the rest of society.

Moreover, national statistics mask variation at the local level. Hauser and associates (2001), for example, report much higher dropout rates across grades 10–12 in central cities than in their suburban rings. Over the decade of the 1990s, dropout averaged 18.0% in the nation's 17 largest cities (including Baltimore) versus 10.2% in the suburbs surrounding them.

Estimates of school system "holding power" (i.e., the number of graduates as a percentage of the ninth grade enrollment 4 years prior) show even more dramatic differences. Though strictly speaking not a measure of dropout (e.g., the calculation makes no allowance for transfers in and out), holding power certainly reflects on a school's or school system's health and over a period of years likely parallels dropout patterns (e.g., Balfanz and Legters 2001). Versus a school district holding power average of 78.8% statewide in 1997/98, Baltimore's holding power that year stood at 35.7%, 30 percentage points below the next lowest average (for Caroline County; Maryland State Department of Education 1999). Moreover, within the city system, nonselective zoned high schools, those where attendance is determined by place of residence, trailed the rest. They averaged 26% as against 76% for academically selective magnet schools, 52% for vocational schools, and 62% for alternative schools.

Analyzing like data from the early 1990s, Balfanz and Legters (2001) find that almost half of all high schools in the nation's 35 largest cities (exclusive of Los Angeles, for which the requisite information was unavailable) have holding power ratios under 50%. And in large schools (enrolling 900 or more) with high minority enrollments (90% or greater), over two-thirds of schools have low levels of holding power.

This litany of statistics supports two conclusions: (1) Determining exact levels of dropout is exceedingly difficult because the numbers differ, depending on the definition of dropout, age range, time frame, administrative unit selected, and a whole host of other considerations.[3] (2) Despite all this, it seems safe to say that dropout remains at epidemic levels in high-poverty communities such as Baltimore. In 1989, over a fourth of Baltimoreans age 25–29 were out of school and without degrees (U.S. Census Bureau 1992). In raw numbers, that translates into almost 20,000 young adults without degrees trying to establish a toehold in an inhospitable urban economy.

But even these last figures do not tell the whole story because they mix regular high school degrees with GEDs. Nationally, about half of all dropouts eventually obtain high school certification (U.S. Department of Education 1998), so indeed there is opportunity to reverse course. In fact, GED holders as a percentage of all high school degree recipients have increased in recent years, from 4.2% among 18- to 24-year-olds in 1988 to 10.1% in 1998 (U.S. Department of Education 2000b: 23). Still, a high school degree seems to enhance employment and earnings prospects when compared to a GED (e.g., Cameron and Heckman 1993; Murnane, Willett, and Boudett 1995; Murnane, Willett and Tyler 2000).

The best outcome, of course, would be for more youth to realize success in school the first time through, rather than need to recover by way of uncertain "second chance" opportunities. Unfortunately, in high-poverty school systems typically 30%–50% of children drop out (Council of Great City Schools 1994; Education Week 1998); and in individual schools there may be no ceiling – for example, Balfanz and Legters (2001) describe a large zoned Baltimore high school (1,407 students in 1996/97) with just 20% holding power (see also Fine 1991;

[3] The lament is a familiar one, similar to that discussed earlier regarding the lack of high-quality, comparable data on grade retention at the local level: "Dropout data probably are the least reliable information available today regarding the reality of schools" (Frymier 1997: 4).

Hammack 1986; Kelly 1988). The dropout "crisis" in these localities is of the present, not the past. One estimate for 1990 puts the dropout rate in Baltimore at 40% (Bomster,1992). In the Beginning School Study (BSS) it is 42%. Details follow.

The Timing and Extent of Dropout in the BSS

Dropout as used here means leaving school at least once for an extended period prior to graduation. The withdrawal may be temporary or permanent, and whether dropouts later are certified is a separate matter. We identify dropouts through self-reports and school records with questions first posed of BSS students in the spring of 1991 (ninth grade for those not held back) and repeated annually thereafter through fall 1999 at age 22–23 (5 years after the group's expected high school graduation in spring 1994). Questioning covers the instance and timing of dropout, along with subsequent degree completion.[4] Weaving together sources, dropout status is known for 92.3% of the original cohort (729 of 790). According to these self-reports, 41.6% of the group ($N = 303$) dropped out of school at some point.[5]

And what of high school completion? Through fall 1999, 9.2% of BSS dropouts returned to school and completed high school degrees. Another 30.4% obtained the GED, setting high school completion among dropouts at 39.6%,[6] close to the 44% figure registered by dropouts

---

[4] A typical dropout question, asked in interviews administered in late spring of Year 12 (12th grade for those on time), asked, "Are you currently attending high school?" Response options were (caps in original) as follows:

   1. Yes, I was in school for the whole year.
   2. No, I attended some of this year, but dropped out DURING the 1993–94 school year.
   3. No, I received a high school diploma early (NOT A GED) DURING the 1993–1994 school year.
   4. No, I dropped out BEFORE the start of the 1993–94 school year.
   5. No, I received a high school diploma (NOT A GED) BEFORE the start of the 1993–94 school year.

[5] Not all panel members were interviewed each year. To construct dropout histories, up to nine responses were reviewed and checked for consistency. Members of the panel whose graduation status could not be determined ($N = 61$) resemble dropouts more than graduates across a range of criteria. This suggests that more dropouts are missed than graduates, but patterns relating risk factors to dropout have proved robust in attrition analyses (Alexander et al. 1997).

[6] These calculations exclude 10 dropouts for whom reenrollment could not be determined. The base N thus is 293.

TABLE 11.1. *Timing of First Dropout*

Grade Level Attained	Year Left School								Total N	%
	8	9	10	11	12	13	14	15	N	%
6	1								1	0.3
7	1		3						4	1.3
8	1	9	5						15	5.0
9		11	32	36	2	1			82	27.2
10			13	37	30	7	1		88	29.2
11				22	31	12	4	1	70	23.2
12					18	16	6	1	41	13.6
Total N	3	20	53	95	81	36	11	2	301	100.0
%	1.0	6.6	17.6	31.6	26.9	12.0	3.6	0.7	100.0	
On-Time	1	11	13	22	18	0	0	0	65	21.6
Off-Time	2	9	40	73	63	36	11	2	236	78.4
% Off-Time	66.6	45.0	75.5	76.8	77.8	100.0	100.0	100.0		
	52% On-Time		23% On-Time			0% On-Time				

nationally (U.S. Department of Education 1998: 10) despite very different baseline levels of dropout in the two instances (42% in the BSS versus 21% nationally).[7]

Combining regular degrees and GEDs, high school completion as of age 22–23 stands at 76% in the BSS. The noncompletion figure of 24%, about the same level as indicated in Census data from 1989 for Baltimore as a whole, is a vastly better showing than when dropout is the standard. Still, if a fourth of Baltimore's young people are struggling to make their way in the world without high school certification, that proportion is far too high.

The timing of dropout in the BSS is organized in Table 11.1 according to *year* and *grade* of dropout.[8] The two accounting schemes would align perfectly if all children progressed through school in lockstep, but we know from Chapter 4 that grade retention and time in special education slow many children's progress. The implications for dropout show up in Table 11.1 as misalignment.

---

[7] The national figure is for the NELS88 eighth grade panel. It represents certification obtained as of 1994, 2 years after the group's expected graduation in spring 1992. The corresponding figure was 30% in the earlier High School and Beyond project (U.S. Department of Education 1989: 35–36), but in that panel high school completion increased to 46% after 4 years.

[8] The figures in Table 11.1 are based on N = 301, as the timing of dropout could not be determined in two instances.

About 35% of BSS dropouts, amounting to 14% of the entire co-hort, leave school having attained less than a 10th grade education, the standard in the literature for identifying "early leavers" (e.g., Rumberger 1995; Schneider et al. 1994). Here again experience in the BSS aligns with national estimates (in this instance for 16- to 24-year-olds: U.S. Department of Education 1997: 15). However, the mismatch in Table 11.1 between "grade attained at dropout" and "year left school" indicates that most of these early leavers repeated one or more grades before with-drawing – we say this because all of them started first grade together in fall 1982. "During Year 11" ($N = 95$) is the modal *year* of dropout in Table 11.1; 10th grade ($N = 88$) is the modal *grade* attained by dropouts. In fact, of the 95 who leave during Year 11, more are in 9th ($N = 36$) and 10th ($N = 37$) grades at the time than are "on-time" 11th graders ($N = 22$).[9]

Sixteen is the earliest age at which students may leave school legally in Maryland; at about that age children who are 2 years behind are making the transition from middle school to high school. For these students, the stresses of being off-time relative to grade level expectation add to the pressures surrounding school transitions that challenge children generally (e.g., Eccles et al. 1991). This confluence of forces apparently drives up dropout rates (e.g., Roderick 1995a; Roderick and Camburn 1999), especially when academic performance and school attachment are marginal, as is true for many repeaters (e.g., Alexander, Entwisle, and Kabbani 2002).

However, the hazard of dropping out is also high around the time of the next school transition, which is high school graduation. It may seem odd that so many students leave as 12th graders ($N = 41$, almost 14% of the total),[10] with the finish line seemingly so near, but this assumes the line is fixed, and that may not be the case. Only 18 of the 41 12th grade dropouts are in their 12th year of school at the time. The others are in their 13th, 14th, even 15th year, and we know from talking with

---

[9] Grade of dropout in Table 11.1 is defined in terms of children's grade level at the time of departure – those who leave during 10th grade or after completing 10th grade but before starting 11th grade are considered 10th grade dropouts. This is a bit different from the convention frequently used with Census data (Hauser et al. 2000; Kominski 1990), which identifies as 10th grade dropouts those who leave school after completing 9th grade or during 10th grade. Our interest in the alignment between year and grade of dropout recommends the present approach. Under the alternative construction, the BSS grade distribution of dropout is as follows: 7th, 0.3%; 8th, 4.3%; 9th, 25.2%; 10th, 25.9%; 11th, 26.2%; 12th, 17.9%.

[10] Using the Census definition, which counts as 12th grade dropouts those who finish 11th grade but do not begin 12th, the figure increases to 17.9%.

them that many saw ahead not caps and gowns, but yet another year in 12th grade – surely a discouraging prospect. Altogether, roughly 16% of BSS dropouts ($N = 49$) leave school *after* completing 12 years. These late dropouts demonstrate impressive commitment to school, but having already repeated at least one grade, they apparently decide it is time to try another tack.[11]

So, whereas many dropouts in the BSS leave at the earliest opportunity, others persevere but leave eventually anyway. Dropout rates appear to peak in 9th and 10th grades, and though they are high at those points, the mode of presentation used in Table 11.1 obscures a slight upward trend across grades that extends at least through 11th grade. This is because simple percentaging does not adjust for shrinkage over time in the population base as dropouts leave. For example, 10.4% of the entire cohort ($N = 729$) leave in 9th grade, 11.2% in 10th grade, and 8.8% in 11th grade. However, there are 170 fewer students still in school at the start of 11th grade than at the start of the 9th, so the 70 who leave then are a larger fraction of the "survivor" pool than are the 82 9th grade dropouts at the time of their departure. With the base appropriately adjusted, we get the following risk distribution (with calculations under the Census definition in parentheses): 6th grade, .14%; 7th, .55% (.14%); 8th, 2.1% (1.79%); 9th, 11.57% (10.63%); 10th, 14.04% (12.21%); 11th, 13.98% (14.08%); 12th, 8.74% (11.20%).

National estimates of dropout timing show a steady increase with ascending grade levels (e.g., Anderson 1999; Hauser et al. 2001; U.S. Department of Education 1997). The pattern in the BSS is a bit different, but we see the entire picture: "outflow" begins as a trickle in middle school, holds steady at high levels over grades 9–11, and then falls off a bit in 12th grade. The scheduling of dropout in relation to "push–pull" considerations has received scant attention in the literature (Anderson 1999, is an exception), but one suspects the circumstances surrounding early and late dropout must differ (African-American dropouts, for example, tend to leave later than do White dropouts, a pattern evident in the BSS as well as the nation, e.g., Hauser and Phang 1993; Kominski 1990). Here, though, we are more interested in commonalities than differences. Grade retention lurks behind the time line of dropout in the BSS; that much is clear from Table 11.1. But to move it into the foreground requires a different approach. The next section evaluates risk factors for dropout,

---

[11] This is not to say that school policy plays no role. Some late dropouts leave after being turned away when they try to transfer schools; others are denied admission to so-called second chance alternative schools. School practices that have the effect of pushing students out are discussed in Bowditch (1993) and Riehl (1999).

and in particular whether early grade retention plays a distinctive role in elevating dropout risk.

Grade Retention and Dropout

The 1997 edition of the Department of Education's annual series on high school dropout devotes an entire section to the grade retention–dropout connection. That a government report usually focused on prevalence statistics should venture so into "risk factors" is noteworthy. And what does the report's compilation of statistics show? Against a 1995 (status) dropout rate of 12% for never retained 16- to 24-year-olds, repeaters weigh in at 24.1%, a percentage that breaks down to 22.4% for single repeaters and 39.3% for multiple repeaters (U.S. Department of Education 1997: 46–47). Grade retention is associated with a two- to threefold elevation of dropout risk in much other research also (for overview and review, see Jimerson 2000).

These differences are large and troubling, but are they causal? That is the key question for policy. Is grade retention itself an impetus to dropout, or can the association between grade retention and dropout be traced to other factors that contribute to both, such as a history of poor school adjustment and low levels of achievement? To achieve clarity, the standard analytic remedy is to adjust statistically for common causes that might explain the association. There are many such studies – indeed early grade retention is perhaps the best documented school-based risk factor for dropout (e.g., Brooks-Gunn et al. 1993; Grissom and Shepard 1989; Jimerson 1999; Rumberger 1995; Rumberger and Larson 1998; Temple, Reynolds, and Miedel 2000) – but because of research design constraints most studies do not provide broad coverage of potential confounds, especially risks incurred in the early years. Again quoting the Goal 2 Work Group (1993: 18): "Few retention studies follow students throughout their school careers, especially studies beginning in the early elementary grades where retention is most likely to occur." The BSS is an exception. Data gathering for the BSS began before anyone was held back, and this depth puts us in a position to pursue the matter with a measure of authority.

Risk Factors for Dropout

The likelihood of dropping out is distinctly nonrandom, and BSS analyses have identified numerous early precursors to dropout. Children's conduct and school performance *as first graders* forecast dropout risk, for example (e.g., Alexander et al. 1997), as do later academic experiences, including grade retention (Alexander, Entwisle, and Kabbani 2001). The context of children's early schooling is implicated in non-BSS research, also (e.g., Brooks-Gunn et al. 1993; Ensminger and Slusarcick 1992; Garnier, Stein, and Jacobs 1997).

Family background and the out-of-school context also weigh heavily on graduation prospects in the BSS, including family socioeconomic level, family structure, mother's age, family stress, and maternal employment (Alexander et al. 2001), a listing familiar from many other studies (for overviews see Rumberger 1987; 2001; Wagenaar 1987).[12] Of these, family socioeconomic status (SES) dominates the list, with a fourfold difference in dropout rates across the socioeconomic "extremes" in the BSS: 60% of children we classify as lower-SES (half the panel, whose mothers average a 10th grade education) drop out at some point, as against 15% of those we classify as upper-SES (one-fourth of the panel, whose mothers average some college) (Alexander et al. 2001).[13]

Dropout risk is nonrandom by retention status also. Table 11.2 shows the basic information, for dropout (leaving school at least once without a degree) on the left column and high school noncompletion (failure to obtain certification by *any* route as of age 22–23) on the right. Trends are similar for the two, although at much lower levels for noncompletion.

The relevant figures samplewide are 42% dropout and 24% noncompletion. Grade retention greatly increases the risk of both. Two-thirds of

[12] Race/ethnicity is an exception. In the BSS the Black–White difference in dropout rates is not significant. However, African-American and White high school completion rates are also close nationally (e.g., Day and Curry 1998; Hauser et al. 2001; U.S. Department of Education 1998). The parity seen here could well be characteristic of disadvantaged urban populations generally (e.g., McDonald and LaVeist 2001), as the Whites who attend Baltimore's public schools – just 11.3% of the city system enrollment in 1999 (Maryland State Department of Education 2000) – are mostly low-income and so are at high risk of dropout for that reason. Moreover, Bauman (1998) reports that African-Americans achieve higher levels of education than Whites when SES is controlled (an advantage that extends back at least to the 1950s in his results).

[13] Our measure of family SES is computed as the average of up to five items (after conversion to standard scores): mother's education, father's education, mother's occupational status, father's occupational status, and family income, as indicated by participation in the federally subsidized school meal program for low-income households. When the scale is trichotomized such that roughly half the cohort is classified "low(er)" and a fourth "high(er)," mother's education in the lower-SES group averages 10 years and 95% of lower SES families qualify for subsidized school meals; in the higher-SES group, mother's education averages 14.6 years and 13% receive reduced price meals. These distinctions capture the range of family standing in Baltimore's public school enrollment, but that range embraces few genuinely upper-SES, wealthy households. The "lower"–"higher" descriptors in that sense are context bound.

TABLE 11.2. *Dropout Risk by Retention Status*

	% Dropout[a]	% Noncomplete[b]
All Rets[c]	67.3	45.5
	(287)	(286)
All Never Ret	24.2	10.3
	(430)	(429)
Never Ret, sans	22.0	09.0
Comparison Gp	(337)	(334)
Comparison Gp	32.3	14.7
	(93)	(95)
Ret 1	67.8	43.0
	(115)	(114)
Ret 2	58.1	46.0
	(62)	(63)
Ret 3	73.8	36.6
	(42)	(41)
Ret 4–7	70.6	54.4
	(68)	(68)
Spec Ed	53.1	38.8
	(49)	(49)
Spec Ed & Mult	61.5	47.4
Ret	(39)	(38)
Mult Ret	74.3	52.7
	(74)	(74)
Mult Ret	88.6	58.3
(No Spec Ed)	(35)	(36)

[a] *Dropout* means left school at some point without a degree.
[b] *Noncompletion* means has not obtained high school certification by any route as of age 22–23.
[c] *All Rets* are children held back through Year 7; *All Never Ret* are children not held back through Year 7; children held back in years 1, 2, 3, and 4 through 7 are identified, respectively, as *Ret 1, Ret 2, Ret 3,* and *Ret 4–7*; *Spec Ed* are children assigned to separate special education classes at some point over years 1–7 but not held back; *Spec Ed and Mult Ret* are double-repeaters who also were assigned to special education classes at some point; *Mult Ret (No Spec Ed)* are double-repeaters who were not assigned to special education; *Mult Ret* includes all double-repeaters.

repeaters leave school at some point, and even as young adults almost half still are without degrees. By way of comparison, a fourth of the never-retained group drops out and only 10 percent remain degreeless at age 22–23.[14]

[14] By way of comparison, the Chicago Longitudinal Study (CLS) has tracked the schooling of a low-income panel, mostly African-American, over roughly the same time frame as the BSS, from kindergarten to age 21–22. That group's dropout rate is 50.6% overall,

Repeaters in the BSS thus drop out at a rate approximately 2.8 times that of never-retained children, and the disparity for noncompletion is larger still, amounting to more than a fourfold difference. Are all classes of repeaters at similar risk? Apparently not. Double repeaters are at especially high risk, for example, as three-fourths of them leave school before graduation (including 89% of double repeaters who avoid special education).[15] A time trend also is evident in Table 11.2: children held back after second grade are more prone to dropout than are first and second grade repeaters, and those in grades 4–7 are at an especially high risk of noncompletion (54.4%).

Higher rates of dropout are also seen for later repeaters in national data (e.g., U.S. Department of Education 1997: 41). The situation of children held back in the upper grades is intriguing, as their school performance, we have seen, ranks well above early retainees' (i.e., those held back in grades 1–3). In light of their better grades and test scores, their exceeding others in terms of dropout and noncompletion seems odd.

The experience of children in the poor-performing promoted group also warrants comment. These youth had low CAT scores in first grade, but not as low as those of repeaters – the latter fall so far off the never-retained standard that a close match could not be achieved. If the comparison group were truly comparable and prior academic problems were the driving force behind dropout, then the poor performers would be expected to leave school in about the same numbers as repeaters. Instead, their dropout rate is much lower, and though the implication of this difference is clouded by the weak CAT match, the contrasts still are impressive: dropout level among comparison group children is roughly half again the level of other never-retained students (32% versus 22%), but less than half the level of repeaters (67%). Differences involving noncompletion are similar.

Adjusting for Potential Confounds

In agreement with virtually every study of this question, Table 11.2 establishes that repeaters in the BSS are a high-risk group for dropout.

including 69.7% of repeaters and 43.4% of nonrepeaters. Dropout risk in the CLS thus is about the same as in the BSS for repeaters, but higher for promoted children. However, in Chicago, it appears few dropouts go on to obtain alternative certification. High school noncompletion in the CLS is 47.4% overall, 67.4% for repeaters, and 39.9% for promoted youth (Temple et al. 2001).

[15] Exceptionally high levels of dropout among double repeaters are seen, too, in other local studies (e.g., Cairns and Cairns 1994; Fine 1991), as well as in national statistics (U.S. Department of Education 1997).

But is this "excess" dropout rate due to their status as repeaters, or is it traceable to other considerations involving repeaters' preretention risk profile, such as family hardship or achievement shortfall in the early years? Simple percentage comparisons, as in Table 11.2, cannot resolve the question, and certainly not when the "comparables" are not truly comparable. We know from Chapter 5 that BSS repeaters are drawn disproportionately from lower-income and minority households, and we have seen throughout this volume that before they are held back repeaters lag in school performance far behind promoted students.

One way to take account of these differences is to use statistical adjustments. The approach used in this section parallels that used earlier to estimate retainee/promoted differences on academic and attitudinal outcomes. Here, however, because dropout and noncompletion are both measured as simple dichotomies (i.e., 0–1 contrasts), the adjustments are implemented via logistic regression, whereas in previous chapters ordinary least squares (OLS) regression was used.

Dropout and noncompletion are analyzed separately and in parallel. Repeaters first are compared against all promoted children, then against the poor-performing but promoted subsample. Results reported in Table 11.3 are odds ratios. This is a different metric from the regression coefficients used in previous chapters to capture retainee–promoted (adjusted) outcome differences. Odds ratios express the conditionality of dropout or noncompletion on retention. To illustrate, Table 11.2 shows that roughly two-thirds of repeaters leave school without a degree. Accordingly, the odds of dropout given retention are 2.030 to 1 (i.e., $0.67/0.33 = 2.03$). The corresponding odds for children not held back are 0.316 to 1 (i.e., $0.24/0.76$). The ratio of these two odds (i.e., $2.030/0.316 = 6.42$) gives the difference in the relative risk of dropout associated with grade retention: repeaters' odds of dropping out in relation to never-retained students' odds. Note that simple odds are always represented as a likelihood with respect to 1 – odds are 2.030 to 1 or 0.316 to 1. The odds ratio is derived by dividing the simple odds, from which it follows that a value of 1.0 signifies "no difference" – that is, the odds for the groups being compared are the same.

Table 11.3 reports odds ratios for the several repeater groups relative to the never-retained group, before and after adjusting for possible confounding factors. The first set of statistical adjustments takes account of CAT scores from first grade and a by now familiar set of demographic factors (e.g., race/ethnicity, gender, mother's age, lunch subsidy status, number of siblings, household type, and age as of the fall of first grade). The second set highlights the experience of one-time repeaters

TABLE 11.3. *Odds Ratios Predicting Dropout and High School Completion: Repeaters vs. All Never-Retained and Repeaters vs. Poor-Performing Comparison Group*

	All Never Ret		Poor-Perf Comp Gp	
	HS Dropout[a]	HS Noncomplete[b]	HS Dropout[a]	HS Noncomplete[b]
With No Adjustments[c]				
Ret 1	8.89**	9.29**	5.25**	4.56**
Ret 2	5.47**	8.52**	3.23**	4.18**
Ret 3	6.58**	3.33*	3.89**	1.64
Ret 4–7	6.74**	12.08**	3.98**	5.93**
With Fall CAT and Demographic Adjustments[d]				
Ret 1	4.79**	4.33**	4.04**	3.25**
Ret 2	3.15**	4.83**	2.56*	3.45**
Ret 3	3.29**	1.49	2.59	1.16
Ret 4–7	4.30**	8.18**	3.45**	6.10**
With Double-Ret and Special Ed Adjustments[e]				
Ret 1	4.32**	3.64**	3.56**	2.63*
Ret 2	2.96**	4.29**	2.36	2.99*
Ret 3	2.65*	1.28	2.11	0.97
Ret 4–7	4.03**	7.78**	3.27**	5.72**
Spec Ed Only	0.64	1.02	0.62	1.05
Spec Ed & Ret	0.95	1.42	0.96	1.48
2d Ret	6.63*	1.84	7.43*	2.04

[a] *Dropout* means left school at some point without a degree.

[b] *Noncompletion* means has not obtained high school certification by any means as of age 22–23.

[c] These regressions adjust only for differences among the several retainee groups and between retainees and those never retained.

[d] These regressions adjust additionally for CAT scores from the fall of Year 1 and for demographic factors: race/ethnicity, gender, mother's education, lunch subsidy status (eligible or not), number of siblings, age as of the fall of first grade, and living in a two-parent household at the start of first grade.

[e] These regressions adjust additionally for differences associated with special education alone, double retention alone, or both.

* $p \leq .05$

** $p \leq .01$

never in special education by adjusting additionally for double retention and receipt of special education services (the same approach used in Chapters 7–9).

Entries in the top panel of Table 11.3 implement no such controls, however. Instead, they adjust only for the scheduling of retention (first grade repeaters versus the never retained, second grade repeaters versus the never retained, etc.),[16] showing all classes of repeaters at elevated risk of dropout relative to that of the never retained. The disadvantages suffered by repeaters are both broad-based and substantial, with the odds ratios generally larger for noncompletion than for dropout (the exception are third grade repeaters), for the earliest and latest retainees (as opposed to second and third grade repeaters), and when repeaters are compared against all never-retained children (as opposed to the poor-performing comparison group). Among first grade repeaters, for example, the odds of dropout are about nine times the odds among all never-retained youth.

This is a tremendous disparity, and even the smaller differences in the top panel of Table 11.3 (e.g., second grade repeaters against the poor-performing comparison group at 3.23) imply large differences in relative prospects across the retained–promoted divide. However, as we have cautioned throughout, these first entries in Table 11.3 simply describe the association between retention and dropout. Gauging retention's unique role as an *impetus* to dropout (i.e., as an effect on dropout) requires a more refined approach, one that takes into account other possible causes. Estimates in the second panel implement the adjustments that are needed and so are our best evidence of retention's effects in the "impetus" sense. Through statistical means, these comparisons equate repeaters and never retained in terms of first grade CAT scores and sociodemographic risk factors.

These adjustments do reduce retention differentials somewhat, but not enough to alter the essential conclusion: grade retention continues to stand out as a distinctive risk factor for dropout. In the case of first grade repeaters, for example, an unadjusted 9-to-1 risk in the odds of dropping out reduces to roughly a 5-to-1 risk after adjustment. Most of the retention coefficients in Table 11.3 are statistically significant and large, and they remain large also in analyses we have performed with even more expansive controls, including measures of school performance through Year 9 (and so closer in proximity to the time of dropout, e.g., Alexander et al. 2001; 2002). According to all these results, grade retention indeed diverts children from the path to high school graduation, and in terms of at least noncompletion, it is late retainees, those held back in grades 4 through 7, who are set back most by the experience.

[16] The odds ratios, though, are not identical to those that could be calculated from Table 11.2 because case coverage differs in the two instances – Table 11.3 screens out cases with missing data on any of the control variables used in the analysis.

The last panel of results separates out effects of double retention and receipt of special education services. Three points stand out here. First, these further adjustments do not have much effect on estimates of the four main repeater groups' dropout risk relative to that of those not retained. The figures from the middle panel generally shrink a little, but not much, indicating that even one-time repeaters who have been spared special education interventions are at elevated risk for dropout and noncompletion (third grade retainees are a possible exception). Second, double repeaters are at especially high risk of dropout (although they are not noticeably disadvantaged with respect to high school completion). Third, when allowance is made for prior levels of test performance and background risk factors, children who receive special education services, whether held back or not, do *not* have especially high odds of dropout; nor do they fall noticeably short in terms of eventual degree completion. Here the statistical adjustments do matter, as special education students in general have higher dropout rates than do general education students (e.g., McDonnell, McLaughlin, and Morison 1997: 95–96). However, the present findings accord with results from the Chicago Longitudinal Study (CLS) (e.g., Temple et al. 2000), a panel study of low-income Chicago schoolchildren that has many parallels to the BSS. In the BSS there is no *added risk* traceable specifically to placement in special education. Not so for retention, however, as repeaters' levels of dropout and noncompletion are far beyond expectation given their risk profile. This, too, accords with results from the CLS.

Discussion

This chapter finds that children held back in the upper grades and multiple repeaters are especially prone to leave school without degrees, but because single repeaters are also at elevated risk, grade retention seemingly alters children's school trajectories across the board. In previous chapters we concluded that double repeaters and first grade repeaters were helped least by repeating a grade, so their elevated levels of dropout and noncompletion are perhaps not surprising. But single repeaters held back in second grade also drop out in numbers greater than expected, and in at least one instance so do third grade repeaters. Earlier we concluded that single repeaters profited from an extra year in grade. If repeating a grade in elementary school boosts school performance and shores up children's self-regard, as it appears to do for BSS youth, why would it later drive up dropout risk?

The problem seems most pronounced for repeaters held back in grades 4–7, and this timing may hold a clue. When designated for retention, children held back in grades 4–7 are not as far behind their promoted classmates academically as are first and second grade repeaters at the time of their retention. Were grade retention simply a proxy for predisposing academic difficulties, first grade retention would be more problematic for dropout than later retention. Why is this not the case? Something other than retention's academic consequences must be at issue, but if not academics, what then? Repeaters' off-time status seems a likely candidate.

Schooling in the United States is strongly age-graded, and falling off the prescribed timetable of grade progressions creates problems for repeaters. For one thing, it makes them conspicuous. For another, it complicates social integration with classmates. In grades 4 to 7 children are making the elementary to middle school transition. Transitions are much more difficult without close friends to ease the path, and repeaters over the first three grades have had time to make new friends.

Being "out of step" can cause problems at any age, but conditions peculiar to late retention may well heighten them. The adolescent middle grade years (typically age 12–14) are a time of heightened self-consciousness, when "fitting in" is paramount. But for recent repeaters, the separation from their friends is still fresh, and "fitting in" may not be easy. They find themselves thrust into the company of younger children at a time in life when an age difference of a year or two counts for a great deal (physically, emotionally, and socially). Students who are struggling academically sometimes find refuge in the social side of schooling, the extracurriculum (Mahoney and Cairns 1997; McNeal 1995) and strong friendships (Hymel, Comfort, Schonert-Reichl, and McDougall 1996), but because repeaters are overage for grade, these sources of attachment to school may be difficult to attain. And with grade repetition less common in the upper elementary and middle school years, unlike early repeaters, these children lack the refuge (and anonymity) afforded by large numbers.

And what lies ahead? For late repeaters, it is the middle school to high school transition. In previous chapters we saw repeaters' standing begin to slide when they move from elementary to middle school and it is reasonable to anticipate even greater challenges at the next level. Educational transitions are hard on children generally (Belsky and Mackinnon 1994; Dunn 1988; Eccles et al. 1991; Entwisle and Alexander 1989; Simmons and Blyth 1987), and the high school transition is no exception (Roderick 1995a). Consider this one "symptom": in their ninth year of school, future dropouts in the BSS averaged 46.8 absences. This figure compares with an average of 13.5 absences among nondropouts. With 47 *recorded* absences, these dropouts-to-be were missing about 1 day of every 4 – fade-out segueing to dropout, hardly an auspicious way to start high school.

Moreover, the timetable of schooling puts late repeaters in a vastly different situation from that, say, of elementary school repeaters within a year or two of their retention. The problems surrounding later retentions all are fresh when the time arrives to contemplate what life in high school might hold, and for those approaching age 16 "exit" is an option. They can leave a situation that many no doubt find punishing for a world outside school that may seem to hold greater promise. Because dropout risk is elevated for late retainees specifically, it appears many avail themselves of that option (Grissom and Shepard [1989] and Roderick [1994] advance similar interpretations of the retention–dropout link).

The situation of late repeaters holds important lessons as a result of such timing considerations, but it would be a mistake to overstate their distinctiveness – the differences between them and early repeaters are matters of degree, not of kind. All the retentions examined in this chapter precede high school, and so all have the effect of putting children off-time when making the transition from middle school to high school. Indeed, even so-called academic redshirts appear to be at high risk of dropout as a result of their off-time standing (Roderick 1993; 1994). These children are overage for grade because they started school late, not because they were retained, but they confront the same sort of adjustment challenges. Recent retentions may be more salient, and hence more difficult, but our interpretation points to social pressures that apply broadly when children find themselves off-time in making school transitions, and especially children whose school performance and attachment already are shaky.

Dropout rates at the levels experienced by the BSS panel and other poor urban students are a tragedy. Grade retention may be a contributing factor, but problems associated with rigid age grading have little relation to the conventional lines of debate – that is, does retention help or hurt academically; is it stigmatizing? And if the diagnosis is different, then what of remedies? These are taken up in the concluding chapter.

12

The Retention Puzzle

Problem, Solution, or Signal?

This volume began by asking whether retention helps children, as intended, or harms them, as critics of the practice believe. In hindsight, the question seems too simplistic, as is the expectation that there will be a simple answer to it.

For measures of school performance and attitudes, retention for many BSS children has mainly positive consequences. Positive effects are clearest for one-time repeaters and children held back *after* first grade. The children not helped, multiple repeaters and first grade repeaters, have severe problems that predate their retention, and so the implications of less favorable results for them are clouded. First grade repeaters in particular are caught in a web of low-level track placements over their entire school career: most are assigned to special education, most are in low first grade reading groups, and their reading level is low all along the way. Further, when they get to middle school it is "more of the same" – they are assigned to low-level academic courses. These children's academic and adjustment difficulties predate their retention, overlap the time of their retention, and continue after their retention, as do their low-level track placements. Repeating a grade has not helped these children (at least over the long term) – that much seems clear – but can it really be said that retention is the source of their problems? Any such conclusion takes us out of the realm of evidence and into the realm of opinion, preconception, or worldview.

And what of those situations in which repeating seems to help? Here, too, claims require qualification, even if one is willing to grant that technical problems are not distorting the picture. For one thing, the benefits that follow from an extra year in grade are not "across the board."

Despite the academic boost and associated improvements in attitude that result from doing better in school after retention, many of these children still do not finish high school. Given what we now know about the long-term costs of high school dropout, this is a very serious consequence indeed. The distinction between "solution" and "some help" becomes critical here, and glossing over it is a source of much confusion. The academic and socioemotional boost BSS repeaters get from an extra year in grade is real but limited: most one-time repeaters derive some benefit but afterward still lag behind their agemates and grademates. Should grade retention be faulted for their continuing difficulties or credited for their progress? It is a question with no certain answer.

Conflicting Views on Grade Retention

Except for our findings related to dropout, conclusions in this volume are at odds with the view of retention that dominates academic research circles, namely, that retention impedes children's academic development and assaults their sense of self. Our conclusions about retention accord well with practitioners' understandings, though, as numerous surveys report that teachers see a useful role for retention in helping poor-performing students overcome problems before they fall too far behind (e.g., Byrnes 1989; Lombardi et al. 1990; Smith 1989; Smith and Shepard 1988; Tomchin and Impara 1992). Why such wildly discrepant perceptions? In Chapter 2 we reviewed some of the technical problems that detract from research on retention's effects. High-quality studies in fact are few, and not all such studies find against retention. In fact, there is less of a sound foundation supporting negative views than many suppose, and it does not help that some of the more influential reviews harbor a decidedly negative bias. A fair reading of this body of research turns up more questions than answers, but this is not reflected in scholarly commentary on the topic.

Studies that match repeaters with control youngsters and then track for a year or two afterward how the two groups are faring – the most common research paradigm – do not give a proper accounting of retention's effects. Repeaters have multiple problems. After retention their test scores are depressed, their marks are low, and they are prone to problem behaviors, but these problems all are discernible *before* retention. It is understandable that people concerned about retainees' welfare would find the picture troubling on the face of it. It also is understandable that retention would be faulted if just the "after" problems are perceived, as in everyday, casual observation. It is much less understandable that most matched-control studies also only look forward from the point of failure, with the result that they too lack perspective on repeaters' earlier problems.

Few studies are like the present one, in which future repeaters are "captured" by taking a random sample from a well-defined cohort of students and then monitored in terms of academic progress and personal development over a long interval that predates and follows the retention experience. An outstanding exception is the Chicago Longitudinal Study (CLS), to which we have referred several times in this volume. The CLS targets a poverty-level, entirely African-American, inner-city population, tracking their experiences, so far, from kindergarten to age 21–22. Grade retention is less common in the CLS than in the BSS (28% through eighth grade), but otherwise the two projects share many commonalities.

Two CLS reports examine performance outcomes and attitudes (McCoy and Reynolds 1999; Reynolds 1992), as well as teacher ratings of children's school competence. The more recent study, which takes stock of early repeaters' standing in fourth grade, also assesses self-reported delinquent behaviors.[1] The earlier report (Reynolds 1992) finds positive retention effects on pupil attitudes, no effect on teacher ratings, no achievement differences in same-grade comparisons, and large repeater shortfall in same-age comparisons (all after adjusting statistically for background characteristics, preretention achievement scores, and more).

In the BSS, we, too, find large same-age achievement deficits in the spring of Year 4, at least among first grade repeaters. In the BSS, though, these differences sometimes are considerably less than repeaters' shortfall prior to their retention. By taking a more appropriate baseline – the level where children were before retention – the BSS shows retention in a favorable light even when same-age (and sometimes same-grade) comparisons show repeaters lagging behind. This key comparison, unfortunately, is not made in the CLS report through fourth grade; nor is it provided in the later report that monitors children's progress through 8 years.[2]

---

[1] Other CLS reports address high school dropout (e.g., Temple, Reynolds, and Ou 2000).
[2] The 1992 CLS report scales achievement scores in grade-equivalent units. Though a perfectly fine frame of reference for locating repeaters' standing relative to that of others at the same grade level, that calibration is not well suited for judging changes in repeaters'

The achievement results in McCoy and Reynolds (1999) are consistently negative: repeaters are behind in both reading and math. However, differences involving teacher ratings of school competence and self-reported delinquency are negligible (this pattern holds with and without adjustment for placement in special education). Repeater–promoted differences in the CLS, assessed at the end of seventh grade in the same-grade format and at age 14 in the same-age format, are as follows (after statistical adjustments): Reading, -4.60 same-grade, -9.50 same-age, both significant; Math, -1.30 same-grade, -8.90 same-age, the second significant. Three of the four comparisons show repeaters significantly behind, with differences as large as half a standard deviation. Still, the CLS finds no differences on nonacademic criteria, potentially a positive finding. (Recall our earlier discussion: if a gap favoring promotion is expected, then a finding of "no difference" can be said to reflect positively on retention's contribution.)

The more recent CLS report compares its findings against ours as published in the first edition of this volume. Here is what McCoy and Reynolds (1999) say:

In their Baltimore study Alexander, Entwisle, and Dauber (1994)... reported some positive effects of retention on second- and third-grade children, such that the achievement gap between retained and nonretained children prior to retention narrowed substantially in the years following retention. This occurred both for same-age and same-grade comparisons. Nevertheless, they also reported that retained children consistently lagged behind their same-age and same-grade promoted peers by the eighth-grade year, even after accounting for differences in preretention achievement levels and other factors. Finally our findings that grade retention was unrelated to social–psychological behavior at ages 12–14 occupy the intermediate position between studies showing positive effects (Alexander et al. 1994; Gottfredson et al. 1994) and negative effects (Meisels and Liaw 1993; Roderick 1994).

The summary of their results and ours seems fair, but with at least one correction (i.e., some adjusted same-grade BSS comparisons in the upper grades favor repeaters). More important, without before–after comparisons from the CLS we do not know how well results from the two projects align from that perspective. Nevertheless, the CLS summary also accords with our sense of the literature generally – the evidence is mixed and not consistently against retention. Much hinges on

own standing over time. The 1999 report shifts to standard scores (centered on 100) as the achievement metric. This scaling is better suited to pre-/postcomparisons of the sort we favor, but the CLS report still does not look at its data that way.

the outcome domains at issue, the exact method by which comparisons are structured, and when in students' careers comparisons are made. We already have pointed out, for example, that repeaters' situation looks worse in middle school than in the primary grades, a conclusion to which we return shortly.

The life course perspective that is missing from the CLS reports is missing from most other retention evaluations also. House (1989) attributes teachers' favorable view of retention to their short time horizon – for example, teachers do not see repeaters' problems that emerge after the repeated year. His point is well taken and is borne out in the BSS: the sizable repeated-year rebound that retention confers does not hold up well over time. However, for a proper reading of retention's effects, the time frame needs to stretch in *both* directions. Most retention evaluations gloss over problems that exist before children are held back, an oversight that seriously compromises the integrity of findings. As already pointed out, if after retention repeaters are doing less well than promoted children, they still may be doing better than they would have otherwise.

Also ignored in most commentary and research on retention are other tracklike interventions that retainees experience – such as low reading-group placements in first grade, low course placements in middle school, and special education placements. These placements may be even more relevant to children's daily routine and experience at school than their standing as retainees and are much more common for repeaters than for promoted students. Special education probably alters the daily routine most dramatically (e.g., Carrier 1986; Richardson 2000), but high and low reading groups in elementary school and high-and low-track classes in middle school also differ markedly in status as seen by students, parents, and classmates, with obvious implications for the social relations of schooling. Such placements also introduce differences between retainees and nonretainees in the pace of instruction, in the structure of the subject matter, and in the extent of the curriculum that is actually taught (e.g., Barr and Dreeben 1983; Dougherty 1996; Oakes et al. 1992).

Retention studies are rarely sensitive to this broader organizational context, a potentially serious oversight. The "pathways" of Chapter 4 and the "bundling" of track placements in Chapter 10 establish that retainees often are consigned to low tracks, yet most evaluations of retention ignore tracking within grades. Consequences of low placements and special education are not separated out. They are even seen as consequences of retention rather than concomitants. The point is that retention is only one of many administrative arrangements commonly used, and the various arrangements overlap in ways likely to slow retainees' progress.

Finally, preconceptions play a strong role. Much critical commentary on retention reflects a hostile predisposition partly grounded in equity or fairness concerns of the sort reviewed in Chapter 1. We share these concerns and respect those who are moved by them, but they are no warrant for a premature rush to judgment.

In the BSS and elsewhere minority and disadvantaged children tend to be overrepresented in lower-track placements and are more likely to be held back than Whites or children from higher socioeconomic status (SES) families. When children are separated along racial/ethnic and economic lines (even if the separation is based on educationally appropriate criteria) and then assigned disproportionately to tracks low in the school's hierarchy of prestige, the risk of harm is real.

The other risk, though, is that of accepting evidence too readily only because it accords with one's wish for equity. Not all "separations" are bad, and a reflexive inclination toward leveling can do more harm than good in the absence of superior alternatives. Consider, for example, recent experience with so-called detracking initiatives. As an abstraction the concept has great appeal, but evidence on its hidden risks is beginning to mount – the promised benefits are not always realized and students' progress sometimes is slowed (e.g., Gamoran and Weinstein 1998; Loveless 1999; Rosenbaum 1999–2000).

Today's tension between forces committed to ending grade retention and those committed to ending social promotion likewise offers much promise but also much risk. The healthy result would be an energetic search for workable, effective alternatives to both these "remedies" (e.g., Alexander et al. 1999; Darling-Hammond 1998; U.S. Department of Education 1999), neither of which in actuality is a remedy for anything. But partisanship can cloud thinking, and sweeping policy pronouncements that go beyond the evidence, or distort it, risk making matters worse, not better.

Whether a child should repeat a grade is the implicit question in most evaluations of retention. Had we started at the point when children were held back, as most research does, we would have missed not just the depth of their earlier problems, but also the course they were running prior to retention. Without this perspective, the turnaround reflected in children's progress during the repeated year would have been obscured. And even when repeaters' standing slipped after retention, in many comparisons these children still were better off than they were before repeating. Retainees only rarely kept up, in the sense of having test scores or marks at the level of promoted children's. Sometimes the comparisons were not favorable, as in the case of first grade repeaters (and others) when they arrived at the middle school period. But after adjusting repeaters' later performance for their standing before retention, in same-grade comparisons they often were ahead of expectation for children "like them."

Our data show little harm from retention, and we see no reason for expecting social promotion – that is, moving children ahead regardless of their preparation – to repair anything. Let us be clear: we are not enthusiasts for grade retention, especially traditional grade repetition without supplemental services. In the ideal, options other than retention and social promotion would be available, and we need to work energetically toward that end. But for educators, administrators, and parents confronted with an immediate problem, the theoretical ideal may have little relevance. Statements about effectiveness hold "on average," and that means there are exceptions. The practical question is how best to help specific children who are struggling in light of (1) the nature of their problems and (2) the resources available. In places like Baltimore, the decision often is whether to promote or retain. Would first grade repeaters in the BSS really have been better off being moved ahead? And how would it affect the schooling of other children in the classes they joined if so many additional classmates were performing at such low levels? To the first question, the answer is "almost certainly not"; to the second, we would have to say we really do not know, but such potential tradeoffs have to be balanced every day by administrators, teachers, and other school personnel, and members of the research community ought to be mindful of them (for relevant comment, see Natriello 1998). Our advice under such circumstances is to judge each case on its merits; sometimes retention may be the more appropriate course.

There are at least two problems when critics say, in blanket terms, that grade retention is harmful: (1) they deflect attention from the real problems identified in this volume, those confused with retention; (2) they deny the gift of time to those who might benefit from it. Children's rates of development are highly variable. A good example is early language development: some children are speaking in paragraphs at age 2; others have yet to utter more than single words at age 3; both are equally verbal by the time they start first grade. Parents see the benefits for redshirting when they make this decision. Why cannot a similar decision be made by the school without prejudice for the child?

The Gift of Time: Grade Retention and the Pace of Schooling

Not all children struggle at school for the same reason, as recognized in a Department of Education report on social promotion (1999: 32):

Some students have learning disabilities, others have behavioral problems, are not ready for school, or face other challenges in their families and in their lives outside school. Some students barely miss meeting the standards, while others perform at levels considerably behind their peers. The point is that in order to help all students meet standards, educators must understand the nature of children's difficulties, and they must do so early.

Across the board solutions will not work, and the available research offers little guidance for determining individual placements. To know the best course in the individual case requires understanding of what underlies a particular child's difficulties. And context must be factored in. We would not expect problems surrounding retention to be the same in high-poverty schools with many children at risk of failure as in low-poverty schools with few children at risk.

The "Retention/Promotion Checklist" (Grant and Richardson 1998) is the rare instance of a research-informed diagnostic inventory. It encourages thinking of retention, when it seems advised, as "additional learning time for misplaced students" (Kelly 1999: 1). These six words shift the onus from the child to the school and banish the black cloud. What kinds of children might be candidates for additional learning time? The "younger students in a class, emotionally immature children of average or high ability, and children who are small for their age" (Kelly 1999: 2; see also Grant and Richardson 1999). That kind of guidance is sorely needed, but global research on retention's effectiveness is not well suited to the task.

In reality, though, the problem is as much organizational as it is personal. What grade retention "buys" is time, but it is extra time within the framework of traditional scheduling and calendar constraints. All children are expected to be "ready" for first grade at age 6; they are expected to move in lockstep annually thereafter from one grade to the next; and within the school year, they are expected to master the curriculum in the same time frame – 9 months, fall to spring. This calendar-driven model of schooling sets a severe pace: children who are not up to speed when the teacher is obliged to move on to the next lesson are left behind, and if they are far behind when the final bell sounds for the year, what then? Should they be moved ahead anyway? Should they be held back?

Because the curriculum in the primary grades is the foundation for all later learning, children need to master it before moving on. But children do not all mature on the same schedule; they do not all learn at the same pace; and they do not all develop in the same way. Mastering the curriculum takes longer for some than for others. This simple insight is certainly not original with us. Here is how the National Education Commission on Time and Learning (1994: p. 7) puts it:

Decades of school improvement efforts have foundered on a fundamental design flaw, the assumption that learning can be doled out by the clock and defined by the calendar.... Some students take three to six times longer than others to learn the same thing. Yet students are caught in a time trap – processed on an assembly line to the minute. Our usage of time virtually assures the failure of many students.

The challenge – a daunting one – is to build more flexibility into the system without the stigma and other problems associated with being "off-time." We return to this point later, in our concluding remarks.

Marginal Students and Educational Transitions

The value of a "gift of time" when it is needed is one point missed by critics of retention. Another point is that by faulting retention for children's difficulties, they advance an implicit remedy that misdiagnoses the problem. The problems our analyses identify have little to do with retention itself, so simply moving children ahead will not solve those problems. Our results, rather, point to the burdens that weigh on children at key educational transition points: when they start formal schooling, when they move from the elementary grades into middle school, and then later when it is time for them to make transitions into and out of high school. There can be little doubt that the way children weather these transitions is more important for their well-being than any issues involving retention policy. A life-course perspective identifies transitions as times of stress in people's lives (for a general overview see Elder 1998). The life transitions that usually come to mind are situated in adulthood (e.g., Elder 1991) – marrying, becoming a parent, embarking on a new career, entering retirement. But children's role transitions can be as dramatic as, as challenging as, and possibly more overwhelming than those experienced by adults because children have less control over their lives and fewer resources to meet challenges. Some are better positioned than others to manage transition difficulties. Those not well positioned may need extra help.

This volume has considered two in-school transitions: into full-time schooling, representing children's first encounter with the student role and its associated bureaucratic trappings; and the transition from elementary to middle school, when the role demands and the bureaucracy undergo significant changes. Both transitions are harder on repeaters – in the first instance, because they are already shaky academically; in the latter, because being off-time or overage for grade causes them additional problems. And in a more subtle way, these children have been forced to make a third transition. Being held back means the "normal" passage from one grade to the next is replaced by a "backward" move with the need to adjust to new peers and classrooms. Repeating a grade poses many of the same transitional pressures as moving from one school to the next.

The Beginning School Transition and Early School Failure

The relevance of transition pressures at the time of school entry is obvious. Indeed, failure in the early grades is prima facie evidence of unsuccessful adaptation to the student role. Time and again in this volume striking parallels emerge between the severity of children's difficulties and the scheduling of their retention. Can that be coincidental? First grade retainees, the largest single repeater group by far in the BSS, are also the most severely stressed. And this pattern is not the rule just in Baltimore, as retention rates are the highest in first grade throughout the country (Chapter 1). In many localities kindergarten retention is also common (especially if pre–first transition years are counted).

The beginning school period entails a transition into a new social world (Entwisle and Alexander 1989; 1993). Children add "schoolchild" to their role set and must learn to function in an institutional context governed by conventions different from those at home. Parent–child and pupil–teacher relations are very different: the latter is instrumental, impersonal, and achievement oriented (e.g., Dreeben 1968). These new and different role relationships challenge all youngsters, but to children with few resources outside school who have grown up outside the middle-class mainstream, home and school may seem to be different worlds.

Differences across class lines in family socialization practices and resources give children from higher-SES families an academic advantage before they begin school, and a continuing advantage through all their school years (e.g., Hess and Holloway 1984; Slaughter and Epps 1987). Children who lack these advantages often get off to a shaky start academically, and once they have fallen behind, their prospects for recovery are not good. Achievement trajectories are established early (e.g., Bloom 1964; Kraus 1973): children who lose ground in terms of test scores and marks over the first few years tend to stay behind all along the way. Retention calls attention to children's academic problems, but does it cause them? Not for the BSS children, so far as we can tell.

Academic failure and weak attachment to school are the root problems that need fixing. The price that many children pay for growing up in highly stressed home and community circumstances is academic failure. All BSS children began first grade in 1982. Most of their parents were in their 20s. During this time (and still today) being young, poorly educated, a single parent, or African-American often also meant living in poverty or at its edge. In Baltimore, as in other old-line cities, Whites and the well-to-do have been abandoning the city, moving out in large numbers and taking neighborhood institutions, such as banks, schools, community centers, Little League sports, and Scout troops, along with them. In 1980, near the time when the BSS started, Baltimore's population was 55% African-American, up from 47% a decade earlier. The White population remaining was much older than the African-American population (median ages of 37.0 versus 26.2: U.S. Census Bureau 1973; 1983). Forty-one percent of Baltimore households with children under 18 were headed by a female, and half of them fell below the poverty line. Overall, 19% of families were living in poverty, and about the same percentage receiving public assistance. Nearly a third of 16- to 19-year-olds were identified as not enrolled in school and not high school graduates, and more than half of adults 25 years and older had not completed high school (U.S. Census Bureau 1983). Baltimore placed 14th among the nation's 15 largest cities in 1983 in the percentage of 20- to 24-year-olds who complete high school (Szanton 1986).

These conditions during the early 1980s were the community backdrop to BSS youngsters' elementary schooling, and the situation locally has not improved much since. Baltimore continues to have one of the highest dropout rates in the country (Bomster, 1992; Bowie, 1998; Casey Foundation 1997; Kelly 1989). In 1990, its childhood poverty rate was 32.5% for children 18 and younger (39.1% among African-Americans), as against 15.2% for the nation's 200 largest cities (Children's Defense Fund 1992); in that same year Baltimore ranked 11th among the nation's 100 largest cities in terms of poverty concentration (Kasarda 1993: Table A.1). By 1997 it placed second highest among U.S. cities in the percentage of births to teen mothers and infant mortality rate, and its juvenile arrest rate led the nation (Casey Foundation 1997).

The population served by the public schools is even more disadvantaged now than it was two decades ago, and the immediate family context of most BSS children offers more of the same. In 1999, two-thirds of Baltimore City Public School (BCPS) students received free or reduced price meals at school, an indication of low income relative to family size (Maryland State Department of Education 1999), and in more than half the city's elementary schools low-income enrollments exceeded 80% (*Baltimore Sun* 1999).

On the home front, as first graders 47% of BSS children were in single-parent households; two-thirds received free or reduced price meals at school; and just below 40% of their mothers had no high school degree. First grade benchmarks for children who remained in city schools over the 8 years covered in this volume are even more sobering as a result of the outward migration reviewed in Chapter 4: 52% in single-parent households, 76% low-income, and 42% high school dropout mothers – all well documented academic risk factors.

For youngsters who are not regularly promoted over the first three grades, failure is not a sharply demarcated experience that occurs when they are held back. Rather, they have been "failing" or "near-failing" all along. Children's early struggles with the demands of schooling put far too many at risk, but programs to help young people manage this difficult time in their lives are not well described. Head Start, the only federally funded preschool program for poor children, serves about one in five children in poor families, and at present just 52% of poverty level 3- to 5-year-olds obtain any kind of center-based care as against 62% of nonpoverty-level children (Federal Interagency Forum on Child and Family Statistics 2000: 47).

Kindergarten follows preschool, and though kindergarten now is practically universal, many children – over 40% – still only attend half the day (U.S. Census Bureau 1999). Programs to ease school adjustment during kindergarten generally are piecemeal and rarely represent formal policy. Although most school personnel do not view kindergarten adjustment as especially difficult, according to Love and Logue's National Transition Study (1992) the data indicate otherwise. A third of schools in which half or more of students qualify for free meals report that children have great difficulty in adjusting. These schools also report more transition classes (e.g., an extra year between kindergarten and first grade) and retention. Whatever the merits of such practices, their being disproportionate in schools that enroll low-income children aligns with the high rate of early failure in the BSS: too many children start school unprepared or not well enough prepared for what awaits them.

The Middle School Transition and the Fading of Retention's Benefits

Getting off to a bad start in school is the backdrop to early retention. Recovering from early failure is hard, but single repeaters do recover to some extent after being held back a year. The recovery is not complete, though, because most retainees remain behind both their previous classmates and their new ones. The recovery also is only temporary.

The gains children realize by repeating a grade are hard won, and costly, so to see them fade over time is a disappointment. In fact, though, most interventions designed to shore up the academic skills of at-risk children have transient effects. Preschool programs for the disadvantaged such as Head Start raise test scores only temporarily.[3] Such children usually show a significant intelligence quotient (IQ) spurt in the year after participation, but after a couple of years their scores typically are no better than those of children with no preschool (e.g., Currie and Thomas 1995; Lazar and Darlington 1982; Schweinhart, Berrueta-Clement, Barnett, Epstein, and Weikart 1985; Schweinhart and Weikart 1985).[4] A similar "spurt–fade-out" pattern likewise is seen in comparisons of half-day versus full-day kindergarten programs (Entwisle, Alexander, Cadigan, and Pallas 1987; Karweit 1989) and in assessments of Chapter 1 (now Title 1), the major federal program for assisting

---

[3] This may be due to problems with the schools disadvantaged preschoolers later attend, and not the quality of their preschool experience (e.g., Currie and Thomas 1998; Lee, Brooks-Gunn, Schnur, and Liaw 1990).

[4] Gains in IQ and achievement may be transient, but that hardly makes them inconsequential. They could, for example, be the reason poor preschooled children are less often held back or assigned to special education. Retention rates are highest in first grade, so an edge at this point could tip the scales. Woodhead (1988: 447–448) discusses how such temporary improvement can "trigger a more positive cycle of achievement and expectation [and] carry the child through the later grades long after the original cognitive benefits had washed out." Then, too, IQ gains and performance on standardized tests are not the only considerations. The same research shows that preschooled children are less likely to be held back and assigned to special education. Follow-up studies that track children beyond high school also find that participants more often graduate from high school, are less likely to experience unemployment and to be on public assistance, are more likely to be living with a spouse or companion, and are less likely to be in jail (for overview, see Barnett 1995).

schools that service large numbers of poverty-level children (e.g., Carter 1984; Borman and D'Agostino 2001).[5]

None of these efforts to help children represents a well-defined intervention model. Head Start and Chapter 1/Title 1 are mainly funding pipelines. The way moneys are deployed is largely a local matter. Similarly, extending kindergarten to a full day simply buys more time for children in school; the use to which that time is put is not standardized.[6] Indeed, in all of these areas attempts to inform future planning by isolating program features critical to program effectiveness have not been especially successful (e.g., Karweit 1989; Schweinhart, Weikart, and Larner 1986; White 1985–1986; White, Taylor, and Moss 1992; but see Frede 1995 and Entwisle 1995).

Retention, too, lacks programmatic coherence, and exactly why this experience helps children has yet to be isolated. Many localities provide supplemental services for retainees, but systematic comparisons of alternative service models are rarely attempted. Retention-plus plans, that is, retention coupled with other services such as one-on-one instruction and smaller class sizes, seem to work better than simple grade repetition, but little is certain. Grade retention "helps some" in the short term, but absent an effective program to consolidate and sustain children's improved performance, its advantages do not last. To that extent, the evidence on retention parallels that for other "buying time" interventions.

Our results tell us a little more, however. Retainees' academic standing in some instances shows improvement several years after retention, an uncommonly long interval, or, equivalently, an uncommonly slow fade. Moreover, in several comparisons the fade is abrupt, not gradual, and performance and attitudes drop off most noticeably in grades 6–8, or middle school. "Settling in" issues arise whenever children switch schools, and the elementary to middle school move is no exception.

---

[5] This holds, too, for evaluations of the Project Follow Through planned variation experiment (Stebbins, St. Pierre, Proper, Anderson, and Cerva 1977). Follow Through was a federal program intended to build on the successes of Head Start by providing extra services and resources to children during the early elementary years. Even though funding for Follow Through waned during the 1970s, controversy raged for years over whether different Follow Through sites differed in effectiveness and whether specific effective program features could be identified (e.g., Bereiter and Kurland 1981–82; Gersten 1984; House, Glass, McLean, and Walker 1978).

[6] More generally, time logs document very low rates of productive or engaged time in the typical classroom (e.g., Yair 2000).

Having to learn one's way around a new physical plant, getting to know new teachers and administrators, being separated from one's long-time friends, and going from the top to the bottom of the school's social hierarchy are very real concerns for children. All of these problems are magnified when the move is from a smaller school to a bigger one, as is typical with the middle grades and high school transitions.

But size is not the only factor that changes in moving up. Compared with elementary schools, middle and junior high schools are larger and more departmentalized, teaching is more specialized, standards of performance are higher, and academic achievement is emphasized more, all of which encourage a more competitive atmosphere. There are also differences in the character of pupil–teacher relations: teachers tend to be more distant and controlling; whole-class instruction is the norm; evaluation is more public; and tracking tends to be more formalized and rigid.

This middle school or junior high environment is very different from that of the primary grades. The very features of schooling in the middle grades that are new in children's experience run counter to their needs as adolescents. Eccles and Midgley (1989: 141) describe the situation as follows:

These changes are *particularly* harmful at early adolescence in that they emphasize competition, social comparison and ability self-assessment at a time of heightened self-focus; they decrease decision-making and choice when the desire for control is growing; and they disrupt social networks at a time when adolescents are especially concerned with peer relationships and may be in special need of close adult friendships.

The middle grades transition is hard on children, and it is a problem shared by middle schools and junior highs alike (e.g., Cuban 1992; Eccles et al. 1991).[7] Children's attitudes toward self and school, along with their performance, tend to deteriorate as they move from the primary grades to later ones (for an overview see Eccles and Midgley 1989; Stipek 1984; Weisz and Cameron 1985), but there is an especially precipitous decline right around the middle grades transition. And probably low achievers are the ones most challenged by the more

---

[7] This conclusion may be too sweeping, however. Although Epstein and MacIver (1990) conclude that most middle schools "have not yet developed educational programs based on recommended practices for the middle grades" (p. 73), some differences indicate more responsive practices in middle schools. These include more opportunities for remedial instruction, activities designed to ease transition pressures, and a greater commitment to interdisciplinary teaming.

elaborated bureaucracy that characterizes school organization in the upper grades (e.g., Entwisle 1990).

The experience of the BSS youngsters suggests that the middle school transition especially challenges elementary school repeaters. Retainees are off-time (and older) when making the middle school transition, so for them the adolescent and school transitions may still overlap.[8] Though these children were doing better in the postretention period than before, they still were performing marginally, so it is reasonable to suppose that any of several middle school features mentioned – elevated standards, a more rigid tracking system, or the larger, more impersonal bureaucracy – could set them back. These are problems for everyone, but repeaters are not as well positioned as other students to manage them.

If the performance and affective "dips" experienced by repeaters in the Beginning School Study at the time of the middle school transition mark this as a time of particular vulnerability, then repeaters' later dropout statistics are its logical culmination. Two-thirds of BSS repeaters leave school without degrees, and the percentages are higher still for double retainees and children held back toward the end of elementary school. At first blush, this seems a terrible indictment of grade retention, and certainly dropout figures anywhere near these levels are a tragedy – who could think otherwise? But apparently dropout rates are elevated among repeaters as a result of context rather than adverse effects on children's academic development, an important distinction. This perspective sheds light on the counterintuitive observation that most dropouts are *not* failing at the time they drop out. Rather, dropout risk is elevated by problems of social and personal adjustment.

The present volume finds smaller but still significant repeater–promoted dropout differences when relevant preretention measures are controlled, and other BSS research shows much the same when the counterpart postretention measures are added as controls (Alexander et al. 2000; 2001). What seems to be happening in the BSS is that being out of step adds to repeaters' difficulties at a time when they already are fragile. The fragility aspect of the problem hardly is peculiar to repeaters, though. There is a broader need to help all students fit in comfortably, while providing academic supports to keep them moving ahead. It is an agenda familiar to those involved in dropout reduction through school reform at the upper grades (e.g., Wehlage, Rutter, Smith, Lesko, and Fernandez 1989), and early retention has little to do with it.

---

[8] The timing issue is complicated for girls by the drop in average age of menarche in recent years.

Breaking Out of the Retain–Promote Box: A Proactive, Early Intervention Approach

Because we do not come out foursquare against retention, we sometimes are misread as enthusiasts for the practice. This is decidedly *not* the case. Grade retention, especially without supplemental services, should be a last recourse, as even the most favorable evidence does not show that repeaters catch up with their promoted classmates. Additionally, it is expensive (the cost of a year's per pupil expenditures); it costs children a year of their lives; and it separates children from their agemates, a practice that under present organizational arrangements apparently creates problems for them later.

Common sense suggests we ought to be able to do better, and we can. School systems throughout the country – including Baltimore's (e.g., Bowie 2001) – are experimenting, ambitiously and energetically, with alternatives both to grade repetition and to social promotion for children in the early grades who are not keeping up (see Kelly 1999). These programs often incorporate research-based "best practice" principles – such as summer programs (Cooper et al. 2000), reduced class size (Grissmer 1999), and one-on-one or small group supplemental instruction (Farkas 1998; Wasik and Slavin 1993) – and preliminary results in many instances are encouraging.[9]

Chicago's public school system has been in the vanguard of this movement. Mandatory summer school is the cornerstone of Chicago's reform package, but it includes many other kinds of support in addition to summer school (e.g., after-school enrichment programs and small transition schools for overage ninth graders who fall short of promotion standards; see Toch 1998). Promotion is determined, first and foremost, by performance on the Iowa Test of Basic Skills (ITBS). Flunking reading or math is another road to summer school, as are 20 or more unexcused absences for children whose test scores fall below the national average for their grade (Catalyst 1998).

The record for the first 2 years of Chicago's experiment is that about half the third, sixth, and eighth graders assigned to mandatory summer school come close enough to meeting the "pass" criteria to be moved

---

[9] McCay's collection of readings (2001) nicely surveys the relevant landscape, with separate papers on summer programs, year-round schooling, looping, one-on-one tutoring, and high school transition programs (see, also, American Association of School Administrators 1998; Medway 1985; U. S. Department of Education 1999).

up to the next grade (e.g., Chicago Public Schools 1998).[10] Such results demonstrate that an intensive, coordinated package of supplemental services can help a great many at-risk children avoid failure, even in the most challenging of circumstances (in 1996/97, 85% of Chicago's public school enrollment was low-income: Chicago Public Schools 1999).

We should take heart in that realization, as such victories are hard-won. But another implication of the 50% success rate is less cheery: the other 50% still fall short. Children who are far behind academically are not good prospects to spurt ahead suddenly, but a spurt is what it takes to catch up. Obviously, it is much better for children to keep pace all along and not have to catch up, but in Chicago, Baltimore, and other poverty-stricken urban centers, too many children cannot keep up on their own. Children at risk of academic failure require early and ongoing interventions. Addressing their needs effectively calls for a more comprehensive reform agenda than resolving the promotion–retention conundrum.

It is important to recognize that most "school problems" do not originate there. Low achievement, underachievement, and other problems reach public attention in schools, but these problems trace mainly to resource shortfall in children's home and community environments (e.g., Entwisle, Alexander, and Olson 1997, 2000b; Frymier 1992; 1997; Hart and Risley 1995). The first priority is not so much to find a formula for effective *remediation*, as to find a formula for effective *education*, so that there will be less need later for the kind of rear-guard heroics exemplified in Chicago's reforms.

Children need to start school with the skills to succeed. Minority youth and those of lower-SES households who begin school already behind (West et al. 2000) in particular need extra help. Scientifically impeccable evidence shows that good preschools can improve disadvantaged children's later school success, not just in terms of test performance, but also in terms of reduction of retention risk, assignment to special education, and cutting of dropout rates (Ramey, Campbell, and Blair 1998; Schweinhart and Weikart 1998; Temple, Reynolds, and Ou 2000).[11]

---

[10] The Chicago Consortium on School Research has released an evaluation of the first 2 years of the Chicago reforms (Roderick et al. 1999). It finds that pass rates in grades 3, 6, and 8 are up overall (compared with prereform benchmarks), that the largest gains are registered by the poorest-performing children, and that summer school helped many children, especially sixth and eighth graders. However, children held back under the new plan are not faring well despite supplemental services and resources.

[11] For a general overview, see Barnett (1995).

At present, though, disadvantaged children are the ones least likely to attend preschool (National Center for Education Statistics 1998). (For further comment, see Alexander, Entwisle, and Olson 2001.)

Inoculation is not enough, however. High-quality preschool experiences need to be followed by high-quality, full-day kindergarten. Most children now attend full-day programs (59% in 1998, e.g., U.S. Census Bureau 1999) – more lower-income than upper-income as a result of targeted federal (e.g., Title 1) and state supplemental funding (e.g., Rothenberg 1995; U.S. Census Bureau 1999).[12] Does this matter? The benefits of full-day as compared to half-day kindergartens for BSS children are considerable. With family background and many other variables allowed for, first graders who attended full-day kindergarten were absent fewer days in first grade, were less often retained, and earned higher marks and test scores over first grade than half-day attendees (Entwisle et al. 1987; see also Cryan, Sheehan, Weichel, and Bandy-Hedden 1992; Karweit 1989).

Preschool and kindergarten can help children arrive at first grade ready to succeed, but to help them keep up, extra resources and enrichment experiences will be needed all along the way. The Chicago Longitudinal Study shows that intense supplementation of learning resources in the early grades helps poor children maintain the academic edge they get from attending a good preschool *and* that these benefits then continue into the upper grades (Temple, Reynolds, and Ou 2000; Reynolds and Temple 1998). Importantly, in the Chicago study neither preschool alone nor school year supplementation alone proved sufficient. Rather, they are most effective in combination, one building on the other. After strong programmatic support leading up to first grade, "just in time" interventions are needed to catch problems early (see American Federation of Teachers 1997: 24–25). Third grade, the first of Chicago's "promotion gates," almost certainly is too late.

For a large group of children, perhaps 20% nationally and an even larger fraction in high-poverty school districts, regular schooling at present simply is not doing the job, and there is no sure blueprint now in hand to address their needs effectively (e.g., Deschenes, Cuban, and Tyack 2001). Reform models that combine "best practice" lessons from basic research on student learning and classroom process have

---

[12] Half-day programs remained the majority into the early 1990s (e.g., Love and Logue 1992; U.S. Department of Education 1992).

demonstrated effectiveness (e.g., Crane 1998; Farkas, Fischer, Dosher, and Vicknair 1998; Pinnell, Lyons, DeFord, Bryk, and Seltzer 1994; Ross, Smith, Casey, and Slavin 1995), but even the best of these programs leave many children behind. More radical reforms may be necessary. Cuban (1989), for example, believes that nothing short of dismantling graded schooling will work, and he may be right.

Schools are rigidly age-graded, as pointed out earlier when we observed that repeaters have a hard time "fitting in" socially in the upper grades. However, rigid age grading in the early years is problematic, too, for at least two reasons. One is that when children move annually from one grade to the next, they make a minitransition. Starting with a new teacher(s) each fall is anxiety provoking. The other is that although it is not widely appreciated, age itself makes little if any difference in children's ability to profit from schooling. BSS children and those in other studies who are the youngest (say 5 years, 8 months when they start first grade) gain as much on achievement tests over the first grade year as do their classmates who are 6 years 8 months at the start (Entwisle et al. 2000b). So age grading triggers more transitions and apparently contributes little to cognitive growth.

Examples of reforms that promise to loosen the stranglehold of the clock and calendar include multiage or nongraded classes (e.g., Goodlad and Anderson 1987; Gutierrez and Slavin 1992; Lloyd 1999; Veenman 1995; Willis 1991), in which placement is determined by skill level rather than age, and extended year and summer program alternatives to the archaic 9-month school calendar (e.g., Cooper et. al. 2000; Gándara and Fish 1994). Multiage classes offer the additional advantage of reducing the number of grade-to-grade minitransitions.

The pace of schooling under present organizational arrangements also poses serious obstacles. Age is used to calibrate the pace of instruction but is virtually irrelevant, at least in terms of 12-month units, as presently is the case. An extra few months or summer session could probably help some youngsters who need more time and together with reforms like those being tested in Chicago and elsewhere might well reduce the need for retention.[13] Until school reform addresses the pace of instruction in a serious way, too many of our children will continue to fall behind.

---

[13] We thank Jim Grant (personal communication) for this insight. It is tempting, and easy, to talk in terms of alternatives to grade retention, but the more realistic goal is "retention reduction."

Is it possible to create learning environments in the primary grades in which 6-, 7-, and 8-year-olds can be working on the same material without anyone's taking notice and in which everyone's developmental needs are met? How can we construct middle schools and high schools that encourage workplace experience without detracting from academics and that seriously involve students in school governance? Those questions go far beyond the scope of this volume, but visionary reforms along these lines might make a real difference in the lives of young people who find themselves at high risk of retention.

However, there are barriers to be overcome before such reforms can even get a fair hearing. "Age" and "grade" are so closely aligned in the way we think about schooling today that it is hard even to conceive of separating them. That is one barrier, perhaps the most formidable one. Standardized organizational forms like the age graded classroom constitute elements of what Tyack and colleagues refer to as a "grammar of schooling" (Tyack and Cuban 1995; Tyack and Tobin 1994). Once institutionalized as the understood way of doing things, such practices are highly resistant to change. That is why "break the mold" changes in school organization may be needed.

In the primary grades today multiage classes are considered extraordinary, but class mixing of this sort is routine in high school and college, so long as prerequisites are satisfied. There are restrictions, to be sure, but typically they are not defined around age. Not anyone can take upper-division college courses, but an 18-year-old who has satisfied the prerequisites generally will be admitted, and without prejudice. With prerequisites appropriately defined, would similar organizational arrangements be workable in the primary grades with less mature pupils?

And what of age grading beyond the elementary level? Overage high schoolers are made to feel out of place, but do they have to be? At issue here is the 4-year, full-time schedule, along with the expectation that high school is a place for "kids," not adults. But this sense of the nature of high school is antiquated. Across the United States in 1994 about 7% of all public school 12th graders were age 19 and above (Portner 1996), and much the same is evident in the experience of the BSS panel: 27% were still enrolled beyond their "expected" graduation, including 16% of (eventual) dropouts.

Schools to date have done little to accommodate age heterogeneity, but experience at the postsecondary level may hold lessons about how to meet the needs of "mature" students. Colleges, too, once labored under the "4-year program" fiction,[14] but that fiction dissolved once the 1980s "baby-bust" generation created financial pressures that made colleges more accommodating to nontraditional students – including mature adults who had to juggle work and school, "reentry" women seeking to upgrade their skills after a spell at full-time parenting, and students who took a year off, moved from one college to the next, or insisted on more flexible class schedules. Part-time programs proliferated, and suddenly it was not so odd that 30-year-olds were studying alongside traditional college-age students. Just 36% of students who received the B.A. degree in 1992–93 finished within 4 years of their initial enrollment and one in six was age 30 or older at graduation (National Center for Education Statistics 1996) – hardly the traditional college profile.

Is the secondary landscape really all that different from the postsecondary? Today almost all high school students juggle school and work at some point (e.g., Committee on the Health and Safety Implications of Child Labor 1998), and many shoulder heavy family responsibilities. These students already have begun to fill adult roles. Still, programs to help them balance their in-school and out-of-school obligations are rare (for additional comment see Entwisle et al. 2000b). Beyond that, it is asking a great deal of someone who has heavy work or parenting responsibilities, as many repeaters do, to accommodate to an 8:00 A.M to 3:00 P.M school schedule and to blend in with a student body preoccupied with the traditional concerns of adolescence – hardly a congenial fit.

Current arrangements segregate and marginalize youth who are off-time. Part-time programs of study might help, along with leaves of absence with flexible return provisions and an expanded horizon that makes 5 and even 6 years to degree completion an unexceptional circumstance as it is in college. But in order for any such reforms to work the tight link between age and grade must be relaxed. From our perspective, the kernel of the problem is not grade retention so much as the institutional structure within which grade retention is embedded. At present, this structure makes deviants of otherwise "normal" children while failing to accomplish the aims it was designed to fulfill.

---

[14] Eckland (1964), for example, reports that only about 30% of a sample of first-year college students in 1952 graduated 4 years later from the same institution in which they enrolled initially.

Concluding remarks

The retention question can be framed narrowly or broadly. By standards of a narrow assessment, we ask whether poor-performing children are better or worse off after they have been held back and find in favor of retention. Retention helps BSS children recover in the short term, and for a number of years afterward, it keeps many above the level projected for them on the basis of their earlier performance trajectories. This is the sense in which we judge retention a qualified success – the "success of failure" alluded to in this volume's title.

The qualification is critical, though. Regardless of exactly how the comparisons are made (whether through statistical adjustments or comparison groups), evaluations of retention basically compare retainees' standing after retention with that of promoted children with a similar academic profile or prognosis. We accept this as a reasonable standard for judging retention's effectiveness. It is the "industry standard," subscribed to (if only implicitly) by almost everyone who does research in this area. But it is a low standard, too low. Going beyond the narrow question of whether retention helps or hurts, one has to question a system of education that leaves so many children, retained and promoted alike, so far behind.[15]

The prognosis for poor-performing children altogether is not good, and we should not be content to see repeaters just keep pace if the pace itself is unacceptable. Retention does not turn failures into academic superstars, or even into average students. At best it helps them hang on, and when they (eventually) make it to middle school, most are relegated to remedial, slow-track courses; then later many leave school without a degree. It is useful to know that repeaters' low middle school placements trace to weak academic skills and that their elevated risk of dropout has more relation to age grading than to retention, but this knowledge is small comfort if the goal is to launch as many children as possible into successful middle school and high school trajectories.

Policies need to be especially conscious of difficulties surrounding educational transitions, when problems tend to mount. Performing at acceptable levels before a transition is key, in our view. Retention supplies additional time for some students, but a general solution requires much more than simply going over the same material twice.

[15] Similar concerns have been raised by Travers (1982: 273) in commenting on the debate over special education versus regular placement, and by Hebbeler (1985) regarding the effectiveness of preschool programs.

Appendix

Authors Meet Critics, Belatedly

After publication of the first edition of *On the Success of Failure*, Shepard and colleagues (1996, hereafter SSM) published a critical review of the book. Our initial response (Alexander 1998) sought to correct what seemed to us the review's chief flaw, its misrepresentations of our conclusions and interpretations (e.g., SSM's assertion that we express "outright enthusiasm for retention"). Since then numerous references to the first version of *Success* have included disclaimers citing SSM as identifying technical flaws and suggesting that SSM's "reanalysis" of the data yielded different conclusions (e.g., Hauser 1999; Rury 1999; Thompson and Kolb 1999; Viadero 2000). Shepard, Smith, and Marion (1998) also claim they reanalyzed the data in their published rejoinder to our response. Further, they say the original review "pointed out errors in [the] analyses that allowed [Alexander and coworkers] to see some benefits for retention that were not there once their data were rescaled and appropriately analyzed" (Shepard et al. 1998: 404). In hindsight, it was a mistake not to address their technical criticisms in our rejoinder. Their criticism rests mainly on interpretation, not new evidence: SSM did no reanalysis of the data in the book; nor did they discover flaws in our analyses.

To restore balance to the discussion surrounding the book, we turn now to SSM's specific criticisms. To do so, we return to their original review, pointing out areas of agreement and disagreement. For each subsection of SSM's review we first summarize their argument, then respond to their main points. Their subheadings are used for the convenience of readers who have the original review. Unless otherwise specified, all page numbers from *Success* refer to the first edition.

Dismissal of Previous Research

Their Argument

SSM claim that we "attempt to dismiss" past research on the effects of retention, calling prior studies "bad science." They go on to describe Holmes's (1989) meta-analysis of more than 60 studies, in which he concludes that retention fails to boost children's academic achievement. SSM single out one criticism of prior research from *Success*, the problem with constructing an adequate comparison group. They point out that it is sometimes possible to match retained students with poorly performing students who were not retained, perhaps because of differences in teaching philosophy. Next they present more specific data from the Holmes (1989) study: in the six "most tightly controlled" studies the retained students' achievement levels lagged comparable promoted students' by roughly a quarter of a standard deviation. One tightly controlled study did show favorable effects of retention, and SSM point out that this study was singled out for praise in *Success* despite the greater weight of evidence in the opposite direction.

Our Response

Success does criticize prior research, pointing out problems with the logic of many studies, including the lack of an appropriate comparison group, short-term follow-ups (typically a year or less), and designs that examine students' status after retention, with no preretention baseline data. We also pointed out that many of the studies included in the reviews are quite old, and that many (the majority in the Holmes review, for example) are unpublished. But even more serious is the one-sidedness that characterizes many reviews of retention research, that is, presenting the results of the many constituent studies as unequivocally opposing retention. Much of that material is repeated in this edition of *Success*, along with an expanded review of more recent studies.

Here is what we said at the time (*Success*, p. 13): "Most of the studies covered in the three reviews actually show insignificant differences between retained and nonretained children; some studies favor retention by a small margin, others do not, and significant differences point in both directions. More studies find in favor of promotion, but there are many exceptions." We are not the only ones to point this out. As noted in Chapter 2 of the second edition, Reynolds (1992) also finds Holmes's (1989) meta-analysis problematic, concluding that "this hardly constitutes conclusive evidence for or against retention." Every research area has studies that can be criticized, of course. Our primary complaint is not with individual studies, however flawed; it is, rather, with researchers who summarize the studies in ways that slight contradictory evidence and that argue for much stronger conclusions than the evidence warrants.

Design and Inferences

Their Argument

The BSS design differs from previous research in a number of respects. One major one is that the BSS is a prospective study of achievement that starts in first grade; that means achievement patterns before retention can be compared to those after retention (except for first grade retainees). The more typical matched-group design starts at the time of retention, selecting apparently similar promoted students for comparison with repeaters. SSM describe the BSS design and then point out that despite "rejecting" a matched-group design, we did construct a "poorly performing comparison group" of never retained students. The BSS comparison group was not well matched with the focal retained groups, leading SSM to conclude that the comparison group does "not help to evaluate the effects of retention" (SSM, p. 252).

Our Response

Success does not advocate any one design type (except perhaps an unlikely experimental design). Absent the ideal experiment, what should researchers do? Our approach is to triangulate, taking advantage of the considerable strengths of the BSS's prospective design. For each set of issues we identify alternative comparison groups and analyses that speak to different issues, present these analyses, and consider the resulting corpus of evidence, relying on no single analysis, comparison group, or interpretation in isolation when taking stock.

A word is in order about our comparison group, however. Because *Success* uses data from children's first through eighth years of school, we constructed a single comparison group of low-performing never-retained students, rather than groups of low-performing but promoted students from each grade. This is a large distinction. Had we created a comparison group for first grade retainees from the pool of promoted first graders, it almost surely would have included many children destined for retention later, in second grade and beyond. Excluding those children, as we did, makes it harder (perhaps impossible) to achieve a close match in the comparison group. With cumulative retention rates of 50% or more common in high-poverty schools, unless steps are taken to guard against this eventuality, it seems certain that many studies include "hidden" eventual repeaters in their comparison groups.

The presence of hidden repeaters would tend to reduce differences between retained and comparison groups, in terms of social background characteristics associated with retention and of academic performance indicators (by depressing average scores in the comparison group). As Shepard notes with regard to social promotion, retained students one year may be "socially promoted" in subsequent years, especially if their academic performance continues to lag prevailing standards (Shepard 2000). The same can be said for promoted children. Our inability to achieve a good match is one reason we rely mainly on statistical adjustments for assessing retention's effects, adjustments that SSM also criticize (discussed later).

Test Scores before and after Retention: Is There a Pattern?

Their Argument

SSM reproduce Figure 4.1 (*Success*, p. 75; in the second edition, Figure 6.1), which shows California Achievement Test Reading Comprehension (CAT-R) gains in grades 1, 2, 3, and 4 through 7 for all of the retained groups, as well as the never-retained students and the poorly performing comparison group students. In the figure, retained students' gains are "stacked up" in the grade that they repeated. That is, gains from the second time through the repeated grade are depicted on top of gains from the first time through the repeated year.

SSM then identify "the most serious problem" with *Success*: our being "alternatively aware and unaware of the implications of the decelerating score scale" (SSM, p. 253). The argument is that there are two ways of interpreting decelerating test scores over time, and the implications for the way you interpret relative gains differ, depending on which of these you choose. The book argues, as SSM note, that the rate of cognitive growth decreases over time (that is, that decelerating gains reflect real changes in the rate of achievement growth over the elementary years). SSM do not agree, arguing instead that decreases are across grade (not time or age) and are built in by the test makers. The interpretation of Table 4.3 is at issue (Table 6.3 in the current edition).

In Table 4.3 the "pace" of growth between the never-retained and retained students is compared. It is based on different grades, but on the same amount of time. If decreases across grade are built in to the test scores, then retained students, who are a year behind never retained students in same-grade comparisons, are advantaged because the tests allow more growth during the earlier grades. So, for example, consider the case of first grade repeaters in the last column of comparisons in Table 4.3, which examines 3 year gains through and after year 3. Since the first grade repeaters spent two years in first grade, they will only be in third through fifth grades in the "post" years (years 4, 5, and 6). The never-retained students, by contrast, are completing fourth through sixth grades in the "post" years. If gains are artificially constrained in higher grades as a result of test construction, then the first grade re-peaters are advantaged because they are taking tests for earlier grade levels (third through fifth versus fourth through sixth for the never re-tained children). The same advantage would hold for the second and third grade repeaters. The comparisons in Table 4.3 in this way artifi-cially inflate the relative rate of growth of retained students.

SSM then propose a "more appropriate picture of relative standing across grades." In their Figure 2, SSM recalibrate the trend data from Table 4.a1 by converting the scale scores to within-grade *t* scores (they say in the review that the data are from *Success,* Figure 4.1, but since they are original scale scores, not gain scores, we assume they mean Table 4.a1). They conclude from this exercise that "retention clearly im-proves achievement test scores during the repeated year" (SSM, p. 254), and they agree with our interpretation of results for first and fourth through seventh grade retainees. They disagree with our interpretation of the second and third grade retainees' results, however. They reject the argument that these two groups had steadily downward performance trajectories prior to retention and that retention slowed this downward spiral. SSM argue instead that the second and third grade retainees' achievement boost reflects regression to the mean.

SSM conclude this section by noting that they accept the attrition checks reported in *Success* (which indicate that students who stay in the study do not have different achievement levels from those who exit) but then mention that fluctuations in sample size due to missing data are not described.

Our Response
SSM are correct in questioning conclusions based on the single table they criticize (Table 4.3 in *Success*). It is, as they point out, hard to know whether the decline in average gains with time are real or built into the

test. We do not know which interpretation is more correct, and neither do SSM. However, Table 4.3 is one of five tables that address the same issue (in Chapter 4, Test Scores before and after Retention). Chapter 4 provides a detailed description of how CAT gains trend over time for different groups, which are defined and compared in different ways. Tables 4.1 and 4.2 report same-grade comparisons, and Tables 4.4 and 4.5 present results from both same-grade and same-age comparisons. The deceleration issue does not enter into same-grade comparisons, and SSM neither criticize nor mention these tables in their review. In discussing our conclusions about test score gains before and after retention, we were careful to consider evidence from all the analyses in Chapter 4, not the single analysis that SSM chose to discuss. Together these analyses paint a quite consistent picture. Except for first grade repeaters, postretention achievement gaps tend to be smaller than those before retention, and second and third grade repeaters' gains are very similar to the never-retained patterns.

We are puzzled by the recalibration of test scores in SSM's Figure 2. This recalibration is merely a conversion that accentuates the dip and recovery pattern that would be obtained by plotting the original data in Table 4.1a. SSM's criticism in this exercise is one of interpretation, not analysis. In fact, their own words serve our purpose: "the second and third-grade graphs lend themselves to two very different interpretations" (SSM, p. 254). Their interpretation is that the pattern in their Figure 2 reflects regression to the mean, rather than a positive effect of retention. That is, because students "were selected for retention at an all-time low," they would likely regress to the mean in subsequent periods merely as a research artifact.

Although regression to the mean is always possible, we believe their recalibration supports our original conclusion: that retention stops the free-fall in test scores evident before retention. Before retention the to-be-retained students are falling further and further off the never-retained standard (in a pattern that includes at least three waves of test scores, not just the single data point that coincides with the decision to retain). After retention (with the exception of the first grade retainees) the achievement gap is smaller, and it remains smaller for a number of years.

The trend line before retention gives a frame of reference for interpreting the after retention pattern. We do not understand how anyone could look at SSM's Figure 2 for second and third grade repeaters and not see recovery from a precipitous downward trajectory. Their own "picture" belies a regression toward the mean interpretation, which hinges on repeaters' retention year test score's being an aberrant data point. In fact, everything we know about these students suggests that their retention year test scores are not aberrant. The evidence presented throughout the book suggests that these students were retained after accumulating a portfolio of poor performance.

As for the small point about missing data, most missing data are due to Exiting (which is thoroughly described in the attrition analysis), and the N's across years in Table 4.2a are very close after various exclusions. We do not believe that missing data have compromised the analyses in any way; nor, we gather, do SSM.

Statistical Adjustments

Their Argument
SSM dismiss the multivariate analyses in Chapter 5, suggesting that the regression model says "in effect that if retained students had entered school white, middle class, higher performing and non-handicapped they would have come closer to the achievement levels of the non-retained comparison groups." SSM claim that the analyses in Chapter 5 "provide no new insights" for "evaluating the effects of retention" (SSM, p. 257). Later, they say that they are going to ignore the last set of adjustments that control for special education placement and double retention, suggesting that those adjustments incorrectly minimize repeaters' problems by blaming them on special education and double repeaters.

SSM focus on the results adjusted only for the demographic characteristics and achievement test scores from the fall of the retention decision year. They suggest that we inadvertently misread the table when we concluded that "when first grade repeaters move to second grade . . . and after adjustments are made for other factors that damp scores, the retainees actually surpass their classmates" (SSM, p. 257). (This reflects a misunderstanding by SSM. They interpret the phrase "when first grade repeaters move to second grade" as the end of second grade, hence their citing the end of second grade numbers for first grade repeaters. The text refers to the end of first grade figures, which with adjustments favor first grade repeaters.)

Finally, SSM bring up what we consider the most important argument in their review, the interpretation of the patterning of results before and after retention. In some ways this returns to the regression to the mean argument, but it extends beyond that, as well. The central argument here surrounds the following question: What patterns would one expect if retention had a positive effect? SSM say that we "see very positive benefits for second- and third-grade retainees...because they take the no-difference findings after retention and compare them to the significantly negative adjusted scores obtained for these groups at the end of their retention-decision year" (SSM, p. 258). Moreover, they claim that the statistical analysis asks the question "How would retained and never-retained groups compare if they are equated on demographic variables and immediately prior achievement?" (SSM, p. 258). The answer, they claim, is "the same." Since prior test scores are controlled, they read the results as saying that retained students would have scored essentially the same after retention whether they were retained or not. Retention, according to this view, has no effect.

Our Response
The statistical adjustments in Chapter 5 are standard practice, and they help put retention into context. SSM's dismissive stance regarding statistical adjustments as a method for addressing possible confounds is hard to fathom, especially since Shepard employs essentially the same approach in her oft-cited analysis of high school dropout in relation to grade retention (Grissom and Shepard 1989). The reality of the situation is that retention happens to children with a bundle of risk factors that weigh on their school performance independently of retention. That is why matched-control studies match; it is also why statistical adjustments are made. Adjusting for these other factors acknowledges an empirical reality: for all children, whether retained or not, other factors depress or boost test scores. Adjusting for those affords a more accurate assessment of the effects of retention.

We also treat analyses controlling for double retention and special education with care, noting that "whether or not the problems peculiar to double repeaters and special education youngsters should be separated out in this way is arguable" (*Success*, p. 116). We include these analyses because they contribute to the larger picture. It is perhaps worth mentioning that analyses of retention's effects reported by the Chicago Longitudinal Study also adjust for children's special education placements (e.g., McCoy and Reynolds 1999).

Part of the reality of retention is that some retainees are so far behind that their situation prompts further administrative action. We know of no other study that contextualizes retained students' experiences to the extent done in *Success*. Having said that, most of the discussion in Chapter 5 focuses on analyses that do not include this adjustment. Some of the analyses with background and preretention achievement controls reflect positively on retention; others are significantly negative. Even those that are significantly negative, however, generally involve smaller differences than the preretention differences. Given the wide differences at the beginning, and the groups' divergent preretention trajectories, controls for prior achievement would not necessarily anticipate parity.

Although the SSM review gives the impression that we emphasize positive benefits of retention in this chapter, a careful reading of Chapter 5 shows otherwise. Summarizing the results for first grade retainees we note: "Not only do they trail badly, but they do so by more after being held back than they had before.... Aside from some scattered gains in the short term, up through seventh grade, retention cannot be said to have helped first grade repeaters" (*Success*, p. 120). Our summaries for second and third grade retainees, although finding positive effects, are not nearly as one-sided and enthusiastic as SSM portray:

When allowance is made for their problems before retention, they do better than would be predicted.... But retainees continue to suffer from their early difficulties, which retention does not erase. Most retainees never catch up once they have fallen behind, but for many the free-fall is slowed, possibly even stopped; at least this appears to be the case for second and third grade repeaters. Short of actually getting them up to the level of their promoted agemates, this seems an impressive showing. (*Success*, p. 132)

Report Card Marks

Their Argument
SSM criticize the crude scale of marks, arguing that "by definition" retained students are assigned marks of 1 (unsatisfactory) on a 4-point scale. They go on to say that, in these particular analyses, levels of explained variance achieved and the "lack of much statistical adjustment," which we take to mean very little difference between the coefficients before and after controlling for special education assignment, "suggest that grades do not validly rank students' achievement" (SSM, p. 258). They then describe the pattern for first grade, second grade, and third grade repeaters' marks, concluding, "We do not see positive benefits here." After statistical adjustment for confounds, first grade repeaters' marks are significantly behind those of the control groups, and second and third grade repeaters' marks are equal to the control groups' marks after retention. From that, they conclude, retention depresses first grade

repeaters' marks and has no effect on second and third grade repeaters' marks.

Our Response

Success does not treat marks as objective evidence of achievement, but rather as teacher judgments of performance relative to the local context within which marks are assigned. This is discussed at length in Chapter 6. Nor do we understand SSM's assessment of the results presented in Chapter 6, which evaluates marks across the elementary and middle school years. For example, SSM note that first grade repeaters' marks rose from 1.0 in the spring of their failed first grade year, to 1.9, 1.9, 1.8, 1.9, 2.1, 1.9, and 1.9 in each of the successive years. They then say, "We do not see positive benefits here." They go on to say, "When statistical adjustments are applied, first-grade retainees are still significantly behind control groups.... Thus, retention hurts the performance of first graders." The data do not conform to that interpretation, regardless of the way one measures positive benefits.

Tables 6.1 and 6.2 show clear improvement after retention. First grade retainees at the end of elementary school are on a par with the poorly performing comparison group in both math and reading even with no adjustments and are only a quarter of a mark behind all never-retained children when fall test scores and social background are controlled. There is some slippage during the middle school years, but considering where first grade repeaters started, we fail to see how SSM reached the conclusion that "retention hurts the performance of first graders." Results for second and third grade repeaters are even more favorable (see Chapter 6 for more information about report card marks).

Self-Esteem and Attitudes

Their Argument

The next section of the review takes up our treatment of self-esteem and attitudes. Here SSM begin by reproducing Figure 7.1 from the text (*Success*, p. 158), which focuses on academic self-esteem. They point out that retainees gained on average 1 point on a 25-point scale. They go on to say that "without signaling its implications, the authors have moved from a same-grade to a same-age comparison" (SSM, p. 260). They then recalibrate the data, transforming the figure from a same-age comparison to a same-grade comparison, which they present as their Figure 5. They interpret their new figure as showing that gains in attitudes are of shorter duration than presented in the book.

SSM finish up this section by agreeing with the book's conclusion that there is no evidence that retention harms academic self-esteem or other measures of attitudes toward school. They dispute, instead, the "more elaborate causal claims" leading from improved performance to improvements in self-esteem and confidence.

Our Response

Although SSM seem to dismiss a 1-point gain on a 25-point scale, that gain is noteworthy in the context of the academic self-image data. Moreover, although the self-image data tend to be skewed high overall, they also are patterned in meaningful ways. The 1-point gain in academic self-image for first grade repeaters reduces by half the initial disparity in academic self-image between first grade repeaters and never-retained students. Since the never-retained students' self-image declines between the first and second years, the difference is actually reduced even more, to less than 0.5 point from 2 points initially (see original Figure 7.1; Figure 9.1 in the present edition). Although it would be tempting to dismiss as suspect a single instance of this dip–recovery pattern, the totality of evidence in Chapter 7 supports the conclusion that first grade retainees' sense of self, initially the lowest of all groups, recovers considerably over the repeated year. Their self-image remains lower than the never-retained groups' throughout elementary school, but it is not significantly lower. Their self-regard again takes a turn for the worse during middle school, however.

Because of the timing of data collection for the attitude data, we are unable to monitor changes in self-regard across both the first and the second time through the repeated grade for other than first grade repeaters. For that reason, the same-age format is used for these analyses, and it is SSM's major criticism of this chapter. Their recalibration of our data is intended to approximate same-grade contrasts by shifting the annual data points reported in our graphs. Unfortunately, in doing so, they present the "grade" data as if they are measured at the same time of the year for everybody. Through the fourth grade this is true: all the data are from the spring. After fourth grade, however, the data are from the fall (this is clear in the text and in the original Figure 7.1). Thus, SSM's "sixth grade" points for the never-retained and poorly performing comparison groups are closer to the end of fifth grade than to spring of sixth grade; first grade retainees' seventh grade is fall seventh grade; and so on. Rather than present data as if they could unproblematically mimic the same-grade comparisons of test scores and marks, we chose instead to present the data as accurately as possible, showing their original data collection periods.

Perhaps more to the point, by shifting the analysis SSM have effectively eliminated what we see as a major benefit of our longitudinal data: the ability to see preretention patterns as a basis for evaluating postretention results. SSM's Figure 5 reduces repeaters' low academic self-esteem Year 1 spring score to a dot on the vertical axis, which they ignore in their narrative. First graders' "recovery" between first and second grades is evident in SSM's Figure 4, but their mode of presentation makes it less prominent.

On the basis of their Figure 5, SSM conclude, "Short term gains in attitudes for retainees fell off sooner than the authors admit." This conclusion is unwarranted, however. Since no data were collected between the spring of their repeated first grade year and the spring of the fourth year in school (the end of third grade for first grade repeaters), the timing of the decline is ambiguous regardless of whether same-age or same-grade comparisons are made. Moreover, we are not convinced that the same-grade logic works well here. Is it grade specific experience that matters to feelings of self? Or is it maturation or ongoing school experiences and feedback about current performance? The pattern of results suggests to us that students react to their school experiences. We do not perceive this line of reasoning as particularly "elaborate." Instead, it seems to us quite sensible and straightforward. Retained children go from failing miserably the year the retention decision is made to receiving markedly better academic feedback the following year. Why should they not, as a result, feel better about themselves as students and more inclined to academic work?

Generalization Issues

Their Argument
SSM criticize us for making claims about the generalizability of the study, saying we likely could make inferences from the study to the Baltimore city population, but no further. In fact, they say, "there is nothing in the procedures of this study that warrants generalizations past the boundaries of the system" (SSM, p. 260). They point out that we were careful to say the study could only be generalized to other

urban school systems similar to Baltimore's and note our speculation that the findings about self-esteem may have some relation to the local context: that is, where high proportions of one's classmates are retained, the blows to one's ego may be less sharp. But then they say, in a comment that seems unrelated, "in their deprecation of the existing research literature they say only that other studies are inadequate and misleading and fail to acknowledge that the Baltimore study might simply be an outlier of the literature as a whole."

Finally, SSM conclude that we express "outright enthusiasm for retention by the end," quoting from the book where we say that "retention has mainly positive effects." Then they say that we dismiss the negative results for the first grade retainees and "fail to mention the flat achievement trajectories of fourth-through-seventh-grade retainees." They finish by saying that their reading of the results is that retention neither harms nor helps, so our conclusion that retention has positive benefits is "a statement of belief not an empirical conclusion."

Our Response

The BSS has been used to study some of the most pressing issues in urban education today: among them retention, summer learning loss, dropout, and minority–majority achievement gaps. We recognize that along with the considerable benefits of a longitudinal study such as ours are limitations. In this and all other studies using BSS data we are very careful to make those clear. Nevertheless, we do not agree with the implications of SSM's claims here, since they would appear to dismiss virtually all empirical research that does not use nationally representative samples. We stand by our original statements about the limited generalizability of the results: we should be cautious about generalizing the results beyond urban school districts like Baltimore's, districts with high-poverty, high-minority populations, and a high cumulative retention rate. On the other hand, one should also be cautious in concluding that effects of retention *on average* necessarily apply to students in poverty areas where large numbers of classmates are also retained.

The remainder of the section on "Generalization Issues" formed the basis for our original response to the SSM review (Alexander 1998). The distortion of our view of retention was so egregious in the original review that we chose to focus on it rather than the technical issues addressed in this response. We decline to join in the pro- or antiretention rhetoric. Instead, we have tried to take a balanced approach based on our analyses of BSS data. To the extent that our analyses are technically correct – and nothing in the SSM review challenges the appropriateness or accuracy of our treatment of the data – our disagreements with SSM lie in interpretations of results. We do not, as SSM claim, express "outright enthusiasm" for retention in the original volume. We do, however, question whether a policy that does not harm retained students, and in some cases clearly benefits them, should be eliminated from the arsenal of tools to help poorly performing students. We very clearly state that retention is not the answer to all academic problems. A fair reading of the data available to us when we wrote the first volume of *Success* argues against dismissing retention as one possible strategy for helping children succeed in school. Those, to return to SSM's terms, are our "empirical conclusions."

Policy Implications

Their Argument

In the final section, SSM return to their interpretation of the results, which leads them to reject retention as one possible response to dismal academic achievement. They reiterate that their reading of *Success* suggests that retention does "no harm" and ask whether school systems should, on this basis, retain poorly performing students. They argue that we ignore two important policy issues: the financial costs associated with adding a year to the cost of educating a child and the link between retention and dropout. They conclude by praising the detail and extensive analyses included in the book but dismiss the conclusions as unwarranted.

Our Response

We disagree with SSM's interpretation of the data (a point to which we return in our concluding remarks). If, as we believe our data show, retention has some positive benefits, then the rest of SSM's argument rests on mistaken assumptions. Clearly if retention neither harms nor helps retained students, then there would be little point either in incurring the financial burden of retaining large numbers of students or in increasing the probability of students' eventually dropping out of school. But if retention does succeed in some measure to help struggling students make up some lost ground, then it is properly a strategy that ought to be considered, among others, as a response to struggling students' academic problems. Our results and our interpretation of those results do not in any way argue for retention as *the* strategy of choice. They merely give policymakers and practitioners some data from which to evaluate their choices. Providing relevant data and the various perspectives they allow seems to us a sensible and useful way for educational researchers to approach real world issues. The second edition of *Success* goes further than the first in pointing to troubling links between retention and dropout. These links identify additional serious issues that policymakers need to consider in weighing their options. Our analyses point to both positive and negative consequences of retention, reflecting the complexity of the issues involved.

Concluding Remarks

For the most part, SSM do not disagree with our treatment of the data. They may prefer to display data differently for descriptive purposes, to make a different point. We have no problem with that use of our data. Where we differ is in interpretation, and in assumptions about the kinds of "effects" retention is likely to yield. It should be clear from both the first and the second editions of *On the Success of Failure* that retention has not solved the problems of the poorly performing children in the BSS. That said, our evidence indicates that retention helped stem the downward spiral that children were experiencing before retention. The picture from the first edition of *Success* is complicated, and now that we have analyzed data related to dropout it has become even more so. We conclude, as we did previously in our earlier response to SSM, by inviting those with an interest in the issues to judge for themselves how well our conclusions and interpretations accord with the evidence presented.

References

Abercrombie, K. L. (1999, 23 June). Programs that promote summer learning gain popularity. *Education Week on the Web* [Online] 18(41). Available: http://www.edweek.org.

Abidin, R. R., Golladay, W. M., & Howerton, A. L. (1971). Elementary school retention: An unjustifiable, discriminatory and noxious policy. *Journal of School Psychology, 9*, 410–417.

Alexander, K. L. (1998). Response to Shepard, Smith, and Marion. *Psychology in the Schools, 35*, 402–404.

Alexander, K. L., & Cook, M. A. (1982). Curricula and coursework: A surprise ending to a familiar story. *American Sociological Review, 47*, 626–640.

Alexander, K. L., & Entwisle, D. R. (1996). Educational tracking during the early years: First grade placements and middle school constraints. In A. C. Kerckhoff (Ed.), *Generating social stratification: Toward a new research agenda* (pp. 83–113). New York: Westview Press.

Alexander, K. L., Entwisle, D. R., & Bedinger, S. D. (1994). When expectations work: Race and socioeconomic differences in school performance. *Social Psychology Quarterly, 57*(4), 283–299.

Alexander, K. L., Entwisle, D. R., & Dauber, S. L. (1993). First grade classroom behavior: Its short- and long-term consequences for school performance. *Child Development, 64*(3), 801–814.

Alexander, K. L., Entwisle, D. R., & Dauber, S. L. (1994). *On the success of failure: A reassessment of the effects of retention in the primary grades.* Cambridge: Cambridge University Press.

Alexander, K. L., Entwisle, D. R., & Dauber, S. L. (1996). Children in motion: School transfers and elementary school performance. *Journal of Educational Research, 90*(1), 3–12.

Alexander, K. L., Entwisle, D. R., Dauber, S. L., & Kabbani, N. (2000, 18–19 October). *Dropout in relation to grade retention: An accounting from the Beginning School Study.* Presented at the National Invitational Conference: Can Unlike Children Learn Together? Grade Retention, Tracking, and Grouping. Alexandria, VA.

Alexander, K. L., Entwisle, D. R., & Horsey, C. (1997). From first grade forward: Early foundations of high school dropout. *Sociology of Education, 70*(2), 87–107.

Alexander, K. L., Entwisle, D. R., & Kabbani, N. (2002). Grade retention, social promotion and "third way" alternatives. In A. J. Reynolds, H. J. Walberg, & M. C. Wang (Eds.), *Early childhood programs for a new century* (pp. 185–224). Washington, D.C.: Child Welfare League of America.

Alexander, K. L., Entwisle, D. R., & Kabbani, N. (2001). The dropout process in life course perspective: Early risk factors at home and school. *Teachers College Record, 103*, 760–822.

Alexander, K. L., Entwisle, D. R., & Legters, N. (1998, August). *On the multiple faces of first grade tracking.* Presented at the American Sociological Association annual meeting. San Francisco.

Alexander, K. L., Entwisle, D. R., & Olson, L. S. (2001). Schools, achievement and inequality: A seasonal perspective. *Educational Evaluation and Policy Analysis, 23*, 171–191.

American Association of School Administrators. (1998). *The School Administrator, 7*(55).

American Federation of Teachers. (1997). *Passing on failure: District promotion policies and practices.* Washington, D.C.: Author.

Anderson, D. K. (1999, 6–10 August). *The timing of high school dropout.* Presented at the American Sociological Association annual meeting. Chicago.

Astone, N. M., & McLanahan, S. S. (1994). Family structure, residential mobility, and school dropout: A research note. *Demography, 31*(4), 575–584.

Balfanz, R., & Legters, N. (2001, 13 January). *How many central city high schools have a severe dropout problem, where are they located, and who attends them? Initial estimates using the Common Core of Data.* Presented at the The Civil Rights Project: Dropouts in America: How Severe Is the Problem? What Do We Know about Intervention and Prevention? Cambridge, MA.

Baltimore Sun. (1999). *The ultimate guide to Baltimore schools.* Baltimore: Author.

Barcai, A. (1971). Attendance, achievement and social class: The differential impact of non attendance upon school achievements in different social classes. *Acta Paedopsychiatrica, 38*, 153–159.

Barnett, K. P., Clarizio, H. F., & Payette, K. A. (1996). Grade retention among students with learning disabilities. *Psychology in the Schools, 33*(4), 285–293.

Barnett, W. S. (1995). Long-term effects of early childhood care and education on disadvantaged children's cognitive development and school success. *The Future of Children, 5*(3), 25–50.

Barr, R., & Dreeben, R. (1983). *How schools work.* Chicago: University of Chicago Press.

Bauman, K. J. (1998). Schools, markets, and family in the history of African-American education. *American Journal of Education, 106*(4), 500–531.

Belsky, J., & MacKinnon, C. (1994). Transition to school: Developmental trajectories and school experiences. *Early Education and Development, 5*(2), 106–119.

Bereiter, C., & Kurland, M. (1981–1982). A constructive look at follow through results. *Interchange, 12*, 1–22.

Bianchi, S. M. (1984). Children's progress through school: A research note. *Sociology of Education, 57*, 184–192.

Blake, J. (1989). *Family size and achievement.* Berkeley: University of California Press.

Bloom, B. B. (1964). *Stability and change in human characteristics.* New York: John Wiley.

Blumenfeld, P. C., Pintrich, P. R., Meece, J., & Wessels, K. (1982). The formation and role of self perceptions of ability in elementary classrooms. *The Elementary School Journal, 82,* 401–420.

Bomster, M. (1992, 18 September). City's dropout rate ranked 9th-worse in nation in 1990. *The Baltimore Sun,* C1–4.

Borman, G. D., & D'Agostino, J. V. (2001). Title I and student achievement: A quantitative synthesis. In G. D. Borman, S. C. Stringfield, & R. E. Slavin (Eds.), *Title I: Compensatory education at the crossroads* (pp. 25–57). Mahwah, NJ: Lawrence Erlbaum Associates.

Bowditch, C. (1993). Getting rid of troublemakers: High school disciplinary procedures and the production of dropouts. *Social Problems, 40*(4), 493–509.

Bowie, L. (1998, 9 February). Board looking at radical cures for city schools. *The Baltimore Sun,* Final ed., Sec. A, pp. 1, 4.

Bowie, L. (2001, 7 June). 30,000 facing summer school. *The Baltimore Sun,* Sec. A, pp. 1, 6.

Bowler, M. (1994, 27 November). Right of passage to the next grade may be failing Maryland students. *The Baltimore Sun,* Sec. A, pp. 1, 26.

Brooks-Gunn, J., Guo, G., & Furstenberg Jr., F. F. (1993). Who drops out and who continues beyond high school? A 20-year follow-up of black urban youth. *Journal of Research on Adolescence, 3*(3), 271–294.

Byrnes, D. A. (1989). Attitudes of students, parents and educators toward repeating a grade. In L. A. Shepard & M. L. Smith (Eds.), *Flunking grades: Research and policies on retention* (pp. 108–131). London: Falmer Press.

Byrnes, D. A., & Yamamoto, K. (1996). Views on grade repetition. *Journal of Research and Development in Education, 20*(1), 14–20.

Cairns, R. B., & Cairns, B. D. (1994). *Lifelines and risks: Pathways of youth in our time.* Cambridge: Cambridge University Press.

Cairns, R. B., Cairns, B. D., & Neckerman, H. J. (1989). Early school dropout: Configurations and determinants. *Child Development, 60,* 1437–1452.

California Achievement Test. (1979). *California achievement tests: Norms tables, level 18, forms C and D.* Monterey, CA: CTB/McGraw Hill.

Cameron, S. V., & Heckman, J. J. (1993). The nonequivalence of high school equivalents. *Journal of Labor Economics, 11*(1), 1–47.

Card, D. (1999). The causal effect of education on earnings. In O. Ashenfelter & D. Card (Eds.), *Handbook of labor economics* (vol. 3A, pp. 1801–1863). New York: Elsevier Science.

Carrier, J. G. (1986). Sociology and special education: Differentiation and allocation in mass education. *American Journal of Education, 94,* 281–312.

Carter, L. F. (1984). The sustaining effects study of compensatory and elementary education. *Educational Researcher, 13,* 4–13.

Casey Foundation, A. E. (1997). *Kids count data book: State profiles of child well-being.* Baltimore: Annie E. Casey Foundation.

Catalyst. (1998, September). CPS policies: Elementary school promotion policy. Available: http://www.catalyst-chicago.org.

Catterall, J. S. (1987). On the social costs of dropping out. *The High School Journal, 20,* 19–30.

Catterall, J. S. (1998, February). Risk and resilience in student transitions to high school. *American Journal of Education, 106,* 302–333.

Center for Policy Research in Education. (1990). *Repeating grades in school: Current practice and research evidence* (Tech. Rep. No. RB-04-1/90). New Brunswick, NJ: Author.

Chen, X., Kaufman, P., & Frase, M. (1997). *Risk and resilience: The effects on dropping out of school.* Presented at the American Educational Research Association annual meeting. Chicago.

Chicago Public Schools. (1998, 21 August). Chicago Public Schools has successful summer school. In CPS press release [Online]. Available: http://www.cps.k12.il.us.

Chicago Public Schools. (1999). Student characteristics. Available: http://www.cps.k12.il.us.

Children's Defense Fund. (1992). *City poverty data from 1990 census.* Washington, D.C.: Author.

Clinton, W. J. (1998). *State of the Union Address.* Washington, D.C.: Department of State, Bureau of Public Affairs.

Clinton, W. J. (1999). *State of the Union Address.* Washington, D.C.: Department of State, Bureau of Public Affairs.

Coleman, J. S., Campbell, E. Q., Hobson, C. J., McPartland, J., Mood, A., Weinfeld, F. D., & York, R. L. (1966). *Equality of educational opportunity.* Washington, D.C.: U.S. Government Printing Office.

Committee on the Health and Safety Implications of Child Labor. (1998). *Protecting youth at work.* Washington, D.C.: National Academy Press.

Cooper, C. (1979). *The relationship between early identification of potential learning problems using the Maryland Systematic Teaching Observation Instrument and later reading achievement in elementary school.* Unpublished doctoral dissertation, University of Maryland.

Cooper, H., Charlton, K., Valentine, J. C., & Muhlenbruck, L. (2000). Making the most of summer school: A meta-analytic and narrative review. *Monograph Series for the Society for Research in Child Development.* Ann Arbor, MI: Society for Research in Child Development.

Corman, H. (2001). *The effects of state policies, individual characteristics, family characteristics, and neighborhood characteristics on grade repetition in the United States.* Final report to the American Educational Research Association Washington, D.C.

Council of Great City Schools. (1994). *National urban education goals: 1992–1993 indicators report.* Washington, D.C.: Author.

Crandall, V. C., Katkovsky, W., & Crandall, V. (1965). Children's beliefs in their own control of reinforcement in intellectual-achievement situations. *Child Development, 36,* 91–109.

Crane, J. (1998). *Social programs that work.* New York, NY: Russell Sage Foundation.

284   *References*

Cryan, J., Sheehan, R., Weichel, J., & Bandy-Hedden, I. (1992). Success outcomes of full-day kindergarten: More positive behavior and increased achievement in the years after. *Early Childhood Research Quarterly, 7*(2), 187–203.

Cuban, L. (1989). The 'at-risk' label and the problem of urban school reform. *Phi Delta Kappan, 70*, 780–801.

Cuban, L. (1992). What happens to reforms that last? The case of the junior high school. *American Educational Research Journal, 29*, 227–251.

Currie, J., & Thomas, D. (1995). Does Head Start make a difference? *American Economic Review, 85*(3), 341–364.

Currie, J., & Thomas, D. (1998). *School quality and the longer-term effects of head start* (Working paper No. 6362). Cambridge, MA: National Bureau of Economic Research.

Darling-Hammond, L. (1998). Alternatives to grade retention. *The School Administrator, 55*(7), 18–23.

Dauber, S. L., Alexander, K. L., & Entwisle, D. R. (1993). Characteristics of retainees and early precursors of retention in grade: Who is held back? *Merrill-Palmer Quarterly, 39*(3), 326–343.

Dauber, S. L., Alexander, K. L., & Entwisle, D. R. (1996). Tracking and transitions through the middle grades: Channeling educational trajectories. *Sociology of Education, 69*, 290–307.

Dawson, P. (1998a). A primer on student grade retention: What the research says. *NASP Communique, 26*(8), 28–30.

Dawson, P. (1998b). "On the success of failure": A reassessment of the effects of retention in the primary grades. *NASP Communique, 26*(5), 1–5.

Day, J., & Curry, A. (1998). *Educational attainment in the United States: March 1997* (#P20–505). Washington, D.C.: U.S. Census Bureau. Current Population Reports: Population Characteristics.

Denton, D. (2001). *Finding alternatives to failure: Can states end social promotion and reduce retention rates?* Atlanta: Southern Regional Education Board.

Deschenes, S., Cuban, L., & Tyack, D. (2001). Mismatch: Historical perspectives on schools and students who don't fit them. *Teachers College Record, 103*(4), 525–547.

Dougherty, K. J. (1996). Opportunity-to-learn standards: A sociological critique. *Sociology of Education*, Extra issue, 40–66.

Dreeben, R. (1968). *On what is learned in school.* Reading, MA: Addison-Wesley.

Dreeben, R. (1984). First-grade reading groups: Their formation and change. In P. L. Peterson, L. C. Wilkinson, & M. Hallinan (Eds.), *The social context of instruction: Group organization and group process* (pp. 69–84). San Diego: Academic Press.

Dunn, J. (1988). Normative life events as risk factors in childhood. In M. Rutter (Ed.), *Studies of psychosocial risk: The power of longitudinal data* (pp. 227–244). Cambridge: Cambridge University Press.

Dworkin, A. G., Lorence, J., Toenjes, L. A., Hill, A. N., Perez, N., & Thomas, M. (1999a). *Comparisons between the TAAS and norm-references tests: Issues of criterion-related validity.* Houston: Sociology of Education Research Group, University of Houston.

Dworkin, A. G., Lorence, J., Toenjes, L. A., Hill, A. N., Perez, N., & Thomas, M. (1999b). *Elementary school retention and social promotion in Texas: An assessment of students who failed the reading section of the TAAS.* Houston: Sociology of Education Research Group, University of Houston.

Dyer, P. C., & Binkney, R. (1995). Estimating cost-effectiveness and educational outcomes: Retention, remediation, special education, and early intervention. In R. L. Allington & S. A. Walmsley (Eds.), *No quick fix: Rethinking literacy programs in America's elementary schools* (pp. 61–77). New York: Teachers College Press.

Eccles, J. S., Lord, S., & Midgley, C. (1991). What are we doing to early adolescents? The impact of educational contexts on early adolescents. *American Journal of Education, 99*(4), 521–542.

Eccles, J. S., & Midgley, C. (1989). Stage/environment fit: Developmentally appropriate classrooms for early adolescents. In R. E. Ames & C. Ames (Eds.), *Research on Motivation in Education* (pp. 139–186). New York: Academic Press.

Eccles, J. S., & Midgley, C. (1990). Changes in academic motivation and self-perception during early adolescence. In R. Montemayor, G. R. Adams, & T. P. Gullotta (Eds.), *From childhood to adolescence: A transitional period?* (pp. 134–155). Newbury Park, CA: Sage.

Eccles, J. S., Midgley, C., & Adler, T. (1984). Grade-related changes in the school environment: Effects on achievement motivation. In J. G. Nicholls (Ed.), *The development of achievement motivation* (pp. 283–331). Greenwich, CT: JAI Press.

Eckland, B. K. (1964). Social class and college graduation: Some misconceptions corrected. *American Journal of Sociology, 70*(1), 36–50.

Eder, D. (1986). Organizational constraints on reading group mobility. In J. Cook-Gumperz (Ed.), *The social constraints of literacy* (pp. 138–155). Cambridge: Cambridge University Press.

Education Week. (1998, January). Quality counts, '98: An Education Week Pew Charitable Trust report on education in the 50 states. *Education Week, 17*(17).

Educational Testing Service. (1995). *Dreams deferred: High school dropouts in the United States.* Princeton, NJ: Educational Testing Service, Policy Information Service.

Elder, G. H., Jr. (1991). Family transitions, cycles, and social changes. In P. A. Cowan & M. Hetherington (Eds.), *Family transitions* (pp. 31–56). Hillsdale, NJ: Erlbaum.

Elder, G. H., Jr. (1998). The life course and human development. In R. M. Lerner and W. Damon (Eds.), *Handbook of child psychology. Vol. I. Theoretical models of human development* (pp. 939–991). New York: Wiley.

Ensminger, M. E., & Slusarcick, A. L. (1992, April). Paths to high school graduation or dropout: A longitudinal study of a first-grade cohort. *Sociology of Education, 65*(2), 95–113.

Entwisle, D. R. (1990). Schools and the adolescent. In S. S. Feldman & G. R. Elliott (Eds.), *At the threshold: The developing adolescent* (pp. 197–224). Cambridge, MA: Harvard University Press.

Entwisle, D. R. (1995, Winter). The role of schools in sustaining benefits of early childhood programs. *The Future of Children, 5*(3), 133–144.

Entwisle, D. R., & Alexander, K. L. (1989). Early schooling as a "critical period" phenomenon. In K. Namboodiri & R. Corwin (Eds.), *Sociology of education and socialization* (pp. 27–55). Greenwich, CT: JAI Press.

Entwisle, D. R., & Alexander, K. L. (1993). Entry into schools: The beginning school transition and educational stratification in the United States. In *Annual Review of Sociology* (Vol. 19, pp. 401–423). Palo Alto, CA: Annual Reviews.

Entwisle, D. R., Alexander, K. L., Cadigan, D., & Pallas, A. M. (1987). Kinder-garten experience: Cognitive effects or socialization? *American Educational Research Journal, 24,* 337–364.

Entwisle, D. R., Alexander, K. L., & Olson, L. S. (1997). *Children, schools and inequality.* Boulder, CO: Westview Press.

Entwisle, D. R., Alexander, K. L., & Olson, L. S. (2000a). Summer learning and home environment. In R. D. Kahlenberg (Ed.), *A notion at risk: Preserving public education as an engine for social mobility* (pp. 9–30). New York: Century Foundation Press.

Entwisle, D. R., Alexander, K. L., & Olson, L. S. (2000b, August). *Urban teenagers: Work and dropout.* Presented at the American Sociological Association annual meeting. Washington, D.C.

Entwisle, D. R., & Hayduk, L. A. (1978). *Too great expectations: The academic outlook of young children.* Baltimore: The Johns Hopkins University Press.

Entwisle, D. R., & Hayduk, L. A. (1982). *Early schooling: Cognitive and affective outcomes.* Baltimore: The Johns Hopkins University Press.

Epstein, J. L., & MacIver, D. J. (1990). *Education in the middle grades: National trends and practices.* Columbus, OH: National Middle School Association.

Epstein, J. L., & McPartland, J. M. (1976). The concept and measurement of the quality of school life. *American Educational Research Journal, 13,* 15–30.

Epstein, K. K. (1987, 5 April). Latest trend: Flunking kids in first grade. *The Baltimore Sun,* C5.

Farkas, G. (1998). Reading one-to-one: An intensive program serving a great many students while still achieving large effects. In J. Crane (Ed.), *Social programs that work* (pp. 75–109). New York: Russell Sage.

Farkas, G., Fischer, J., Dosher, R., & Vicknair, K. (1998). Can all children learn to read at grade-level by the end of third grade? In D. Vannoy & P. J. Dubeck (Eds.), *Challenges for work and family in the twenty-first century* (pp. 143–165). New York: Aldine de Gruyter.

Federal Interagency Forum on Child and Family Statistics. (2000). *America's children: Key national indicators of well-being, 2000.* Washington, D.C.: U.S. Government Printing Office.

Felner, R. D., & Adan, A. M. (1988). The school transitional environment project: An ecological intervention and evaluation. In R. Price, E. L. Cowen, R. P. Lorion, & J. Ramos-McKay (Eds.), *Fourteen ounces of prevention: A casebook for practitioners* (pp. 111–122). Washington, D.C.: American Psychological Association.

Felner, R. D., Ginter, M., & Primavera, J. (1982). Primary prevention during school transitions: Social support and environmental structure. *American Journal of Community Psychology, 10,* 277–290.

Fine, M. (1991). *Framing dropouts: Notes on the politics of an urban public high school.* Albany, NY: State University of New York Press.

Finlayson, H. J. (1977). Non-promotion and self-concept development. *Phi Delta Kappan, 59,* 205–206.

Finn, C. E., Jr. (1987, Spring). The high school dropout puzzle. *The Public Interest, 87,* 3–22.

Frede, E. C. (1995). The role of program quality in producing early childhood program benefits. *Long-term Outcomes of Early Childhood Programs, 5*(3), 115–132.

Frymier, J. (1992). *Growing up is risky business, and schools are not to blame.* Bloomington, IN: Phi Delta Kappa.

Frymier, J. (1997, February/March). Characteristics of students retained in grade. *The High School Journal, 80*(3), 184–192.

Gallup Organization. (2001, 24 January). Poll Releases. Available: http://www.gallup.com.

Gamoran, A. (1989). Rank, performance and mobility in elementary school grouping. *Sociological Quarterly, 30,* 109–123.

Gamoran, A. (1992). Access to excellence: Assignment to honors English classes in the transition to high school. *Educational Evaluation and Policy Analysis, 14,* 185–204.

Gamoran, A., & Weinstein, M. (1998, May). Differentiation and opportunity in restructured schools. *American Journal of Education, 106,* 385–414.

Gándara, P., & Fish, J. (1994). Year-round schooling as an avenue to major structural reform. *Educational Evaluation and Policy Analysis, 16,* 67–85.

Garnier, H. E., Stein, J. A., & Jacobs, J. K. (1997). The process of dropping out of high school: A 19-year perspective. *American Educational Research Journal, 34*(2), 395–419.

Gersten, R. (1984). Follow through revisited: Reflections on the site variability issue. *Educational Evaluation and Policy Analysis, 6,* 411–423.

Gewertz, C. (2000, 7 June). More districts add summer coursework. *Education Week on the Web* [Online] 19(39). Available: http://www.edweek.org.

Goal 2 Work Group. (1993). *Reaching the goals: Goal 2, high school completion.* Washington, D.C.: Office of Educational Research and Improvement, U.S. Department of Education.

Goethals, G. R. (1987). Social comparison theory: Psychology from the lost and found. *Personality and Social Psychology Bulletin, 12,* 261–278.

Goodlad, J. I., & Anderson, R. H. (1987). *The nongraded elementary school.* New York: Teachers College Press.

Gottfredson, D. C., Fink, C. M., & Graham, N. (1994). Grade retention and problem behavior. *American Educational Research Journal, 31,* 761–784.

Gottfried, A. E. (1985). Academic intrinsic motivation in elementary and junior high school students. *Journal of Educational Psychology, 77*(6), 631–645.

Grant, J., & Richardson, I. (1998). *The retention/promotion checklist.* Peterborough, NH: Crystal Springs Books.

Grant, J., & Richardson, I. (1999). One more year. *High School Magazine, 7*(4), 9–13.

Graue, M. E., & DiPerma, J. (2000). Redshirting and early retention: Who gets the gift of time and what are its outcomes? *American Educational Research Journal, 37,* 509–534.

Greene, J. P. (2000). The Texas school miracle is for real. *City Journal, 10*(3), 74–81.

Griliches, Z. (1977). Estimating the returns to schooling: Some econometric problems. *Econometrica, 45*(1), 1–22.

Grissmer, D. (Ed.). (1999). *Educational Evaluation and Policy Analysis.* Vol. 21: *Class size: Issues and new evidence.* [Special issue]. Washington, D.C.: American Educational Research Association.

Grissmer, D., & Flanagan, A. (1998). *Exploring rapid achievement gains in North Carolina and Texas.* Washington, D.C.: National Education Goals Panel.

Grissom, J. B., & Shepard, L. A. (1989). Repeating and dropping out of school. In L. A. Shepard & M. L. Smith (Eds.), *Flunking grades: Research and policies on retention* (pp. 34–63). London: Falmer Press.

Gutierrez, R., & Slavin, R. E. (1992). Achievement effects of nongraded elementary schools: A best evidence synthesis. *Review of Educational Research, 62,* 333–376.

Haddad, W. D. (1979). *Educational and economic effects of promotion and repetition practices* (Staff Working Paper No. 319). Washington, D.C.: The World Bank.

Hallinan, M. T. (1992, April). The organization of students for instruction in the middle school. *Sociology of Education, 65,* 114–127.

Hallinan, M. T. (1996). Track mobility in secondary school. *Social Forces, 74*(3), 983–1002.

Hallinan, M. T., & Sørensen, A. B. (1983). The formation and stability of instructional groups. *American Sociological Review, 48,* 838–851.

Hammack, F. M. (1986). Large school system's dropout reports: An analysis of definitions, procedures, and findings. *Teachers College Record, 87,* 324–341.

Haney, W. (2000, 19 August). The myth of the Texas miracle in education. *Education Policy Analysis Archives* [Online] 8(41). Available: http://epaa.asu.edu/epaa.

Hart, B., & Risley, T. R. (1995). *Meaningful differences in the everyday experience of young American children.* Baltimore: Paul H. Brookes.

Harvard Education Letter. (1986). Repeating a grade: Does it help? *Harvard Education Letter, 2,* 1–4.

Harvard Education Letter. (1992a, September–October). After tracking – what? Middle schools find new answers. *Harvard Education Letter, 8,* 1–5.

Harvard Education Letter. (1992b, January–February). The seventh-grade slump and how to avoid it. *Harvard Education Letter, 8*(1), 1–4.

Harvard Education Letter. (1992c, May/June). The tracking wars: Is anyone winning? *Harvard Education Letter, 8,* 1–4.

Hauser, R. M. (1999, 7 April). What if we ended social promotion? *Education Week on the Web* [Online] 18(30). Available: http://www.edweek.org.

Hauser, R. M. (2001). Should we end social promotion? Truth and consequences. In G. Orfield & M. Kornhaber (Eds.), *Raising standards or raising barriers? Inequality and high stakes testing in public education* (pp. 151–178). New York: Century Foundation.

Hauser, R. M., Pager, D. I., & Simmons, S. J. (2000, 18–19 October). *Race-ethnicity, social background, and grade retention.* Presented at the National Invitational Conference: Can Unlike Children Learn Together? Grade Retention, Tracking, and Grouping. Alexandria, VA.

Hauser, R. M., & Phang, H. S. (1993). *Trends in High School Dropout among White, Black and Hispanic Youth, 1973–1989* (Discussion Paper No. 1007-93). Madison, WI: Institute for Research on Poverty.

Hauser, R. M., Simmons, S. J., & Pager, D. I. (2001, 13 January). *High school dropout, race-ethnicity, and social background from the 1970s to the 1990s.* Presented at the The Civil Rights Project: Dropouts in America: How Severe Is the Problem? What Do We Know About Intervention and Prevention? Cambridge, MA.

Hebbeler, K. (1985). An old and a new question on the effects of early education for children from low income families. *Educational Evaluation and Policy Analysis, 7*, 207–216.

Henry, W. A., III. (1994). *In defense of elitism.* New York: Doubleday.

Herrnstein, R. J., & Murray, C. (1994). *The bell curve: Intelligence and class structure in American life.* New York: The Free Press.

Hess, R. D., & Holloway, S. D. (1984). Family and school as educational institutions. In R. D. Parke (Ed.), *Review of child development research.* Vol. 7: *The family* (pp. 179–222). Chicago: University of Chicago Press.

Hetherington, E. M., Camara, K. A., & Featherman, D. L. (1983). Achievement and intellectual functioning in one-parent families. In J. Spence (Ed.), *Achievement and achievement motives* (pp. 205–284). San Francisco: W. H. Freeman.

Heubert, J. P., & Hauser, R. M. (1999). *High stakes: Testing for tracking, promotion, and graduation.* Washington, D.C.: National Academy Press.

Heyns, B. (1978). *Summer learning and the effects of schooling.* New York: Academic Press.

Heyns, B. (1987). Schooling and cognitive development: Is there a season for learning? *Child Development, 58*, 1151–1160.

Hill, A. N., Lorence, J., Dworkin, A. G., Toenjes, L. A., Perez, N., Thomas, M., & Segvic, D. (1999). *Educational practices applied to Texas elementary students retained in grade.* Houston: Sociology of Education Research Group, University of Houston.

Holmes, C. T. (1989). Grade level retention effects: A meta-analysis of research studies. In L. A. Shepard & M. L. Smith (Eds.), *Flunking grades: Research and policies on retention* (pp. 16–33). London: Falmer Press.

Holmes, C. T., & Matthews, K. (1984). The effects of nonpromotion on elementary and junior high school pupils: A meta-analysis. *Review of Educational Research, 54*, 225–236.

House, E. R. (1989). Policy implications of retention research. In L. A. Shepard & M. L. Smith (Eds.), *Flunking grades: Research and policies on retention* (pp. 202–213). London: Falmer Press.

House, E. R., Glass, G., McLean, L., & Walker, D. (1978). No simple answer: Critique of the "Follow Through" evaluation. *Harvard Educational Review, 48*, 128–160.

Husén, T. (1976). The equality-meritocracy dilemma in education. In N. F. Ashline, T. R. Pezzullo & C. I. Norris (Eds.), *Education, inequality, and national policy* (pp. 45–59). Lexington, MA: Lexington Books.

Hymel, S., Comfort, C., Schonert-Reichl, K., & McDougall, P. (1996). Academic failure and school dropout: The influence of peers. In J. Juvonen & K. R. Wentzel (Eds.), *Social motivation: Understanding children's school adjustment* (pp. 313–345). Cambridge: Cambridge University Press.

Ingersoll, G. M., Scamman, J. P., & Eckerling, W. D. (1989). Geographic mobility and student achievement in an urban setting. *Educational Evaluation and Policy Analysis, 11*(2), 143–149.

Jackson, G. B. (1975). The research evidence on the effects of grade retention. *Review of Educational Research, 45*, 613–635.

Jencks, C. (1985). How much do high school students learn? *Sociology of Education, 58*, 128–153.

Jimerson, S. (1999). On the failure of failure: Examining the association between early grade retention and education and employment outcomes during late adolescence. *Journal of School Psychology, 37*(3), 243–272.

Jimerson, S. (2000, 18–19 October). *Meta-analysis of the effects of grade retention 1990–1999: A basis for moving beyond grade retention and social promotion.* Presented at the National Invitational Conference: Can Unlike Children Learn Together? Grade Retention, Tracking, and Grouping. Alexandria, VA.

Jimerson, S., Carlson, E., Rotert, M., Egeland, B., & Sroufe, L. A. (1997). A prospective, longitudinal study of the correlates and consequences of early grade retention. *Journal of School Psychology, 35*(1), 3–25.

Jimerson, S., Egeland, B., Sroufe, L. A., & Carlson, B. (2000). A prospective, longitudinal study of high school dropouts: Examining multiple predictors across development. *Journal of School Psychology, 38*(6), 525–549.

Karweit, N. (1989). Effective kindergarten practices for students as risk. In R. E. Slavin, N. L. Karweit, & N. A. Madden (Eds.), *Effective programs for students at risk* (pp. 103–142). Boston: Allyn & Bacon.

Karweit, N. (1992). Retention policy. In M. Alkin (Ed.), *Encyclopedia of educational research* (pp. 1114–1118). New York: Macmillan.

Karweit, N. L. (1999). *Grade retention: Prevalence, timing, and effects* (Report No. 33). Baltimore: Johns Hopkins University, CRESPAR.

Kasarda, J. D. (1993). Inner-city concentrated poverty and neighborhood distress: 1970 to 1990. *Housing Policy Debate, 4*(3), 253–302.

Kaufman, P., Bradby, D., & Owings, J. (1992). *National Education National Education Longitudinal Study of 1988: Characteristics of at-Risk Students in NELS:88* (Contractor Report, NCES 92-042). Washington, D.C.: U.S. Department of Education, Office of Educational Research and Improvement, National Center for Education Statistics.

Kaufmann, R. (1982). *An investigation of the relationship between early identification procedures during kindergarten and subsequent third grade reading* (Dissertation Abstracts International, 42, 1909A, University Microfilms No. 8226474).

Kellam, S. G. (1994). The social adaptation of children in classrooms: A measure of family childrearing effectiveness. In R. D. Parke & S. G. Kellam (Eds.),

Exploring family relationships with other social contexts (pp. 147–168). Hillsdale, NJ: Lawrence Erlbaum Associates.

Kellam, S. G., Branch, J., Agrawal, K., & Ensminger, M. E. (1975). *Mental health and going to school: The Woodlawn program of assessment, early intervention, and evaluation.* Chicago: University of Chicago Press.

Kellam, S. G., Werthamer-Larsson, L., Dolan, L. J., Brown, C. H., Laudolff, J., Edelsohn, G., & Wheeler, L. (1991). Developmental epidemiologically-based preventive trials: Baseline modeling of early target behaviors and depressive symptoms. *American Journal of Community Psychology, 19*, 563–584.

Kelly, K. (1999). Retention vs. social promotion: Schools search for alternatives. *Harvard Education Letter, 15*(1), 1–3.

Kelly, S. P. (1988, 8 February). 46% of Baltimore 9th-graders drop out before graduation. *The Evening Sun*, Sect. A, pp. 1, 5.

Kelly, S. P. (1989, 25 July). 15,000 city students failed despite debate over promotions. *The Evening Sun*, C1.

Keogh, B. K. (1986). Temperament and schooling: Meaning of "goodness of fit." In J. V. Lerner & R. M. Lerner (Eds.), *Temperament and social interaction during infancy and childhood* (pp. 89–108). San Francisco: Jossey-Bass.

King, P., & McCormick, J. (1998, 15 June). Politics of promotion. *Newsweek, 131*, 27.

Klein, S. P., Hamilton, L. S., McCaffrey, D. F., & Stecher, B. M. (2000, 26 October). What do test scores in Texas tell us? *Education Policy Analysis Archives* [Online] 8(49). Available: http://epaa.asu.edu/epaa.

Kominski, R. (1990). Estimating the national high school dropout rate. *Demography, 27*(2), 303–311.

Kraus, P. E. (1973). *Yesterday's children.* New York: Wiley.

Larabee, D. F. (1984). Setting the standard: Alternative policies for student promotion. *Harvard Educational Review, 54*, 67–87.

Lawton, M. (1997, 11 June). Promote or retain? Pendulum for students swings back again. *Education Week on the Web* [Online]. Available: http://www.edweek.org.

Lazar, I., & Darlington, R. (1982). Lasting effects of early education: A report from the Consortium for Longitudinal Studies. *Monographs of the Society for Research in Child Development, 47*(2–3), ix–139.

Lee, V. E., Brooks-Gunn, J., Schnur, E., & Liaw, F.-R. (1990). Are Head Start effects sustained? A longitudinal follow-up comparison of disadvantaged children attending Head Start, no preschool, and other preschool programs. *Child Development, 61*, 495–507.

Lerner, J. V., Lerner, R. M., & Zabski, S. (1985). Temperament and elementary school children's actual and rated academic performance: A test of a "goodness-of-fit" model. *Journal of Child Psychology and Psychiatry, 26*(1), 125–136.

Levin, H. M. (1972). *The costs to the nation of inadequate education: Report to the Select Committee on Equal Educational Opportunity in the United States.* Washington, D.C.: U. S. Government Printing Office.

Lloyd, D. N. (1978). Prediction of school failure from third-grade data. *Educational and Psychological Measurement, 38*, 1193–1200.

Lloyd, L. (1999). Multi-age classes and high ability students. *Review of Educational Research, 69*(2), 187–212.

Lockheed, M. E., & Verspoor, A. M. (1991). *Improving primary education in developing countries.* Washington, D.C.: Oxford University Press for the World Bank.

Lombardi, T. P., Odell, K. A., & Novotny, D. E. (1990). Special education and students at risk: Findings from a national study. *Remedial and Special Education, 12,* 56–62.

Lorence, J., Dworkin, A. G., Toenjes, L. A., & Hill, A. N. (2002). Grade retention and social promotion in Texas 1994–1999: An assessment of academic achievement among elementary school students. In *Brookings papers on education policy 2002* pp. 13–67. Washington, D.C.: Brookings Institution Press.

Love, J. M., & Logue, M. E. (1992). *Transitions to kindergarten in American schools: Executive summary* (Final report to the Office of Policy and Planning, Contract No. LC88089001). Washington, D.C.: U.S. Department of Education.

Loveless, T. (1999). *The tracking wars: State reform meets school policy.* Washington, D.C.: Brookings Institution Press.

Lucas, S. R. (1999). *Tracking inequality: Stratification and mobility in American high schools.* New York: Teachers College Press.

Madaus, G., & Clarke, M. (2001). The adverse impact of high stakes testing on minority students: Evidence from 100 years of test data. In G. Orfield & M. L. Kornhaber (Eds.), *Raising standards or raising barriers? Inequality and high-stakes testing in public education* (pp. 85–106). New York: Century Foundation.

Mahoney, J. L., & Cairns, R. B. (1997). Do extracurricular activities protect against early school dropout? *Developmental Psychology, 33*(2), 241–253.

Mantzicopoulos, P., & Morrison, D. (1992). Kindergarten retention: Academic and behavioral outcomes through the end of second grade. *American Educational Research Journal, 29,* 182–198.

Markey, J. P. (1988). The labor market problems of today's high school dropouts. *Monthly Labor Review, 111,* 36–43.

Maryland State Department of Education. (1999). *The fact book, 1998–1999.* Baltimore: Author.

Maryland State Department of Education. (2000). *The fact book, 1999–2000.* Baltimore, MD: Author.

Mathews, J. (2000, 13 June). Hot debate on value of summer school: Some educators say it helps skills; others call it unproductive. *Washington Post* Final ed., Sec. A, p. 24.

McCay, E. (2001). *Moving beyond retention and social promotion.* Bloomington, IN: Phi Delta Kappa International.

McCoy, A. R., & Reynolds, A. J. (1999). Grade retention and school performance: An extended investigation. *Journal of School Psychology, 37*(3), 273–298.

McDill, E. L., Natriello, G., & Pallas, A. M. (1986). A population at risk: Potential consequences of tougher school standards for student dropouts. *American Journal of Education, 94*(2), 135–181.

McDonald, K. B., & LaVeist, T. A. (2001). Black educational advantage in the inner city. *Review of Black Political Economy, 29*(1).

McDonnell, L. M., McLaughlin, M. J., & Morison, P. (1997). *Educating one and all: Students with disabilities and standards-based reform.* Washington, D.C.: National Academy Press.

McLanahan, S. S., & Sandefur, G. (1994). *Growing up with a single parent: What hurts, what helps.* Cambridge, MA: Harvard University Press.

McLaughlin, M. J. (1990, 3 August). High school dropouts: How much of a crisis? *Backgrounder* [Online] 781. Available: www.heritage.org/library/archives/backgrounder.

McLeskey, J., & Grizzle, K. L. (1992). Grade retention rates among students with learning disabilities. *Exceptional Children, 58,* 548–554.

McNeal Jr., R. B. (1995). Extracurricular activities and high school dropout. *Sociology of Education, 68,* 62–81.

McNeil, L., & Valenzuela, A. (2001). The harmful impact of the TAAS system of testing in Texas: Beneath the accountability rhetoric. In G. Orfield & M. L. Kornhaber (Eds.), *Raising standards or raising barriers? Inequality and high-stakes testing in public education* (pp. 127–150). New York: Century Foundation.

McPartland, J. M., Coldiron, J. R., & Braddock, J. H. (1987). *School structures and classroom practices in elementary, middle and secondary schools* (Report No. 14). Baltimore: The Johns Hopkins University, Center for Research on Elementary and Middle Schools.

Medway, F. (1985). To promote or not to promote? *Principal, 64,* 22–25.

Meisels, S. J. (1992). Doing harm by doing good: Iatrogenic effects of early childhood enrollment and promotion policies. *Early Childhood Research Quarterly, 7,* 155–174.

Meisels, S. J., & Liaw, F.-R. (1993). Failure in grade: Do retained students catch up? *Journal of Educational Research, 87*(2), 69–77.

Miller, S. M. (1976). Types of equality: Sorting, rewarding, performing. In N. F. Ashline, T. R. Pezzullo, & C. I. Norris (Eds.), *Education, inequality, and national policy* (pp. 15–43). Lexington, KY: Lexington Books.

Mischel, W., Zeiss, R., & Zeiss, A. (1974). Locus of control: Current trends in theory and research. *Journal of Personality and Social Psychology, 29,* 265–278.

Mishel, L., & Bernstein, J. (1994). *The state of working America.* New York: Economic Policy Institute.

Morris, D. R. (1993). Patterns of aggregate grade-retention rates. *American Educational Research Journal, 30,* 497–514.

Mueller, E. (1989, March). *The long-term effects on reading achievement of failing first grade.* Presented at the AERA meeting. San Francisco.

Murnane, R. J., Willett, J. B., & Boudett, K. P. (1995). Do high school dropouts benefit from obtaining a GED? *Educational Evaluation and Policy Analysis, 17*(2), 133–147.

Murnane, R. J., Willett, J. B., & Tyler, J. H. (2000). Who benefits from obtaining a GED? Evidence from high school and beyond. *Review of Economics and Statistics, 82*(1), 23–37.

Murphy, J., & Hallinger, P. (1989). Equity as access to learning: Curricular and instructional treatment differences. *Journal of Curriculum Studies, 21,* 129–149.

National Center for Education Statistics. (1990). *A profile of the American eighth grader: NELS88 student descriptive summary* (U.S. Department of Education,

Office of Educational Research and Improvement). Washington, D.C.: U.S. Department of Education, National Center for Education Statistics.

National Center for Education Statistics. (1996). *A descriptive summary of 1992–1993 bachelor's degree recipients one year later* (NCES 96-158). Washington, D.C.: U.S. Department of Education, National Center for Education Statistics.

National Center for Education Statistics. (1998). *The condition of education 1998* (NCES 98-013). Washington, D.C.: U.S. Department of Education, National Center for Education Statistics.

National Commission on Excellence in Education. (1983). *A nation at risk: The imperative for educational reform.* Washington, D.C.: Department of Education.

National Education Commission on Time and Learning. (1994). *Prisoners of time.* Washington, D.C.: Author.

National Education Goals Panel. (1999). *The National Education Goals report: Building a nation of learners, 1999.* Washington, D.C.: U.S. Government Printing Office.

National Research Council. (1993). *Losing generations: Adolescents in high-risk settings.* Washington, D.C.: National Academy Press.

Natriello, G. (1998, August). Failing grades for retention. *The School Administrator, 55*(7), 14–17.

Natriello, G., & Pallas, A. M. (2001). The development and impact of high stakes testing. In G. Orfield & M. L. Kornhaber (Eds.), *Raising standards or raising barriers? Inequality and high-stakes testing in public education* (pp. 19–38). New York: Century Foundation.

Nicholls, J. G. (1978). The development of the concepts of effort and ability, perception of academic attainment, and the understanding that difficult tasks require more ability. *Child Development, 49,* 800–814.

Oakes, J. (1988). Tracking in mathematics and science education: A structural contribution to unequal schooling. In L. Weis (Ed.), *Class, race and gender in American education* (pp. 106–125). Albany: State University of New York Press.

Oakes, J. (1989/1990). Opportunities, achievement and choice: Women and minority students in science and mathematics. *Review of Research in Education, 16,* 153–222.

Oakes, J., Gamoran, A., & Page, R. N. (1992). Curriculum differentiation: Opportunities, outcomes and meanings. In P. W. Jackson (Ed.), *Handbook of research on curriculum* (pp. 570–608). New York: Macmillan.

Olson, L. (1990, 16 May). Education officials reconsider policies on grade retention. *Education Week on the Web* [Online] May 16. Available: http://www.edweek.org.

Pallas, A. M., Entwisle, D. R., Alexander, K. L., & Stluka, M. F. (1994). Ability-group effects: Instructional, social or institutional? *Sociology of Education, 67,* 27–46.

Pallas, A. M., Natriello, G., & McDill, E. L. (1987). The high costs of high standards: School reform and dropouts. *Urban Education, 22,* 103–114.

Pallas, A. M., Natriello, G., & McDill, E. L. (1989). The changing nature of the disadvantaged population: Current dimensions and future trends. *Educational Researcher, 18,* 16–22.

Parsons, J. E., & Ruble, D. N. (1977). The development of achievement-related expectancies. *Child Development, 48,* 1075–1079.

Patterson Research Institute. (1999). *Two decades of progress: African Americans moving forward in higher education.* Fairfax, VA: United Negro College Fund.

Peng, S. S. (1985). *High school dropout: A national concern.* Washington, D.C.: U.S. Government Printing Office.

Peterson, S. E., DeGracie, J. S., & Ayabe, C. R. (1987). A longitudinal study of the effects of retention/promotion on academic achievement. *American Educational Research Journal, 27,* 107–118.

Pianta, R. C., Tietbohl, P., & Bennett, E. (1997). Differences in social adjustment and classroom behavior between children retained in kindergarten and groups of age and grade matched peers. *Early Education and Development, 8,* 137–152.

Pierson, L. H., & Connell, J. P. (1992). Effect of grade retention on self-system processes, school engagement and academic performance. *Journal of Educational Psychology, 84,* 300–307.

Pinnell, G. S., Lyons, C. A., DeFord, D. E., Bryk, A. S., & Seltzer, M. (1994). Comparing instructional models for the literacy education of high-risk first graders. *Reading Research Quarterly, 29*(1), 9–39.

Portner, J. (1996, 18 September). Older students make presence felt in classes. *Education Week* [Online] 16. Available: http://edweek.com/ew/vol-16/03older.h16.

Public Agenda. (2000). *Survey finds little sign of backlash against academic standards or standardized tests.* New York: Author.

Ramey, C. T., Campbell, F. A., & Blair, C. (1998). Enhancing the life course for high-risk children: Results from the Abecedarian Project. In J. Crane (Ed.), *Social programs that work* (pp. 163–183). New York: Russell Sage Foundation.

Reaney, L. M., West, J., & Denton, K. L. (2001, 11 April). *Is time a gift? Cognitive performance of kindergarten children who repeat kindergarten or whose entry is delayed.* Presented at the American Educational Research Association annual meeting. Seattle, WA.

Reynolds, A. J. (1992). Grade retention and school adjustment: An explanatory analysis. *Educational Evaluation and Policy Analysis, 14*(2), 101–121.

Reynolds, A. J. (1994). Effects of a preschool plus follow-on intervention for children at risk. *Developmental Psychology, 30,* 787–804.

Reynolds, A. J., & Temple, J. A. (1998). Extended early childhood intervention and school achievement: Age thirteen findings from the Chicago Longitudinal Study. *Child Development, 69*(1), 231–246.

Reynolds, A., Temple, J., & McCoy, A. (1997, 17 September). Grade retention doesn't work. *Education Week on the Web* [Online] 17(3). Available: http://www.edweek.org.

Richardson, J. G. (2000). The variable construction of educational risk. In M. T. Hallinan (Ed.), *Handbook of the sociology of education* (pp. 307–323). New York: Kluwer Academic/Plenum Publishers.

Richer, S. (1976). Reference-group theory and ability grouping: A convergence of sociological theory and educational research. *Sociology of Education, 49,* 65–71.

Riehl, C. (1999). Labeling and letting go: An organizational analysis of how high school students are discharged as dropouts. *Research in Sociology of Education and Socialization, 12,* 231–268.

Roderick, M. (1993). *The path to dropping out: Evidence for intervention.* Westport, CT: Auburn House.

Roderick, M. (1994). Grade retention and school dropout: Investigating the association. *American Educational Research Journal, 31*(4), 729–759.

Roderick, M. (1995a, December). Grade retention and school dropout: Policy debate and research questions. *Research Bulletin, Phi Delta Kappa Center for Evaluation, Development, and Research* [Online] 15. Available: http://www.pdkintl.org/edres/resbul15.htm.

Roderick, M. (1995b). School transitions and school dropout. *Advances in Educational Policy, 1,* 135–185.

Roderick, M., Bryk, A. S., Jacob, B. A., Easton, J. Q., & Allensworth, E. (1999). *Ending social promotion: Results from the first two years.* Chicago: Chicago Consortium on School Research.

Roderick, M., & Camburn, E. (1999). Risk and recovery from course failure in the early years of high school. *American Educational Research Journal, 36*(2), 303–343.

Roemer, J. E. (2000). Equality of opportunity. In K. Arrow, S. Bowles & S. Durlauf (Eds.), *Meritocracy and economic inequality* (pp. 17–32). Princeton, NJ: Princeton University Press.

Rosenbaum, J. E. (1976). *Making inequality: The hidden curriculum of high school tracking.* New York: Wiley.

Rosenbaum, J. E. (1999/2000, Winter). If tracking is bad, is detracking better? *American Educator,* 24–29, 47.

Ross, S. M., Smith, L. J., Casey, J., & Slavin, R. E. (1995). Increasing the academic success of disadvantaged children: An examination of alternative early intervention programs. *American Educational Research Journal, 32*(4), 773–800.

Rothenberg, D. (1995, May). Full-day kindergarten programs. ERIC Digest. *ERIC Digests* [Online] ED382410. Available: www.ed.gov/databases/ERIC_Digests.

Rothstein, R. (1998, November). Where is Lake Wobegon anyway? The controversy surrounding social promotion. *Phi Delta Kappan, 80*(3), 195–198.

Rotter, J. B. (1966). Generalized expectancies for internal versus external control of reinforcement. *Psychology Monographs: General and Applied, 80,* 1–28.

Royce, J. M., Darlington, R. B., & Murray, H. W. (1983). Pooled analyses: Findings across studies. In The Consortium for Longitudinal Studies (Ed.), *As the twig is bent: Lasting effects of preschool programs.* Hillsdale, NJ: Erlbaum.

Ruble, D. N. (1982). The development of social-comparison processes and their role in achievement-related self-socialization. In E. T. Higgins, D. N. Ruble, & W. W. Hartup (Eds.), *Social cognition and social development: A sociocultural perspective* (pp. 134–157). Cambridge: Cambridge University Press.

Rumberger, R. W. (1987). High school dropouts: A review of issues and evidence. *Review of Educational Research, 57*(2), 101–121.

Rumberger, R. W. (1995). Dropping out of middle school: A multilevel analysis of students and schools. *American Educational Research Journal, 32*(3), 583–625.

Rumberger, R. W. (2001, 13 January). *Why students drop out of school and what can be done.* Presented at the The Civil Rights Project: Dropouts in America: How

Severe Is the Problem? What Do We Know about Intervention and Prevention? Harvard University, Cambridge, MA.

Rumberger, R. W., & Larson, K. A. (1998, November). Student mobility and the increased risk of high school dropout. *American Journal of Education, 107,* 1–35.

Rury, J. L. (1999). Historians and policy making. *American Journal of Education, 107,* 321–327.

Sahagun, L. (1999, 17 April). L.A. school district curtails plan to end social promotions. *Los Angeles Times,* 1.

Schneider, B. L. (1980). *Production analysis of gains in achievement.* Presented at the the American Educational Research Association annual meeting. Boston.

Schneider, B., Stevenson, D., & Link, J. (1994, April). *Social and cultural capital: Differences between students who leave school at different periods in their school careers.* Presented at the American Educational Research Association annual meeting. New Orleans, LA.

Schrag, P. (2000, 15 March). Bush's "Texas miracle" in schools? TAAS tells. *Sacramento Bee,* Sec. Capitol Alert.

Schweinhart, L. J., Berrueta-Clement, J., Barnett, W., Epstein, A., & Weikart, D. P. (1985). The promise of early education. *Phi Delta Kappan, 66,* 548–551.

Schweinhart, L. J., & Weikart, D. P. (1985, April). Evidence that good early childhood programs work. *Phi Delta Kappan, 66,* 545–548.

Schweinhart, L. J., & Weikart, D. P. (1998). High/Scope Perry Preschool Program effects at age twenty-seven. In J. Crane (Ed.), *Social programs that work* (pp. 148–183). New York: Russell Sage.

Schweinhart, L. J., Weikart, D. P., & Larner, M. B. (1986). Consequences of three preschool curriculum models through age 15. *Early Childhood Research Quarterly, 1,* 15–45.

Sen, A. (2000). Merit and justice. In K. Arrow, S. Bowles, & S. Durlauf (Eds.), *Meritocracy and economic inequality* (pp. 5–16). Princeton, NJ: Princeton University Press.

Shepard, L. A. (2000, 18–19 October). *Understanding research on the consequences of retention.* Presented at the National Invitational Conference: Can Unlike Students Learn Together? Grade Retention, Tracking, and Grouping. Alexandria, VA.

Shepard, L. A., & Smith, M. L. (1988). Escalating academic demand in kindergarten: Counterproductive policies. *The Elementary School Journal, 89*(2), 135–145.

Shepard, L. A., & Smith, M. L. (1989). *Flunking grades: Research and policies on retention.* London: The Falmer Press.

Shepard, L. A., Smith, M. L., & Marion, S. F. (1996). Failed evidence on grade retention. *Psychology in the Schools, 33*(3), 251–261.

Shepard, L. A., Smith, M. L., & Marion, S. F. (1998). "On the success of failure": A rejoinder to Alexander. *Psychology in the Schools, 35,* 404–406.

Simmons, R. G., & Blyth, D. A. (1987). *Moving into adolescence: The impact of pubertal change and school context.* Hawthorn, NY: Aldine de Gruyter.

Slaughter, D. T., & Epps, E. G. (1987). The home environment and academic achievement of black American children and youth: An overview. *Journal of Negro Education, 56*, 3–20.

Smith, M. L. (1989). Teachers' beliefs about retention. In L. A. Shepard & M. L. Smith (Eds.), *Flunking grades: Research and policies on retention* (pp. 132–150). London: Falmer Press.

Smith, M. L., & Shepard, L. A. (1987). What doesn't work: Explaining policies of retention in the early grades. *Phi Delta Kappan, 66*(2), 129–134.

Smith, M. L., & Shepard, L. A. (1988). Kindergarten readiness and retention: A qualitative study of teachers' beliefs and practices. *American Educational Research Journal, 25*, 307–333.

Sørensen, A. B. (1970). Organizational differentiation of students and educational opportunity. *Sociology of Education, 43*, 355–376.

Sørensen, A. B. (1987). The organizational differentiation of students in schools as an opportunity structure. In M. T. Hallinan (Ed.), *The social organization of schools: New conceptualizations of the learning process* (pp. 103–129). New York: Plenum.

Stebbins, L. B., St. Pierre, R. G., Proper, E. C., Anderson, R. B., & Cerva, T. R. (1977). *A planned variation model.* Vol. IV-A. *Effects of follow through models.* Washington, D.C.: U.S. Office of Education.

Stenvall, M. J. (2001, 23 May). Is summer school the answer or the problem? *Education Week on the Web* [Online] 20(37). Available: http://www.edweek.org.

Stephens, J. M. (1956). *Educational psychology.* New York: Holt, Rinehart & Winston.

Stevenson, D. L., Schiller, K. S., & Schneider, B. (1994). Sequences of opportunities for learning. *Sociology of Education, 67*, 184–198.

Stipek, D. J. (1984). The development of achievement motivation. In R. Ames & C. Ames (Eds.), *Research on motivation in education.* Vol. 1. *Student motivation* (pp. 145–174). Orlando, FL: Academic Press.

Stipek, D. J., & Ryan, R. H. (1997). Economically disadvantaged preschoolers: Ready to learn but further to go. *Developmental Psychology, 33*(4), 711–723.

Stipek, D. J., & Weisz, J. R. (1981). Perceived personal control and academic achievement. *Review of Educational Research, 51*, 101–137.

Stroup, A. L., & Robins, L. N. (1972). Elementary school predictors of high school dropout among black males. *Sociology of Education, 45*(2), 212–222.

Suhorsky, J., & Wall, R. (1978). *A validation study of early identification and intervention program screening instruments: A longitudinal study.* Baltimore, MD: Maryland State Department of Education (ERIC Document Reproduction Service No. ED 171 777).

Suls, J. (1993). *Psychological perspectives on the self,* Vol. 4. Hillsdale, NJ: Lawrence Erlbaum.

Swanson, C. B., & Schneider, B. (1999). Students on the move: Residential and educational mobility in America's schools. *Sociology of Education, 72*(1), 54–67.

Szanton, P. L. (1986). *Baltimore 2000: A choice of futures.* Baltimore: Morris Goldseker Foundation.

Tanner, C. K., & Galis, S. A. (1997). Student retention: Why is there a gap between the majority of research findings and school practice? *Psychology in the Schools, 34*(2), 107–114.

Temple, J. A., & Reynolds, A. J. (1999). School mobility and achievement: Longitudinal findings from an urban cohort. *Journal of School Psychology, 37*(4), 355–377.

Temple, J. A., Reynolds, A. J., & Miedel, W. T. (2000). Can early intervention prevent high school dropout? Evidence from the Chicago child-parent centers. *Urban Education, 35*(1), 31–56.

Temple, J., Ou, S.-R., & Helevy, S. (2001, 31 May). *Grade retention, special education, and high school dropout.* Presented at the Society for Prevention Research annual meeting. Washington, D.C.

Temple, J., Reynolds, A. J., & Ou, S.-R. (2000, 18–19 October). *Grade retention and school dropout: Another look at the evidence.* Presented at the National Invitational Conference: Can Unlike Students Learn Together? Grade Retention, Tracking, and Grouping. Alexandria, VA.

Thompson, C. L., & Kolb, E. F. (1999). *Research on Retention and Social Promotion: Synthesis and Implications for Policy* (NCERC Policy Brief). Chapel Hill: North Carolina Education Research Council.

Toch, T. (1998, 5 October). Making the grade harder. *U.S. News and World Report, 125*, 59–60.

Tomchin, E. M., & Impara, J. C. (1992). Unraveling teachers' beliefs about grade retention. *American Educational Research Journal, 29*, 199–223.

Travers, J. R. (1982). Testing in educational placement: Issues and evidence. In K. A. Heller, W. H. Holtzman, & S. Messick (Eds.), *Children in special education: A strategy for equity* (pp. 230–261). Washington, D.C.: National Academy Press.

Tyack, D., & Cuban, L. (1995). *Tinkering toward Utopia: A century of public school reform.* Cambridge, MA: Harvard University Press.

Tyack, D., & Tobin, W. (1994, Fall). The grammar of schooling: Why has it been so hard to change? *American Educational Research Journal, 31*, 453–479.

UNESCO. (2000). *World education report 2000.* Paris: Author.

U.S. Bureau of Labor Statistics. (2001). *College enrollment and work activity of year 2000 high school graduates* (News release No. USDL 01-94). Washington, D.C.: Author.

U.S. Census Bureau. (1973). Characteristics of the population. Part 22. Maryland. In *Census of the population: 1970, Vol. 1.* Washington, D.C.: U.S. Government Printing Office.

U.S. Census Bureau. (1983). *Census of population: 1980. Vol 1. Characteristics of the population.* Washington, D.C.: U.S. Government Printing Office.

U.S. Census Bureau. (1992). *Census of population and housing, 1990: 5% Public use microdata samples U.S..* Washington, D.C.: U.S. Government Printing Office.

U.S. Census Bureau. (1999). *School enrollment – social and economic characteristics of students (update): October 1998* (current population reports No. P20–521). Washington, D.C.: U.S. Government Printing Office.

U.S. Census Bureau. (2000). *Money income in the United States: 1999* (Current population reports No. P60–209). Washington, D.C.: U.S. Government Printing Office.

U.S. Department of Education. (1989). *Dropout rates in the United States: 1988* (NCES 89–609 by Mary J. Frase). Washington, D.C.: U.S. Department of Education, National Center for Education Statistics.

U.S. Department of Education. (1992). *Experiences in child care and early childhood programs of first and second graders* (NCES 92-005, by Jerry West, Elvie G. Hausken, Kathryn Chandler, & Mary Collins). Washington, D.C.: U.S. Department of Education, National Center for Education Statistics.

U.S. Department of Education. (1997). *The condition of education 1997* (NCES 97388). Washington, D.C.: U.S. Department of Education, National Center for Education Statistics.

U.S. Department of Education. (1998). *National education longitudinal study of 1988 (NELS:88) base year through second follow-up: Final methodology report* (Working Paper No. 98–06 by Steven J. Ingels, Leslie A. Scott, John R. Taylor, Jeffrey Owings (Project Officer), & Peggy Quinn). Washington, D.C.: U.S. Department of Education, National Center for Education Statistics.

U.S. Department of Education. (1999). *Digest of education statistics, 1998* (NCES 1999–036 by Thomas D. Snyder (Production Manager), Charlene M. Hoffman (Program Analyst), & Clair M. Geddes). Washington, D.C.: U.S. Department of Education, National Center for Education Statistics.

U.S. Department of Education. (2000a). *The condition of education 2000* (NCES 2000-062). Washington, D.C.: Department of Education, National Center for Education Statistics.

U.S. Department of Education. (2000b). *Digest of education statistics, 1999* (NCES 2000–031). Washington, D.C.: U.S. Department of Education, National Center for Education Statistics.

U.S. Department of Education. (2000c). *Dropout rates in the United States: 1998* (Tech. Rep. No. NCES 2000–022) (NCES 2000-022, by Phillip Kaufman, Jin Y. Kwon, & Steve Klein). Washington, D.C.: U.S. Department of Education, National Center for Education Statistics.

U.S. Department of Education. (2001). *The condition of education 2001* (Tech. Rep. No. NCES 2001-072). Washington, D.C.: U.S. Department of Education, National Center for Education Statistics.

U.S. Department of Health and Human Services. (2000). *Trends in the well-being of America's children and youth: 2000.* Washington, D.C.: Author.

U.S. House of Representatives. (2000). *2000 Green book, 17th ed.* Washington, D.C.: Author.

Veenman, S. (1995). Cognitive and noncognitive effects of multigrade and multi-age classes: A best-evidence synthesis. *Review of Educational Research, 65*(Winter), 319–381.

Viadero, D. (2000, 15 March). Ending social promotion. *Education Week* [Online] 19(27). Available: http://www.edweek.org.

Wagenaar, T. C. (1987). What do we know about dropping out of high school? In A. C. Kerckhoff (Ed.), *Research on sociology of education and socialization* (Vol. 7, pp. 161–190). Greenwich, CT: JAI Press.

Wasik, B. A., & Slavin, R. E. (1993). Preventing early reading failure with one-to-one tutoring: A review of five programs. *Reading Research Quarterly, 28*(2), 179–200.

Wehlage, G. G., Rutter, R. A., Smith, G., Lesko, N., & Fernandez, R. (1989). *Reducing the risk: Schools as communities of support.* Philadelphia: Falmer Press.

Weiss, J. A., & Gruber, J. E. (1987). The managed irrelevance of federal education statistics. In W. Alonso & P. Starr (Eds.), *The politics of numbers* (pp. 363–391). New York: Russell Sage Foundation.

Weisz, J. R., & Cameron, A. (1985). Individual differences in the student's sense of control. In C. Ames & R. Ames (Eds.), *The classroom milieu.* Vol. 2. *Research on motivation in education* (pp. 93–139). Orlando, FL: Academic Press.

Weitzman, M., Klerman, L. V., Lamb, G. A., Kane, K., Geromini, K. R., Kayne, R., Rose, L., & Alpert, J. J. (1985). Demographic and educational characteristics of inner city middle school problem absence students. *American Journal of Orthopsychiatry, 55*(3), 378–383.

West, J., Denton, K., & Germino-Hausken, E. (2000). *America's Kindergartners: Findings from the Early Childhood Longitudinal Study, Kindergarten Class of 1998–99, Fall 1998* (NCES 2000-070). Washington, D.C.: U.S. Department of Education, National Center for Education Statistics.

Weston, W. J. (1989). *Education and the American family.* New York: New York University Press.

White, K. A., & Johnston, R. C. (1999, September 22). Summer school: Amid successes, concerns persist. *Education Week on the Web* [Online] 19(3). Available: http://www.edweek.org.

White, K. R. (1985/1986). Efficacy of early intervention. *Journal of Special Education, 19,* 401–416.

White, K. R., Taylor, M. J., & Moss, V. D. (1992). Does research support claims about the benefits of involving parents in early intervention programs? *Review of Educational Research, 62,* 91–125.

Wildavsky, B. (1999, 19 July). When Johnny can't read – try tough love. *U.S. News and World Report, 127,* 24–25.

Willis, S. (1991). Breaking down grade barriers: Interest in nongraded classrooms on the rise. *ASCD Update, 33,* 1–4.

Wilson, M. (1990). Book review of "Flunking Grades: Research and policies on retention." *Educational Evaluation and Policy Analysis, 12,* 228–230.

Wood, D., Halfon, N., Scarlata, D., Newacheck, P., & Nissim, S. (1993). The impact of family relocation on children's growth and development, school function, and behavior. *Journal of the American Medical Association, 270,* 1334–1338.

Woodhead, M. (1988). When psychology informs public policy: The case of early childhood intervention. *American Psychologist, 43,* 443–454.

Woodward, S. K., & Kimmey, T. M. (1997). *The impact of repeating a grade: A review of research in the 90s* (Tech. Rep. No. Occasional Paper No. 25). Orono, ME: Center for Research and Evaluation, University of Maine.

World Bank. (2001). *World development indicators 2001.* Washington, D.C.: Author.

Yair, G. (2000). Not just about time: Instructional practices and productive time in school. *Educational Administration Quarterly, 36*(4), 485–512.

Zill, N. (1996). Family change and student achievement: What we have learned, what it means for schools. In A. Booth & J. F. Dunn (Eds.), *Family-school links: How do they affect educational outcomes?* (pp. 139–174). Mahwah, NJ: Erlbaum.

Zill, N., Loomis, L. S., & West, J. (1997). *The elementary school performance and adjustment of children who enter kindergarten late or repeat kindergarten: Findings from national surveys* (NCES 98-097). Washington, D.C.: U.S. Department of Education, National Center for Education Statistics. National Center for Education Statistics Statistical Analysis Report.

Author Index

Subject Index